View From New Salem Hill

THE LIFE OF
ABRAHAM LINCOLN

Volume One

THE MACMILLAN COMPANY
NEW YORK · BOSTON · CHICAGO · DALLAS
ATLANTA · SAN FRANCISCO

MACMILLAN & CO., Limited
LONDON · BOMBAY · CALCUTTA
MELBOURNE

THE MACMILLAN CO. OF CANADA, Ltd.
TORONTO

EARLIEST LINCOLN PORTRAIT.

THE LIFE OF ABRAHAM LINCOLN

Drawn from Original Sources and Containing Many Speeches, Letters, and Telegrams Hitherto Unpublished

ILLUSTRATED

With Many Reproductions from Original Photographs, Paintings, etc.

BY

IDA M. TARBELL

IN TWO VOLUMES

VOLUME ONE

NEW YORK
THE MACMILLAN COMPANY
1928

All rights reserved

Copyright, 1895, 1896, 1898, 1899
By The S. S. McClure Co.

Copyright, 1900
By Doubleday & McClure Co.

Copyright, 1900
By McClure, Phillips & Co.

Copyright, 1917
By The Macmillan Company

Copyright, 1924
By The Lincoln History Society

New Edition In Two Volumes
Published, October, 1928

PRINTED IN THE UNITED STATES OF AMERICA
BY T. MOREY & SON

To my Father

CONTENTS

Volume One

	PAGE
Preface	xi
Preface to Revised Edition	xv

CHAPTER

I. The Origin of the Lincoln Family—The Lincolns in Kentucky—Birth of Abraham Lincoln 1

II. The Lincolns Leave Kentucky for Southern Indiana—Conditions of Life in Their New Home 21

III. Abraham Lincoln's Early Opportunities—The Books He Read—Trips to New Orleans—Impression He Made on His Friends . . 32

IV. The Lincolns Leave Indiana—The Journey to Illinois—Abraham Lincoln Starts Out for Himself 51

V. Lincoln Secures a Position—He Studies Grammar—First Appearance in Politics . . 67

VI. The Black Hawk War—Lincoln Chosen Captain of a Company—Re-enlists as an Independent Ranger—End of the War . . 85

VII. Lincoln Runs for State Assembly and is Defeated—Storekeeper—Student—Postmaster—Surveyor 103

VIII. Electioneering in Illinois in 1834—Lincoln Reads Law—First Term as Assemblyman—Lincoln's First Great Sorrow . . . 125

IX. Lincoln is Re-elected to the Illinois Assembly—His First Published Address—Protests against Pro-slavery Resolutions of the Assembly 144

vii

CONTENTS

CHAPTER		PAGE
X.	Lincoln Begins to Study Law—Mary Owens—A Newspaper Contest—Growth of Political Influence	170
XI.	Lincoln's Engagement to Mary Todd—Breaking of the Engagement—Lincoln-Shields Duel	196
XII.	Lincoln Becomes a Candidate for Congress and is Defeated—On the Stump in 1844—Nominated and Elected to the 30th Congress	223
XIII.	Lincoln in Washington in 1847—He Opposes the Mexican War—Campaigning in New England	241
XIV.	Lincoln at Niagara—Secures a Patent for an Invention—Abandons Politics and Decides to Devote Himself to the Law	262
XV.	Lincoln on the Circuit—His Humor and Persuasiveness—His Manner of Preparing Cases, Examining Witnesses, and Addressing Juries	280
XVI.	Lincoln's Important Law Cases—Defence of a Slave Girl—The McCormick Case—The Armstrong Murder Case—The Rock Island Bridge Case.	298
XVII.	Lincoln Re-enters Politics	324
XVIII.	The Lincoln-Douglas Debates.	348
XIX.	Lincoln's Nomination in 1860	388
XX.	The Campaign of 1860	418

LIST OF ILLUSTRATIONS

Early Portrait of Lincoln	*Frontispiece*
	FACING PAGE
Land Warrant	2
Home of Abraham Lincoln's Grandfather	4
Will of Joseph Hanks	8
House where Thomas Lincoln and Nancy were Married	10
Lincoln Country of Kentucky	11
Marriage Bond	13
Return of Marriage Bond	14
Appointment of Thomas Lincoln as Road Surveyor	15
House in which Lincoln was Born	16
Rock Spring Farm	24
Rock Spring	24
Record in Family Bible by Lincoln	27
Lincoln's Indiana Farm	30
Thomas Lincoln's Bible	32
Lincoln's Exercise Book	35
Abraham Lincoln's Indiana Home	36
Lincoln Working by Firelight	36
Facsimile Lines from Copy-book	47
Swimming Hole	52
Buckthorn Valley	52
Grave of Nancy Hanks Lincoln	54
New Salem Mill	64
Mouth of Anderson Creek	64
Map, New Salem	69

LIST OF ILLUSTRATIONS

	FACING PAGE
Lincoln's First Vote	70
Kirkham Grammar	76
Black Hawk	86
Map of Illinois	99
Discharge from Service in Black Hawk War	100
Facsimile of an Election Return	104
Berry and Lincoln Store	106
Facsimile of Letter by Postmaster Lincoln	112
Court House at Petersburg	116
Report of Road Survey	118
Map by Lincoln	119
State House, Vandalia	120
Lincoln's Surveying Instruments	120
Bowling Green's House	128
Grave of Ann Rutledge	140
Joshua Speed and Wife	148
Map of Albany, Ill.	153
Map of Illinois	157
Walnut Cabinet Made by Lincoln	172
Lincoln's Saddle-Bags	172
Page from Stuart and Lincoln Fee Book	178
Stuart and Lincoln Law Office	184
Harrison Badge of 1840	192
Stuart and Lincoln Adv. Card	195
Invitation to Cotillion	197
Mary Todd Lincoln	198
Portrait of Shields	214
Lincoln's Marriage License	220
Earliest Portrait of Lincoln	226
Crawford Well	230
Crawford House	230
Log Cabin in Hodgenville Temple	240
Thomas Lincoln's Home in Illinois	256
Model of Lincoln's Patent	264

LIST OF ILLUSTRATIONS

FACING PAGE

Map of Lincoln Law Circuit	*page* 283
Lincoln Memorandum	*page* 291
Lincoln in 1857	296
Lincoln's Office	300
Photo of Joseph Medill	342
Photo of H. C. Whitney	342
Lincoln in 1857	346
Stephen A. Douglas	350
Lincoln-Douglas Meeting at Galesburg	354
Lincoln in 1858	360
Lincoln Letter about Lincoln-Douglas Debate	364
Lincoln in 1858, Age 49	368
Lincoln in 1859	372
Lincoln, 1860, at time of Cooper Union Speech	380
Lincoln in 1860	394
Chair at Republican Convention	*page* 405
Wigwam, Chicago	406
William H. Seward-Salmon P. Chase	412
Edward Bates-Simon Cameron	412
Jesse W. Fell-Horace Greeley	416

PREFACE

The collection of the material for the work here offered the public was begun in 1894 at the suggestion of Mr. S. S. McClure and Mr. J. S. Phillips, editors of "McClure's Magazine." Their desire was to add to our knowledge of Abraham Lincoln by collecting and preserving the reminiscences of such of his contemporaries as were then living. In undertaking the work it was determined to spare neither labor nor money and in this determination Mr. McClure and his associates never wavered. Without the sympathy, confidence, suggestion and criticism which they gave the work it would have been impossible. They established in their editorial rooms what might be called a Lincoln Bureau and from there an organized search was made for reminiscences, pictures and documents. To facilitate the work all persons possessing or knowing of Lincoln material were asked through the magazine to communicate with the editor. The response was immediate and amazing. Hundreds of persons from all parts of the country replied. In every case the clews thus obtained were investigated and if the matter was found to be new and useful, was secured. The author wrote thousands of letters and travelled thousands of miles in collecting the material which came to the editors simply as a result of this request in the magazine. The work thus became one in which the whole country co-operated.

At the outset it was the intention of the editors to use the results of the research simply as a series of unpublished reminiscences, but after a few months the new material gathered, while valuable, seemed to them too fragmentary to be published as it stood, and the author was asked to prepare a series of articles on Lincoln covering his life up to 1858 and embodying as far as possible the unpublished material collected. These articles, which appeared in "McClure's Magazine" for 1895 and 1896, were received favorably, and it was decided to follow them by a series on the later life of Lincoln. This latter series was concluded in September, 1899, and both series, with considerable supplementary matter, were later published in book form.

It is impossible in this brief preface to mention all who aided in the work, but there are a few whose names must not be omitted, so essential was their assistance to the enterprise.

From the beginning Mr. J. McCan Davis of Springfield, Illinois, was of great service, particularly in examining the files of Illinois newspapers and in interviewing. It is to Mr. Davis's intelligent and patient research that we owe the report of Lincoln's first published speech, the curious letters on the Adams law case, most of the documents of Lincoln's early life in New Salem and Springfield, such as his first vote, his reports and maps of surveys, his marriage certificate and many of the letters printed in the appendix. Mr. William H. Lambert of Philadelphia also assisted us constantly by his sympathy and suggestions, and his large and valuable Lincoln

PREFACE

collection was put at our disposal. Other collections that were generously opened were those of O. H. Oldroyd of Washington, R. T. Durrett, Louisville, Ky., C. F. Gunther, Chicago, Ill., and Louis Vanuxem, Philadelphia, Pa. The War Department of the United States Government extended many courtesies, the War Records being freely opened and the members of the War Records Commission aiding us in every way in their power. The librarians of the War Department, of the Congressional Library, of the Boston Public Library and of the Astor Library of New York, were also most helpful.

The chief obligation which any student of Abraham Lincoln owes is to the great work of Messrs. Nicolay and Hay. In it are collected nearly all the documents essential to a study of Lincoln's life. Their History has been freely consulted in preparing this work and whenever letters and speeches of Lincoln appearing in their collection of his writings have been quoted, their version has been followed. Other lives of Lincoln that have been found useful are those of W. H. Herndon, W. O. Stoddard, John T. Morse, Isaac Arnold, Ward H. Lamon, H. C. Whitney, and J. G. Holland.

The new material collected will, we believe, add considerably to our knowledge of Lincoln's life. Documents are presented establishing clearly that his mother was not the nameless girl that she has been so generally believed. His father, Thomas Lincoln, is shown to have been something more than a shiftless "poor white," and Lincoln's early life, if hard and crude, to have been full of honest, cheerful effort at betterment. His struggles for a livelihood and his intellectual development from the time he started out for himself until he was admitted to the bar are traced with more detail than in any other biography, and considerable new light is thrown on this period of his life. The sensational account of his running away from his own wedding, accepted generally by historians, is shown to be false. To the period of Lincoln's life from 1849, when he gave up politics, until 1858, the period of the Lincoln and Douglas Debates, the most important contribution made is the report of what is known as the "Lost Speech."

The fourth volume of the Life contains as an appendix 150 pages of letters, telegrams and speeches which do not appear in Lincoln's "Complete Works," published by his private secretaries, Messrs. Nicolay and Hay. The great majority of these documents were first published in this work. The source from which they have been obtained is given in each case.

No attempt has been made to cover the history of Lincoln's times save as necessary in tracing the development of his mind and in illustrating his moral qualities. It is Lincoln the man, as seen by his fellows and revealed by his own acts and words, that the author has tried to picture.

I. M. T.

1900.

PREFACE TO REVISED EDITION

There is no man in American history with whom people so desire intimate acquaintance as they do with Abraham Lincoln. This is true in spite of the fact that no man's life has undergone so close a scrutiny. His tragic death in 1865 set his contemporaries telling what they knew and thought of him. The more they told the more men demanded to know. As time went on he who had known Lincoln became a special and revered figure in his community. He was pressed to tell and retell his recollections. These recollections finding their way into print brought out other recollections—an unbroken stream even to-day. Nothing genuine has ever been too slight to find its way into Lincoln literature.

His letters and speeches were gathered into volumes years ago and have been added to from time to time so that it has come to be that we have practically all that he ever set down on paper. No one was ever so bared by his associates. No one's words were ever so spread before the world. And never has a man's life in so short a period been so many times written and rewritten, unless possibly it is that of Napoleon Bonaparte.

The man has stood the test. He comes out of each examination and re-examination still sound, wise, honest, humorous, merciful. The more we know of him the less desire we have to treat him as a heroic figure—he is too strong and good a human being to be obscured by idealism. We want him as he was, one of our kind. It is good to see what a man can make of heart and brain if he will set himself for life to the task—what can be done in spite of multiplied handicaps.

He found the essentials for both citizenship and leadership in a democracy. Born close to the time of the making of the Republic he shared the faith of the Fathers in the soundness of the undertaking. He saw it as an experiment, something for which men must work if its promises were to be redeemed. He asked chiefly of the new government that it give him full opportunity to work for its realization.

The closer one studies his life the clearer it becomes that he had a definite idea of what a man in a democracy should be. He should have knowledge of the things that he proposed to work for. It is significant that throughout his life he regarded knowing, not guessing, a matter of primary individual responsibility in public affairs. Follow his life from start to finish and you find him faithful to this conviction that a man's opinion must be built on what he has been able to learn, and if he learns that which changes the case then he must change his view. "I shall adopt new views so fast as they shall appear to be true views," he told Horace Greeley in 1862. This was only another way of saying what he had said thirty years before, in his first public address, "So soon as I discover my opinions to be erroneous, I shall be ready to renounce them."

The duty to labor in order to know held a high place in his creed. He was willing to work to get facts; willing to take time to digest them. His mastery of the question of slavery extension came from years of study and pondering. He went to the sources of information for his knowledge, never evaded a new fact or argument of an opponent, was never satisfied that he knew all. Confronted early in the Civil War with the necessity of making decisions in military matters, he found time in the frightful pressure of affairs to read numbers of works on military science. Nothing which would help him better to discharge his duties was neglected, whatever the labor. "This man was all right for labor," said Ralph Waldo Emerson, "and liked nothing so well," and added, "A good worker is so rare."

He did not see the possibility of self-government without character. Character meant to him truthfulness, frankness, willingness to give up personal ambition if by so doing he could make the truth of the thing he was working for more clear, and charity for all men—charity for them in their views, their stupidities, even their crimes.

His fidelity to this code was natural. He could do no other way. It led him again and again to sacrifice his hopes—put him out of politics in 1849—defeated him for senatorship in 1858—imperilled his re-election in 1864. But personal victory was never his first aim—his first aim was making clear what he believed —what he would do if given power.

He understood men and could work with them. He never held himself aloof from anyone, high or low. If you want to have a government in which all take part you must work with all. He made his way around or through the superciliousness, the ignorance, the intrigue, the meanness of men, found in each that which was sound, and depended on that. It made him a past master in handling men.

His confidence in the right thinking of the mass never was shaken; it was that to which he steadily appealed through defeat after defeat. "He never appeals to any vulgar sentiment," James Russell Lowell said of him, "he never alludes to the humbleness of his origin; it probably never occurred to him, indeed, that there was anything higher to start from than manhood; and he put himself on a level with those he addressed, not by going down to them, but only by taking it for granted that they had brains and would come up to a common ground of reason."

No career in our history so justifies the democratic theory that men can be depended upon to do the righteous thing if leaders have the patience and the intelligence to demonstrate what is righteous.

No man's leadership has furnished stronger argument for the value of mercifulness in public life. By nature he was kindly—liked people—dreaded to hurt them. His hard-fought battles with men—constant through the last ten years of his life—are free from malice. "What I deal with is too vast for malicious dealings," he said once when Horace Greeley was badgering him. Victory brought him no exultation over his enemies. He never got satisfaction, he said, from knowing that somebody had been disappointed or pained by his success. When he told the North

PREFACE

that the war should be wound up "with malice toward none, with charity for all," he was but expressing the deepest thing in him—the greatest thing he had learned in his years of struggle.

There is no life in our history better fitted than Abraham Lincoln's to show men and women what they should be if they are to help this country work out the aims of democracy; and there is none that shows better the courage, the labor, the sacrifice, the human sympathy it requires to be the kind of man he was.

The hold he has on the world is as strong an argument as we have for believing that his faith in men's ability to govern themselves was not misplaced. So long as men honor, study and hold up Abraham Lincoln as a model, so long we may be sure they understand the quality of manhood which is essential for self-government.

IDA M. TARBELL.

November, 1924.

THE LIFE
OF
ABRAHAM LINCOLN

LIFE OF LINCOLN

CHAPTER I

THE ORIGIN OF THE LINCOLN FAMILY—THE LINCOLNS IN KENTUCKY—BIRTH OF ABRAHAM LINCOLN

BETWEEN the years 1635 and 1645 there came to the town of Hingham, Massachusetts, from the west of England, eight men named Lincoln. Three of these, Samuel, Daniel, and Thomas, were brothers. Their relationship, if any, to the other Lincolns who came over from the same part of England at about the same time, is not clear. Two of these men, Daniel and Thomas, died without heirs; but Samuel left a large family, including four sons. Among the descendants of Samuel Lincoln's sons were many good citizens and prominent public officers. One was a member of the Boston Tea Party, and served as a captain of artillery in the War of the Revolution. Three served on the brig *Hazard* during the Revolution. Levi Lincoln, a great-great-grandson of Samuel, born in Hingham in 1749, and graduated from Harvard, was one of the minute-men at Cambridge immediately after the battle of Lexington, a delegate to the convention in Cambridge for framing a state constitution, and in 1781 was elected to the Continental Congress, but declined to serve. He was a member of the House of Representatives and of the Senate of Massachusetts, and was appointed Attorney General of the United States by Jefferson; for a few months preceding the arrival of Madison he was Secretary of State, and in 1807 he was elected Lieutenant Governor of Massachusetts. In 1811 he was appointed Associate Justice of the United States Supreme Court by President Madison, an office which he declined. From the close of the Revolutionary War he was considered the head of the Massachusetts bar.

His eldest son, Levi Lincoln, born in 1782, had also an honorable career. He was a Harvard graduate, became Governor of the State of Massachusetts, and held other important public offices. He received the degree of LL.D. from both Williams College and Harvard College.

Another son of Levi Lincoln, Enoch Lincoln, served in Congress from 1818 to 1826. He became Governor of Maine in 1827, holding the position until his death in 1829. Enoch Lincoln was a writer of more than ordinary ability.

The fourth son of Samuel Lincoln was called Mordecai. Mordecai was a "blacksmith," as an ironmaster was called in those days. Besides setting up a smelter where he made iron, and a forge with a trip hammer where he beat out nails, bolts, shovels, and tongs, he ran a sawmill and a gristmill. His business prospered for when he died in 1727 he left an estate, large for that day, of something over £3,000. Two of his children, Mordecai and Abraham, did not remain in Massachusetts, but removed to New Jersey, and thence to Pennsylvania, where both prospered,

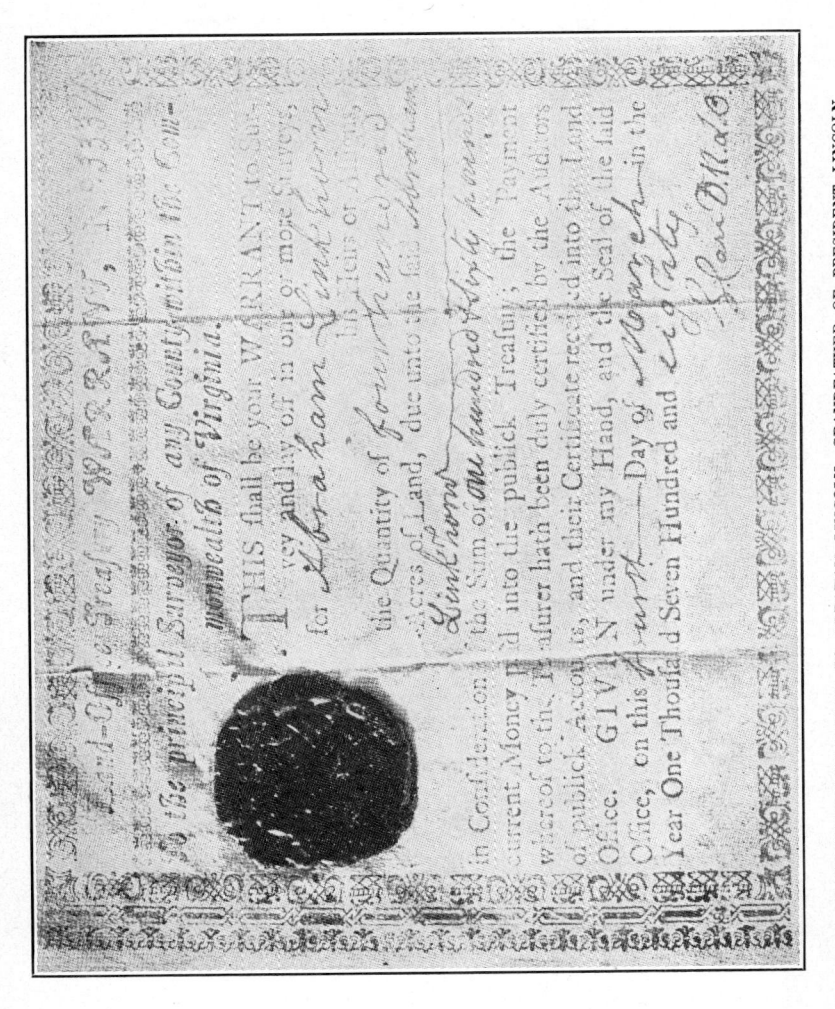

LAND WARRANT ISSUED TO ABRAHAM LINCOLN, GRANDFATHER OF PRESIDENT LINCOLN.

and dying, left considerable estates to their children. Their descendants in Pennsylvania have continued to this day to be well-to-do people, some of them having taken prominent positions in public affairs. Abraham Lincoln, of Berks County, who was born in 1736 and died in 1806, filled many public offices, being a member of the General Assembly of Pennsylvania, of the State Convention of 1787, and of the State Constitutional Convention in 1790.

One of the sons of this second Mordecai, John, received from his father "three hundred acres of land, lying in the Jerseys." But evidently he did not care to cultivate his inheritance, for about 1768 he removed to Virginia. "Virginia John," as this member of the family was called, had five sons one of whom, Jacob, entered the Continental Army and served as a lieutenant at Yorktown. The third son, named Abraham, was twenty-four years old when John Lincoln moved into the Shenandoah Valley. He made his way quickly in the neighborhood, for by 1770 he had married into a prominent family, the Herring's, and had been made a captain in the local militia; later he was elected a judge advocate of the military court. In 1773 his father gave him a tract of 210 acres of land in what is now Rockingham County, Virginia. But though Abraham Lincoln prospered and added to these acres he was not satisfied to remain many years in Virginia. It was not strange. The farm on which he lived lay close to the track of one of the earliest of those wonderful western migrations which from time to time have taken place in this country. Soon after John Lincoln came into Virginia vague rumors began to be circulated there of a rich western land called Kentucky. These rumors rapidly developed into facts, as journeys were made into the new land by John Finley, Daniel Boone and other adventure-loving men, and settlers began to move thither from Pennsylvania, Virginia and North Carolina. There were but two roads by which Kentucky could be reached then, the national highway from Philadelphia to Pittsburgh and thence by the Ohio, and the highway which ran from Philadelphia south-westward through the Virginia Valley to Cumberland Gap and thence by a trail called the Wilderness Road, northwest to the Ohio at Louisville. The latter road was considered less dangerous and more practical than the former and by it the greater part of the emigrants journeyed. Now this road lay through Rockingham County. Abraham Lincoln was thus directly under the influence of a moving procession of restless seekers after new lands and unknown goods. The spell came upon him and, selling two hundred and forty acres of land in Rockingham County for five thousand pounds of the current money of Virginia—a sum worth at that time not more than one hundred and twenty-five pounds sterling—he joined a party of travelers to the Wilderness. Returning a few months later he moved his whole family, consisting of a wife and five children, into Kentucky.

Abraham Lincoln was ambitious to become a landed proprietor in the new country, and he entered a generous amount of land—four hundred acres on Long Run, in Jefferson County; eight hundred acres on Green River, near the Green River lick; five hun-

THE HOME OF ABRAHAM LINCOLN, GRANDFATHER OF THE PRESIDENT.

Hughes' Station, on Floyd's Creek, Jefferson County, Kentucky. From original owned by R. T. Durrett, LL.D., Louisville.

See page 5.

dred acres in Campbell County. He settled near the first tract, where he undertook to clear a farm. It was a dangerous task, for the Indians were still troublesome, and the settlers, for protection, were forced to live in or near forts or stations. In 1784, when John Filson published his "History of Kentucky," though there was a population of thirty thousand in the territory, there were but eighteen houses outside of the stations. Of these stations, or stockades, there were but fifty-two. According to the tradition in the Lincoln family, Abraham Lincoln lived at Hughes Station on Floyd Creek in Jefferson County.

All went well with him and his family at the start. Then, one day, while he and his three sons were at work in their clearing, an unexpected Indian shot killed the father. His death was a terrible blow to the family. The large tracts of land which he had entered were still uncleared, and his personal property was necessarily small. The difficulty of reaching the country at that date, as well as its wild condition made it impracticable for even a wealthy pioneer to own more stock or household furniture than was absolutely essential. Abraham Lincoln was probably as well provided with personal property as most of his neighbors. The inventory of his estate, still to be seen in the court-house at Bardstown, Kentucky, formerly county seat of Washington, now of Nelson County, was returned by the appraisers on March 10, 1789. It gives a clearer idea of the condition in which he left his wife and children, than any description could do:

	£	s.	d.
One Sorrel Horse Appraised to	8	0	0
Black Horse	9	10	0
One Red Cow & Calf	4	10	0
Brindle Cow & Calf	4	10	0
Red Cow & Calf	5		
Brindle bull yearling	1	0	0
Brindled heifer yearling	1	0	0
Bar Shear plow and Tackling	2	5	0
Three Weeding hoes	0	7	6
Flax wheel	0	6	0
Pair of Smoothing Irons	0	15	0
One Dozen pewter plates	1	10	0
Two pewter Dishes	0	17	6
Dutch Oven and Cale (sic) Weighing 15 lbs.	1	15	0
Small Iron Kettle and Cale weighing 12 lbs.	1	12	0
Foot adds	0	10	0
Hand saw	0	5	0
One Inch Auger	0	6	0
Three quarter Do	0	4	6
Half Inch Do	0	3	0
Drawing knife	0	3	0
Curring Knife	0	10	0
Curriers Hook and barking Iron	0	6	0
Old Smooth bore Gun	0	10	0
Riffle do	5	0	0
do do	3	10	0
Two pott Trammells	0	14	0
One Feather Bead & furniture	5	10	0
Ditto	8	5	0
One Bed of Turkey feathers and furniture	1	10	0
Stakeing Iron	0	1	6
Candlestick	0	1	6
One Ax	0	9	0
	£68	16s.	6d.

Soon after the death of Abraham Lincoln, his widow moved from Jefferson County to Washington County. Here the eldest son, Mordecai, who is supposed to have inherited nearly all of the large estate, became a well-to-do and popular citizen. The deed-book of Washington County contains a number of records of lands bought and sold by him. At one time he was sheriff of his county and according to a tradition of his descendants a member of the Kentucky Legislature. His name is not to be found however in the journals of the Kentucky legislature. Mordecai Lincoln is remembered especially for his sporting tastes, his bitter hatred of the Indians and his ability as a story-teller. He remained in Kentucky until late in life, when he removed to Hancock County, Illinois.

Of Josiah, the second son, we know very little more than that the records show that he owned and sold land. He left Kentucky when a young man to settle on the Blue River, in Harrison County, Indiana, and there he died. The two daughters married into well-known Kentucky families; the elder, Mary, marrying Ralph Crume; the younger, Nancy, William Brumfield.

The death of Abraham Lincoln was saddest for the youngest of the children, a lad of eight years at the time, named Thomas, for it turned him adrift early to become a "wandering laboring-boy." If Thomas inherited any part of his father's estate which is now believed probable, although until recently denied, he did not receive it until he was of age. That meant that at the start he was obliged to shift for himself.

For several years he supported himself by rough farm work of all kinds, learning, in the meantime, the trade of carpenter and cabinet-maker. According to one of his acquaintances, "Tom had the best set of tools in what was then and now Washington County," and was "a good carpenter for those days, when a cabin was built mainly with the axe, and not a nail or bolt-hinge in it; only leathers and pins to the door, and no glass." Although a skilled craftsman for his day, he never became a thrifty or ambitious man. "He would work energetically enough when a job was brought to him, but he would never seek a job." But if Thomas Lincoln plied his trade spasmodically, he shared the pioneer's love for land, for in 1803 when but twenty-three years old and still without the responsibility of a family, he bought a farm in Hardin County, Kentucky. This fact is of importance, proving as it does that Thomas Lincoln was not the altogether shiftless man he has been pictured. Certainly he must have been above the grade of the ordinary country boy to have had the energy and ambition to learn a trade and secure a farm through his own efforts by the time he was twenty-three. He was illiterate, never doing more "in the way of writing than to bunglingly write his own name." Nevertheless, he had the reputation in the country of being good-natured and obliging and possessing what his neighbors called "good strong horse-sense." Although he was a "very quiet sort of a man," he was known to be determined in his opinions and quite competent to defend his rights by force if they were too flagrantly

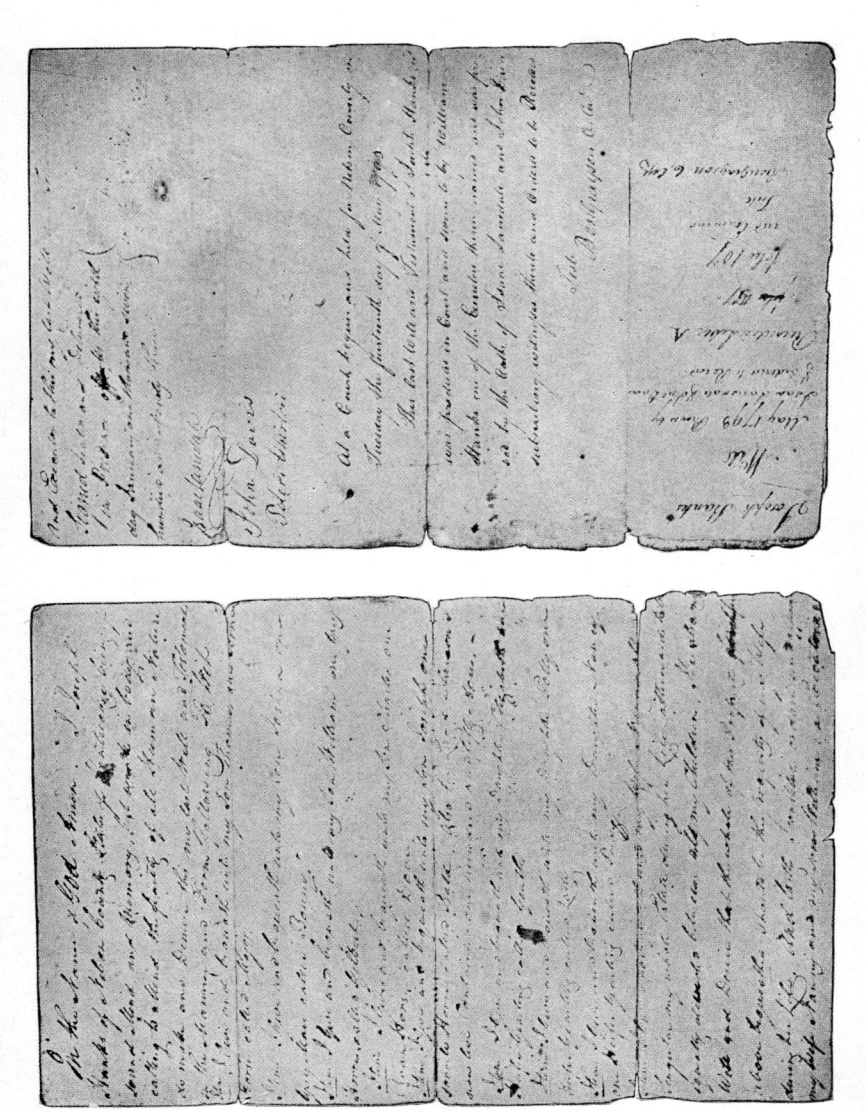

FACSIMILE OF WILL LEFT BY JOSEPH HANKS.

violated. He was a moral man, and religious, a faithful Baptist.

In 1806 Thomas Lincoln was married to a young woman of the neighborhood, Nancy Hanks. The genealogy of the Hanks family in America has never been satisfactorily completed. It is certain, however, that they have been almost as long in America as the Lincolns. Mordecai Lincoln, the iron master of Scituate, had as a neighbor in Plymouth, Mass., a Benjamin Hanks, though it has not been proved that Nancy Hanks descended from him. It is probable, though still not proved, that a neighbor of the Pennsylvania Lincolns, one John Hanks, who later moved into the Shenandoah Valley, was an ancestor of hers. In the records of several counties of western Virginia there are traces of Hanks. Members of the family certainly came early into Kentucky, among them one Joseph Hanks, who settled in Nelson County. The will of this Joseph Hanks, still to be seen in the courthouse in Bardstown, shows him to have left a large family as well as some property.

The youngest child recognized in his will was named Nancy. It has not been conclusively proved —though it seems to the writer probable—that this was the Nancy that Thomas Lincoln married in 1806; she was certainly closely connected with this family.

The earliest reliable traditions that we have of Nancy Hanks place her in the family of one Richard Berry who owned a farm in Washington County near Springfield. There was a large number of related people in this neighborhood and it is believed that

Nancy was brought up by them. She grew into a sweet-tempered and beautiful woman whom tradition paints not only as the center of all the country merrymaking but as a famous spinner and housewife.

It was probably at the house of Richard Berry that Thomas Lincoln met Nancy Hanks, for he doubtless spent more or less time nearby with his oldest brother, Mordecai Lincoln, who was a resident of Washington County and a friend and neighbor of the Berrys. He may have seen her, too, at the home of her relative—possibly her brother—Joseph Hanks, in Elizabethtown. This Joseph Hanks was a carpenter who had inherited the old home of the family and it was from him that Thomas Lincoln learned his trade. At all events, the two young people became engaged and on June 10, 1806, their marriage bond was issued according to the law of the time. Two days later, according to the marriage returns of the Reverend Jesse Head, they were married,—a fact duly attested also by the marriage certificate made out by the officiating minister.

The marriage took place at the home of Richard Berry, near Beechland in Washington County, Kentucky. It was celebrated in the boisterous style of one hundred years ago and was followed by an infare given by the bride's guardian. To this celebration came all the neighbors, and, according to an entertaining Kentucky centenarian, Dr. Christopher Columbus Graham, even those who happened in the neighborhood were made welcome. He tells how he heard of the wedding while "out hunting for roots," and went "just to get a good supper. I saw Nancy

HOUSE NEAR BEECHLAND, KENTUCKY, WHERE THOMAS LINCOLN AND NANCY HANKS WERE MARRIED.

From a photograph in the collection of O. H. Oldroyd, preserved in the house in which Lincoln died, Washington, D. C.

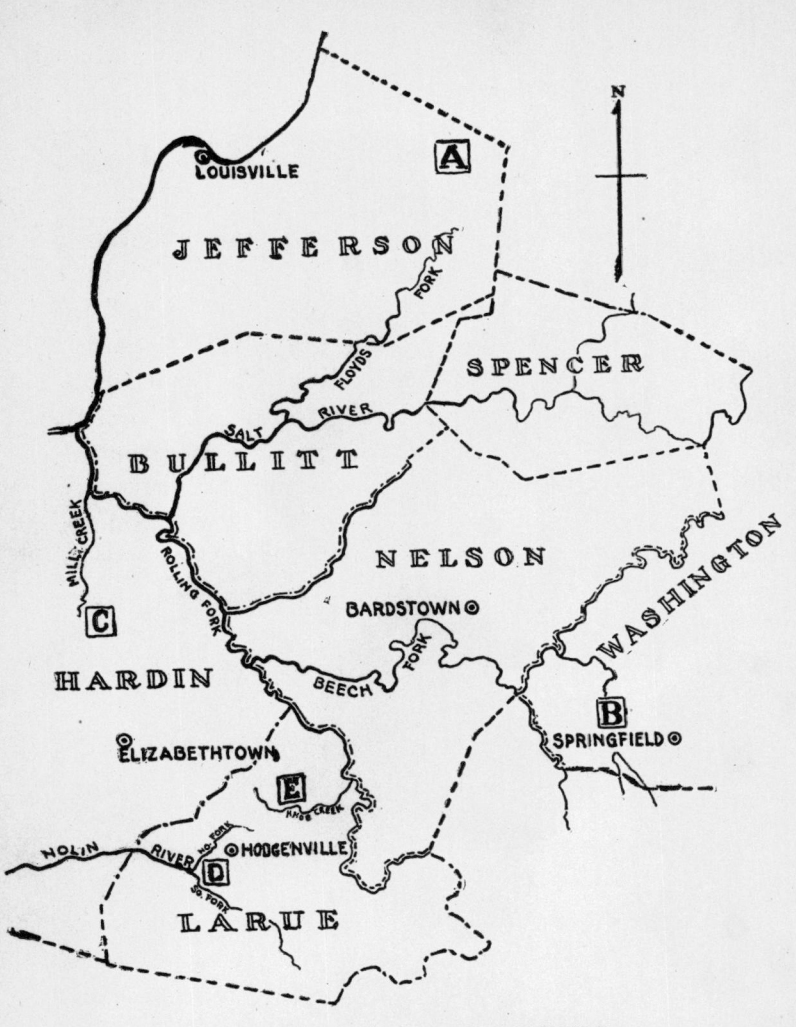

THE LINCOLN COUNTRY OF KENTUCKY

A.—Here Abraham Lincoln, Sr., was building his first cabin in Kentucky when killed by Indians before the eyes of his little sons. B.—The first permanent home of the Lincolns in Kentucky. C.—First land owned by Thomas Lincoln, bought and paid for in 1803. D.—Birthplace of Abraham Lincoln. E.—First home Abraham Lincoln remembered.

Interesting documents connected with the history of Abraham Lincoln and his family are to be seen in the court houses at Bardstown, Springfield and Elizabethtown.

Hanks Lincoln at her wedding," continued Mr. Graham, "a fresh looking girl, I should say over twenty. I was at the infare, too, given by John H. Parrott, her guardian—and only girls with money had guardians appointed by the court. We had bear meat; ... venison; wild turkey and ducks; eggs, wild and tame, so common that you could buy them at two bits a bushel; maple sugar, swung on a string, to bite off for coffee or whiskey; syrup in big gourds; peach-and-honey; a sheep that the two families barbecued whole over coals of wood burned in a pit and covered with green boughs to keep the juice in; and a race for the whiskey bottle."

After his marriage Thomas Lincoln settled in Elizabethtown. His home was a log cabin, but at that date few people in the state had anything else. Kentucky had been in the union only fourteen years. When admitted, the few brick structures within its boundaries were easily counted, and there were only log school-houses and churches. Fourteen years had brought great improvements, but the majority of the population still lived in log cabins, so that the home of Thomas Lincoln was as good as most of his neighbors. Little is known of his position in Elizabethtown, though we have proof that he had credit in the community, for the descendants of two of the early storekeepers still remember seeing on their grandfathers' account books sundry items charged to T. Lincoln. Tools and groceries were the chief purchases he made, though on one of the ledgers a pair of "silk suspenders," worth one dollar and fifty cents, was entered. He not only enjoyed a certain credit with the

Know all men by these presents that we Thomas Lincoln and Richard Berry   are held and firmly bound unto his Excellency the governof Kentucky for the use and benefit of fifty pounds currant money to the payment of which we bind ourselves to be made to the said governor and his successors for the use bind our heirs our his &c Jointly and severally firmly by these presents sealed with our seals and dated this 10th day of June. 1806 The Condition of this obligation is such that whereas there is a marriage shortly entended between the above bound Thomas Lincoln and Nancy Hanks   for which there is no lawful cause to obstruct the said Marriage then this obligation to be Void or else to remain in full force &Virtue in law

Witness
John H. Parrott

Thomas Lincoln (Seal)
Richard Berry jr. (Seal)
guardan

FACSIMILE OF THE MARRIAGE BOND OF THOMAS LINCOLN.

Washington Co.

I do hereby certify that the following is a true list of Marriages Solemnized by me in Serving from the 28th of April 1806 until the date hereof

June 26th 1806 Joined together in the Holy estate of Matrimony agreeable to the rules of the M.E.C.

Morris Berry & Peggy Simms,
Nov 27th 1806 David Mize & Hanah Xter
March 5th 1807 Charles Ridge & Anna Davis
March 24th 1807 John Head & Sally Clark
March 27th Benjamin Clark & Polly Head
Jany 14th Edward Dyle & Rosanah McMahon
Dec 22nd 1806 Silas Chamberlin & Betsey West
Jun 17th 1806 John Springer & Elizebeth Ingram
Jun 12th 1806 Thomas Lincoln & Nancy Hanks
September 23 1806 John Cambron & Hanah White
October 2nd 1806 Anthony Lypey & Keziah Pettit
October 23rd 1806 Aron Harding & Hanah Hottot
April 5th 1807 Daniel Payne & Christeena Pierce
July 26th 1806 Benjamin Clark & Polly Clark
May — 1806 Hugh Haskins & Betsey Dyer
September 25th 1806 John Graham & Cathrine Jones

Given under my hand this 22nd day of April 1807

John Head D.M.E.Co.

RETURN OF MARRIAGE OF THOMAS LINCOLN AND NANCY HANKS.

From a tracing of the original, made by Henry Whitney Cleveland. This certificate was discovered about 1885 by W. F. Booker, Esq., Clerk of Washington County, Kentucky.

ORIGIN OF THE LINCOLN FAMILY 15

people of Elizabethtown; he was sufficiently respected by the public authorities to be appointed in 1816 a road surveyor, or, as the office is known in some localities, supervisor. It was not, to be sure, a position of great importance, but it proved that he was considered fit to oversee a body of men at a task of considerable value to the community. Indeed, all of the many documents mentioning Thomas Lincoln which have

FACSIMILE OF THE APPOINTMENT OF THOMAS LINCOLN AS ROAD SURVEYOR.

been discovered show him to have had a much better position in Hardin County than he has been credited with.

It was at Elizabethtown that the first child of the Lincolns, a daughter, was born. Soon after this event Thomas Lincoln decided to combine farming with his trade and moved to a farm on the Big South fork of Nolin Creek, in Hardin County, now La Rue County, three miles from Hodgensville, and about fourteen miles from Elizabethtown. Here he was living when, on February 12, 1809, his second child, a boy, was born. The little newcomer was called Abraham, after his grandfather—a name which had persisted through many preceding generations in both the Lincoln and Hanks families.

The home into which the child came was the ordinary one of the poorer western pioneer—a one-roomed cabin with a huge outside chimney, a single window, and a rude door. The descriptions of its squalor and wretchedness, which are so familiar, have been overdrawn. Dr. Graham, than whom there is no better authority on the life of that day, and who knew Thomas Lincoln well, declares energetically that "It is all stuff about Tom Lincoln keeping his wife in an open shed in a winter. The Lincolns had a cow and calf, milk and butter, a good feather bed—for I have slept on it. They had home-woven 'kiverlids,' big and little pots, a loom and wheel. Tom Lincoln was a man and took care of his wife."

The Lincoln home was undoubtedly rude and in many ways uncomfortable, but it sheltered a happy family, and its poverty affected the new child but little. He grew to be robust and active and soon learned how endless are the delights and interests the country offers to a child. He had several companions. There was his sister Nancy, or Sarah—both names are given her—two years his senior; there was a cousin of his mother, ten years older, Dennis Friend (commonly called Dennis Hanks), an active and ingenious leader in sports and mischief; and there were the neighbors' boys. One of the latter, Austin Gollaher, lived to be over ninety years of age and to his death related with pride how he played with young Lincoln in the shavings of his father's carpenter shop, hunted

LOG CABIN IN WHICH ABRAHAM LINCOLN WAS BORN.

In 1808 Thomas Lincoln moved his family into this cabin which stood on a farm 2½ miles from Hodgenville, La Rue Co., Ky. Here on February 12th, 1809, Abraham Lincoln was born. The cabin was at one time exhibited in various cities of the United States but was finally returned to the original site, and there stood when the above photograph was taken some 30 years ago. It now stands within a beautiful Temple—a national memorial to Lincoln at Hodgenville, Ky.

coons and ran the woods with him, and once even saved his life.

"Yes," Mr. Gollaher was accustomed to say, "the story that I once saved Abraham Lincoln's life is true. He and I had been going to school together for a year or more and had become greatly attached to each other. Then school disbanded on account of there being so few scholars, and we did not see each other much for a long while. One Sunday my mother visited the Lincolns, and I was taken along. Abe and I played around all day. Finally we concluded to cross the creek to hunt for some partridges young Lincoln had seen the day before. The creek was swollen by a recent rain and, in crossing on the narrow footlog, Abe fell in. Neither of us could swim. I got a long pole and held it out to Abe, who grabbed it. Then I pulled him ashore. He was almost dead, and I was badly scared. I rolled and pounded him in good earnest. Then I got him by the arms and shook him, the water meanwhile pouring out of his mouth. By this means I succeeded in bringing him to, and he was soon all right.

"Then a new difficulty confronted us. If our mothers discovered our wet clothes they would whip us. This we dreaded from experience and determined to avoid. It was June, the sun was very warm, and we soon dried our clothing by spreading it on the rocks about us. We promised never to tell the story, and I never did until after Lincoln's tragic end."

When the little boy was about four years old the first real excitement of his life occurred. His father moved from the farm on Nolin Creek to another some fifteen miles northeast on Knob Creek, and here the child began to go to school. At that day the schools in the West were usually accidental, depending upon the coming of some poor and ambitious young man who was willing to teach a few terms while he looked for an opening to something better. The terms were irregular, their length being decided by the time the settlers felt able to board the master and pay his small salary. The chief qualifications for a schoolmaster seem to have been enough strength to keep the "big boys" in order, though one high authority affirms that pluck went "for a heap sight more'n sinnoo with boys."

Many of the itinerant masters were Catholics, strolling Irishmen from the colony in Tennessee, or French priests from Kaskaskia. Lincoln's first teacher, Zachariah Riney, was a Catholic and a man of considerable cultivation, it is believed, probably connected with one of the important institutions which the Church had already founded in that part of the world. His second teacher, Caleb Hazel, was a neighbor of the Lincolns, his farm adjoining theirs. The records of the county show that Hazel dealt in lands and was active in various county affairs. That is, both men were something more than wandering schoolmasters. Mr. Gollaher says that Abraham Lincoln, in those days when he was his schoolmate, was "an unusually bright boy at school and made splendid progress in his studies. Indeed, he learned faster than any of his schoolmates. Though so young, he studied very hard. He would get spicewood bushes, hack them up on a log, and burn them two or three together for the purpose of giving light by which he might pursue his studies."

Probably the boy's mother had something to do

with the spicewood illuminations. Tradition has it that Mrs. Lincoln took great pains to teach her children what she knew, and that at her knee they heard all the Bible lore, fairy tales, and country legends that she had been able to gather in her poor life.

Besides the "A B C schools," as Lincoln called them, the only other medium of education in the country districts of Kentucky in those days was "preaching." Itinerants like the schoolmasters, the preachers, of whatever denomination, were often though not always uncouth and illiterate; the code of morals they taught was mainly a healthy one, and they, no doubt, did much to keep the consciences of the pioneers awake. It is difficult to believe that they ever did much for the moral training of young Lincoln, though he certainly got his first notion of public speaking from them; and for years of his boyhood one of his chief delights was to gather his playmates about him and preach and thump until he had his auditors frightened or in tears.

As soon as the child was strong enough to follow his father in the fields he was put to work at simple tasks—bringing tools, carrying water, picking berries, dropping seeds. He learned to know his father's farm from line to line and years after, when President of the United States, he recalled in a conversation at the White House, in the presence of Dr. J. J. Wright of Emporia, Kansas, the arrangement of the fields and an incident of his own childish experience as a farmer's son. "Mr. President," one of the visitors had asked, "how would you like when the war is over to visit your old home in Kentucky?" "I would like it very much," Mr. Lincoln replied. "I remember that old home very well. Our farm was composed of three fields. It lay in the valley surrounded by high hills and deep gorges. Sometimes when there came a big rain in the hills the water would come down through the gorges and spread all over the farm. The last thing that I remember of doing there was one Saturday afternoon; the other boys planted the corn in what we called the big field; it contained seven acres —and I dropped the pumpkin seed. I dropped two seeds every other hill and every other row. The next Sunday morning there came a big rain in the hills, it did not rain a drop in the valley, but the water coming down through the gorges washed ground, corn, pumpkin seeds and all clear off the field."

CHAPTER II

THE LINCOLNS LEAVE KENTUCKY FOR SOUTHERN INDIANA—CONDITIONS OF LIFE IN THEIR NEW HOME

In 1816 a great adventure came to the little boy. His father emigrated from Knob Creek to Indiana. "This removal was partly on account of slavery, but chiefly on account of the difficulty in land titles in Kentucky," says his son. It was due, as well, no doubt, to the fascination which an unknown country has always for the adventurous, and to that restless pioneer spirit which drives even men of sober judgment continually towards the frontier, in search of a place where the conflict with nature is less severe—some spot farther on to which a friend or a neighbor has preceded and from which he sends back glowing reports. It may be that Thomas Lincoln was tempted into Indiana by the reports of his brother Josiah who had settled on the Big Blue River in that state. At all events, in the fall of 1816 he started with wife and children and household stores to journey by horseback and by wagon from Knob Creek to a farm selected on a previous trip he had made. This farm, located near Little Pigeon Creek, about fifteen miles north of the Ohio River, and a mile and a half east of Gentryville, Spencer County, was in a forest so dense that the road for the travellers had to be hewed out as they went.

To a boy of seven years, free from all responsibility

and too vigorous to feel its hardships, such a journey must have been a long delight and wonder. Life suddenly ceased its routine, and every day brought forth new scenes and adventures. Little Abraham saw forests greater than he had ever dreamed of, peopled by strange birds and beasts, and he crossed a river so wide that it must have seemed to him like the sea. To Thomas and Nancy Lincoln the journey was probably a hard and anxious one; but to the children beside them it was a wonderful journey into the unknown.

On arriving at the new farm an axe was put into the boy's hands, and he was set to work to aid in clearing a field for corn, and to help build the "half-face camp" which for a year was the home of the Lincolns. There were few more primitive homes in the wilderness of Indiana in 1816 than this of young Lincoln, and there were few families, even in that day, who were forced to practice more make-shifts to get a living. The cabin which took the place of the "half-face camp" had but one room, with a loft above. For a long time there was no window, door, or floor; not even the traditional deer-skin hung before the exit; there was no oiled paper over the opening for light; there was no puncheon covering on the ground.

The furniture was of their own manufacture. The table and chairs were of the rudest sort—rough slabs of wood in which holes were bored and legs fitted in. Their bedstead, or, rather bed-frame, was made of poles held up by two outer posts, and the ends made firm by inserting the poles in auger-holes that had been bored in a log which was a part of the wall of the cabin; skins were its chief covering. Little Abraham's bed was even more primitive. He slept on a heap of dry leaves in the corner of the loft, to which he mounted by means of pegs driven into the wall.

Their food, if coarse, was usually abundant; the chief difficulty in supplying the larder was to secure variety. Of game there was plenty—deer, bear, pheasants, wild turkeys, ducks, birds of all kinds. There were fish in the streams and wild fruits of many kinds in the woods in the summer, and these were dried for winter use; but the difficulty of raising and milling corn and wheat was great. Indeed, in many places in the west the first flour cake was an historical event. Corn-dodger was the every-day bread of the Lincoln household, the wheat cake being a dainty reserved for Sunday mornings.

Potatoes were the only vegetable raised in any quantity, and there were times in the Lincoln family when they were the only food on the table; a fact proved to posterity by the oft-quoted remark of Abraham to his father after the latter had asked a blessing over a dish of roasted potatoes—"that they were mighty poor blessings." Not only were they all the Lincolns had for dinner sometimes; one of their neighbors tells of calling there when raw potatoes, pared and washed, were passed around instead of apples or other fruit. They even served as a kind of pioneer chauffrette—being baked and given to the children to carry in their hands as they started to school or on distant errands in winter time.

The food was prepared in the rudest way, for the supply of both groceries and cooking utensils was limited. The former were frequently wanting entirely, and as for the latter, the most important item was the Dutch oven. An indispensable article in the primitive kitchen outfit was the "gritter." It was made by flattening out an old piece of tin, punching it full of holes, and nailing it on a board. Upon this all sorts of things were grated, even ears of corn, in which slow way enough meal was sometimes secured for bread. Old tin was used for many other contrivances besides the "gritter," and every scrap was carefully saved. Most of the dishes were of pewter; the spoons, iron; the knives and forks horn-handled.

The Lincolns of course made their own soap and candles, and if they had cotton or wool to wear they had literally to grow it. It is probable that young Abraham Lincoln wore little cotton or linsey-woolsey. His trousers were of roughly tanned deer-skin, his foot-covering a home-made moccasin, his cap a coon-skin; it was only the material for his blouse or shirt that was woven at home. If this costume had some obvious disadvantages, it was not to be despised. So good an authority as Governor Reynolds says of one of its articles—the linsey-woolsey shirt—"It was an excellent garment. I have never felt so happy and healthy since I put it off."

These "pretty pinching times," as Abraham Lincoln once described the early days in Indiana, lasted until 1819. The year before Nancy Lincoln had died, and for many months no more forlorn place could be conceived than this pioneer home bereft of its guiding spirit; but finally Thomas Lincoln went back to Kentucky and returned with a new wife—Sally Bush

VIEW OF ROCK SPRING FARM, WHERE PRESIDENT LINCOLN WAS BORN.
From a photograph taken in September, 1895. The house in which Lincoln was born is seen to the right, in the background.

ROCK SPRING, ON THE FARM WHERE LINCOLN WAS BORN.
From a photograph taken in September, 1895.

Johnston, a widow with three children, John, Sarah, and Matilda. The new mother came well provided with household furniture, bringing many things unfamiliar to little Abraham—"one fine bureau, one table, one set of chairs, one large clothes-chest, cooking utensils, knives, forks, bedding, and other articles." She was a woman of energy, thrift, and gentleness, and at once made the cabin homelike and taught the children habits of cleanliness and comfort. Abraham was ten years old when his new mother came from Kentucky, and he was already an important member of the family. He was remarkably strong for his years, and the work he could do in a day was a decided advantage to Thomas Lincoln. The axe which had been put into his hand to help in making the first clearing, he had never been allowed to drop; indeed, as he says himself, "from that till within his twenty-third year he was almost constantly handling that most useful instrument." Besides, he drove the team, cut the elm and linn brush with which the stock was often fed, learned to handle the old shovel-plough, to wield the sickle, to thresh the wheat with a flail, to fan and clean it with a sheet, to go to mill and turn the hard-earned grist into flour. In short, he learned all the trades the settler's boy must know, and so well that when his father did not need him he could hire him to the neighbors. Thomas Lincoln also taught him the rudiments of carpentry and cabinet-making and kept him busy much of the time as his assistant in his trade. There are houses still standing, in and near Gentryville, on which it is said he worked.

As he grew older he became one of the strongest and most popular "hands" in the vicinity, and much of his time was spent as a "hired boy" on some neighbor's farm. For twenty-five cents a day—paid to his father—he was hostler, ploughman, wood-chopper, and carpenter, besides helping the women with the "chores." For them he was ready to carry water, make the fire, even tend the baby. No wonder that a laborer who never refused to do anything asked of him, who could "strike with a maul heavier blows" and "sink an axe deeper into the wood" than anybody else in the community, and who at the same time was general help for the women, never lacked a job in Gentryville.

Of all the tasks his rude life brought him, none seems to have suited him better than going to the mill. It was, perhaps, as much the leisure enforced by this trip as anything else that attracted him. The machinery was primitive, and each man waited his turn, which sometimes was long in coming. A story is told by one of the pioneers of Illinois of going many miles with a grist and waiting so long for his turn that when it came, he and his horse had eaten all the corn and he had none to grind. This waiting with other men and boys on like errands gave an opportunity for talk, story-telling, and games, which were Lincoln's delight.

If Abraham Lincoln's life was rough and hard it was not without amusements. At home the rude household was overflowing with life. There were Abraham and his sister, a stepbrother and two stepsisters, and a cousin of Nancy Hanks Lincoln, Dennis

FACSIMILE OF THE RECORD OF THE LINCOLN FAMILY MADE BY ABRAHAM LINCOLN IN THE FAMILY BIBLE.
From original in possession of C. F. Gunther, Esq., Chicago.

By permission, from Herndon and Weik's "Life of Abraham Lincoln."
Copyright 1892, by D. Appleton & Co.

(Friend) Hanks, whom misfortune had made an inmate of the Lincoln home—quite enough to plan sports and mischief and keep time from growing dull. Thomas Lincoln and Dennis Hanks were both famous story-tellers, and the Lincolns spent many a cozy evening about their cabin fire repeating the stories they knew.

Of course the boys hunted. Not that Abraham ever became a true sportsman; indeed, he seems to have lacked the genuine sporting instinct. In a curious autobiography, written entirely in the third person, which Lincoln prepared at the request of a friend in 1860, he says of his exploits as a hunter: "A few days before the completion of his eighth year, in the absence of his father, a flock of wild turkeys approached the new log cabin; and Abraham with a rifle, standing inside, shot through a crack and killed one of them. He has never since pulled the trigger on any larger game." This exploit is confirmed by Dennis Hanks, who says: "No doubt about A. Lincoln's killing the turkey. He done it with his father's rifle, made by William Lutes of Bullitt County, Kentucky. I have killed a hundred deer with her myself; turkeys too numerous to mention."

But there were many other country sports which he enjoyed to the full. He went swimming in the evenings; fished with the other boys in Pigeon Creek, wrestled, jumped, and ran races at the noon rests. He was present at every country horse-race and fox-chase. The sports he preferred were those which brought men together; the spelling-school, the husking-bee; the "raising"; and of all these he was the life by his wit, his stories, his good nature, his doggerel verses, his practical jokes, and by a rough kind of politeness—for even in Indiana in those times there was a notion of politeness, and one of Lincoln's schoolmasters had given "lessons in manners." Lincoln seems to have profited in a degree by them, for Mrs. Crawford, at whose home he worked for some time, declares that he always "lifted his hat and bowed" when he made his appearance.

Fun and frolic, courting and mating, of course went on among these young people of southwestern Indiana. Lincoln's old comrades and friends have left many tales of how he "went to see the girls," of how he brought in the biggest back-log and made the brightest fire; of how the young people, sitting around it watching the way the sparks flew, told their fortunes. He helped pare apples, shell corn and crack nuts. He took the girls to meeting and to spelling-school, though he was not often allowed to take part in the spelling-match, for the one who "chose first" always chose "Abe Lincoln," and that was equivalent to winning, as the others knew that "he would stand up the longest."

The nearest approach to sentiment at this time, of which we know, is recorded in a story Lincoln once told to an acquaintance in Springfield. It was a rainy day, and he was sitting with his feet on the window-sill, his eyes on the street, watching the rain. Suddenly he looked up and said:

"Did you ever write out a story in your mind? I did when I was a little codger. One day a wagon with a lady and two girls and a man broke down near us, and while they were fixing up, they cooked in our kitchen. The woman had books and read us stories, and they were the first I had ever heard. I took a great fancy to one of the girls; and when they were gone I thought of her a great deal, and one day when I was sitting out in the sun by the house I wrote out a story in my mind. I thought I took my father's horse and followed the wagon, and finally I found it, and they were surprised to see me. I talked with the girl and persuaded her to elope with me; and that night I put her on my horse, and we started off across the prairie. After several hours we came to a camp; and when we rode up we found it was the one we had left a few hours before, and we went in. The next night we tried again, and the same thing happened—the horse came back to the same place; and then we concluded that we ought not to elope. I stayed until I had persuaded her father to give her to me. I always meant to write that story out and publish it, and I began once; but I concluded that it was not much of a story. But I think that was the beginning of love with me."

His life had its tragedies as well as its touch of romance—tragedies so real and profound that they gave dignity to all the crudeness and poverty which surrounded him and quickened and intensified the melancholy temperament which he inherited from his mother. Away back in 1816, when Thomas Lincoln had started to find a farm in Indiana, bidding his wife be ready to go into the wilderness on his return, Nancy Lincoln had taken her boy and girl to a tiny grave, that of her youngest child; and the three had there said good-by to a little one whom the children had scarcely known, but for whom the mother's grief was so keen that the boy never forgot the scene.

Two years later he saw his father make a green pine box and put his dead mother into it, and he saw her

VIEW OF LINCOLN FARM IN INDIANA IN 1895.

A marble tablet now marks the site of the Lincoln Cabin, every vestige of which has disappeared. Thomas Lincoln selected this tract in 1816, and, to identify it, he blazed the trees and piled up brush at the corners to establish boundary lines. When he returned with his family he was obliged to cut his way to the spot chosen for his cabin and to fell trees to find space for the "half-face camp," in which he first lived. This land was entered October 15, 1817, under the old credit system. Later Mr. Lincoln gave up to the United States the east half, and the amount paid on it was passed to his credit to complete paying for the west half. The patent issued for the latter tract was dated June 6, 1827.

buried not far from their cabin, almost without prayer. Young as he was, it was his efforts, it is said, which brought a parson from Kentucky three months later to preach the sermon and conduct the service which seemed to the child a necessary honor to the dead. As sad as the death of his mother was that of his only sister, Sarah. Married to Aaron Grigsby in 1826, she had died a year and a half later in childbirth, a death which to her brother must have seemed a horror and a mystery.

Apart from these family sorrows there was all the crime and misery of the community—all of which came to his ears and awakened his nature. He even saw in those days one of his companions go suddenly mad. The young man never recovered his reason but sank into idiocy. All night he would croon plaintive songs, and Lincoln himself tells how, fascinated by this mysterious malady, he used to rise before daylight to cross the fields to listen to this funeral dirge of the reason. In spite of the poverty and rudeness of his life the depths of his nature were unclouded. He could feel intensely, and his imagination was quick to respond to the touch of mystery.

CHAPTER III

ABRAHAM LINCOLN'S EARLY OPPORTUNITIES—THE BOOKS HE READ—TRIPS TO NEW ORLEANS—IMPRESSION HE MADE ON HIS FRIENDS

WITH all his hard living and hard work, Lincoln was getting, in this period, a desultory kind of education. Not that he received much schooling. He went to school "by littles," he says; "in all it did not amount to more than a year." And, if we accept his own description of the teachers, it was perhaps just as well that it was only "by littles." No qualification was required of a teacher beyond "readin', writin' and cipherin' to the rule of three." If a straggler supposed to know Latin happened to sojourn in the neighborhood, he was looked upon as a "wizard." But more or less of a school-room is a matter of small importance if a boy has learned to read and to think of what he reads. And that, this boy had learned. His stock of books was small, but he knew them thoroughly, and they were good books to know: the Bible, "Æsop's Fables," "Robinson Crusoe," Bunyan's "Pilgrim's Progress," a "History of the United States," Weems's "Life of Washington," and the "Statutes of Indiana."* These are the chief ones we

* The first authorized sketch of Lincoln's life was written by the late John L. Scripps of the Chicago "Tribune," who went to Springfield at Mr. Lincoln's request, and by him was furnished the data for a campaign biography. In a letter written to Mr. Herndon after the death of Lincoln, which Herndon turned over to me, Scripps relates that in writing

THOMAS LINCOLN'S BIBLE.

EARLY OPPORTUNITIES

know about. Some of these books he borrowed from the neighbors; a practice which resulted in at least one casualty, for Weems's "Life of Washington" he allowed to get wet, and to make good the loss he had to pull fodder three days. No matter. The book became his then, and he could read it as he would. Fortunately he took this curious work in profound seriousness, which a wide-awake boy would hardly be expected to do to-day. Washington became an exalted figure in his imagination. He always contended later, when the question of the real character of the first President was brought up, that it was wiser to regard him as a godlike being, heroic in nature and deeds, as Weems does, than to contend that he was only a man who, if wise and good, still made mistakes and was guilty of follies, like other men.

Besides these books he borrowed many others. He once told a friend that he "read through every book he had ever heard of in that country, for a circuit of fifty miles." From everything he read he made long extracts with his turkey-buzzard pen and brier-root ink. When he had no paper he would write on a board and thus preserve his selections until he secured a copybook. The wooden fire-shovel was his usual slate, and on its back he ciphered with a charred stick,

his book he stated that Lincoln as a youth read Plutarch's "Lives." This he did simply because, as a rule, every boy in the West in the early days did read Plutarch. When the advance sheets of the book reached Mr. Lincoln, he sent for the author and said gravely: "That paragraph wherein you state that I read Plutarch's 'Lives' was not true when you wrote it, for up to that moment in my life I had never seen that early contribution to human history; but I want your book, even if it is nothing more than a campaign sketch, to be faithful to the facts; and in order that the statement might be literally true, I secured the book a few weeks ago, and have sent for you to tell you that I have just read it through."—Jesse W. Weik.

shaving it off when it had become too grimy for use. The logs and boards in his vicinity he covered with his figures and quotations. By night he read and worked as long as there was light, and he kept a book in the crack of the logs in his loft, to have it at hand at peep of day. When acting as ferryman on the Ohio, in his nineteenth year, anxious, no doubt, to get through the books of the house where he boarded before he left the place, he read every night until midnight.

Every lull in his daily labor he used for reading, rarely going to his work without a book. When ploughing or cultivating the rough fields of Spencer County, he found frequently a half hour, for at the end of every long row the horse was allowed to rest and Lincoln had his book out and was perched on stump or fence almost as soon as the plough had come to a standstill. Captain John Lamar, one of the few people remembering Lincoln who was living in Spencer County when the material for this book was gathered, used to tell of riding to mill with his father and seeing, as he drove along, a boy sitting on the top rail of an old-fashioned stake-and-rider worm fence, reading so intently that he did not notice their approach. His father, turning to him, said: "John, look at that boy yonder, and mark my words, he will make a smart man out of himself. I may not see it, but you'll see if my words don't come true." "That boy was Abraham Lincoln," Mr. Lamar would add impressively.

In his habits of reading and study the boy had little encouragement from his father, but his stepmother

An army of a 1000 men having plundered a city, took so much money, that when it was shared among them, each man had 27£. I demand how much money was taken in all

$$\begin{array}{r} 1000 \\ 27 \\ \hline 7000 \\ 2000 \\ \hline 27000 \end{array}$$

Abraham Lincoln His Book

FRAGMENT FROM A LEAF IN LINCOLN'S EXERCISE-BOOK.

did all she could for him. Indeed, between the two there soon grew up a relation of touching gentleness and confidence. In one of the interviews a biographer of Mr. Lincoln sought with her before her death, Mrs. Lincoln said:

"I induced my husband to permit Abe to read and study at home, as well as at school. At first he was not easily reconciled to it, but finally he too seemed willing to encourage him to a certain extent. Abe was a dutiful son to me always, and we took particular care when he was reading not to disturb him—would let him read on and on till he quit of his own accord." This consideration of his stepmother won the boy's confidence, and he rarely copied anything that he did not take it to her to read, asking her opinion of it; and often, when she did not understand it, explaining the meaning in his plain and simple language.

Among the books which fell into young Lincoln's hand when he was about eighteen years old was a copy of the "Revised Statutes of Indiana."* We know from Dennis Hanks and from Mr. Turnham of Gentryville, to whom the book belonged, and from other associates of Lincoln at the time, that he read

* The book was owned by Mr. David Turnham of Gentryville, and was given by him in 1865 to Mr. Herndon, who placed it in the Lincoln Memorial collection of Chicago. In December, 1894, this collection was sold in Philadelphia, and the "Statutes of Indiana" was bought by Mr. William Hoffman Winters, Librarian of the New York Law Institute, where it now may be seen. The book is worn, the title page is gone, and a few leaves from the end are missing. The title page of a duplicate volume reads: "The Revised Laws of Indiana, adopted and enacted by the General Assembly at their eighth session. To which are prefixed the Declaration of Independence, the Constitution of the United States, the Constitution of the State of Indiana, and sundry other documents connected with the Political History of the Territory and State of Indiana. Arranged and published by authority of the General Assembly. Corydon: Printed by Carpenter and Douglass, 1824."

ABRAHAM LINCOLN'S INDIANA HOME.

After an old photograph showing the cabin as it appeared in 1869. Thomas Lincoln built this house in 1817, and moved into it about a year after he reached his farm. At first it had neither windows, doors, nor floor; but after the advent of Sally Bush Lincoln it was greatly improved. When he decided to leave Indiana he was preparing the lumber for a better house.

LINCOLN WORKING BY THE FIRELIGHT.

EARLY OPPORTUNITIES 37

the book intently and discussed its contents intelligently. It was a remarkable volume for a thoughtful lad whose mind had already been fired by the "Life of Washington." It opened with that wonderful document, the Declaration of Independence, following the Declaration of Independence was the Constitution of the United States, the Act of Virginia passed in 1783 by which the "Territory North Westward of the River Ohio" was conveyed to the United States, and the Ordinance of 1787 for governing this territory, containing that clause on which Lincoln in the future based many an argument on the slavery question. This article, No. 6 of the Ordinance, reads:

"There shall be neither slavery nor involuntary servitude in the said territory, otherwise than in the punishment of crimes, whereof the party shall have been duly convicted: provided always, that any person escaping into the same, from whom labor or service is lawfully claimed in any one of the original States, such fugitive may be lawfully reclaimed and conveyed to the person claiming his or her labor or service, as aforesaid."

Following this was the Constitution and the Revised Laws of Indiana, three hundred and seventy-five pages, of five hundred words each, of statutes. When Lincoln finished this book, as he had probably before he was eighteen, we have reason to believe that he understood the principles on which the nation was founded, how the State of Indiana came into being, and how it was governed. His understanding of the subject was clear and practical, and he applied it in his reading, thinking, and discussion. After he had read the Statutes of Indiana, Lincoln had free access to the library of an admirer, Judge John Pitcher of Rockport, Indiana, where he examined many books.

Although so far away from the center of the world's activity, he was learning something of current history. One man in Gentryville, Mr. Jones, the storekeeper, took a Louisville paper, and here Lincoln went regularly to read and discuss its contents. All the men and boys of the neighborhood gathered there, and everything which the paper printed was subjected to their keen, shrewd common sense. It was not long before young Lincoln became the favorite member of the group, the one listened to most respectfully. Politics were warmly discussed by these Gentryville citizens, and it may be that, sitting on the counter of Jones's grocery, Lincoln even argued on slavery. It certainly was one of the live questions in Indiana at that date.

For several years after the organization of the Territory, and in spite of the Ordinance of 1787, a system of thinly disguised slavery had existed; and it took a sharp struggle to bring the state in without some form of the institution. So uncertain was the result that, when decided, the word passed from mouth to mouth all over Hoosierdom, "She has come in free, she has come in free!" Even in 1820, four years after the admission to statehood, the census showed one hundred and ninety slaves, nearly all of them in the southwest corner, where the Lincolns lived, and it was not, in reality, until 1821 that the State Supreme Court put an end to the question. In

Illinois in 1822-1824 there was carried on one of the most violent contests between the friends and opponents of slavery which occurred before the repeal of the Missouri Compromise. The effort to secure slave labor was nearly successful. In the campaign, pamphlets pro and con literally inundated the state; the pulpits took it up; and "almost every stump in every county had its bellowing, indignant orator." So violent a commotion so near at hand could hardly have failed to reach Gentryville.

There had been other anti-slavery agitation going on within hearing for several years. In 1804 a number of Baptist ministers of Kentucky started a crusade against the institution, which resulted in a hot contest in the denomination, and the organization of the "Baptist Licking-Locust Association Friends of Humanity." The Rev. Jesse Head, the minister who married Thomas Lincoln and Nancy Hanks, talked freely and boldly against slavery; and one of their old friends, Christopher Columbus Graham, the man who was present at their wedding, says: "Tom and Nancy Lincoln and Sally Bush were just steeped full of Jesse Head's notions about the wrong of slavery and the rights of man as explained by Thomas Jefferson and Thomas Paine." In 1806 Charles Osborne began to preach "immediate emancipation" in Tennessee. Ten years later he started a paper in Ohio, devoted to the same idea, and in 1819 he transferred his crusade to Indiana. In 1821 Benjamin Lundy started in Tennessee the famous "Genius," devoted to the same doctrine; and in 1822, at Shelbyville, only about one hundred miles from Gentryville, was started a paper similar in its views, the "Abolition Intelligencer."

At that time there were in Kentucky five or six abolition societies, and in Illinois was an organization called the "Friends of Humanity." Probably young Lincoln heard but vaguely of these movements; but of some of them he must have heard, and he must have connected them with the "Speech of Mr. Pitt on the Slave Trade"; with Merry's elegy, "The Slaves," and with the discussion given in his "Kentucky Preceptor," "Which has the Most to Complain of, the Indian or the Negro?" all of which tradition declares he was fond of repeating. It is not impossible that, as Frederick Douglass first realized his own condition in reading a school-speaker, the "Columbian Orator," so Abraham Lincoln first felt the wrong of slavery in reading his "Kentucky" or "American Preceptor."

Lincoln was not only winning in these days in the Jones grocery store a reputation as a talker and a story-teller; he was becoming known as a kind of backwoods orator. He could repeat with effect all the poems and speeches in his various school readers, he could imitate to perfection the wandering preachers who came to Gentryville, and he could make a political speech so stirring that he drew a crowd about him every time he mounted a stump. The applause he won was sweet; and frequently he indulged his gifts when he ought to have been working—so thought his employers and Thomas, his father. It was trying, no doubt, to the hard-pushed farmers to see the men who ought to have been cutting grass or chopping

EARLY OPPORTUNITIES

wood throw down their scythes or axes and group around a boy whenever he mounted a stump to develop a pet theory or repeat with variations yesterday's sermon. In his fondness for speech-making young Lincoln attended all the trials of the neighborhood and frequently walked fifteen miles to Boonville to attend court.

He wrote as well as spoke, and some of his productions were printed through the influence of his admiring neighbors. Thus a local Baptist preacher was so struck with one of Abraham's essays on temperance that he sent it to Ohio, where it is said to have appeared in a newspaper. Another article on "National Politics" so pleased a lawyer of the vicinity that he declared the "world couldn't beat it."

In considering the different opportunities for development which the boy had at this time it should not be forgotten that he spent many months at one time or another on the Ohio and Mississippi rivers. In fact, all that Abraham Lincoln saw of men and the world outside of Gentryville and its neighborhood until after he was twenty-one years of age he saw on these rivers. For many years the Ohio and the Mississippi were the Appian Way, the one route to the world for the western settlers. To preserve it they had been willing in early times to go to war with Spain or with France, to secede from the Union, even to join Spain or France against the United States if either country would insure their right to the highway. In the long years in which the ownership of the great river was unsettled, every man of them had come to feel with Benjamin Franklin, "a neighbor might as well ask me to sell my street door." In fact, this water-way was their "street door," and all that many of them ever saw of the world passed here. Up and down the rivers was a continual movement. Odd craft of every kind possible on a river went by: "arks" and "sleds," with tidy cabins where families lived, and where one could see the washing stretched, the children playing, the mother on pleasant days rocking and sewing; keel-boats, which dodged in and out and turned inquisitive noses up all the creeks and bayous; great fleets from the Alleghenies, made up of a score or more of timber rafts, and manned by forty or fifty rough boatmen; "Orleans boats," loaded with flour, hogs, produce of all kinds; pirogues, made from great trees; "broad-horns;" curious nondescripts worked by a wheel; and, after 1812, steamboats.

All this traffic was leisurely. Men had time to tie up and tell the news and show their wares. Even the steamboats loitered as it pleased them. They knew no schedule. They stopped anywhere to let passengers off. They tied up wherever it was convenient to wait for fresh wood to be cut and loaded, or for repairs to be made. Waiting for repairs seems, in fact, to have absorbed a great deal of the time of these early steamers. They were continually running onto "sawyers," or "planters," or "wooden islands," and they blew up with a regularity which was monotonous. Even as late as 1842, when Charles Dickens made the trip down the Mississippi, he was often gravely recommended to keep as far aft as possible, "because the steamboats generally blew up forward."

With this varied river life Abraham Lincoln first

EARLY OPPORTUNITIES

came into contact in 1826 when he spent several months as a ferryman at the mouth of Anderson Creek, where it joins the Ohio. This experience suggested new possibilities to him. It was a practice of the farmers of Ohio, Indiana and Illinois at this date to raft their yearly crop down the river, selling it on the way. Young Lincoln saw this and wanted to try his fortune as a produce merchant. An incident of his projected trip he related once to Mr. Seward:

"Seward," he said, "did you ever hear how I earned my first dollar?"

"No," said Mr. Seward.

"Well," replied he, "I was about eighteen years of age, and belonged, as you know, to what they call down south the 'scrubs'; people who do not own land and slaves are nobody there; but we had succeeded in raising, chiefly by my labor, sufficient produce, as I thought, to justify me in taking it down the river to sell. After much persuasion I had got the consent of my mother to go, and had constructed a flatboat large enough to take the few barrels of things we had gathered to New Orleans. A steamer was going down the river. We have, you know, no wharves on the western streams, and the custom was, if passengers were at any of the landings they were to go out in a boat, the steamer stopping, and taking them on board. I was contemplating my new boat, and wondering whether I could make it stronger or improve it in any part, when two men with trunks came down to the shore in carriages and, looking at the different boats, singled out mine, and asked, 'Who owns this?' I answered modestly, 'I do.' 'Will you,' said one of them, 'take us and our trunks out to the steamer?' 'Certainly,' said I. I was very glad to have the chance of earning something, and supposed that each of them would give me a couple of bits. The trunks were put in my boat, the passengers seated themselves on them, and I sculled them out to the steamer. They got on board, and I lifted the trunks and put them on the deck. The steamer was about to put on steam again, when I called out, 'You have forgotten to pay me.' Each of them took from his pocket a silver half-dollar and threw it on the bottom of my boat. I could scarcely believe my eyes as I picked up the money. You may think it was a very little thing, and in these days it seems to me like a trifle, but it was a most important incident in my life. I could scarcely credit that I, the poor boy, had earned a dollar in less than a day; that by honest work I had earned a dollar. I was a more hopeful and thoughtful boy from that time."

Soon after this, while he was working for Mr. Gentry, the leading citizen of Gentryville, his employer decided to send a load of produce to New Orleans, and chose young Lincoln to go as "bowhand," "to work the front oars." For this trip he received eight dollars a month and his passage back. Who can believe that he could see and be part of this river life without learning much of the ways and thoughts of the world beyond him? Every time a steamboat or a raft tied up near Anderson Creek and he with his companions boarded it and saw its mysteries and talked with its crew, every time he rowed out with passengers to a passing steamer, who can doubt that he came back with new ideas and fresh energy? The trips to New Orleans were, to a thoughtful boy, an education of no mean value. It was the most cosmopolitan and brilliant city of the United States at that date, and there young Lincoln saw life at its intensest.

Such was Abraham Lincoln's life in Indiana; such were the avenues open to him for study and for seeing the world. In spite of the crudeness of it all; in spite of the fact that he had no wise direction, that he was brought up by a father with no settled purpose, and that he lived in a pioneer community where a young man's life at best is but a series of makeshifts, Lincoln soon developed a determination to make something out of himself and a desire to know, which led him to neglect no opportunity to learn.

The only unbroken outside influence which directed and stimulated him in these ambitions was that coming first from his mother, then from his stepmother. These two women, both of them of unusual earnestness and sweetness of spirit, were one or the other of them at his side throughout his youth and young manhood. The ideal they held before him was the simple ideal of the early American—that if a boy is upright and industrious he may aspire to any place within the gift of the country. The boy's instinct told him they were right. Everything he read confirmed their teachings, and he cultivated, in every way open to him, his passion to know and to rise. His zeal in study, his ambition to excel, made their impression on his acquaintances. Even then they pointed him out as a boy who would "make something" of himself. In 1865, thirty-five years after he left Gentryville, Wm. H. Herndon, for many years a law partner of Lincoln, anxious to save all that was known of Lincoln in Indiana, went among his old associates, and with a sincerity and thoroughness worthy of grateful respect, interviewed them. At that time there were still living numbers of the people with whom Lincoln had been brought up. They all remembered something of him.

It is curious to note that these people tell of his doing something different from what other boys did, something sufficiently superior to have made a keen impression upon them. In almost every case each person had his own special reason for admiring Lincoln. Facility in making rhymes and writing essays was the admiration of many, who considered it the more remarkable because "essays and poetry were not taught in school," and "Abe took it up on his own account."

Many others were struck by the clever application he made of this gift for expression. At one period he was employed as a "hand" by a farmer who treated him unfairly. Lincoln took a revenge unheard of in Gentryville. He wrote doggerel rhymes about his employer's nose—a long and crooked feature about which the owner was very sensitive. The wit he showed in taking revenge for a social slight by a satire on the Grigsbys, who had failed to invite him to a wedding, made a lasting impression in Gentryville. That he should write so well as to be able to humiliate his enemies more deeply than if he had resorted to the method of taking revenge current in the country and thrashed them, seemed to his friends a mark of surprising superiority.

His schoolmates all remembered his spelling. He invariably stood at the head of his class and so often did he spell the school down that finally, tradition says, he was no longer allowed to take part in the matches.

Many of his old neighbors recalled his reading habits and how well stored his mind was with information. His explanations of natural phenomena were so unfamiliar to his companions that he sometimes was jeered at for them, though as a rule his listeners were sympathetic, taking a certain pride in the fact that one of their number knew as much as Lincoln did. "He was better read than the world knows or is likely to know exactly," said one old acquaintance.

*Abraham Lincoln
his hand and pen.
he will be good but
god knows When*

FACSIMILE OF LINES FROM LINCOLN'S COPY BOOK.

"He often and often commented or talked to me about what he had read—seemed to read it out of the book as he went along—did so with others. He was the learned boy among us unlearned folks. He took great pains to explain; could do it so simply. He was diffident, then, too."

One man was impressed by the character of the sentences Lincoln had given him for a copybook. "It was considered at that time," said he, "that Abe was the best penman in the neighborhood. One day, while he was on a visit at my mother's, I asked him to write some copies for me. He very willingly consented.

He wrote several of them, but one of them I have never forgotten, although a boy at that time. It was this:

> " 'Good boys who to their books apply
> Will all be great men by and by.' "

His wonderful memory was recalled by many. To save that which he found to his liking in the books he borrowed, Lincoln committed much to memory. He knew many long poems, and most of the selections in the "Kentucky Preceptor." By the time he was twenty-one, his mind was well stored with verse and prose.

All of his comrades remembered his stories and his clearness in argument. "When he appeared in company," says Nat Grigsby, "the boys would gather and cluster around him to hear him talk. Mr. Lincoln was figurative in his speech, talks, and conversation. He argued much from analogy and explained things hard for us to understand by stories, maxims, tales, and figures. He would almost always point his lesson or idea by some story that was plain and near us, that we might instantly see the force and bearing of what he said." This ability to explain clearly and to illustrate by simple figures of speech must be counted as the chief mental gain of Lincoln's boyhood. It was a power which he gained by hard labor. Years later he related his experience to an acquaintance who had been surprised by the lucidity and simplicity of his speeches and who had asked where he was educated.

"I never went to school more than six months in my life," he said, "but I can say this: that among my earliest recollections I remember how, when a mere child, I used to get irritated when anybody talked to me in a way I could not understand. I do not think I ever got angry at anything else in my life; but that always disturbed my temper, and has ever since. I can remember going to my little bedroom, after hearing the neighbors talk of an evening with my father, and spending no small part of the night walking up and down and trying to make out what was the exact meaning of some of their, to me, dark sayings.

"I could not sleep, although I tried to, when I got on such a hunt for an idea until I had caught it; and when I thought I had got it, I was not satisfied until I had repeated it over and over; until I had put it in language plain enough, as I thought, for any boy I knew to comprehend. This was a kind of passion with me, and it has stuck by me; for I am never easy now, when I am handling a thought, till I have bounded it north and bounded it south, and bounded it east and bounded it west."

Mr. Herndon in his interviewing in Indiana found that everywhere Lincoln was remembered as kind and helpful. The man or woman in trouble never failed to receive all the aid he could give him. Even a worthless drunkard of the village called him friend, as well he might, Lincoln having gathered him up one night from the roadside where he lay freezing and carried him on his back a long distance to a shelter and a fire. The thoughtless cruelty to animals so common among country children revolted the boy. He wrote essays on "cruelty to animals," harangued his playmates, protested whenever he saw any wanton abuse of a dumb creature. This gentleness made a lasting impression on his mates, coupled as it was with the physical strength and courage to enforce his doctrines. Stories of his good heart and helpful life might be multiplied, but they are summed up in what his stepmother said of the boy:

"Abe was a good boy, and I can say what scarcely one woman—a mother—can say in a thousand: Abe never gave me a cross word or look, and never refused, in fact or appearance, to do anything I requested him. I never gave him a cross word in all my life. . . . His mind and mine—what little I had—seemed to run together. He was here after he was elected president. He was a dutiful son to me always. I think he loved me truly. I had a son, John, who was raised with Abe. Both were good boys; but I must say, both now being dead, that Abe was the best boy I ever saw, or expect to see."

CHAPTER IV

THE LINCOLNS LEAVE INDIANA—THE JOURNEY TO ILLINOIS—ABRAHAM LINCOLN STARTS OUT FOR HIMSELF

In the spring of 1830 when Abraham Lincoln was twenty-one years old, his father, Thomas Lincoln, decided to leave Indiana. The reason Dennis Hanks gives for this removal was a disease called the "milksick." Abraham Lincoln's mother, Nancy Hanks Lincoln, and several of their relatives who had followed them from Kentucky had died of it. The cattle had been carried off by it. Neither brute nor human life seemed to be safe. As Dennis Hanks says: "This was reason enough (ain't it) for leaving?"

But there were other reasons. Spencer County had not progressed as rapidly as it promised to do in the first years after its settlement. Immigration had almost entirely stopped. Settlers now were moving west into Illinois or north into Michigan, so that when the country was again attacked by the disease which had already wrought such disaster in the Lincoln family it is not to be wondered that Thomas Lincoln, natural pioneer that he was, should have joined a migration passing almost by his door and including members of his first wife's family as well as former Kentucky neighbors.

The place chosen for their new home was the

Sangamon country in central Illinois. It was at that day a country of great renown in the West, the name meaning "The land where there is plenty to eat." One of the family—John Hanks, a cousin of Abraham's mother—was already there, and the inviting reports he had sent to Indiana were no doubt what led the Lincolns to decide on Illinois as their future home. Gentryville saw young Lincoln depart with genuine regret, and his friends gave him a score of rude proofs that he would not be forgotten. After he was gone, one of these friends planted a cedar tree in his memory. It still marks the site of the Lincoln home—the first monument erected to the memory of a man to whom the world will never cease to raise monuments.

The spot on the hill overlooking Buckthorne Valley, where the Lincolns said good-by to their old home and to the home of Sarah Lincoln Grigsby, to the grave of the mother and wife, to all their neighbors and friends, is still pointed out. Buckthorne Valley held many recollections dear to them all, but to no one of the company was the place dearer than to Abraham. It is certain that he felt the parting keenly and that he never forgot his years in the Hoosier State. One of the most touching experiences he relates in all his published letters is his emotion at visiting his old Indiana home fourteen years after he had left it. So strongly was he moved by the scenes of his first conscious sorrows, efforts, joys, ambitions, that he put into verse the feelings they awakened.

While he never attempted to conceal the poverty and hardship of these days and would speak humor-

THE OLD SWIMMING HOLE.

A secluded part of Little Pigeon Creek, not far from Gentryville, where Lincoln, Dennis Hanks, John Johnston, the Gentry boys, and others of the neighborhood, used to bathe. It is still pointed out as "the place where Abe went in swimming."

BUCKTHORN VALLEY, WHERE LINCOLN WORKED AND HUNTED.

In this valley are located nearly all the farms on which Lincoln worked in his boyhood, including the famous Crawford place, where he and his sister Sarah were both employed as "help." Visitors to the locality have pointed out to them numberless items associated with his early life—fields he helped to clear and till, fences he built, houses he repaired, wells he dug, paths he walked, playgrounds he frequented. Indeed, the inhabitants of Buckthorn Valley take the greatest pride, and very properly, in Lincoln's connection with it.

ously of the "pretty pinching times" he experienced, he never regarded his life at this time as mean or pitiable. Frequently he talked to his friends in later days of his boyhood, and always with apparent pleasure. "Mr. Lincoln told this story (of his youth)," says Leonard Swett, "as the story of a happy childhood. There was nothing sad or pinched, and nothing of want, and no allusion to want in any part of it. His own description of his youth was that of a happy, joyous boyhood. It was told with mirth and glee, and illustrated by pointed anecdotes, often interrupted by his jocund laugh."

And he was right. There was nothing ignoble or mean in this Indiana pioneer life. It was rude, but only with the rudeness which the ambitious are willing to endure in order to push on to a better condition than they otherwise could know. These people did not accept their hardships apathetically. They did not regard them as permanent. They were only the temporary deprivations necessary in order to accomplish what they had come into the country to do. For this reason they endured hopefully all that was hard. It is worth notice, too, that there was nothing belittling in their life; there was no pauperism, no shirking. Each family provided for its own simple wants and had the conscious dignity which comes from being equal to a situation. If their lives lacked culture and refinement, they were rich in independence and self-reliance.

The company which emigrated to Illinois included the family of Thomas Lincoln and those of Dennis Hanks and Levi Hall, married to Lincoln's stepsisters—thirteen persons in all. They sold land, cattle and grain, and much of their household goods, and were ready in March of 1830 for their journey. All the possessions which the three families had to take with them were packed into big wagons, to which oxen were attached, and the caravan was ready. The weather was still cold, the streams were swollen, and the roads were muddy; but the party started out bravely. Inured to hardships, alive to all the new sights on their route, every day brought them amusement and adventures, and especially to young Lincoln the journey must have been of keen interest.

He drove one of the teams, he tells us, and, according to a story current in Gentryville, he succeeded in doing a fair peddler's business on the route. Captain William Jones, in whose father's store Lincoln had spent so many hours in discussion and in story-telling, and for whom he had worked the last winter he was in Indiana, says that before leaving the state Abraham invested all his money, some thirty-odd dollars, in notions. Though the country through which they expected to pass was but sparsely settled, he believed he could dispose of them. "A set of knives and forks was the largest item entered on the bill," says Captain Jones; "the other items were needles, pins, thread, buttons, and other little domestic necessities. When the Lincolns reached their new home near Decatur, Illinois, Abraham wrote back to my father stating that he had doubled his money on his purchases by selling them along the road. Unfortunately we did not keep that letter, not thinking how highly we would have prized it in years afterwards."

THE GRAVE OF NANCY HANKS LINCOLN.

STARTS OUT FOR HIMSELF

The pioneers were a fortnight on their journey. All we know of the route they took is from a few chance remarks of Lincoln's to his friends to the effect that they passed through Vincennes, where he saw a printing-press for the first time, and through Palestine, where he saw a juggler performing sleight-of-hand tricks. They reached Macon County, their new home, from the south. Mr. H. C. Whitney says that once, when he and Lincoln were passing the courthouse in Decatur together, "Lincoln walked out a few feet in front and, after shifting his position two or three times, said, as he looked up at the building, partly to himself and partly to me: 'Here is the exact spot where I stood by our wagon when we moved from Indiana twenty-six years ago; this isn't six feet from the exact spot.' . . . He then told me he had frequently thereafter tried to locate the route by which they had come, and that he had decided that it was near the main line of the Illinois Central Railroad."

The party settled some eight miles west of Decatur, in Macon County. Here John Hanks had the logs already cut for their new home, and Lincoln, Dennis Hanks, and Hall soon had a cabin erected. Mr. Lincoln says in his short autobiography of 1860: "Here they built a log cabin into which they removed, and made sufficient of rails to fence ten acres of ground, fenced and broke the ground, and raised a crop of sown corn upon it the same year. These are, or are supposed to be, the rails about which so much is being said just now, though these are far from being the first or only rails ever made by Abraham." If they were far from being his "first and only rails," they certainly were the most famous ones he or anybody else ever split.

This was the last work Lincoln did for his father, for in the summer of that year (1830) he exercised the right of majority and started out to shift for himself. When he left his home, he went empty-handed. He was already some months over twenty-one, but he had nothing in the world, not even a suit of respectable clothes; and one of the first pieces of work he did was "to split four hundred rails for every yard of brown jeans dyed with white-walnut bark that would be necessary to make him a pair of trousers." He had no trade, no profession, no spot of land, no patron, no influence. Two things recommended him —he was strong and he was a good fellow.

His strength made him a valuable laborer. Not that he was fond of hard labor. One of his Indiana employers says: "Abe was no hand to pitch into work like killing snakes;" but when he did work, it was with an ease and effectiveness which compensated his employer for the time he spent in practical jokes and extemporaneous speeches. He could lift as much as three ordinary men, and "My, how he would chop," says Dennis Hanks. "His axe would flash and bite into a sugar-tree or sycamore and down it would come. If you heard him fellin' trees in a clearin', you would say there was three men at work by the way the trees fell."

Standing six feet four, he could out-lift, out-work and out-wrestle any man he came in contact with. Friends and employers were proud of his prowess and boasted of it, never failing to pit him against any hero whose strength they heard vaunted. He himself was proud of it, and throughout his life was fond of comparing himself with tall and strong men. When the committee called on him in Springfield in 1860 to notify him of his nomination as President, Governor Morgan, of New York, was of the number, a man of great height and brawn. "Pray, Governor, how tall may you be?" was Mr. Lincoln's first question. There is a story told of a poor man seeking a favor from him once at the White House. He was overpowered by the idea that he was in the presence of the President, and, his errand done, was edging shyly away, when Mr. Lincoln stopped him, insisting that he "measure" with him. The man was the taller, as Mr. Lincoln had thought, and he went away evidently as much abashed that he dared be taller than the President of the United States as that he had dared to venture into his presence.

Governor Hoyt tells an excellent story illustrating this interest of Lincoln's in physical strength. In 1859, after he had delivered a speech at the Wisconsin State Agricultural Fair in Milwaukee, Governor Hoyt asked him to make the rounds of the exhibits, and they went into a tent to see a "strong man" perform. He went through the ordinary exercises with huge iron balls, tossing them in the air and catching them and rolling them on his arms and back; and Mr. Lincoln, who evidently had never before seen such a combination of agility and strength, watched him intently, ejaculating under his breath now and then: "By George! By George!" When the performance was over, Governor Hoyt, seeing Mr. Lincoln's interest, suggested that he speak to the athlete. He did so and, as he stood looking down musingly on the man, who was very short, and evidently wondering that one so much smaller than he could be so much stronger, suddenly broke out with one of his quaint speeches. "Why," he said, "why, I could lick salt off the top of your hat."

His strength won him popularity, but his good-nature, his wit, his skill in debate, his stories, were still more efficient in gaining him good-will. People liked to have him around and voted him a good fellow to work with. Yet such were the conditions of his life at this time that, in spite of his popularity, nothing was open to him but hard manual labor. To take the first job which he happened upon—rail-splitting, ploughing, lumbering, boating, store-keeping—and make the most of it, thankful if thereby he earned his bed and board and yearly suit of jeans, was apparently all there was before Abraham Lincoln in 1830 when he started out for himself.

Through the summer and fall of 1830 and the early winter of 1831, Mr. Lincoln worked in the vicinity of his father's new home, usually as a farm-hand and rail-splitter. Most of his work was done in company with John Hanks. Before the end of the winter he secured employment of which he has given an account himself, though in the third person:

"During that winter, Abraham, together with his stepmother's son, John D. Johnston, and John Hanks, yet residing in Macon County, hired themselves to Denton Offutt to take a flatboat from Beardstown, Illinois, to New Orleans, and for that purpose were to join him—Offutt—at Springfield, Illinois, as soon as the snow should go off. When it did go off, which was about the first of March, 1831, the country was so flooded as to make traveling by land impracticable; to obviate which difficulty they purchased a large canoe and came down the Sangamon River in it. This is the time and manner of Abraham's first entrance into Sangamon County. They found Offutt at Springfield, but learned from him that he had failed in getting a boat at Beardstown. This led to their hiring themselves to him for twelve dollars per month each, and getting the timber out of the trees, and building a boat at old Sangamon town, on the Sangamon River, seven miles northwest of Springfield, which boat they took to New Orleans, substantially on the old contract."

Sangamon town, where Lincoln built the flatboat, has, since his day, completely disappeared from the earth, but then it was one of the flourishing settlements on the river of that name. Lincoln's advent in the town did not go unnoticed. In a small community, cut off from the world, as old Sangamon was, every newcomer is scrutinized and discussed before he is regarded with confidence. Lincoln did not escape this scrutiny. His appearance was so striking that he attracted everybody's attention. "He was a tall, gaunt young man," says Mr. John Roll of Springfield, then a resident of Sangamon, "dressed in a suit of blue homespun jeans, consisting of a roundabout jacket, waistcoat, and breeches which came to within about four inches of his feet. The latter were encased in rawhide boots, into the tops of which, most of the time, his pantaloons were stuffed. He wore a soft felt hat which had at one time been black, but now, as its owner dryly remarked, 'was sun-burned until it was a combine of colors.'"

It took some four weeks to build the raft, and in that period Lincoln succeeded in captivating the entire village by his story-telling. It was the custom in Sangamon for the "men-folks" to gather at noon and in the evening in a convenient lane near the mill. They had rolled out a long peeled log, on which they lounged while they whittled and talked. Lincoln had not been long in Sangamon before he joined this circle. At once he became a favorite by his jokes and good-humor. As soon as he appeared at the assembly ground the men would start him to story-telling. So irresistibly funny were his "yarns" that, says Mr. Roll, "whenever he'd end up in his unexpected way the boys on the log would whoop and roll off." The result of the rolling off was to polish the log like a mirror. The men, recognizing Lincoln's part in this polishing, christened their seat "Abe's log." Long after Lincoln had disappeared from Sangamon, "Abe's log" remained, and until it had rotted away people pointed it out and repeated the droll stories of the stranger.

When the flatboat was finished Lincoln and his friends prepared to leave Sangamon. Before he started, however, he was the hero of an adventure so thrilling that he won new laurels in the community. Mr. Roll, who was a witness to the whole exciting scene, tells the story:

"It was the spring following the winter of the deep snow.* Walter Carman, John Seamon and myself, and at times others of the Carman boys had helped Abe in building the

* 1830—1831. "The winter of the deep snow" is the date which is the starting point in all calculations of time for the early settlers of

STARTS OUT FOR HIMSELF 61

boat, and when we had finished we went to work to make a dugout, or canoe, to be used as a small boat with the flat. We found a suitable log about an eighth of a mile up the river, and with our axes went to work under Lincoln's direction. The river was very high, fairly 'booming.' After the dugout was ready to launch we took it to the edge of the water and made ready to 'let her go,' when Walter Carman and John Seamon jumped in as the boat struck the water, each one anxious to be the first to get a ride. As they shot out from the shore they found they were unable to make any headway against the strong current. Carman had the paddle, and Seamon was in the stern of the boat. Lincoln shouted to them to 'head up stream,' and 'work back to shore,' but they found themselves powerless against the stream. At last they began to pull for the wreck of an old flatboat, the first ever built on the Sangamon, which had sunk and gone to pieces, leaving one of the stanchions sticking above the water. Just as they reached it Seamon made a grab and caught hold of the stanchion, when the canoe capsized, leaving Seamon clinging to the old timber and throwing Carman into the stream. It carried him down with the speed of a mill-race. Lincoln raised his voice above the roar of the flood and yelled to Carman to swim for an old tree which stood almost in the channel, which the action of the high water had changed.

"Carman, being a good swimmer, succeeded in catching a branch and pulled himself up out of the water, which was very cold, and had almost chilled him to death; and there he sat shivering and chattering in the tree. Lincoln, seeing Carman safe, called out to Seamon to let go the stanchion and swim for the tree. With some hesitation he obeyed and struck out, while Lincoln cheered and directed him from the bank. As Seamon neared the tree he made one grab for a branch, and, missing it, went under the water. Another desperate lunge was successful, and he climbed up beside

Illinois, and the circumstance from which the old settlers of Sangamon County receive the name by which they are generally known, "Snowbirds."

Carman. Things were pretty exciting now, for there were two men in the tree, and the boat was gone.

"It was a cold, raw April day, and there was great danger of the men becoming benumbed and falling back into the water. Lincoln called out to them to keep their spirits up and he would save them. The village had been alarmed by this time, and many people had come down to the bank. Lincoln procured a rope and tied it to a log. He called all hands to come and help roll the log into the water, and after this had been done, he, with the assistance of several others, towed it some distance up the stream. A daring young fellow by the name of 'Jim' Dorrell then took his seat on the end of the log, and it was pushed out into the current, with the expectation that it would be carried down stream against the tree where Seamon and Carman were.

"The log was well directed and went straight to the tree; but Jim, in his impatience to help his friends, fell a victim to his good intentions. Making a frantic grab at a branch, he raised himself off the log, which was swept from under him by the raging water, and he soon joined the other two victims upon their forlorn perch. The excitement on shore increased, and almost the whole population of the village gathered on the river bank. Lincoln had the log pulled up the stream, and, securing another piece of rope, called to the men in the tree to catch it if they could when he should reach the tree. He then straddled the log himself and gave the word to push out into the stream. When he dashed into the tree, he threw the rope over the stump of a broken limb and let it play until it broke the speed of the log, and gradually drew it back to the tree, holding it there until the three now nearly frozen men had climbed down and seated themselves astride. He then gave orders to the people on the shore to hold fast to the end of the rope which was tied to the log, and, leaving his rope in the tree he turned the log adrift. The force of the current, acting against the taut rope, swung the log around against the bank, and all 'on board' were saved. The excited people, who had watched the dan-

STARTS OUT FOR HIMSELF 63

gerous experiment with alternate hope and fear, now broke into cheers for Abe Lincoln and praises for his brave act. This adventure made quite a hero of him along the Sangamon, and the people never tired telling of the exploit."

The flatboat built and loaded, the party started for New Orleans about the middle of April. They had gone but a few miles when they met with another adventure. At the village of New Salem there was a mill-dam. On it the boat stuck, and here for nearly twenty-four hours it hung, the bow in the air and the stern in the water, the cargo slowly settling backwards —shipwreck almost certain. The village of New Salem turned out in a body to see what the strangers would do in their predicament. They shouted, suggested, and advised for a time, but finally discovered that one big fellow in the crew was ignoring them and working out a plan of relief. Having unloaded the cargo into a neighboring boat, Lincoln had succeeded in tilting his craft. Then, by boring a hole in the end extending over the dam, the water was let out. This done, the boat was easily shoved over and reloaded. The ingenuity which he had exercised in saving his boat made a deep impression on the crowd on the bank, and it was talked over for many a day. The proprietor of boat and cargo was even more enthusiastic than the spectators, and vowed he would build a steamboat for the Sangamon and make Lincoln the captain. Lincoln himself was interested in what he had done, and nearly twenty years later he embodied his reflections on this adventure in a curious invention for getting boats over shoals.

The raft over the New Salem dam, the party went

on to New Orleans, reaching there in May, 1831, and remaining a month. It must have been a month of intense intellectual activity for Lincoln. Since his first visit, made with young Gentry, New Orleans had entered upon her "flush times." Commerce was increasing at a rate which dazzled speculators and drew them from all over the United States. From 1830 to 1840 no other American city increased in such a ratio; exports and imports, which in 1831 amounted to $26,000,000, had more than doubled by 1835. The Creole population had held the sway so far in the city, but now it came into competition, and often into conflict, with a pushing, ambitious and frequently unscrupulous native American party. To these two predominating elements were added Germans, French, Spanish, Negroes and Indians. Cosmopolitan in its make-up, the city was even more cosmopolitan in its life. Everything was to be seen in New Orleans in those days, from the idle luxury of the wealthy Creole to the organization of filibustering juntas. The pirates still plied their trade in the Gulf, and the Mississippi River brought down hundreds of river boatmen—one of the wildest, wickedest sets of men ever gathered in a city.

Lincoln and his companions ran their boat up beside thousands of others. It was the custom to tie such craft along the river front where St. Mary's Market now stands, and one could walk a mile, it is said, over the tops of these boats without going ashore. No doubt Lincoln went too, to live in the boatmen's rendezvous, called the "Swamp," a wild, rough quarter, where roulette, whiskey, and the flint-lock pistol ruled.

THE NEW SALEM MILL FORTY-FIVE YEARS AGO.

After a painting by Mrs. Bennett; reproduced, by permission, from "Menard-Salem-Lincoln Souvenir Album," Petersburg, Illinois, 1893. The Rutledge and Cameron mill, of which Lincoln at one time had charge, stood on the same spot as the mill in the picture, and had the same foundation.

MOUTH OF ANDERSON CREEK, WHERE LINCOLN KEPT THE FERRY-BOAT.

This ferry, at the mouth of Anderson Creek, was first established and owned by James McDaniel, and was afterwards kept by his son-in-law, James Taylor. It was the latter who hired Abraham Lincoln, about 1826, to attend the ferry-boat. As the boat did not keep him busy all the time, he acted as man-of-all-work around the farm. A son of James Taylor, Captain Green B. Taylor of South Dakota, recalled distinctly the months Lincoln spent in his father's employ. Captain Taylor says that Lincoln "slept upstairs" with him, and used to read "till near midnight."

All of the picturesque life, the violent contrasts of the city, he would see as he wandered about, and he would carry away the sharp impressions which are produced when mind and heart are alert, sincere, and healthy.

In this month spent in New Orleans, Lincoln must have seen much of slavery. At that time the city was full of slaves, and the number was constantly increasing; indeed, one-third of the New Orleans increase in population between 1830 and 1840 was in negroes. One of the saddest features of the institution was to be seen there in its aggravated form—the slave market. The better class of slave-holders of the South, who looked on the institution as patriarchal, and who guarded their slaves with conscientious care, knew little, it should be said, of this terrible traffic. Their transfer of slaves was humane, but in the open markets of the city it was attended by shocking cruelty and degradation. Lincoln witnessed in New Orleans for the first time the revolting sight of men and women sold like animals. Mr. Herndon says that he often heard Mr. Lincoln refer to this experience:

"In New Orleans for the first time," he writes, "Lincoln beheld the true horrors of human slavery. He saw 'negroes in chains—whipped and scourged.' Against this inhumanity his sense of right and justice rebelled, and his mind and conscience were awakened to a realization of what he had often heard and read. No doubt, as one of his companions has said, 'slavery ran the iron into him then and there.' One morning in their rambles over the city the trio passed a slave auction. A vigorous and comely mulatto girl was being sold. She underwent a thorough examination at the hands of the bidders; they pinched her flesh, and made her trot up and down the room like a horse to show how she moved, and in order, as the auctioneer said, that 'bidders might satisfy themselves whether the article they were offering to buy was sound or not.' The whole thing was so revolting that Lincoln moved away from the scene with a deep feeling of 'unconquerable hate.' Bidding his companions follow him, he said: 'Boys, let's get away from this. If ever I get a chance to hit that thing' (meaning slavery), 'I'll hit it hard.' "

Mr. Herndon gives John Hanks as his authority for this statement, but, according to Mr. Lincoln's autobiography, Hanks did not go on to New Orleans, but, having a family, and finding that he was likely to be detained from home longer than he had expected, he turned back at St. Louis. Though the story as told above probably grew to its present proportions by much telling, there is reason to believe that Lincoln was deeply impressed on this trip by something he saw in a New Orleans slave market, and that he often referred to it.

CHAPTER V

LINCOLN SECURES A POSITION—HE STUDIES GRAMMAR
—FIRST APPEARANCE IN POLITICS

THE month in New Orleans passed swiftly, and in June, 1831, Lincoln and his companions took passage up the river. He did not return, however, in the usual condition of the river boatman "out of a job." According to his own way of putting it, "during this boat-enterprise acquaintance with Offutt, who was previously an entire stranger, he conceived a liking for Abraham, and, believing he could turn him to account, he contracted with him to act as a clerk for him on his return from New Orleans, in charge of a store and mill at New Salem." The store and mill were, however, so far only in Offutt's imagination, and Lincoln had to drift about until his employer was ready for him. He made a short visit to his father and mother, now in Coles County, near Charleston (fever and ague had driven the Lincolns from their first home in Macon County), and then, in July, 1831, he went to New Salem, where, as he says, he "stopped indefinitely, and for the first time, as it were, by himself."

The village of New Salem, the scene of Lincoln's mercantile career, was one of the many little towns which, in the pioneer days, sprang up along the Sangamon River, a stream then looked upon as navigable and as destined to be counted among the highways of commerce. Twenty miles northwest of Springfield, strung along the left bank of the Sangamon, parted by hollows and ravines, is a chain of hills. On one of these—a long, narrow ridge, beginning with a sharp and sloping point near the river, running south, and parallel with the stream a little way, and then, reaching its highest point, making a sudden turn to the west, and gradually widening until lost in the prairie—stood this frontier village. The crooked river for a short distance comes from the east and, seemingly surprised at meeting the bluff, abruptly changes its course and flows to the north. Across the river the bottom stretches out half a mile back to the highlands. New Salem, founded in 1829 by James Rutledge and John Cameron, and a dozen years later a deserted village, is rescued from oblivion only by the fact that Lincoln was once one of its inhabitants. The town never contained more than fifteen or twenty houses, all of them built of logs, but it had an energetic population of perhaps one hundred persons, among whom were a blacksmith, a tinner, a hatter, a schoolmaster and a preacher. New Salem boasted a gristmill, a sawmill, two stores and a tavern, but its day of hope was short. In 1837 it began to decline and by 1840, Petersburg, two miles down the river, had absorbed its business and population.

Salem Hill was soon only a green cow pasture, and so it remained until fifteen or twenty years ago, when a group of Menard County citizens formed what they called "The Old Salem Lincoln League," devoted to rebuilding the settlement. In 1918 when the State of Illinois celebrated its first centennial the League pro-

FIRST APPEARANCE IN POLITICS   69

duced on the site of the village, a pageant in which Abraham Lincoln and Ann Rutledge were the central figures. For this pageant eight or ten of the

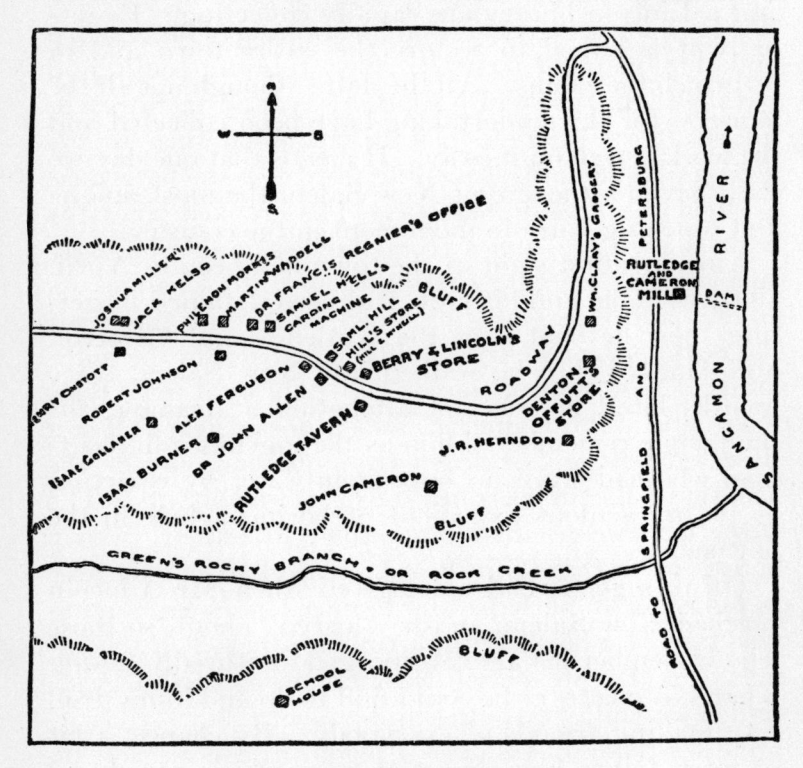

MAP OF NEW SALEM, ILLINOIS.

Drawn for this biography by J. McCann Davis, aided by surviving inhabitants of New Salem. Dr. John Allen, who lived across the road from Berry & Lincoln's store, attended Ann Rutledge in her last illness. None of the buildings are in existence to-day.

cabins as well as the Rutledge tavern were reproduced. So beautifully was the thing done that interest in the project of restoration was stimulated throughout the state. The legislature took the matter up, acquired considerable land in the vicinity and built an admirable stone museum, overlooking the valley of the river. In this museum Lincoln relics and a Lincoln library are rapidly collecting. Eventually it is hoped to restore the entire town and to refurnish the cabins. All the data—though not all the money—for this undertaking have been collected and the work is well on its way. It means that one day we shall have on the site of New Salem the most unique and touching Lincoln monument in the country.

Lincoln's first sight of the town had been in April, 1831, when he and his crew had been detained in getting their flatboat over the Rutledge and Cameron mill-dam. When he walked into New Salem, three months later, he was not altogether a stranger, for the people remembered him as the ingenious flatboatman who had freed his boat from water by resorting to the miraculous expedient of boring a hole in the bottom.

Offutt's goods had not arrived when Mr. Lincoln reached New Salem, and he "loafed" about, so those who remember his arrival say, good-naturedly taking a hand in whatever he could find to do and in his droll way making friends of everybody. By chance, a bit of work fell to him almost at once, which introduced him generally and gave him an opportunity to make a name in the neighborhood. It was election day. In those days elections in Illinois were conducted by the *viva voce* method. The people did try voting by ballot, but the experiment was unpopular. It required too much form and in 1829 the former method of voting was restored. The judges and clerks sat at a

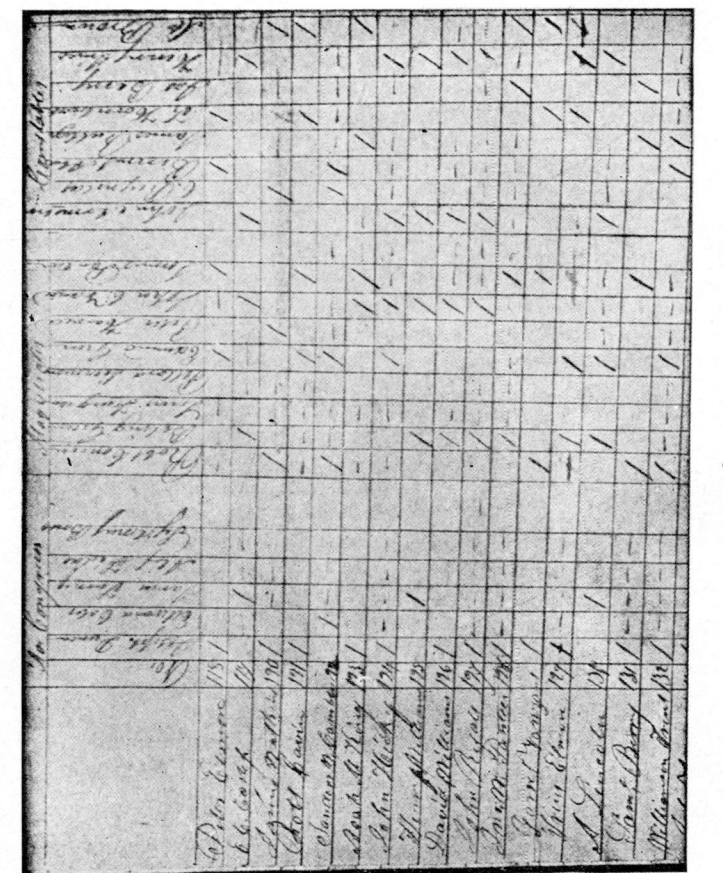

LINCOLN'S FIRST VOTE.

table with a poll-book before them. The voter walked up and announced the candidate of his choice, and it was recorded in his presence. There was no ticket peddling, and ballot-box stuffing was impossible. The village schoolmaster, Mentor Graham by name, was clerk at this particular election, but his assistant was ill. Looking about for some one to help him, Mr. Graham saw a tall stranger loitering around the polling-place and called to him: "Can you write?" "Yes," said the stranger, "I can make a few rabbit tracks." Mr. Graham evidently was satisfied with the answer, for he promptly initiated him; and he filled his place not only to the satisfaction of his employer, but also to the delectation of the loiterers about the polls, for whenever things dragged he immediately began "to spin out a stock of Indian yarns." So droll were they that men who listened to Lincoln that day repeated them long after to their friends. He had made a hit in New Salem, to start with, and here, as in Sangamon town, it was by means of his storytelling.

A few days later he accepted an offer to pilot down the Sangamon and Illinois rivers, as far as Beardstown, a flatboat bearing the family and goods of a pioneer bound for Texas. At Beardstown he found Offutt's goods, waiting to be taken to New Salem. As he footed his way home he found two men with a wagon and ox-team going for the goods. Offutt had expected Lincoln to wait at Beardstown until the ox-team arrived, and the teamsters, not having any credentials, asked Lincoln to give them an order for the goods. This, sitting down by the roadside, he wrote out; one of the men used to relate that it contained a misspelled word, which he corrected.

When the oxen and their drivers returned with the goods, the store was opened in a little log house on the brink of the hill and just above the mill on the river. The precise date of the opening of Denton Offutt's store is not known. We only know that on July 8, 1831, the County Commissioners' Court of Sangamon County granted Offutt a license to retail merchandise at New Salem, for which he paid five dollars, a fee which supposed him to have one thousand dollars' worth of goods in stock.

The frontier store filled a unique place. Usually it was a "general store," and on its shelves were found most of the articles needed in a community of pioneers. But supplying goods and groceries was not its only function; it was the pioneer's intellectual and social center. It was the common meeting-place of the farmers, the happy refuge of the village loungers. No subject was unknown there. The habitués of the place were equally at home in discussing politics, religion, or sports. Stories were told, jokes were cracked, and the news contained in the latest newspaper finding its way into the wilderness was repeated again and again. Lincoln could hardly have chosen surroundings more favorable to the highest development of the art of story-telling, and he had not been there long before his reputation for drollery was established.

But he gained popularity and respect in other ways. There was near the village a settlement called Clary's Grove. The most conspicuous part of the population was an organization known as the "Clary's Grove

FIRST APPEARANCE IN POLITICS 73

Boys." They exercised a veritable terror over the neighborhood, and yet they were not a bad set of fellows. Mr. Herndon, who knew personally many of the "boys," says:

"They were friendly and good-natured; they could trench a pond, dig a bog, build a house; they could pray and fight, make a village or create a state. They would do almost anything for sport or fun, love or necessity. Though rude and rough, though life's forces ran over the edge of the bowl, foaming and sparkling in pure deviltry for deviltry's sake, yet place before them a poor man who needed their aid, a lame or sick man, a defenceless woman, a widow, or an orphaned child, they melted into sympathy and charity at once. They gave all they had and willingly toiled or played cards for more. Though there never was under the sun a more generous parcel of rowdies, a stranger's introduction was likely to be the most unpleasant part of his acquaintance with them."

Denton Offutt, Lincoln's employer, was just the man to love to boast before such a crowd. He seemed to feel that Lincoln's physical prowess shed glory on himself, and he declared the country over that his clerk could lift more, throw farther, run faster, jump higher, and wrestle better than any man in Sangamon County. The "Clary's Grove Boys," of course, felt in honor bound to prove this false, and they appointed their best man, one Jack Armstrong, to "throw Abe." Jack Armstrong was, according to the testimony of all who remember him, a "powerful twister," "square built and strong as an ox," "the best-made man that ever lived"; and everybody knew that a contest between him and Lincoln would be close. Lincoln did not like to "tussle and scuffle," he objected to "woolling and pulling"; but Offutt had gone so far that it became necessary to yield. The match was held on the ground near the grocery. Clary's Grove and New Salem turned out generally to witness the bout, and betting on the result ran high, the community as a whole staking their jack-knives, tobacco plugs, and "treats" on Armstrong. The two men had scarcely taken hold of each other before it was evident that the Clary's Grove champion had met a match. The two men wrestled long and hard, but both kept their feet. Neither could throw the other, and Armstrong, convinced of this, tried a "foul." Lincoln no sooner realized the game of his antagonist than, furious with indignation, he caught him by the throat and, holding him out at arm's length, he "shook him like a child." Armstrong's friends rushed to his aid, and for a moment it looked as if Lincoln would be routed by sheer force of numbers; but he held his own so bravely that the "boys," in spite of their sympathies, were filled with admiration. What bid fair to be a general fight ended in a general hand-shake, even Jack Armstrong declaring that Lincoln was the "best fellow who ever broke into the camp." From that day, at the cock-fights and horse-races which were their common sports, he became the chosen umpire, and when the entertainment broke up in a row—a not uncommon occurrence—he acted the peacemaker without suffering the peacemaker's usual fate. Such was his reputation with the "Clary's Grove Boys," after three months in New Salem, that when the fall muster came off he was elected captain.

FIRST APPEARANCE IN POLITICS 75

Lincoln showed soon that if he was unwilling to indulge in "woolling and pulling" for amusement, he did not object to it in the interests of decency and order. In such a community as New Salem there are always braggarts who can only be made endurable by fear. To them Lincoln soon became an authority more to be respected than sheriff or constable. If they transgressed in his presence he thrashed them promptly with an imperturbable air, half indolent, but wholly resolute which was more baffling and impressive than even his iron grip and well-directed blows. A man came into the store one day and began swearing. Now, profanity in the presence of women, Lincoln never would allow. He asked the man to stop, but he persisted, loudly boasting that nobody should prevent his saying what he wanted to. The women gone, the man began to abuse Lincoln so hotly that the latter said: "Well, if you must be whipped, I suppose I might as well whip you as any other man;" and going outdoors with the fellow, he threw him on the ground and rubbed smart-weed into his eyes until he bellowed for mercy. New Salem's sense of chivalry was touched, and Denton Offutt's clerk became the local hero.

His honesty excited no less admiration. Two incidents seem to have particularly impressed the community. Having discovered on one occasion that he had taken six and one-quarter cents too much from a customer, he walked three miles that evening, after his store was closed, to return the money. Again, he weighed out a half-pound of tea, as he supposed. It was night, and this was the last thing he did before closing up. On entering in the morning he discovered a four-ounce weight in the scales. He saw his mistake and, closing up shop, hurried off to deliver the remainder of the tea. This unusual regard for the rights of others soon won him the title of "Honest Abe."

As soon as the store was fairly under way, Lincoln began to look about for books. Since leaving Indiana in March, 1830, he had had in his drifting life little leisure or opportunity for study, though much for observation of men and of life. His experience had made him realize more and more clearly that power over men depends upon knowledge. He had found that he was himself superior to many of those who were called the "great" men of the country. Soon after entering Macon County, in March, 1830, when he was only twenty-one years old, he had found he could make a better speech than at least one man who was before the public. A candidate had come along where he and John Hanks were at work, and, as John Hanks tells the story, the man made a speech. "It was a bad one, and I said Abe could beat it. I turned down a box, and Abe made his speech. The other man was a candidate, Abe wasn't. Abe beat him to death, his subject being the navigation of the Sangamon River. The man, after Abe's speech was through, took him aside and asked him where he had learned so much, and how he could do so well. Abe replied, stating his manner and method of reading, what he had read. The man encouraged him to persevere."

He studied men carefully, comparing himself with

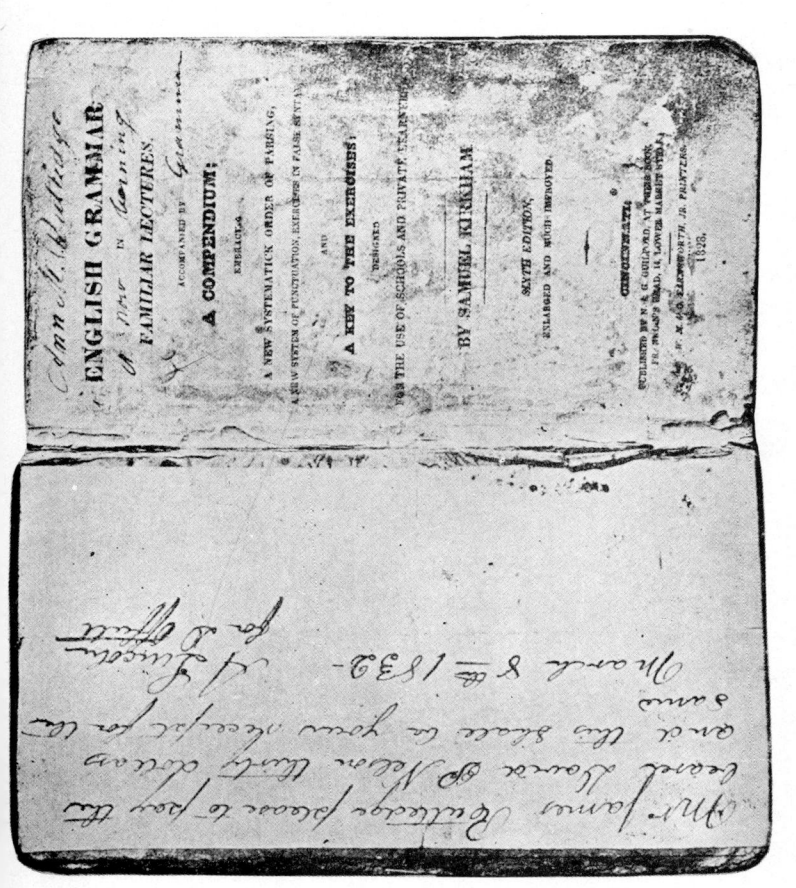

THE KIRKHAM'S GRAMMAR USED BY LINCOLN AT NEW SALEM.

It is said that Lincoln learned this grammar practically by heart. He presented the book to Ann Rutledge. After the death of Ann, it was studied by her brother, Robert, and is now owned by his widow, at Casselton, North Dakota. The words, "Ann M. Rutledge is now learning grammar," were written by Lincoln. The order on James Rutledge to pay Daniel P. Nelson thirty dollars and signed "A. Lincoln for D. Offutt," was pasted upon the front cover of the book by Robert Rutledge.

FIRST APPEARANCE IN POLITICS 77

them. Could he do what they did? He seems never up to this time to have met one who was incomprehensible to him. "I have talked with great men," he told his fellow-clerk and friend Greene, "and I do not see how they differ from others." Then he found, too, that people listened to him, that they quoted his opinions, and that his friends were already saying that he was able to fill any position. Offutt even declared the country over that "Abe" knew more than any man in the United States, and that some day he would be President.

When he began to realize that he himself possessed the qualities which made men great in Illinois, that success depended upon knowledge and that already his friends credited him with possessing more than most members of the community, his ambition was encouraged and his desire to learn increased. Why should he not try for a public position? He began to talk to his friends of his ambition and to devise plans for self-improvement. In order to keep in practice in speaking he walked seven or eight miles to debating clubs. "Practicing polemics," was what he called the exercise. He seems now for the first time to have begun to study subjects. Grammar was what he chose. He sought Mentor Graham, the schoolmaster, and asked his advice. "If you are going before the public," Mr. Graham told him, "you ought to do it." But where could he get a grammar? There was but one, said Mr. Graham, in the neighborhood, and that was six miles away. Without waiting for further information, the young man rose from the breakfast-table, walked immediately to the place and borrowed this rare copy of Kirkham's Grammar. From that time on for weeks he gave every moment of his leisure to mastering the contents of the book. Frequently he asked his friend Greene to "hold the book" while he recited, and, when puzzled by a point, he would consult Mr. Graham.

Lincoln's eagerness to learn was such that the whole neighborhood became interested. The Greenes lent him books, the schoolmaster kept him in mind and helped him as he could, and the village cooper let him come into his shop and keep up a fire of shavings sufficiently bright to read by at night. It was not long before the grammar was mastered. "Well," Lincoln said to his fellow-clerk, Greene, "if that's what they call a science, I think I'll go at another."

Before the winter was ended he had become the most popular man in New Salem. Although he was but twenty-two years of age, in February, 1832, had never been at school an entire year in his life, had never made a speech except in debating clubs and by the roadside, had read only the books he could pick up, and known only the men who made up the poor, out-of-the-way towns in which he had lived, "encouraged by his great popularity among his immediate neighbors," as he says, he decided to announce himself, in March, 1832, as a candidate for the General Assembly of the State.

The only preliminary expected of a candidate for the legislature of Illinois at that date was a statement of his "sentiments with regard to local affairs." The circular in which Lincoln complied with this custom was a document of about two thousand words, in which he plunged at once into the subject he believed most interesting to his constituents—"the public utility of internal improvements."

At that time the State of Illinois—as, indeed, the whole United States—was convinced that the future of the country depended on the opening of canals and railroads, and the clearing out of the rivers. In the Sangamon country the population felt that a quick way of getting to Beardstown on the Illinois River, to which point the steamer came from the Mississippi, was, as Lincoln puts it in his circular, "indispensably necessary." Of course a railroad was the dream of the settlers, but when it was considered seriously there was always, as Lincoln says, "a heart-appalling shock accompanying the amount of its cost, which forces us to shrink from our pleasing anticipations. The probable cost of this contemplated railroad is estimated at two hundred and ninety thousand dollars; the bare statement of which, in my opinion, is sufficient to justify the belief that the improvement of the Sangamon River is an object much better suited to our infant resources."

"Respecting this view, I think I may say, without the fear of being contradicted, that its navigation may be rendered completely practicable as high as the mouth of the South Fork, or probably higher, to vessels of from twenty-five to thirty tons burden, for at least one-half of all common years, and to vessels of much greater burden a part of the time. From my peculiar circumstances, it is probable that for the last twelve months I have given as particular attention to the stage of the water in this river as any other person in the country. In the month of March, 1831, in company with others, I commenced the building of a flatboat on the

Sangamon, and finished and took her out in the course of the spring. Since that time I have been concerned in the mill at New Salem. These circumstances are sufficient evidence that I have not been very inattentive to the stages of the water. The time at which we crossed the mill-dam being in the last days of April, the water was lower than it had been since the breaking of winter in February, or than it was for several weeks after. The principal difficulties we encountered in descending the river were from the drifted timber, which obstructions all know are not difficult to be removed. Knowing almost precisely the height of the water at that time, I believe I am safe in saying that it has as often been higher as lower since.

"From this view of the subject it appears that my calculations with regard to the navigation of the Sangamon cannot but be founded in reason; but, whatever may be its natural advantages, certain it is that it never can be practically useful to any great extent without being greatly improved by art. The drifted timber, as I have before mentioned, is the most formidable barrier to this object. Of all parts of this river, none will require so much labor in proportion to make it navigable as the last thirty or thirty-five miles; and going with the meanderings of the channel, when we are this distance above its mouth we are only between twelve and eighteen miles above Beardstown in something near a straight direction; and this route is upon such low ground as to retain water in many places during the season, and in all parts such as to draw two-thirds or three-fourths of the river water at all high stages.

"This route is on prairie land the whole distance, so that it appears to me, by removing the turf a sufficient width, and damming up the old channel, the whole river in a short time would wash its way through, thereby curtailing the distance and increasing the velocity of the current very considerably, while there would be no timber on the banks to obstruct its navigation in future; and being nearly straight, the timber which might float in at the head would be apt to

FIRST APPEARANCE IN POLITICS 81

go clear through. There are also many places above this where the river, in its zigzag course, forms such complete peninsulas as to be easier to cut at the necks than to remove the obstructions from the bends, which, if done, would also lessen the distance.

"What the cost of this work would be, I am unable to say. It is probable, however, that it would not be greater than is common to streams of the same length. Finally, I believe the improvement of the Sangamon River to be vastly important and highly desirable to the people of the county; and, if elected, any measure in the legislature having this for its object, which may appear judicious, will meet my approbation and receive my support."

Lincoln could not have adopted a measure more popular. At that moment the whole population of Sangamon was in a state of wild expectation. Some six weeks before his circular appeared, a citizen of Springfield had advertised that as soon as the ice went off the river he would bring up a steamer, the "Talisman," from Cincinnati, and prove the Sangamon navigable. The announcement had aroused the entire country, speeches were made, and subscriptions taken. The merchants announced goods direct per steamship "Talisman," and every settlement from Beardstown to Springfield was laid off in town lots. When the circular appeared their excitement was at its height.

Lincoln's comments on two other subjects, on which all candidates of the day were expected to express themselves, are amusing in their simplicity. The practice of loaning money at exorbitant rates was then a great evil in the West. Lincoln proposed that the limits of usury be fixed, and he closed his paragraph on the subject with these words, which sound strange enough from a man who in later life showed so profound a reverence for law:

"In cases of extreme necessity, there could always be means found to cheat the law; while in all other cases it would have its intended effect. I would favor the passage of a law on this subject which might not be very easily evaded. Let it be such that the labor and difficulty of evading it could only be justified in cases of greatest necessity."

A general revision of the laws of the state was the second topic which he felt required a word. "Considering the great probability," he said, "that the framers of those laws were wiser than myself, I should prefer not meddling with them, unless they were first attacked by others; in which case I should feel it both a privilege and a duty to take that stand which, in my view, might tend most to the advancement of justice."

Of course he said a word for education:

"Upon the subject of education, not presuming to dictate any plan or system respecting it, I can only say that I view it as the most important subject which we as a people can be engaged in. That every man may receive at least a moderate education, and thereby be enabled to read the histories of his own and other countries, by which he may duly appreciate the value of our free institutions, appears to be an object of vital importance, even on this account alone, to say nothing of the advantages and satisfaction to be derived from all being able to read the Scriptures, and other works both of a religious and moral nature, for themselves.

"For my part, I desire to see the time when education—

FIRST APPEARANCE IN POLITICS 83

and by its means, morality, sobriety, enterprise, and industry—shall become much more general than at present, and should be gratified to have it in my power to contribute something to the advancement of any measure which might have a tendency to accelerate that happy period."

The audacity of a young man in his position presenting himself as a candidate for the legislature is fully equaled by the humility of the closing paragraphs of his announcement:

"But, fellow-citizens, I shall conclude. Considering the great degree of modesty which should always attend youth, it is probable I have already been more presuming than becomes me. However, upon the subjects of which I have treated, I have spoken as I have thought. I may be wrong in regard to any or all of them; but, holding it a sound maxim that it is better only sometimes to be right than at all times to be wrong, so soon as I discover my opinions to be erroneous, I shall be ready to renounce them.

"Every man is said to have his peculiar ambition. Whether it be true or not, I can say, for one, that I have no other so great as that of being truly esteemed of my fellow-men, by rendering myself worthy of their esteem. How far I shall succeed in gratifying this ambition is yet to be developed. I am young, and unknown to many of you. I was born, and have ever remained, in the most humble walks of life. I have no wealthy or popular relations or friends to recommend me. My case is thrown exclusively upon the independent voters of the county; and, if elected, they will have conferred a favor upon me for which I shall be unremitting in my labors to compensate. But, if the good people in their wisdom shall see fit to keep me in the background, I have been too familiar with disappointments to be very much chagrined."

Very soon after Lincoln had distributed his handbills, enthusiasm on the subject of the opening of the Sangamon rose to a fever. The "Talisman" actually came up the river; scores of men went to Beardstown to meet her, among them Lincoln, of course, and to him was given the honor of piloting her—an honor which made him remembered by many a man who saw him that day for the first time. The trip was made with all the wild demonstrations which always attended the first steamboat. At every stop speeches were made, congratulations offered, toasts drunk, flowers presented. It was one long hurrah from Beardstown to Springfield, and foremost in the jubilation was Lincoln, the pilot. The "Talisman" went to the point on the river nearest to Springfield, and there tied up for a week. When she went back Lincoln again had the conspicuous position of pilot. The notoriety this gave him was probably quite as valuable politically as the forty dollars he received for his service was financially.

While the country had been dreaming of wealth through the opening of the Sangamon, and Lincoln had been doing his best to prove that the dream could be realized, the store in which he clerked was "petering out"—to use his expression. The owner, Denton Offutt, had proved more ambitious than wise, and Lincoln saw that an early closing by the sheriff was probable. But before the store was fairly closed, and while the "Talisman" was yet exciting the country, an event occurred which interrupted all of Lincoln's plans.

CHAPTER VI

THE BLACK HAWK WAR—LINCOLN CHOSEN CAPTAIN OF A COMPANY—REENLISTS AS AN INDEPENDENT RANGER—END OF THE WAR

ONE morning in April a messenger from the governor of the State rode into New Salem, scattering circulars. The circular was addressed to the militia of the northwest section of Illinois, and announced that the British band of Sacs and other hostile Indians, headed by Black Hawk, had invaded the Rock River country, to the great terror of the frontier inhabitants; and it called upon the citizens who were willing to aid in repelling them to rendezvous at Beardstown within a week.

The name of Black Hawk was familiar to the people of Illinois. He was an old enemy of the settlers, and had been a tried friend of the British. The land his people had once owned in the northwest of the present State had been sold in 1804 to the government of the United States, but with the provision that the Indians could hunt and raise corn there until it was surveyed and sold to settlers. Long before the land was surveyed, however, squatters had invaded the country and tried to force the Indians west of the Mississippi. Particularly envious were these whites of the lands at the mouth of the Rock River, where the ancient village and burial place of the Sacs stood, and where they came each year to raise corn. Black Hawk had resisted their encroachments, and many violent acts had been committed on both sides.

Finally, however, the squatters, in spite of the fact that the line of settlement was still fifty miles away, succeeded in evading the real meaning of the treaty and in securing a survey of the desired land at the mouth of the river. Black Hawk, exasperated and broken-hearted at seeing his village violated, persuaded himself that the village had never been sold—indeed, that land could not be sold.

"My reason teaches me," he wrote, "that land cannot be sold. The Great Spirit gave it to his children to live upon, and cultivate, as far as is necessary, for their subsistence; and so long as they occupy and cultivate it they have the right to the soil, but if they voluntarily leave it, then any other people have a right to settle upon it. Nothing can be sold but such things as can be carried away."

Supported by this theory, conscious that in some way he did not understand he had been wronged, and urged on by White Cloud, the prophet, who ruled a Winnebago village on the Rock River, Black Hawk crossed the Mississippi in 1831, determined to evict the settlers. A military demonstration drove him back, and he was persuaded to sign a treaty never to return east of the Mississippi. "I touched the goose-quill to the treaty and was determined to live in peace," he wrote afterwards; but hardly had he "touched the goose-quill" before his heart smote him. Longing for his home, resentment at the whites, obstinacy, brooding over the bad counsels of White Cloud and his disciple, Neapope—an agitating In-

THE BLACK HAWK.

After a portrait by George Catlin, in the National Museum at Washington, D. C., and here reproduced by the courtesy of the director, Mr. G. Brown Goode. Makataimeshekiakiak, the Black Hawk Sparrow, was born in 1767 on the Rock River.

THE BLACK HAWK WAR

dian who had recently been East to visit the British and their Indian allies, and who assured Black Hawk that the Winnebagoes, Ottawas, Chippewas, and Pottawattomies would join him in a struggle for his land, and that the British would send him guns, ammunition, provisions, and clothing early in the spring—all persuaded the Hawk that he would be successful if he made an effort to drive out the whites. In spite of the advice of many of his friends and of the Indian agent in the country, he crossed the river on April 6, 1832, and with some five hundred braves, his squaws and children, marched to the Prophet's town, thirty-five miles up the Rock River.

As soon as they heard of Black Hawk's invasion, the settlers of the northwestern part of the state fled in a panic to the forts, and from there rained petitions for protection on Governor Reynolds. General Atkinson, who was at Fort Armstrong, wrote to the governor for reinforcements; and, accordingly on the 16th of April Governor Reynolds sent out "influential messengers" with a sonorous summons. It was one of these messengers riding into New Salem who put an end to Lincoln's canvassing for the legislature, freed him from Offutt's expiring grocery, and led him to enlist.

There was no time to waste. The volunteers were ordered to be at Beardstown, nearly forty miles from New Salem, on April 22d. Horses, rifles, saddles, blankets, were to be secured, a company formed. It was work of which the settlers were not ignorant. Under the laws of the state every able-bodied male inhabitant between eighteen and forty-five was obliged to drill twice a year or pay a fine of one dollar. "As a dollar was hard to raise," says one of the old settlers, "everybody drilled."

Preparations were quickly made, and by April 22d the men were at Beardstown. The day before, at Richland, Sangamon County, Lincoln was elected captain of the company from Sangamon.

According to his friend Greene it was something beside ambition which led him to seek the captaincy. One of the "odd jobs" which Lincoln had taken since coming into Illinois was working in a saw-mill for a man named Kirkpatrick. In hiring Lincoln, Kirkpatrick had promised to buy him a cant-hook with which to move heavy logs. Lincoln had proposed, if Kirkpatrick would give him the two dollars which the cant-hook would cost, to move the logs with a common hand-spike. This the proprietor had agreed to, but when pay-day came he refused to keep his word. When the Sangamon company of volunteers was formed Kirkpatrick aspired to the captaincy, and Lincoln knowing it, said to Greene: "Bill, I believe I can make Kirkpatrick pay me that two dollars he owes me on the cant-hook. I'll run against him for captain." And he became a candidate. The vote was taken in a field, by directing the men at the command "march" to assemble around the one they wanted for captain. When the order was given, three-fourths of the men gathered around Lincoln. In Lincoln's third-person autobiography he says he was elected "to his own surprise"; and adds, "He says he has not since had any success in life which gave him so much satisfaction."

The company was a motley crowd of men. Each had secured for his outfit what he could get, and no two were equipped alike. Buckskin breeches prevailed, and there was a sprinkling of coon-skin caps. Each man had a blanket of the coarsest texture. Flint-lock rifles were the usual arm, though here and there a man had a Cramer. Over the shoulder of each was slung a powder-horn. The men had, as a rule, as little regard for discipline as for appearances, and when the new captain gave an order were as likely to jeer at it as to obey it. To drive the Indians out was their mission, and any order which did not bear directly on that point was little respected. Lincoln himself was not familiar with military tactics and made many blunders of which he used to tell afterwards with relish. One of these was an early experience in giving orders. He was marching with a front of over twenty men across a field, when he desired to pass through a gateway into the next inclosure.

"I could not for the life of me," said he, "remember the proper word of command for getting my company *endwise,* so that it could get through the gate; so as we came near I shouted: 'This company is dismissed for two minutes, when it will fall in again on the other side of the gate!'"

Nor was it only his ignorance of the manual which caused him trouble. He was so unfamiliar with camp discipline that he once had his sword taken from him for shooting within limits. Another disgrace he suffered was on account of his disorderly company. The men, unknown to him, stole a quantity of liquor one night, and the next morning were too drunk to fall in when the order was given to march. For their lawlessness Lincoln wore a wooden sword two days.

But none of these small difficulties injured his standing with the company. They soon grew so proud of his quick wit and great strength that they obeyed him because they admired him. No amount of military tactics could have secured from the volunteers the cheerful following he won by his personal qualities.

The men soon learned, too, that he meant what he said and would permit no dishonorable performances. A helpless Indian took refuge in the camp one day; and the men, who were inspired by that wanton mixture of selfishness, unreason and cruelty which seems to seize a frontiersman as soon as he scents a red man —were determined to kill the refugee. He had a safe conduct from General Cass; but the men, having come out to kill Indians and not having succeeded, threatened to take revenge on the helpless savage. Lincoln boldly took the man's part, and though he risked his life in doing it, he cowed the company and saved the Indian.

It was on the 27th of April that the force of sixteen hundred men organized at Beardstown started out. The day was cold, the roads heavy, the streams turbulent. The army marched first to Yellow Banks on the Mississippi, then to Dixon on the Rock River, which they reached on May 12. At Dixon they camped, and near here occurred the first bloodshed of the war.

A body of about three hundred and forty rangers, under Major Stillman, but not of the regular army,

THE BLACK HAWK WAR

asked to go ahead as scouts, to look for a body of Indians under Black Hawk, rumored to be about twelve miles away. The permission was given, and on the night of the 14th of May, Stillman and his men went into camp. Black Hawk heard of their presence. By this time the poor old chief had discovered that the promises of aid from the Indian tribes and the British were false, and dismayed, he had resolved to recross the Mississippi. When he heard the whites were near he sent three braves with a white flag to ask for a parley and permission to descend the river. Behind them he sent five men to watch proceedings. Stillman's rangers were in camp when the bearers of the flag of truce appeared. The men were many of them half drunk, and when they saw the Indian trucebearers, they rushed out in a wild mob and ran them into camp. Then catching sight of the five spies, they started after them, killing two. The three who reached Black Hawk reported that the truce-bearers had been killed as well as their two companions. Furious at this violation of faith, Black Hawk "raised a yell," and sallied forth with forty braves to meet Stillman's band, who by this time were out in search of the Indians. Black Hawk, too maddened to think of the difference of numbers, attacked the whites. To his surprise the enemy turned and fled in a wild riot. Nor did they stop at the camp, which from its position was almost impregnable; they fled in complete panic, *sauve qui peut,* through their camp, across prairie and rivers and swamps, to Dixon, twelve miles away. The first arrival reported that two thousand savages had swept down on Stillman's camp and slaughtered all but himself. Before the next night all but eleven of the band had arrived.

Stillman's Defeat, as this disgraceful affair is called, put all notion of peace out of Black Hawk's mind, and he started out in earnest on the warpath. Governor Reynolds, excited by the reports of the first arrivals from the Stillman stampede, made out that night, "by candlelight," a call for more volunteers, and by the morning of the 15th had messengers out and his army in pursuit of Black Hawk. But it was like pursuing a shadow. The Indians purposely confused their trail. Sometimes it was a broad path, then it suddenly radiated to all points. The whites broke their bands and pursued the savages here and there, never overtaking them, though now and then coming suddenly on some terrible evidences of their presence—a frontier home deserted and burned, slaughtered cattle, scalps suspended where the army could not fail to see them.

This fruitless warfare exasperated the volunteers; they threatened to leave, and their officers had great difficulty in making them obey orders. On reaching a point in the Rock River, beyond which lay the Indian country, a company under Colonel Zachary Taylor refused to cross and held a public indignation meeting, urging that they had volunteered to defend the state, and had the right, as independent American citizens, to refuse to go out of its borders. Taylor heard them to the end, and then spoke: "I feel that all gentlemen here are my equals; in reality, I am persuaded that many of them will, in a few years, be my superiors, and perhaps, in the capacity of members of Congress, arbiters of the fortunes and reputation of humble servants of the republic, like myself. I expect then to obey them as interpreters of the will of the people; and the best proof that I will obey them is now to observe the orders of those whom the people have already put in the place of authority to which many gentlemen around me justly aspire. In plain English, gentlemen and fellow-citizens, the word has been passed on to me from Washington to follow Black Hawk and to take you with me as soldiers. I mean to do both. There are the flatboats drawn up on the shore, and here are Uncle Sam's men drawn up behind you on the prairie." The volunteers knew true grit when they met it. They dissolved their meeting and crossed the river without Uncle Sam's men being called into action.

The march in pursuit of the Indians led the army to Ottawa, where the volunteers became so dissatisfied that on May 27 and 28 Governor Reynolds mustered them out. But a force in the field was essential until a new levy was raised; and a few of the men were patriotic enough to offer their services, among them Lincoln, who on May 29 was mustered in at the mouth of the Fox River by a man in whom, thirty years later, he was to have a keen interest—General Robert Anderson, commander at Fort Sumter in 1861. Lincoln became a private in Captain Elijah Iles's company of Independent Rangers, not brigaded—a company made up, says Captain Iles in his "Footsteps and Wanderings," of "generals, colonels, captains, and distinguished men from the disbanded army." General Anderson says that at this muster Lincoln's

LIFE OF LINCOLN

arms were valued at forty dollars, his horse and equipment at one hundred and twenty dollars. The Independent Rangers were a favored body, used to carry messages and to spy on the enemy. They had no camp duties, and "drew rations as often as they pleased." So that as a private Lincoln was really better off than as a captain.*

The achievements and tribulations of this body of rangers to which he belonged are told with interesting detail by its commanding officer, Captain Iles, in his "Footsteps and Wanderings."

"While the other companies were ordered to scout the country," he writes, "mine was held by General Atkinson in camp as a reserve. One company was ordered to go to Rock River (now Dixon) and report to Colonel Taylor (afterwards President) who had been left there with a few United States soldiers to guard the army supplies. The place was also made a point of rendezvous. Just as the company got to Dixon, a man came in and reported that he and six others were on the road to Galena, and, in passing through a point of timber about twenty miles north of Dixon, they were fired on and six killed, he being the only one to make his escape. . . . Colonel Taylor ordered the company to proceed to the place, bury the dead, go on to Galena, and get all the information they could about the Indians. But the company took fright and came back to the Illinois River, helter-skelter.

* William Cullen Bryant, who was in Illinois in 1832 at the time of the Black Hawk War, used to tell of meeting in his travels in the state a company of Illinois volunteers, commanded by a "raw youth" of "quaint and pleasant" speech, and of learning afterwards that this captain was Abraham Lincoln. As Lincoln's captaincy ended on May 27th, and Mr. Bryant did not reach Illinois until June 12th, and as he never came nearer than fifty miles to the Rapids of the Illinois, where the body of rangers to which Lincoln belonged was encamped, it is evident that the "raw youth" could not have been Lincoln, much as one would like to believe that it was.

THE BLACK HAWK WAR 95

"General Atkinson then called on me and wanted to know how I felt about taking the trip; that he was exceedingly anxious to open communication with Galena and to find out, if possible, the whereabouts of the Indians before the new troops arrived. I answered the general that myself and men were getting rusty and were anxious to have something to do, and that nothing would please us better than to be ordered out on an expedition; that I would find out how many of my men had good horses and were otherwise well equipped, and what time we wanted to prepare for the trip. I called on him again at sunset and reported that I had about fifty men well equipped and eager, and that we wanted one day to make preparations. He said go ahead, and he would prepare our orders.

"The next day was a busy one, running bullets and getting our flint-locks in order—we had no percussion locks then. General Henry, one of my privates, who had been promoted to the position of major of one of the companies, volunteered to go with us. I considered him a host, as he had served as lieutenant in the War of 1812, under General Scott, and was in the battle of Lundy's Lane, and several other battles. He was a good drill officer, and could aid me much. . . . After General Atkinson handed me my orders, and my men were mounted and ready for the trip, I felt proud of them, and was confident of our success, although numbering only forty-eight. Several good men failed to go, as they had gone down to the foot of the Illinois rapids, to aid in bringing up the boats of army supplies. We wanted to be as little encumbered as possible, and took nothing that could be dispensed with, other than blankets, tin cups, coffee-pots, canteens, a wallet of bread, and some fat side meat, which we ate raw or broiled.

"When we arrived at Rock River, we found Colonel Taylor on the opposite side, in a little fort built of prairie sod. He sent an officer in a canoe to bring me over. I said to the officer that I would come over as soon as I got my men in camp. I knew of a good spring half a mile above, and

I determined to camp at it. After the men were in camp I called on General Henry, and he accompanied me. On meeting Colonel Taylor (he looked like a man born to command) he seemed a little piqued that I did not come over and camp with him. I told him we felt just as safe as if quartered in his one-horse fort; besides, I knew what his orders would be and wanted to try the mettle of my men before starting on the perilous trip I knew he would order. He said the trip was perilous, and that since the murder of the six men all communications with Galena had been cut off, and it might be besieged; that he wanted me to proceed to Galena, and that he would have my orders for me in the morning, and asked what outfit I wanted. I answered, 'Nothing but coffee, side meat and bread.'

"In the morning my orders were to collect and bury the remains of the six men murdered, proceed to Galena, make a careful search for the signs of Indians, and find out whether they were aiming to escape by crossing the river below Galena, and get all information at Galena of their possible whereabouts before the new troops were ready to follow them.

"John Dixon, who kept a house of entertainment here, and had sent his family to Galena for safety, joined us and hauled our wallets of corn and grub in his wagon, which was a great help. Lieutenant Harris, U. S. A., also joined us. I now had fifty men to go with me on the march. I detailed two to march on the right, two on the left, and two in advance, to act as look-outs to prevent a surprise. They were to keep in full view of us and to remain out until we camped for the night. Just at sundown of the first day, while we were at lunch, our advance scouts came in under whip and reported Indians. We bounced to our feet, and, having a full view of the road for a long distance, could see a large body coming toward us. All eyes were turned to John Dixon, who, as the last one dropped out of sight coming over a ridge, pronounced them Indians. I stationed my men in a ravine crossing the road, where anyone approaching could not see us until within thirty yards; the horses I had driven back out of sight in a valley. I asked General Henry to take command. He said, 'No; stand at your post,' and walked along the line, talking to the men in a low, calm voice. Lieutenant Harris, U. S. A., seemed much agitated; he ran up and down the line and exclaimed, 'Captain, we will catch hell!' He had horse-pistols, belt-pistols, and a double-barreled gun. He would pick the flints, reprime, and lay the horse-pistols at his feet. When he got all ready he passed along the line slowly, and seeing the nerves of the men all quiet—after General Henry's talk to them—said, 'Captain, we are safe; we can whip five hundred Indians.' Instead of Indians, they proved to be the command of General Dodge, from Galena, of one hundred and fifty men, en route, to find out what had become of General Atkinson's army, as, since the murder of the six men, communication had been stopped for more than ten days. My look-out at the top of the hill did not notify us, and we were not undeceived until they got within thirty steps of us. My men then raised a yell and ran to finish their lunch. . . .

"When we got within fifteeen miles of Galena, on Apple Creek, we found a stockade filled with women and children and a few men, all terribly frightened. The Indians had shot at and chased two men that afternoon, who made their escape to the stockade. They insisted on our quartering in the fort, but instead we camped one hundred yards outside, and slept—what little sleep we did get—with our guns on our arms. General Henry did not sleep, but drilled my men all night; so the moment they were called they would bounce to their feet and stand in two lines, the front ready to fire, and fall back to reload, while the others stepped forward to take their places. They were called up a number of times, and we got but little sleep. We arrived at Galena the next day and found the citizens prepared to defend the place. They were glad to see us, as it had been so long since they had heard from General Atkinson and his army. The few Indians prowling about Galena and murdering were simply there as a ruse.

"On our return from Galena, near the forks of the Apple River and Gratiot roads, we could see General Dodge on the Gratiot road, on his return from Rock River. His six scouts had discovered my two men that I had allowed to drop in the rear—two men who had been in Stillman's defeat, and, having weak horses, were allowed to fall behind. Having weak horses they had fallen in the rear about two miles, and each took the other to be Indians, and such an exciting race I never saw, until they got sight of my company; then they came to a sudden halt, and after looking at us a few moments, wheeled their horses and gave up the chase. My two men did not know but that they were Indians until they came up with us and shouted 'Indians!'. They had thrown away their wallets and guns, and used their ramrods as whips.

"The few houses on the road that usually accommodated the travel were all standing, but vacant, as we went. On our return we found them burned by the Indians. On my return to the Illinois River I reported to General Atkinson, saying that, from all we could learn, the Indians were aiming to escape by going north, with the intention of crossing the Mississippi River above Galena. The new troops had just arrived and were being mustered into service. My company had only been organized for twenty days, and as the time had now expired, the men were mustered out. All but myself again volunteered for the third time."

It was the middle of June when Captain Iles and his company returned to Dixon's Ferry from their Indian hunt and were mustered out. On June 20 Lincoln was mustered in again, by Major Anderson, as a member of an independent company under Captain Jacob M. Early. His arms were valued this

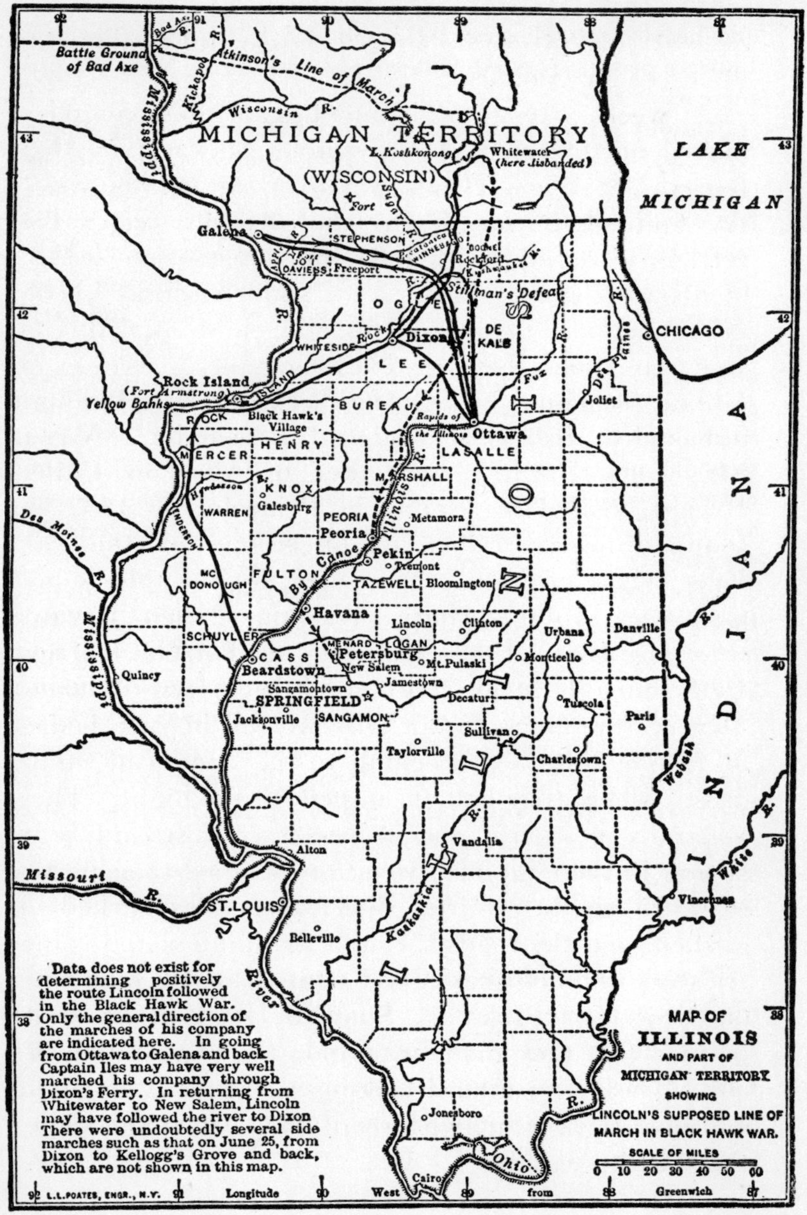
MAP OF
ILLINOIS
AND PART OF
MICHIGAN TERRITORY
SHOWING
LINCOLN'S SUPPOSED LINE OF
MARCH IN BLACK HAWK WAR.
SCALE OF MILES
0 10 20 30 40 50 60
Data does not exist for determining positively the route Lincoln followed in the Black Hawk War. Only the general direction of the marches of his company are indicated here. In going from Ottawa to Galena and back Captain Iles may have very well marched his company through Dixon's Ferry. In returning from Whitewater to New Salem, Lincoln may have followed the river to Dixon There were undoubtedly several side marches such as that on June 25, from Dixon to Kellogg's Grove and back, which are not shown in this map.
MICHIGAN TERRITORY
(WISCONSIN)
LAKE
MICHIGAN
Battle Ground of Bad Axe
Atkinson's Line of March
Wisconsin R.
Kickapoo R.
Mississippi
L. Koshkonong
Whitewater (here disbanded)
Sugar R.
Fort
Galena
STEPHENSON
WINNEBAGO
BOONE
Rockford
Freeport
JO DAVIESS
Stillman's Defeat
OGLE
DE KALB
Dixon
Rock R.
WHITESIDE
LEE
CHICAGO
Des Plaines R.
Fox R.
Joliet
Rock Island
(Fort Armstrong)
Yellow Banks
ROCK ISLAND
Black Hawk's Village
BUREAU
Rapids of the Illinois
Ottawa
LASALLE
MERCER
HENRY
MARSHALL
KNOX
Galesburg
WARREN
Henderson R.
PEORIA
Peoria
Metamora
Illinois R.
Des Moines R.
Pekin
Tremont
By Canoe
FULTON
MC DONOUGH
TAZEWELL
Bloomington
Havana
Lincoln
Clinton
LOGAN
MENARD
Petersburg
New Salem
Mt. Pulaski
SCHUYLER
CASS
Beardstown
Quincy
Sangamontown
Jamestown
SPRINGFIELD
SANGAMON
Jacksonville
Decatur
Urbana
Danville
Monticello
Tuscola
Paris
Sullivan
Charlestown
Taylorville
Wabash R.
Vandalia
Kaskaskia R.
Alton
Missouri R.
ST. LOUIS
Belleville
Vincennes
White R.
River
Jonesboro
Ohio R.
Cairo
ILLINOIS
INDIANA
L. L. POATES, ENGR., N.Y.
Longitude West from Greenwich
92 91 90 89 88 87
43 42 41 40 39 38

time at only fifteen dollars, his horse and equipments at eighty-five dollars.

A week after re-enlistment Lincoln's company moved northward with the army. It was time they moved, for Black Hawk was overrunning the country and scattering death wherever he went. The settlers were wild with fear, and most of the settlements were abandoned. At a sudden sound, at the merest rumor, men, women, and children fled. "I well remember these troublesome times," writes one Illinois woman. "We often left our bread dough unbaked to rush to the Indian fort near by." When Mr. John Bryant, a brother of William Cullen Bryant, visited the colony in Princeton in 1832, he found it nearly broken up on account of the war. Everywhere crops were neglected, for the able-bodied men were volunteering. William Cullen Bryant, who, in June, 1832, traveled on horseback from Petersburg to near Pekin and back, wrote home: "Every few miles on our way we fell in with bodies of Illinois militia proceeding to the American camp, or saw where they had encamped for the night. They generally stationed themselves near a stream or a spring in the edge of a wood and turned their horses to graze on the prairie. Their way was barked or girdled, and the roads through the uninhabited country were as much beaten and as dusty as the highways on New York Island. Some of the settlers complained that they made war upon the pigs and chickens. They were a hard-looking set of men, unkempt and unshaved, wearing shirts of dark calico and sometimes calico capotes."

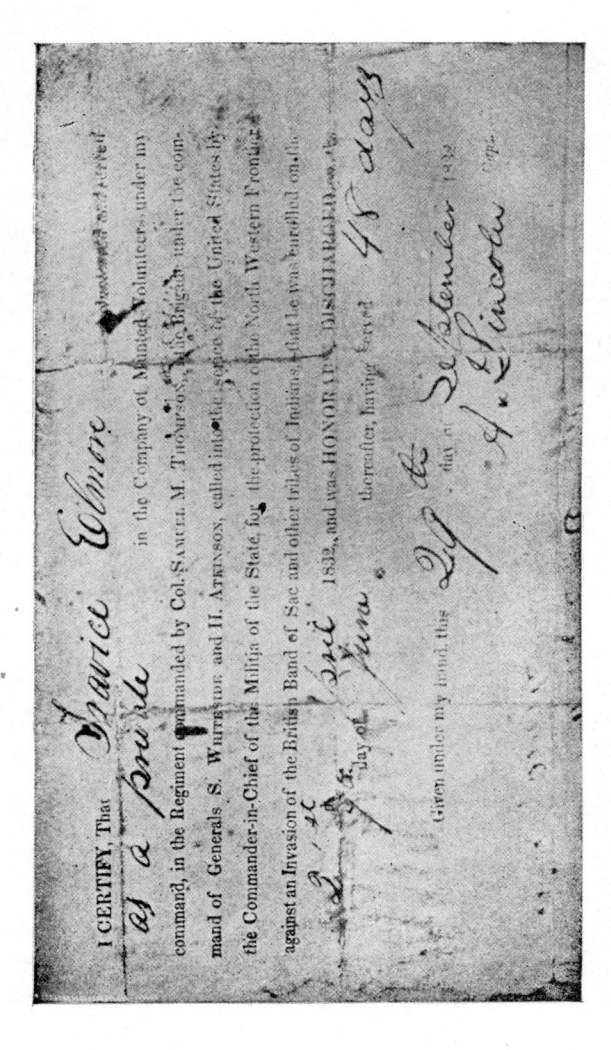

A DISCHARGE FROM SERVICE IN BLACK HAWK WAR SIGNED BY ABRAHAM LINCOLN, AS CAPTAIN.

THE BLACK HAWK WAR 101

Soon after the army moved up the Rock River, the independent spy company, of which Lincoln was a member, was sent with a brigade to the northwest, near Galena, in pursuit of the Hawk. The nearest Lincoln came to an actual engagement in the war was here. The skirmish of Kellogg's Grove took place on June 25; Lincoln's company came up soon after it was over and helped bury the five men killed. It was probably to this experience that he referred when he told a friend once of coming on a camp of white scouts one morning just as the sun was rising. The Indians had surprised the camp and had killed and scalped every man.

"I remember just how those men looked," said Lincoln, "as we rode up the little hill where their camp was. The red light of the morning sun was streaming upon them as they lay heads towards us on the ground. And every man had a round red spot on the top of his head about as big as a dollar, where the redskins had taken his scalp. It was frightful, but it was grotesque; and the red sunlight seemed to paint everything all over." Lincoln paused, as if recalling the vivid picture, and added, somewhat irrelevantly, "I remember that one man had buckskin breeches on."

Early's company, on returning from their expedition, joined the main army on its northward march. By the end of the month the troops crossed into Michigan Territory—as Wisconsin was then called— and July was passed floundering in swamps and stumbling through forests in pursuit of the now nearly exhausted Black Hawk. No doubt Early's company saw the hardest service on the march, for to it was allotted the scouting. The farther the army advanced the more difficult was the situation. Finally the provisions gave out and July 10, three weeks before the last battle of the war, that of Bad Axe, in which the whites finally massacred most of the Indian band, Lincoln's company was disbanded at Whitewater, Wisconsin, and he and his friends started for home. The volunteers in returning suffered much from hunger. More than one of them had nothing to eat on the journey except meal and water baked in rolls of bark laid by the fire. Lincoln not only went hungry on this return; he had to tramp most of the way. The night before his company started from Whitewater he and one of his messmates had their horses stolen; and, excepting when their more fortunate companions gave them a lift, they walked as far as Peoria, Illinois, where they bought a canoe and paddled down the Illinois River to Havana. Here they sold the canoe and walked across the country to New Salem.

CHAPTER VII

LINCOLN RUNS FOR STATE ASSEMBLY AND IS DEFEATED
—STOREKEEPER—STUDENT—POSTMASTER—
SURVEYOR

ON returning to New Salem Lincoln at once plunged into "electioneering." He ran as "an avowed Clay man," and the country was stiffly Democratic. However, in those days political contests were almost purely personal. If the candidate was liked he was voted for irrespective of principle. "The Democrats of New Salem worked for Lincoln out of their personal regard for him," said Stephen T. Logan, a young lawyer of Springfield, who made Lincoln's acquaintance in the campaign. "He was as stiff as a man could be in his Whig doctrines. They did this for him simply because he was popular—because he was Lincoln."

It was the custom for the candidates to appear at every gathering which brought the people out, and, if they had a chance, to make speeches. Then, as now, the farmers gathered at the county-seat or at the largest town within their reach on Saturday afternoons, to dispose of produce, buy supplies, see their neighbors, and get the news. During "election times" candidates were always present, and a regular feature of the day was listening to their speeches. They never missed public sales, it being expected that after the "vandoo" the candidates would take the auctioneer's place.

Lincoln let none of these chances slip. Accompanied by his friends, generally including a few "Clary's Grove Boys," he always was present. The first speech he made was after a sale at Pappsville. What he said there is not remembered, but an illustration of the kind of man he was, interpolated into his discourse, made a lasting impression. A fight broke out in his audience while he was on the stand, and observing that one of his friends was being worsted, he bounded into the group of contestants, seized the fellow who had his supporter down, threw him, according to tradition, "ten or twelve feet," mounted the platform, and finished the speech. Sangamon County could appreciate such a performance; and the crowd at Pappsville that day never forgot Lincoln.

His visits to Springfield were of great importance to him. Springfield was not at that time a very attractive place. Bryant, visiting it in June, 1832, said that the houses were not as good as at Jacksonville, "a considerable proportion of them being log cabins, and the whole town having an appearance of dirt and discomfort." Nevertheless it was the largest town in the county and among its inhabitants were many young men of breeding, education, and energy. One of these men Lincoln had become well acquainted with in the Black Hawk War *—Major John T. Stuart,

* There were many prominent Americans in the Black Hawk War, with some of whom Lincoln became acquainted. Among the best known were General Robert Anderson; Colonel Zachary Taylor; General Scott, afterwards candidate for President, and Lieutenant General; Henry

At an election held at the house of John McNeil in the New Salem precinct in the County of Sangamon and State of Illinois on the 20th day of September in the year of our Lord one thousand eight hundred and thirty two the following named persons received the number of votes annexed to their respective names for Constable —

John Clary had Forty one Votes for Constable
John R. Herndon had Twenty two Votes for Constable
William McNeely had Thirteen Votes for Constable
Baxter B. Berry had Nine — Votes for Constable
Edmund Greer had Four Votes for Constable

James Rutledge
Hugh Armstrong } *Judges of the election*
James White

Attest
A. Lincoln } *Clerks of the election*
William Green

I certify that the above Judges and clerks were qualified according to law
September 20- 1832 *Bowling Green*

FACSIMILE OF AN ELECTION RETURN WRITTEN BY LINCOLN AS CLERK IN 1832.

From the original now on file in the county clerk's office, Springfield, Illinois. The first civil office Lincoln ever held was that of election clerk, and the returns made by him, of which a facsimile is here presented, was his first official document. In the following three or four years, very few elections were held in New Salem at which Lincoln was not a clerk. It is a somewhat singular fact that Lincoln, though clerk of this election, is not recorded as voting.

RUNS FOR STATE ASSEMBLY 105

at that time a lawyer, and, like Lincoln, a candidate for the General Assembly. He met others at this time who were to be associated with him more or less closely in the future in both law and politics, among them Judge Logan and William Butler. With these men the manners which had won him the day at Pappsville were of little value; what impressed them was his "very sensible speech," and his decided individuality and originality.

The election was held on August 6th. Lincoln was defeated. "This was the only time Abraham was ever defeated on a direct vote of the people," says his autobiographical notes. He had a consolation in his defeat, however, for in spite of the pronounced Democratic sentiments of his precinct, he received, according to the official poll-book in the county clerk's office at Springfield, two hundred and twenty-seven votes out of three hundred cast.

This defeat did not take him out of politics. Six weeks later he filled his first civil office, that of clerk of the September election. The report in his hand still exists, his first official document. In the follow-

Dodge, Governor of the Territory of Wisconsin, and United States Senator; Hon. William D. Ewing and Hon. Sidney Breese, both United States Senators from Illinois; William S. Hamilton, a son of Alexander Hamilton; Colonel Nathan Boone, son of Daniel Boone; Lieutenant Albert Sidney Johnston, afterwards a Confederate general; also Jefferson Davis, President of the Southern Confederacy. Davis was at this time a lieutenant stationed at Fort Crawford. According to the muster rolls of his company he was absent on furlough from March 26 to August 18, 1832, but, according to Davis's own statement, corroborated by many of the early settlers of Illinois who served in the Black Hawk War, Davis returned to duty as soon as he found there was to be a war. When Black Hawk was finally captured in August, after the battle of Bad Axe, he was sent down the river to Jefferson Barracks, under the charge of Lieutenant Jefferson Davis. Black Hawk, in his "Life," speaks of Davis as a "good and brave young chief, with whose conduct I was much pleased."

ing years few elections were held in New Salem at which Lincoln did not act as clerk.

The election over, Lincoln began to look for work. One of his friends, an admirer of his physical strength, advised him to become a blacksmith, but it was a trade which afforded little leisure for study and for meeting and talking with men, and he had already resolved, it is evident, that books and men were essential to him. The only employment in New Salem which offered both employment and the opportunities he sought was clerking in a store. Now the stores in New Salem were in more need of customers than of clerks, business having been greatly overdone. In the fall of 1832 four stores offered wares to the one hundred inhabitants. The most pretentious was that of Hill and McNeill, which carried a large line of dry goods. The three others, owned respectively by the Herndon brothers, Reuben Radford, and James Rutledge, were groceries.

Failing to secure employment at any of these establishments, Lincoln resolved to *buy* a store. He was not long in finding an opportunity to purchase. James Herndon had already sold out his half interest in Herndon Brothers' store to William F. Berry; and Rowan Herndon, not getting along well with Berry, was only too glad to find a purchaser of his half in the person of "Abe" Lincoln. Berry was as poor as Lincoln, but that was not a serious obstacle, for their notes were accepted for the Herndon stock of goods. They had barely hung out their sign when something happened which threw another store into their hands. Reuben Radford had made himself obnoxious to the

BERRY AND LINCOLN'S STORE AS IT APPEARED IN 1895.

This little building originally stood in New Salem. It is said to have been sold in 1835 by Lincoln himself. He assisted in moving it to Petersburg—the town which by 1840 had absorbed New Salem, leaving it a mere cow pasture.

"Clary's Grove Boys," and one night they broke in his doors and windows and overturned his counters and sugar barrels. It was too much for Radford, and he sold out next day to William G. Greene for a four-hundred-dollar note signed by Greene. At the latter's request, Lincoln made an inventory of the stock, and offered him six hundred and fifty dollars for it—a proposition which was cheerfully accepted. Berry and Lincoln, being unable to pay cash, assumed the four-hundred-dollar note payable to Radford and gave Greene their joint note for two hundred and fifty dollars. The little grocery owned by James Rutledge was the next to succumb. Berry and Lincoln bought it at a bargain, their joint note taking the place of cash. The three stocks were consolidated. Their aggregate cost must have been not less than fifteen hundred dollars. Berry and Lincoln had secured a monopoly of the grocery business in New Salem. Within a few weeks two penniless men had become the proprietors of three stores and had stopped buying only because there were no more to purchase.

But the partnership, it was soon evident, was unfortunate. Berry, though the son of a Presbyterian minister, was, according to tradition, "a very wicked young man," drinking, gambling, and taking an active part in all the disturbances of the neighborhood. In spite of the bad habits of his partner, Lincoln left the management of the business largely to him. It was his love of books which was responsible for this poor business management. He had soon discovered that store-keeping in New Salem, after all duties were done, left a large amount of leisure on a man's hands.

It was his chance to read, and he scoured the town for books. On pleasant days he spent hour after hour stretched under a tree, which stood just outside the door of the store, reading the works he had picked up. If it rained he simply made himself comfortable on the counter within. It was in this period that Lincoln discovered Shakespeare and Burns. In New Salem there was one of those curious individuals, sometimes found in frontier settlements, half poet, half loafer, incapable of earning a living in any steady employment, yet familiar with good literature and capable of enjoying it—Jack Kelso. He repeated passages from Shakespeare and Burns incessantly over the odd jobs he undertook or as he idled by the streams—for he was a famous fisherman—and Lincoln soon became one of his constant companions.

It was not only Burns and Shakespeare that interfered with the grocery keeping; Lincoln had begun seriously to read law. His first acquaintance with the subject, we have already seen, had been made when, a mere lad, a copy of the "Revised Statutes of Indiana" had fallen into his hands.

But from the time he left Indiana in 1830 he had no legal reading until one day soon after the grocery was started there happened one of those trivial incidents which so often turn the current of a life. It is best told in Mr. Lincoln's own words.* "One day a

* This incident was told by Lincoln to Mr. A. J. Conant, the artist, who in 1860 painted his portrait in Springfield. Mr. Conant, in order to catch Mr. Lincoln's pleasant expression, had engaged him in conversation and had questioned him about his early life, and it was in the course of their conversation that this incident came out. It is to be found in a delightful and suggestive article entitled, "My Acquaintance with Abraham Lincoln," contributed by Mr. Conant to the "Liber Scriptorum."

man who was migrating to the West drove up in front of my store with a wagon which contained his family and household plunder. He asked me if I would buy an old barrel for which he had no room in his wagon, and which he said contained nothing of special value. I did not want it, but to oblige him I bought it, and paid him, I think, half a dollar for it. Without further examination I put it away in the store and forgot all about it. Some time after, in overhauling things, I came upon the barrel and, emptying it upon the floor to see what it contained, I found at the bottom of the rubbish a complete edition of Blackstone's Commentaries. I began to read those famous works, and I had plenty of time, for during the long summer days, when the farmers were busy with their crops, my customers were few and far between. The more I read"—this he said with unusual emphasis—"the more intensely interested I became. Never in my whole life was my mind so thoroughly absorbed. I read until I devoured them."

But all this was fatal to business, and by spring it was evident that something must be done to stimulate the grocery sales. Liquor selling was the expedient adopted, for, on the 6th of March, 1833, the County Commissioners' Court of Sangamon County granted the firm of Berry and Lincoln a license to keep a tavern at New Salem. It is probable that the license was procured not to enable the firm to keep a tavern but to retail the liquors which they had in stock. Each of the three groceries which Berry and Lincoln acquired had the usual supply of liquors and it was only natural that they should seek a way to dispose of the surplus quickly and profitably—an end which could be best accomplished by selling it over the counter by the glass. To do this lawfully required a tavern license, and it is a warrantable conclusion that such was the chief aim of Berry and Lincoln in procuring a franchise of this character. We are fortified in this conclusion by the coincidence that three other grocers of New Salem were among those who took out tavern licenses.

In a community in which liquor drinking was practically universal, at a time when whiskey was as legitimate an article of merchandise as coffee or calico, when no family was without a jug, when the minister of the gospel could take his "dram" without any breach of propriety, it is not surprising that a reputable young man should have been found selling whiskey. Liquor was sold at all groceries, but it could not be lawfully sold in a smaller quantity than one quart. The law, however, was not always rigidly observed, and it was the custom of storekeepers to treat their patrons.

The license issued to Berry and Lincoln read as follows:

Ordered that William F. Berry, in the name of Berry and Lincoln, have a license to keep a tavern in New Salem to continue 12 months from this date, and that they pay one dollar in addition to the six dollars heretofore paid as per Treasurer's receipt, and that they be allowed the following rates (viz.):

French Brandy per ½ pt...................... 25
Peach   "   "   " 18¾
Apple   "   "   "   12
Holland Gin   "   " 18¾

Domestic   "   " 12½
Wine   "   " 25
Rum   "   " 18¾
Whiskey   "   " 12½
Breakfast, dinner or supper.................... 25
Lodging per night.............................. 12½
Horse per night................................ 25
Single feed 12½
Breakfast, dinner or supper for Stage Passengers... 37½
who gave bond as required by law.

At the granting of a tavern license, the applicants therefore were required by law to file a bond. The bond given in the case of Berry and Lincoln was as follows:

Know all men by these presents, we, William F. Berry, Abraham Lincoln and John Bowling Green, are held and firmly bound unto the County Commissioners of Sangamon County in the full sum of three hundred dollars to which payment well and truly to be made we bind ourselves, our heirs, executors and administrators firmly by these presents, sealed with our seal and dated this 6th day of March A. D. 1833. Now the condition of this obligation is such that Whereas the said Berry & Lincoln has obtained a license from the County Commissioners' Court to keep a tavern in the town of New Salem to continue one year. Now if the said Berry & Lincoln shall be of good behavior and observe all the laws of this State relative to tavern keepers—then this obligation to be void or otherwise remain in full force.

ABRAHAM LINCOLN [Seal]
WM. F. BERRY [Seal]
BOWLING GREEN [Seal]

This bond appears to have been written by the clerk of the Commissioners' Court, and Lincoln's name was signed by some other than himself, very likely by his partner Berry.

Business was not so brisk in Berry and Lincoln's grocery, even after the license was granted that the

> Mr. Spears
>
> At your request I send you a receipt for the postage on your paper. I am somewhat surprised at your request. I will however comply with it. The law requires News paper postage to be paid in advance and now that I have waited a full year you choose to wound my feelings by insinuating that unless you get a receipt it will probably make you pay it again—
>
> Respectfully
> A Lincoln
>
> Received of George Spears in full for postage on the Sangamo Journal up to the first of July 1834
> A. Lincoln P.M.

FACSIMILE OF A LETTER WRITTEN BY POSTMASTER LINCOLN.
Reproduced by permission from "Menard-Salem-Lincoln Souvenir Album." Petersburg, 1893.

junior partner did not welcome an appointment as postmaster which he received in May, 1833. The appointment of a Whig by a Democratic administration seems to have been made without comment. "The office was too insignificant to make his politics an objection," say his autobiographical notes. The duties of the new office were not arduous, for letters were few, and their comings far between. At that date the mails were carried by four-horse post-coaches from city to city, and on horseback from central points into the country towns. The rates of postage were high. A single-sheet letter carried thirty miles or under cost six cents; thirty to eighty miles, ten cents; eighty to one hundred and fifty miles, twelve and one-half cents; one hundred and fifty to four hundred miles, eighteen and one-half cents; over four hundred miles, twenty-five cents. A copy of one of the popular magazines sent from New York to New Salem would have cost fully twenty-five cents. The mail was irregular in coming as well as light in its contents. Though supposed to arrive twice a week, it sometimes happened that a fortnight or more passed without any mail. Under these conditions the New Salem post-office was not a serious care.

A large number of the patrons of the office lived in the country—many of them miles away—and generally Lincoln delivered their letters at their doors. These letters he would carefully place in the crown of his hat and distribute them from house to house. Thus it was in a measure true that he kept the New Salem post-office in his hat. The habit of carrying papers in his hat clung to Lincoln, for, many years later, when he was a practising lawyer in Springfield, he apologized for failing to answer a letter promptly, by explaining: "When I received your letter I put it in my old hat and, buying a new one the next day, the old one was set aside, and so the letter was lost sight of for a time."

114   LIFE OF LINCOLN

But whether the mail was delivered by the postmaster himself, or was received at the store it was the habit "to stop and visit awhile." He who received a letter read it and repeated the contents; if he had a newspaper, usually the postmaster could tell him in advance what it contained, for one of the perquisites of the early post-office was the privilege of reading all printed matter before delivering it. Every day, then, Lincoln's acquaintance in New Salem, through his position as postmaster, became more intimate.

As the summer of 1833 went on, the condition of the store became more and more unsatisfactory. As the position of postmaster brought in only a small revenue, Lincoln was forced to take any odd work he could get. He helped in other stores in the town, split rails, and looked after the mill; but all this yielded only a scant and uncertain support, and when in the fall he had an opportunity to learn surveying, he accepted it eagerly.

The condition of affairs in Illinois in the early thirties made a demand for the service of surveyors. The immigration had been phenomenal. There were thousands of farms to be surveyed and thousands of corners to be located. Speculators bought up large tracts and mapped out cities on paper. It was years before the first railroad was built in Illinois, and, as all inland traveling was on horseback or in the stagecoach, each year hundreds of miles of wagon roads were opened through woods and swamps and prairies. As the county of Sangamon was large and eagerly sought by immigrants, the county surveyor in 1833, one John Calhoun, needed deputies, but in a country so new it was no easy matter to find men with the requisite capacity.

With Lincoln, Calhoun had little if any personal acquaintance, for they lived twenty miles apart. Lincoln, however, had made himself known by his meteoric race for the legislature in 1832, and Calhoun had heard of him as an honest, intelligent, and trustworthy young man. One day he sent word to Lincoln by Pollard Simmons, who lived in the New Salem neighborhood, that he had decided to appoint him a deputy surveyor if he would accept the position.

Going into the woods, Simmons found Lincoln engaged in his old occupation of making rails. The two sat down together on a log, and Simmons told Lincoln what Calhoun had said. Now Calhoun was a "Jackson man"; he was for Clay. What did he know about surveying, and why should a Democratic official offer him a position of any kind? He immediately went to Springfield and had a talk with Calhoun. He would not accept the appointment, he said, unless he had the assurance that it involved no political obligation, and that he might continue to express his political opinions as freely and frequently as he chose. This assurance was given. The only difficulty then in the way was the fact that he knew absolutely nothing of surveying. But Calhoun, of course, understood this and agreed that he should have time to learn.

With the promptness of action with which he always undertook anything he had to do, Lincoln procured Flint and Gibson's treatise on surveying, and sought Mentor Graham for help. At a sacrifice of some time, the schoolmaster aided him to a partial mastery of the difficult subject. Lincoln worked literally day and night, sitting up until the crowing of the cock warned him of the approaching dawn. So hard did he study that his friends were greatly concerned at his haggard face. But in six weeks he had mastered all the books within reach relating to the subject—a task which, under ordinary circumstances, would hardly have been achieved in as many months. Reporting to Calhoun for duty (greatly to the amazement of that gentleman), he was at once assigned to the territory in the northwest part of the county, and the first work he did of which there is any authentic record was in January, 1834. In that month he surveyed a piece of land for Russell Godby, dating the certificate January 14, 1834, and signing it "J. Calhoun, S. S. C., by A. Lincoln."

Lincoln was frequently employed in laying out public roads, being selected for that purpose by the County Commissioners' Court. So far as can be learned from the official records, the first road he surveyed was "from Musick's Ferry on Salt Creek, via New Salem, to the county line in the direction of Jacksonville." For this he was allowed fifteen dollars for five days' service, and two dollars and fifty cents for a plat of the new road. The next road he surveyed, according to the records, was that leading from Athens to Sangamon town. This was reported to the County Commissioners' Court November 4, 1834. But road surveying was only a small portion of his work. He was more frequently employed by private individuals.

COURT-HOUSE AT PETERSBURG, MENARD COUNTY, WHERE LINCOLN WAS NOMINATED FOR CONGRESS.

According to tradition, when he first took up the business he was too poor to buy a chain, and instead used a long, straight grape-vine. Probably this is a myth, though surveyors who had experience in the early days say it may be true. The chains commonly used at that time were made of iron. Constant use wore away and weakened the links, and it was no unusual thing for a chain to lengthen six inches after a year's use. "And a good grape-vine," to use the words of a veteran surveyor, "would give quite as satisfactory results as one of those old-fashioned chains."

Lincoln's surveys had the extraordinary merit of being correct. Much of the government work had been rather indifferently done, or the government corners had been imperfectly preserved, and there were frequent disputes between adjacent land-owners about boundary lines. Frequently Lincoln was called upon in such cases to find the corner in controversy. His verdict was invariably the end of the dispute, so general was the confidence in his honesty and skill. Some of these old corners located by him are still in existence. The people of Petersburg proudly remember that they live in a town which was laid out by Lincoln. This he did in 1836, and it was the work of several weeks.

Lincoln's pay as a surveyor was three dollars a day, more than he had ever before earned. Compared with the compensation for like services nowadays it seems small enough, but at that time is was really princely. The Governor of the State received a salary of only one thousand dollars a year, the Secretary of State

To the county commissioner's court for the county of Sangamon—

We the undersigned being appointed to view and relocate a part of the road between Sangamowtown and the town of Athens, respectfully report that we have performed the duty of said appointment according to law—and that we have made the said relocation on good ground—and believe the same to be necessary and proper—

Athens Nov. 4. 1834—

James Shawhedge
Levi Cantrall
A. Lincoln—

Herewith is the map— The court may allow me the following charges if they think proper—

1 day's labour as surveyor — $3.00
Making map — 50
$3.50

A. Lincoln

FACSIMILE OF A REPORT OF A ROAD SURVEY BY LINCOLN.

FACSIMILE OF A MAP MADE BY LINCOLN OF ROAD IN MENARD COUNTY, ILL.

six hundred dollars, and good board and lodging could be obtained for one dollar a week. But even three dollars a day did not enable him to meet all his financial obligations. The heavy debts of the store hung over him. He was obliged to help his father's family. The long distances he had to travel in his new employment had made it necessary to buy a horse, and for it he had gone into debt.

"My father," says Thomas Watkins, of Petersburg, who remembers the circumstances well, "sold Lincoln the horse, and my recollection is that Lincoln agreed to pay him fifty dollars for it. Lincoln was a little slow in making the payments, and after he had paid all but ten dollars, my father, who was a high-strung man, became impatient and sued him for the balance. Lincoln, of course, did not deny the debt, but raised the money and paid it. I do not often tell this," Mr. Watkins adds, "because I have always thought there never was such a man as Lincoln, and I have always been sorry father sued him."

Between his duties as deputy surveyor and postmaster, Lincoln had little leisure for the store, and its management passed into the hands of Berry. The stock of groceries was on the wane. The numerous obligations of the firm were maturing, with no money to meet them. Both members of the firm, in the face of such obstacles, lost courage, and when, early in 1834, Alexander and William Trent asked if the store was for sale, an affirmative answer was eagerly given. A price was agreed upon, and the sale was made. Now, neither Alexander Trent nor his brother had any money, but as Berry and Lincoln had bought

THE STATE-HOUSE AT VANDALIA, ILLINOIS—LATER USED AS A COURT-HOUSE.

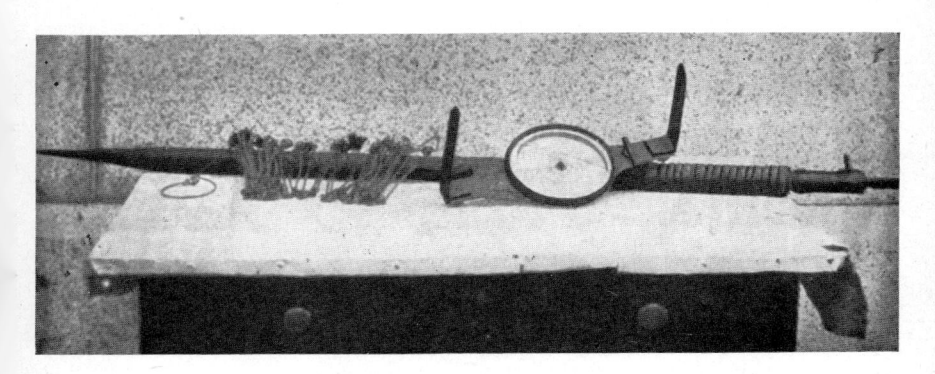

LINCOLN'S SURVEYING INSTRUMENTS.

without money, it seemed only fair that they should be willing to sell on the same terms. Accordingly the notes of the Trent brothers were accepted for the purchase price, and the store was turned over to the new owners. But about the time their notes fell due the Trent brothers disappeared. The few groceries in the store were seized by creditors, and the doors were closed, never to be opened again. Misfortunes now crowded upon Lincoln. His late partner, Berry, soon reached the end of his wild career, and one morning a farmer from the Rock Creek neighborhood drove into New Salem with the news that he was dead.

The appalling debt which had accumulated was thrown upon Lincoln's shoulders. He might have followed a fashion too common then among men mired in debt and in the expressive language of the pioneer "cleared out," as the Trents had done, but this was not Lincoln's way. He quietly settled down among the men he owed, promising to pay them in time. For fifteen years he carried this burden—a load which he cheerfully and manfully bore, but one so heavy that he habitually spoke of it as the "national debt." Talking once of it to a friend, Lincoln said: "That debt was the greatest obstacle I have ever met in life; I had no way of speculating, and could not earn money except by labor, and to earn by labor eleven hundred dollars, besides my living, seemed the work of a lifetime. There was, however, but one way. I went to the creditors and told them that if they would let me alone, I would give them all I could earn over my living, as fast as I could earn it." As late as 1848, so we are informed by Mr. Herndon,

Mr. Lincoln, then a member of Congress, sent home money saved from his salary to be applied on these obligations. All the notes, with interest at the high rates then prevailing, were at last paid.

With a single exception Lincoln's creditors seemed to be lenient. One of the notes given by him came into the hands of a Mr. Van Bergen, who, when it fell due, brought suit. The amount of the judgment was more than Lincoln could pay, and his personal effects were levied upon. These consisted of his horse, saddle and bridle, and surveying instruments. James Short, a well-to-do farmer living on Sand Ridge, a few miles north of New Salem, heard of the trouble which had befallen his young friend. Without advising Lincoln of his plans, he attended the sale, bought in the horse and surveying instruments for one hundred and twenty dollars, and turned them over to their former owner.

Lincoln never forgot a benefactor. He not only repaid the money with interest, but nearly thirty years later remembered the kindness in a most substantial way. After Lincoln left New Salem financial reverses came to James Short, and he removed to the far West to seek his fortune anew. Early in Lincoln's presidential term he heard that "Uncle Jimmy" was living in California. One day Mr. Short received a letter from Washington, D. C. Tearing it open, he read the gratifying announcement that he had been commissioned an Indian agent.

The kindness of Mr. Short was not exceptional in Lincoln's New Salem career. When the store had "winked out," as he put it, and the post-office had been left without headquarters, one of his neighbors, Samuel Hill, invited the homeless postmaster into his store. There was hardly a man or woman in the community who would not have been glad to have done as much. It was a simple recognition on their part of Lincoln's friendliness to them. He was what they called "obliging"—a man who instinctively did the thing which he saw would help another, no matter how trivial or homely it was. In the home of Rowan Herndon, where he had boarded when he first came to town, he had made himself loved by his care of the children. "He nearly always had one of them around with him," says Mr. Herndon. In the Rutledge tavern, where he afterwards lived, the landlord told with appreciation how, when his house was full, Lincoln gave up his bed, went to the store, and slept on the counter, his pillow a web of calico. If a traveler "stuck in the mud" in New Salem's one street, Lincoln was always the first to help pull out the wheel. The widows praised him because he "chopped their wood"; the overworked, because he was always ready to give them a lift. It was the spontaneous, unobtrusive helpfulness of the man's nature which endeared him to everybody and which inspired a general desire to do all possible in return. There are many tales told of homely service rendered him, even by the hard-working farmers' wives around New Salem. There was not one of them who did not gladly "put on a plate" for Abe Lincoln when he appeared, or would not darn or mend for him when she knew he needed it. Hannah Armstrong, the wife of the hero of Clary's Grove, made him one of her family.

"Abe would come out to our house," she said, "drink milk, eat mush, cornbread and butter, bring the children candy, and rock the cradle while I got him something to eat. . . . Has stayed at our house two or three weeks at a time." Lincoln's pay for his first piece of surveying came in the shape of two buckskins, and it was Hannah who "foxed" them on his trousers.

His relations were equally friendly in the better homes of the community; even at the minister's, the Rev. John Cameron's, he was perfectly at home, affectionately calling Mrs. Cameron "Aunt Polly." It was not only his kindly service which made Lincoln loved; it was his sympathetic comprehension of the lives and joys and sorrows and interests of the people. Whether it was Jack Armstrong and his wrestling, Hannah and her babies, Kelso and his fishing and poetry, the schoolmaster and his books—with one and all he was at home. He possessed in an extraordinary degree the power of entering into the interests of others, a power found only in reflective, unselfish natures endowed with a humorous sense of human foibles, coupled with great tenderness of heart.

CHAPTER VIII

ELECTIONEERING IN ILLINOIS IN 1834—LINCOLN READS LAW—FIRST TERM AS ASSEMBLYMAN—LINCOLN'S FIRST GREAT SORROW

Now that the store was closed and his surveying increased, Lincoln had an excellent opportunity to extend his acquaintance by traveling about the country. Everywhere he won friends. The surveyor naturally was respected for his calling's sake, but the new deputy surveyor was admired for his friendly ways, his willingness to lend a hand indoors as well as out, his learning, his ambition, his independence. Throughout the county he began to be regarded as a "right smart young man." Some of his associates appear even to have comprehended his peculiarly great character and to have foreseen a splendid future. "Often," says Daniel Green Burner, at one time clerk in Berry and Lincoln's grocery, "I have heard my brother-in-law, Dr. Duncan, say he would not be surprised if some day Abe Lincoln got to be governor of Illinois. Lincoln," Mr. Burner adds, "was thought to know a little more than anybody else among the young people. He was a good debater, and liked it. He read much, and seemed never to forget anything."

Lincoln was fully conscious of his popularity, and it seemed to him in 1834 that he could safely venture to try again for the legislature. Accordingly he announced himself as a candidate, spending much of the summer of 1834 in electioneering. It was a repetition of what he had done in 1832, though on the larger scale made possible by wider acquaintance. In company with the other candidates he rode up and down the county, making speeches in the public squares, in shady groves, now and then in a log schoolhouse. In his speeches he soon distinguished himself by the amazing candor with which he dealt with all questions, and by his curious blending of audacity and humility. Wherever he saw a crowd of men he joined them, and he never failed to adapt himself to their point of view in asking for votes. If the degree of physical strength was their test for a candidate, he was ready to lift a weight, or wrestle with the countryside champion; if the amount of grain a man could cut would recommend him, he seized the cradle and showed the swath he could cut. The campaign was well conducted, for in August he was elected one of the four assemblymen from Sangamon.

The best thing which Lincoln did in the canvass of 1834 was not winning votes; it was coming to a determination to read law, not for pleasure, but as a business. In his autobiographical notes he says: "During the canvass, in a private conversation, Major John T. Stuart [one of his fellow-candidates] encouraged Abraham to study law. After the election he borrowed books of Stuart, took them home with him and went at it in good earnest. He never studied with anybody." He seems to have thrown himself into the work with almost impatient ardor. As he tramped

ELECTIONEERING IN ILLINOIS

back and forth from Springfield, twenty miles away, to get his law books, he read sometimes forty pages or more on the way. Often he was seen wandering at random across the fields, repeating aloud the points in his last reading. The subject seemed never to be out of his mind. It was the great absorbing interest of his life. The rule he gave twenty years later to a young man who wanted to know how to become a lawyer, was the one he practiced:

"Get books and read and study them carefully. Begin with Blackstone's 'Commentaries,' and after reading carefully through, say, twice, take Chitty's 'Pleadings,' Greenleaf's 'Evidence,' and Story's 'Equity,' in succession. Work, work, work is the main thing."

Having secured a book of legal forms, he was soon able to write deeds, contracts, and all sorts of legal instruments, and he was frequently called upon by his neighbors to perform services of this kind. "In 1834," says Daniel Green Burner, "my father, Isaac Burner, sold out to Henry Onstott, and he wanted a deed written. I knew how handy Lincoln was that way and suggested that we get him. We found him sitting on a stump. 'All right,' said he, when informed what we wanted. 'If you will bring me a pen and ink and a piece of paper I will write it here.' I brought him these articles, and, picking up a shingle and putting it on his knee for a desk, he wrote out the deed."

As there was no practising lawyer nearer than Springfield, Lincoln was often employed to act the part of advocate before the village squire, at that time

Bowling Green. He realized that this experience was valuable, and never, so far as known, demanded or accepted a fee for his services in these petty cases.

Justice was sometimes administered in a summary way in Squire Green's court. Precedents and the venerable rules of law had little weight. The "Squire" took judicial notice of a great many facts, often going so far as to fill, simultaneously, the two functions of witness and court. But his decisions were generally just.

James McGrady Rutledge tells a story in which several of Lincoln's old friends figure and which illustrates the legal practices of New Salem. "Jack Kelso," says Mr. Rutledge, "owned, or claimed to own, a white hog. It was also claimed by John Ferguson. The hog had wandered around Bowling Green's place until he felt somewhat acquainted with it. Ferguson sued Kelso, and the case was tried before 'Squire' Green. The plaintiff produced two witnesses who testified positively that the hog belonged to him. Kelso had nothing to offer, save his own unsupported claim.

"'Are there any more witnesses?' inquired the court.
"He was informed that there were no more.
"'Well,' said 'Squire' Green, 'the two witnesses we have heard have sworn to a —— lie. I know this shoat, and I know it belongs to Jack Kelso. I therefore decide this case in his favor.'"

An extract from the record of the County Commissioners' Court illustrates the nature of the cases that came before the justice of the peace in Lincoln's

BOWLING GREEN'S HOUSE.

Bowling Green's log cabin, half a mile north of New Salem, just under the bluff. It long since ceased to be a dwelling-house, and is now a tumble-down old stable. Here Lincoln was a frequent boarder, especially during the period of his closest application to the study of the law. Stretched out on the cellar door of his cabin, reading a book, he met for the first time "Dick" Yates, then a college student at Jacksonville, and destined to become the great "War Governor" of the State. Yates had come home with William G. Greene to spend his vacation, and Greene took him around to Bowling Green's house to introduce him to "his friend Abe Lincoln." Unhappily there is nowhere in existence a picture of the original occupant of this humble cabin. Bowling Green was one of the leading citizens of the county. He was County Commissioner from 1826 to 1828; he was for many years a justice of the peace; he was a prominent member of the Masonic fraternity, and a very active and uncompromising Whig. The friendship between him and Lincoln, beginning at a very early day, continued until his death in 1842.

J. McCan Davis.

day. It also shows the price put upon the privilege of working on Sunday, in 1832:

"JANUARY 29, 1832.—Alexander Gibson found guilty of Sabbath-breaking and fined 12½ cents. Fine paid into court.
"(Signed) EDWARD ROBINSON, J. P."

The session of the Ninth Assembly began December 1, 1834, and Lincoln went to the capital, then Vandalia, seventy-five miles southeast of New Salem, on the Kaskaskia River, in time for the opening. Vandalia was a town which had been called into existence in 1820 especially to give the State government an abiding place. Its very name had been chosen, it is said, because it "sounded well" for a State capital. As the tradition goes, while the commissioners were debating what they should call the town they were making, a wag suggested that it be named Vandalia, in honor of the Vandals, a tribe of Indians which, he said, had once lived on the borders of the Kaskaskia; this, he argued, would conserve a local tradition while giving a euphonious title. The commissioners, pleased with so good a suggestion, adopted the name. When Lincoln first went to Vandalia it was a town of about eight hundred inhabitants; its noteworthy features, according to Peck's "Gazetteer" of Illinois for 1834, being a brick court-house, a two-story brick edifice "used by State officers," "a neat frame house of worship for the Presbyterian Society, with a cupola and bell," "a frame meeting-house for the Methodist Society," three taverns, several stores, five lawyers, four physicians, a land office, and two newspapers.

It was a much larger town than Lincoln had ever lived in before, though he was familiar with Springfield, then twice as large as Vandalia, and he had seen the cities of the Mississippi.

The Assembly which he entered was composed of eighty-one members—twenty-six senators and fifty-five representatives. As a rule, these men were of Kentucky, Tennessee, or Virginia origin, with here and there a Frenchman. There were but few eastern men, for there was still a strong prejudice in the state against Yankees. The close bargains and superior airs of the emigrants from New England contrasted so unpleasantly with the open-handed hospitality and the easy ways of the Southerners and French, that a pioneer's prospects were blasted at the start if he acted like a Yankee. A history of Illinois in 1837, published evidently to "boom" the state, cautioned the emigrant that if he began his life in Illinois by "affecting superior intelligence and virtue, and catechizing the people for their habits of plainness and simplicity and their apparent want of those things which he imagines indispensable to comfort," he must expect to be forever marked as "a Yankee," and to have his prospects correspondingly defeated. A "hard-shell" Baptist preacher of about this date showed the feeling of the people when he said, in preaching of the richness of the grace of the Lord: "It tuks in the isles of the sea and the uttermust part of the yeth. It embraces the Esquimaux and the Hottentots, and some, my dear brethering, go so far as to suppose that it tuks in the poor benighted Yankees, but *I don't go that fur."* When it came to an election of legislators, many of the people "didn't go that fur" either.

There was a sprinkling of jean suits in the Assembly, and there were occasional coonskin caps and buckskin trousers. Nevertheless, more than one member showed a studied garb and a courtly manner. Some of the best blood of the South went into the making of Illinois, and it showed itself from the first in the Assembly. The surroundings of the legislators were quite as simple as the attire of the plainest of them. The court-house, in good old Colonial style, with square pillars and belfry, was finished with wooden desks and benches. The state furnished her law-makers few perquisites beyond their three dollars a day. A cork inkstand, a certain number of quills, and a limited amount of stationery were all the extras an Illinois legislator in 1834 got from his position. Scarcely more could be expected from a state whose revenues from December 1, 1834, to December 1, 1836, were only about one hundred and twenty-five thousand dollars, with expenditures during the same period amounting to less than one hundred and sixty-five thousand dollars.

Lincoln thought little of these things, no doubt. To him the absorbing interest was the men he met. To get acquainted with them, measure them, compare himself with them, and discover wherein they were his superiors and what he could do to make good his deficiency—this was his chief occupation. The men he met were good subjects for such study. Among them were William L. D. Ewing, Jesse K. Dubois, Stephen T. Logan, Theodore Ford, and Governor Duncan—men destined to play large parts in the history of the state. One whom he met that winter in Vandalia was destined to play a great part in the history of the nation—the Democratic candidate for the office of State Attorney for the first judicial district of Illinois; a man four years younger than Lincoln—he was only twenty-one at the time; a newcomer, too, in the state, having arrived about a year before, under no very promising auspices either, for he had only thirty-seven cents in his pockets, and no position in view; but a man of mettle, it was easy to see, for already he had risen so high in the district where he had settled that he dared contest the office of State Attorney with John J. Hardin, one of the most successful lawyers of the state. This young man was Stephen A. Douglas. He had come to Vandalia from Morgan County to conduct his campaign, and Lincoln met him first in the halls of the old court-house, where he and his friends carried on with success their contest against Hardin.

The ninth Assembly gathered in a more hopeful and ambitious mood than any of its predecessors. Illinois was feeling well. The state was free from debt. The Black Hawk War had brought a large amount of money into circulation. In fact, the greater portion of the eight to ten million dollars the war had cost had been circulated among the Illinois volunteers. Immigration, too, was increasing at a bewildering rate. In 1835 the census showed a population of 269,974. Between 1830 and 1835 two-fifths of this number had come in. In the northeast Chicago had begun to rise. "Even for a western town," its growth had been unusually rapid, declared Peck's "Gazetteer," of 1834; the harbor building there, the proposed Michigan and Illinois canal, the rise in town lots—all promised to the state a great metropolis. To meet the rising tide of prosperity, the legislators of 1834 felt that they must devise some worthy scheme, so they chartered a new state bank, with a capital of one million five hundred thousand dollars, and revived a bank broken twelve years before, granting it a charter of three hundred thousand dollars. There was no surplus money in the state to supply the capital; there were no trained bankers to guide the concern; there was no clear notion of how it was all to be done; but a banking capital of one million eight hundred thousand dollars would be a good thing for the state, they were sure; and if the East could be made to believe in Illinois as much as her legislators believed in her, the stocks would go; and so the banks were chartered.

But even more important to the state than banks was a highway. For thirteen years plans for the Illinois and Michigan Canal had been constantly before the Assembly. Surveys had been ordered, estimates reported, the advantages extolled, but nothing had been done. Now, however, the Assembly, flushed by the first thrill of the coming boom, decided to authorize a loan of a half-million on the credit of the state. Lincoln favored both these measures. He did not, however, do anything especially noteworthy for either of the bills, nor was the record he made in other directions at all remarkable. He was placed on the committee of public accounts and expenditures, and attended meetings with fidelity. His first act as a member was to give notice that he would ask leave to introduce a bill limiting the jurisdiction of justices of the peace—a measure which he succeeded in carrying through. He followed this by a motion to change the rules so that it should not be in order to offer amendments to any bill after the third reading, which was not agreed to, though the same rule, in effect, was adopted some years later, and is to this day in force in both branches of the Illinois Assembly. He next made a motion to take from the table a report which had been submitted by his committee, which met a like fate. His first resolution, relating to a state revenue to be derived from the sales of the public lands, was denied a reference and laid upon the table. Neither as a speaker nor an organizer did he make any especial impression on the body.

In the spring of 1835 the young representative from Sangamon returned to New Salem to take up his duties as postmaster and deputy surveyor, and to resume his law studies. He exchanged his rather exalted position for the humbler one with a light heart. New Salem held all that was dearest in the world to him at that moment, and he went back to the poor little town with a hope, which he had once supposed honor forbade his acknowledging even to himself, glowing warmly in his heart. He loved a young girl of that town, and now for the first time, though he had known her since he first came to New Salem, was he free to tell his love.

One of the most prominent families of the settlement in 1831, when Lincoln first appeared there, was that of James Rutledge. The head of the house was one of the founders of New Salem, and at that time the keeper of the village tavern. He was a high-minded man, of a warm and generous nature, and had the universal respect of the community. Rutledge was a South Carolinian by birth, but had lived many years in Kentucky before coming to Illinois. He came of a distinguished family: one of his ancestors signed the Declaration of Independence; another was chief justice of the Supreme Court of the United States by appointment of Washington, and another was a conspicuous leader in the American Congress.

The third of the nine children in the Rutledge household was a daughter, Ann Mayes, born in Kentucky, January 7, 1813. When Lincoln first met her she was nineteen years old, and as fresh as a flower. Many of those who knew her at that time have left tributes to her beauty and gentleness, and even to-day there are those living who talk of her with moistened eyes and softened tones. "She was a beautiful girl," says her cousin, James McGrady Rutledge, "and as bright as she was beautiful. She was well educated for that early day, a good conversationalist, and always gentle and cheerful. A girl whose company people liked." So fair a maid was not, of course, without suitors. The most determined of those who sought her hand was one John McNeill, a young man who had arrived in New Salem from New York soon after the founding of the town. Nothing was known of his antecedents, and no questions were asked. He was understood to be merely one of the thousands who had come West in search of fortune. That he was intelligent, industrious, and frugal, with a good head for business, was at once apparent, for in four years from his first appearance in the settlement, besides earning a half-interest in a general store, McNeill had acquired a large farm a few miles north of New Salem. His neighbors believed him to be worth about twelve thousand dollars.

John McNeill was an unmarried man—at least so he represented himself to be—and very soon after becoming a resident of New Salem he formed the acquaintance of Ann Rutledge, then a girl of seventeen. It was a case of love at first sight, and the two soon became engaged, in spite of the rivalry of Samuel Hill, McNeill's partner. But Ann was as yet only a young girl, and it was thought very sensible in her and considerate in her lover that both acquiesced in the wishes of Ann's parents that, for some time at least, the marriage be postponed.

Such was the situation when Lincoln appeared in New Salem. He naturally soon became acquainted with the girl. She was a pupil in Mentor Graham's school, where he frequently visited, and rumor says that he first met her there. However that may be, it is certain that in the latter part of 1832 he went to board at the Rutledge tavern and there was thrown daily into her company.

During the next year, 1833, John McNeill, in spite of his fair prospects, became restless and discontented. He wanted to see his people, he said, and before the end of the year he decided to go East for a visit. To secure perfect freedom from his business while gone, he sold out his interest in his store. To Ann he said that he hoped to bring back his father and mother, and to place them on his farm. "This duty done," was his farewell word, "you and I will be married." In the spring of 1834 McNeill started East. The journey overland by foot and horse was in those days a trying one, and on the way McNeill fell ill with chills and fever. It was late in the summer before he reached his home and wrote back to Ann, explaining his silence. The long wait had been a severe strain on the girl, and Lincoln had watched her anxiety with softened heart. It was to him, the New Salem postmaster, that she came to inquire for letters. It was to him she entrusted those she sent. In a way the postmaster must have become the girl's confidant, and his tender heart must have been deeply touched. After the long silence was broken, and McNeill's first letter of explanation came, the cause of anxiety seemed removed, but, strangely enough, other letters followed only at long intervals, and finally they ceased altogether. Then it was that the young girl told her friends a secret which McNeill had confided to her before leaving New Salem.

He had told her what she had never even suspected before, that John McNeill was not his real name, but that it was John McNamar. Shortly before he came to New Salem, he explained, his father had suffered a disastrous failure in business. He was the oldest son, and in the hope of retrieving the lost fortune, he resolved to go West, expecting to return in a few years and share his riches with the rest of the family. Anticipating parental opposition, he ran away from home, and, being sure that he could never accumulate anything with so numerous a family to support, he endeavored to lose himself by a change of name. All this Ann had believed and not repeated; but now, worn out by waiting, she took the story to her friends.

With few exceptions they pronounced the story a fabrication and McNamar an impostor. His excuse seemed flimsy. Why had he worn this mask? At best, they declared, he was a mere adventurer; and was it not more probable that he was a fugitive from justice—a thief, a swindler, or a murderer? And who knew how many wives he might have? With all New Salem declaring John McNamar false, Ann Rutledge could hardly be blamed for imagining that he was dead or had forgotten her.

It was not until McNeill, or McNamar, had been gone many months, and gossip had become offensive, that Lincoln ventured to show his love for Ann, and then it was a long time before the girl would listen to his suit. Convinced at last, however, that her former lover had deserted her, she yielded to Lincoln's wishes and promised, in the spring of 1835, soon after Lincoln's return from Vandalia, to become his wife. But Lincoln had nothing on which to support a family—indeed, he found it no trifling task to support himself. As for Ann, she was anxious to go to school another year. It was decided that in the autumn she should go with her brother to Jacksonville and spend the winter there in the academy. Lincoln was to devote himself to his law studies, and the next spring, when she returned from school and he had been admitted to the bar, they were to be married.

A happy spring and summer followed. New

Salem took a cordial interest in the two lovers and presaged a happy life for them, and all would undoubtedly have gone well if the young girl had not fallen a victim to an epidemic which in the late summer ravaged the community—"Bilious fever" the settlers called it. Every household was afflicted, the Rutledges' among others. It is possible that in her illness Ann was haunted by the memory of her old lover, her fear that she had wronged him, that he might return and claim her. Such torturing conflicts of love, conscience, doubt, are common enough in fever. Such a conflict would account for the tradition long accepted that her illness came from her inability to forget McNamar, although she loved Lincoln. The truth seems to be that fever caused her distress of soul, not distress of soul the fever.

The girl's condition gradually became hopeless, and Lincoln, who had been shut from her, was sent for. The lovers passed an hour alone in an anguished parting, and soon after, on August 25, 1835, Ann died.

The death of Ann Rutledge plunged Lincoln into the deepest gloom. That abiding melancholy, that painful sense of the incompleteness of life which had been his mother's dowry asserted itself. It filled and darkened his mind and his imagination tortured him with its black pictures. One stormy night Lincoln was sitting beside William Greene, his head bowed on his hand, while tears trickled through his fingers; his friend begged him to control his sorrow, to try to forget. "I cannot," moaned Lincoln, "the thought of the snow and rain on her grave fills me with indescribable grief."

For days following Ann's death he was seen walking alone by the river and through the woods, muttering strange things to himself. He seemed to his friends to be in the shadow of madness. They kept a close watch over him, and at last Bowling Green, one of the most devoted friends Lincoln then had, took him home to his little log cabin, half a mile north of New Salem, under the brow of a big bluff. Here, under the loving care of Green, and his good wife Nancy, Lincoln remained until, body and soul rested, he was once more master of himself.

But though he had regained self-control, his grief was deep and bitter. Ann Rutledge was buried in Concord cemetery, a country burying-ground seven miles northwest of New Salem. To this lonely spot Lincoln frequently journeyed to weep over her grave. "My heart is buried there," he said to one of his friends.

When McNamar returned (for McNamar's story was true, and two months after Ann Rutledge died he drove into New Salem with his widowed mother and his brothers and sisters in the "prairie schooner" beside him) and learned of Ann's death, he "saw Lincoln at the post-office," as he afterward said, and "he seemed desolate and sorely distressed." On himself apparently, her death produced no deep impression. Within a year he married another woman, and his conduct toward Ann Rutledge is to this day a mystery.

In later life, when Lincoln's sorrow had become a memory, he told a friend who questioned him: "I really and truly loved the girl and think often of her

GRAVE OF ANN RUTLEDGE IN OAKLAND CEMETERY, PETERSBURG, MENARD CO., ILL.

Ann was first buried in Concord graveyard, several miles from New Salem. In 1890 her remains were removed to Oakland Cemetery and the small stone now at the foot of the grave marked the spot.
The inscription on the bronze tablet of the present monument is by Edgar Lee Masters.

now." There was a pause, and then the President added:

"And I have loved the name of Rutledge to this day."

When the death of Ann Rutledge came upon Lincoln, for a time threatening to destroy his ambition and blast his life, he was in a most encouraging position. Master of a profession in which he had an abundance of work and earned fair fees, hopeful of being admitted in a few months to the bar, a member of the State Assembly with every reason to believe that, if he desired it, his constituency would return him—few men are as far advanced at twenty-six as was Abraham Lincoln.

Intellectually he was far better equipped than he believed himself to be, better than he has ordinarily been credited with being. True, he had had no conventional college training, but he had by his own efforts attained the chief result of all preparatory study, the ability to take hold of a subject and assimilate it —the fact that in six weeks he had acquired enough of the science of surveying to enable him to serve as deputy surveyor shows how well-trained his mind was. The power to grasp a large subject quickly and fully is never an accident. The nights Lincoln spent in Gentryville lying on the floor in front of the fire figuring on the fire-shovel, the hours he passed in poring over the Statutes of Indiana, the days he wrestled with Kirkham's Grammar, alone made the mastery of Flint and Gibson possible. His struggle with Flint and Gibson made easier the volumes he borrowed from Major Stuart's law library.

Lincoln had a mental trait which explains his rapid growth in mastering subjects—seeing clearly was essential to him. He was unable to put a question aside until he understood it. It pursued him, irritated him, until solved. Even in his Gentryville days his comrades noted that he was constantly searching for reasons and that he "explained so clearly." This characteristic became stronger with years. He was unwilling to pronounce himself on any subject until he understood it, and he could not let it alone until he had reached a conclusion which satisfied him.

This seeing clearly became a splendid force in Lincoln, for when he once had reached a conclusion he had the honesty of soul to suit his actions to it. No consideration could induce him to abandon the line of conduct which his reason told him was logical. Joined to these strong mental and moral qualities was that power of immediate action which so often explains why one man succeeds in life while another of equal intelligence and uprightness fails. As soon as Lincoln saw a thing to do he did it. He wants to know; here is a book—it may be a biography, a volume of dry statutes, a collection of verse; no matter, he reads and ponders it until he has absorbed all it has for him. He is eager to see the world; a man offers him a position as a "hand" on a Mississippi flatboat; he takes it without a moment's hesitation over the toil and exposure it demands. John Calhoun is willing to make him a deputy surveyor; he knows nothing of the science; in six weeks he has learned enough to begin his labors. Sangamon County must have representatives, why not he? and his circular goes out. Ambition alone will not explain this power of instantaneous action. It comes largely from that active imagination which, when a new relation or position opens, seizes on all its possibilities and from them creates a situation so real that one enters with confidence upon what seems to the unimaginative the rashest undertaking. Lincoln saw the possibilities in things and immediately appreciated them.

But the position he filled in Sangamon County in 1835 was not all due to these qualities; much was due to his personal charm. By all accounts he was big, awkward, ill-clad, shy—yet his sterling honor, his unselfish nature, his heart of the true gentleman, inspired respect and confidence. Men might laugh at his first appearance, but they were not long in recognizing the real superiority of his nature.

Such was Abraham Lincoln at twenty-six, when the tragic death of Ann Rutledge made all that he had attained, all that he had planned, seem fruitless and empty. He was too sincere and just, too brave a man, to allow a great sorrow permanently to interfere with his activities. He rallied his forces and returned to his law, his surveying, his politics. He brought to his work a new power, that insight and patience which only a great sorrow can give.

CHAPTER IX

LINCOLN IS RE-ELECTED TO THE ILLINOIS ASSEMBLY—
HIS FIRST PUBLISHED ADDRESS—PROTESTS AGAINST
PRO-SLAVERY RESOLUTIONS OF THE ASSEMBLY

THE Ninth General Assembly of Illinois held its opening session in the winter of 1834-35. It was Lincoln's first experience as a legislator and it was rather a tame one, but in December, 1835, the members were called to an extra session which proved to be in every way more exciting and more eventful than its predecessors. The chief reason for its being called was in itself calculated to exhilarate the hopeful young law-givers. A census had been taken since their last session and so large an increase in population had been reported that it was considered necessary to summon the assembly to reapportion the legislative districts. When the reapportionment was made it was found that the General Assembly was increased by fifty members, the number of senators being raised from twenty-six to forty, of representatives from fifty-five to ninety-one. A growth of fifty members in four years excited the imagination of the state. The dignity and importance of Illinois suddenly assumed new importance. It was imagined that the story of New York's growth in wealth and influence was to be repeated in this new country and every ambitious man in the assembly determined to lead in the rise of the state.

The work on internal improvements begun in the previous session took a new form. The governor, in calling the members together, had said: "While I would urge the most liberal support of all such measures as tending with perfect certainty to increase the wealth and prosperity of the state, I would at the same time most respectfully suggest the propriety of intrusting the construction of all such works, where it can be done consistently with the general interest, to individual enterprise." The legislators acquiesced and in this session began to grant a series of private charters for internal improvements which, had they been carried out, would have given the state means of communication in 1840 almost if not quite equal to those of to-day. The map on page 157 shows the incorporations of railroad and canal companies made in the extra session of the Ninth Assembly, 1835-36, and in the regular session of the Tenth, 1836-37; sixteen of the railroads were chartered in the former session.

Lincoln and his colleagues did not devote their attention entirely to chartering railroads. Ten schools were chartered in this same session, some of which exist to-day. In the next session twelve academies and eighteen colleges received charters.

The absorbing topic of the winter, however, and the one in which Lincoln was chiefly concerned was the threatened naturalization of the convention system in Illinois. Up to this time candidates for office in the United States had generally nominated themselves as we have seen Lincoln doing. The only formality they imposed upon themselves was to consult a little unauthorized caucus of personal friends. Unless they were exceptionally cautious persons the disapproval of this caucus did not stand in their way. So long as party lines were indistinct and the personal qualities of a candidate were considered rather than his platform this method of nomination was possible, but with party organization it began to change. In the case of presidential candidates the convention with its delegates and platform had just appeared, the first full-fledged one being held but three years before, in 1832. Along with the presidential convention came the "machine," an organization of all those who belonged to a party, intended to secure unity of effort. By means of primaries and conventions one candidate was put forward by a party instead of a dozen being allowed to offer themselves. The strength which the convention gave the Democratic Party, which first adopted and developed it, was enormous. The Whigs opposed the new institution; they declared it "was intended to abridge the liberties of the people by depriving individuals, on their own mere motion, of the privilege of becoming candidates and depriving each man of the right to vote for a candidate of his own selection and choice."

The efficacy of the new method was so apparent, however, that, let the Whigs preach as they would, it was rapidly adopted. In 1835 the whole machinery was well developed in New England and New York and had appeared in the West. In the north of Illinois the Democrats had begun to organize under the leadership of two men of eastern origin and training, Ebenezer Peck of Chicago, and Stephen A. Douglas

FIRST PUBLISHED ADDRESS 147

of Jacksonville, and at this session of the Illinois legislature the convention system became a subject of discussion.

The Whigs, Lincoln among them, violently opposed the new scheme. It was a Yankee contrivance, they said, favored only by New Englanders like Douglas, or worse still by monarchists like Peck. They recalled with pious indignation that Peck was a Canadian, brought up under an aristocratic form of government, that he had even deserted the Liberal Party to go over to the ultra-monarchists. They declared it a remarkable fact that no man born and raised west of the mountains or south of the Potomac had yet returned to vindicate "the wholesale system of convention." In spite of Whig warnings, however, the convention system was approved by a vote of twenty-six to twenty-five.

The Ninth Assembly expired at the close of this extra session and in June Lincoln announced himself as a candidate for the Tenth Assembly. A few days later the "Sangamon Journal" published his simple platform:

"New Salem, June 13, 1836.
"To the Editor of the 'Journal':

"In your paper of last Saturday I see a communication, over the signature of 'Many Voters,' in which the candidates who are announced in the 'Journal' are called upon to 'show their hands.' Agreed. Here's mine.

"I go for all sharing the privileges of the government who assist in bearing its burdens. Consequently, I go for admitting all whites to the right of suffrage who pay taxes or bear arms (by no means excluding females).

"If elected, I shall consider the whole people of Sangamon

my constituents, as well those that oppose as those that support me.

"While acting as their representative, I shall be governed by their will on all subjects upon which I have the means of knowing what their will is; and upon all others I shall do what my own judgment teaches me will best advance their interests. Whether elected or not, I go for distributing the proceeds of the sales of the public lands to the several States, to enable our State, in common with others, to dig canals and construct railroads without borrowing money and paying the interest on it.

"If alive on the first Monday in November, I shall vote for Hugh L. White for President.

"Very respectfully,

"A. LINCOLN."

The campaign which Lincoln began with this letter was in every way more exciting for him than those of 1832 and 1834. In the reapportionment of the legislative districts which had taken place the winter before Sangamon County's delegation had been enlarged to seven representatives and two senators. This gave new opportunity to political ambition, and doubled the enthusiasm of political meetings.

But the increase of the representation was not all that made the campaign exciting. Party lines had never before been so clearly drawn in Sangamon County, nor personal abuse quite so frank. One of Lincoln's first acts was to answer a personal attack. In his absence from New Salem a rival candidate passing through the place stated that he was in possession of facts which, if known to the public, would entirely destroy Lincoln's prospects at the coming election; but he declared that he thought so much of

JOSHUA F. SPEED AND WIFE.

Lincoln that he would not tell what he knew. Lincoln met this mysterious insinuation with shrewd candor. "No one has needed favors more than I," he wrote his rival, "and generally few have been less unwilling to accept them; but in this case favor to me would be injustice to the public, and therefore I must beg your pardon for declining it. That I once had the confidence of the people of Sangamon County is sufficiently evident; and if I have done anything, either by design or misadventure, which if known would subject me to a forfeiture of that confidence, he that knows of that thing and conceals it is a traitor to his country's interest.

"I find myself wholly unable to form any conjecture of what fact or facts, real or supposed, you spoke; but my opinion of your veracity will not permit me for a moment to doubt that you at least believed what you said. I am flattered with the personal regard you manifested for me; but I do hope that on mature reflection you will view the public interest as a paramount consideration and therefore let the worst come."

Usually during the campaign Lincoln was obliged to meet personal attacks, not by letter, but on the platform. Joshua Speed, who later became the most intimate friend that Lincoln probably ever had, tells of one occasion when he was obliged to act on the spur of the moment. A great mass-meeting was in progress at Springfield, and Lincoln had made a speech which had produced a deep impression.

"I was then fresh from Kentucky," says Mr. Speed, "and had heard many of her great orators. It seemed to me then, as it seems to me now, that I never heard a more effective speaker. He carried the crowd with him and swayed them as he pleased. So deep an impression did he make that George Forquer, a man of much celebrity as a sarcastic speaker and with a great reputation throughout the state as an orator, rose and asked the people to hear *him*. He began his speech by saying that this young man would have to be taken down, and he was sorry that the task devolved upon him. He made what was called one of his 'slasher-gaff' speeches, dealing much in ridicule and sarcasm. Lincoln stood near him, with his arms folded, never interrupting him. When Forquer was done, Lincoln walked to the stand and replied so fully and completely that his friends bore him from the court-house on their shoulders.

"So deep an impression did this first speech make upon me that I remember its conclusion now, after a lapse of thirty-eight years.

" 'The gentleman commenced his speech,' he said, 'by saying that this young man would have to be taken down, and he was sorry the task devolved upon him. I am not so young in years as I am in the tricks and trade of a politician; but live long or die young, I would rather die now than, like the gentleman, change my politics and, simultaneous with the change, receive an office worth three thousand dollars a year, and then have to erect a lightning-rod over my house to protect a guilty conscience from an offended God.'

"To understand the point of this it must be explained that Forquer had been a Whig, but had changed his politics and had been appointed Register of the Land Office; and over his house was the only lightning-rod in the town or county. Lincoln had seen the lightning-rod for the first time on the day before."

This speech has never been forgotten in Springfield, and on my visits there I have repeatedly had the site of the house on which this particular lightning-rod was placed pointed out, and one or another of the many versions which the story has taken related to me.

It was the practice at that date in Illinois for two rival candidates to travel the district together. The custom led to much good-natured raillery between them; and in such contests Lincoln was rarely, if ever, worsted. He could even turn the generosity of a rival to account by his whimsical treatment. On one occasion, says Mr. Weir, a former resident of Sangamon County, he had driven out from Springfield in company with a political opponent to engage in joint debate. The carriage, it seems, belonged to his opponent. In addressing the gathering of farmers that met them, Lincoln was lavish in praise of the generosity of his friend. "I am too poor to own a carriage," he said, "but my friend has generously invited me to ride with him. I want you to vote for me if you will; but if not then vote for my opponent, for he is a fine man." His extravagant and persistent praise of his opponent appealed to the sense of humor in his rural audience, to whom his inability to own a carriage was by no means a disqualification.

The election came off in August and resulted in the choice of a delegation from Sangamon County famous in the annals of Illinois. The nine successful candidates were Abraham Lincoln, John Dawson, Daniel Stone, Ninian W. Edwards, William F. Elkins, R. L. Wilson, Andrew McCormick, Job Fletcher, and Arthur Herndon. Each one of these men was over six feet in height, their combined stature being, it is said, fifty-five feet. "The Long Nine" was the name Sangamon County gave them.

As soon as the election was over Lincoln occupied himself in settling another matter, of much greater moment. He went to Springfield to seek admission to the bar. The "roll of attorneys and counsellors at law," on file in the office of the clerk of the Supreme Court of Springfield, Illinois, shows that his license was dated September 9, 1836, and that the date of the enrollment of his name upon the official list was March 1, 1837. The first case in which he was concerned, as far as we know, was that of Hawthorne against Woolridge. He made his first appearance in court in October, 1836.

Although he had given much time during this year to politics and the law, he had by no means abandoned surveying. Indeed he never had more calls. The grandiose scheme of internal improvements initiated the winter before had stimulated speculation and Lincoln frequently was obliged to be away for three and four weeks at a time, laying out new towns or locating new roads.

Every such trip added to his political capital. Such was his reputation throughout the country that when he got a job, says the Hon. J. M. Ruggles, a friend and political supporter, there was a picnic and jolly time in the neighborhood. Men and boys gathered from far and near, ready to carry chain, drive stakes, and blaze trees, if they could only hear Lincoln's odd stories and jokes. The fun was interspersed with foot races and wrestling matches. To this day the old settlers in many a place of central Illinois repeat the incidents of Lincoln's sojourns in their neighborhood while surveying their town.

Filed for Record June 21st 1836 at 3 o'clock P.M.
Fee $2.50

Map of Albany.

Explanation
Head of Map Due North
Width of Street 66 feet
Do. Alleys 16 do
Front of Lots 66 do
Depth do 124 do
Stone at the S. W.
corner of the Public
square.

Blocks Nos. 1, 2, 3
4, 5. and the Public
Square are situated
on the West half
of the S. E. quarter
of Section 6. and
are the property of
John Wright. Blocks
6 and 7 are situated
on the West half of
the N. E. quarter of
Section 7. and
are the property of
John Donavon. Both tracts are of Township 19 North of Range 3 West.

I hereby certify that the above is a correct Map of the town of Albany, as surveyed by me
June 16th 1836.

A. Lincoln
d for T. M. Neale S.S.C.

FACSIMILE OF A MAP OF ALBANY, ILL., MADE BY LINCOLN.

In December Lincoln put away his surveying instruments to go to Vandalia for the opening session of the Tenth Assembly. Larger by fifty members than its predecessor, this body was as much superior in intellect as in numbers. It included among its members a future President of the United States, a future candidate for the same high office, six future United States Senators, eight future members of the national House of Representatives, a future Secretary of the Interior, and three future Judges of the State Supreme Court. Here sat side by side Abraham Lincoln and Stephen A. Douglas; Edward Dickinson Baker, who represented at different times the States of Illinois and Oregon in the national councils; O. H. Browning, a prospective senator and future cabinet officer, and William L. D. Ewing, who had just served in the senate; John Logan, father of the late General John A. Logan; Robert M. Cullom, father of Senator Shelby M. Cullom; John A. McClernand, afterwards member of Congress for many years, and a distinguished general in the late Civil War, and many others of national repute.

The members came to Vandalia full of hope and exultation. In their judgment it needed only a few months of legislation to put their state by the side of New York; and from the opening of the session they were overflowing with excitement and schemes. In the general ebullition of spirits which characterized the Assembly, Lincoln had little share. Only a week after the opening of the session he wrote to a friend, Mary Owens, at New Salem, that he had been ill, though he believed himself to be about well then; and he added: "But that, with other things I cannot account for, have conspired, and have gotten my spirits so low that I feel I would rather be any place in the world than here. I really cannot endure the thought of staying here ten weeks."

Though depressed, he was far from being inactive. The Sangamon delegation, in fact, had its hands full, and to no one of the nine had more been entrusted than to Lincoln. In common with almost every delegation, they had been instructed by their constituents to adopt a scheme of internal improvements complete enough to give every building town in Illinois easy communication with the world. This for the state in general; for Sangamon County in particular, they had been directed to secure the capital. The change in the state's centre of population made it advisable to move the seat of government northward from Vandalia, and Springfield was anxious to secure it. To Lincoln was entrusted the work of putting through the bill to remove the capital. In the same letter quoted from above he tells Miss Owens: "Our chance to take the seat of government to Springfield is better than I expected." Regarding the internal improvements scheme he feels less confident: "Some of the legislature are for it, and some against; which has the majority, I cannot tell."

It was not long, however, before all uncertainty about internal improvements was over. The people were determined to have them, and the assembly responded to their demands by passing an act which provided, at state expense, for railroads, canals, or river improvements in almost every county in Illinois. No finer bit of imaginative work was ever done, in fact, by a legislative body, than the map of internal improvements laid out by the Tenth Assembly.

With splendid disdain of town settlements and resources they ran the railroads into the counties they thought ought to be opened up, and if there was no terminus they laid out one. They improved the rivers and they dug canals, they built bridges and drained the swamps, they planned to make the waste places blossom and to people the forests with men. This project was to benefit every hamlet of the state, said its defenders, and to compensate the counties which were not to have railroads or canals they voted them a sum of money for roads and bridges.

There was no time to estimate exactly the cost of these fine plans. Nor did they feel any need of estimates; that was a mere matter of detail. They would vote a fund, and when that was exhausted they would vote more; and so they appropriated sum after sum: one hundred thousand dollars to improve the Rock River; one million eight hundred thousand dollars to build a road from Quincy to Danville; four million dollars to complete the Illinois and Michigan Canal; two hundred and fifty thousand for the Western Mail Route—in all, some twelve million dollars. To carry out the elaborate scheme, they provided a commission, one of the first duties of which was to sell the bonds of the state to raise the money for the enterprise. The majority of the Assembly seem not to have entertained for a moment an idea that there would be any difficulty in selling at a premium the bonds of Illinois. "On the contrary," says General Linder, in his

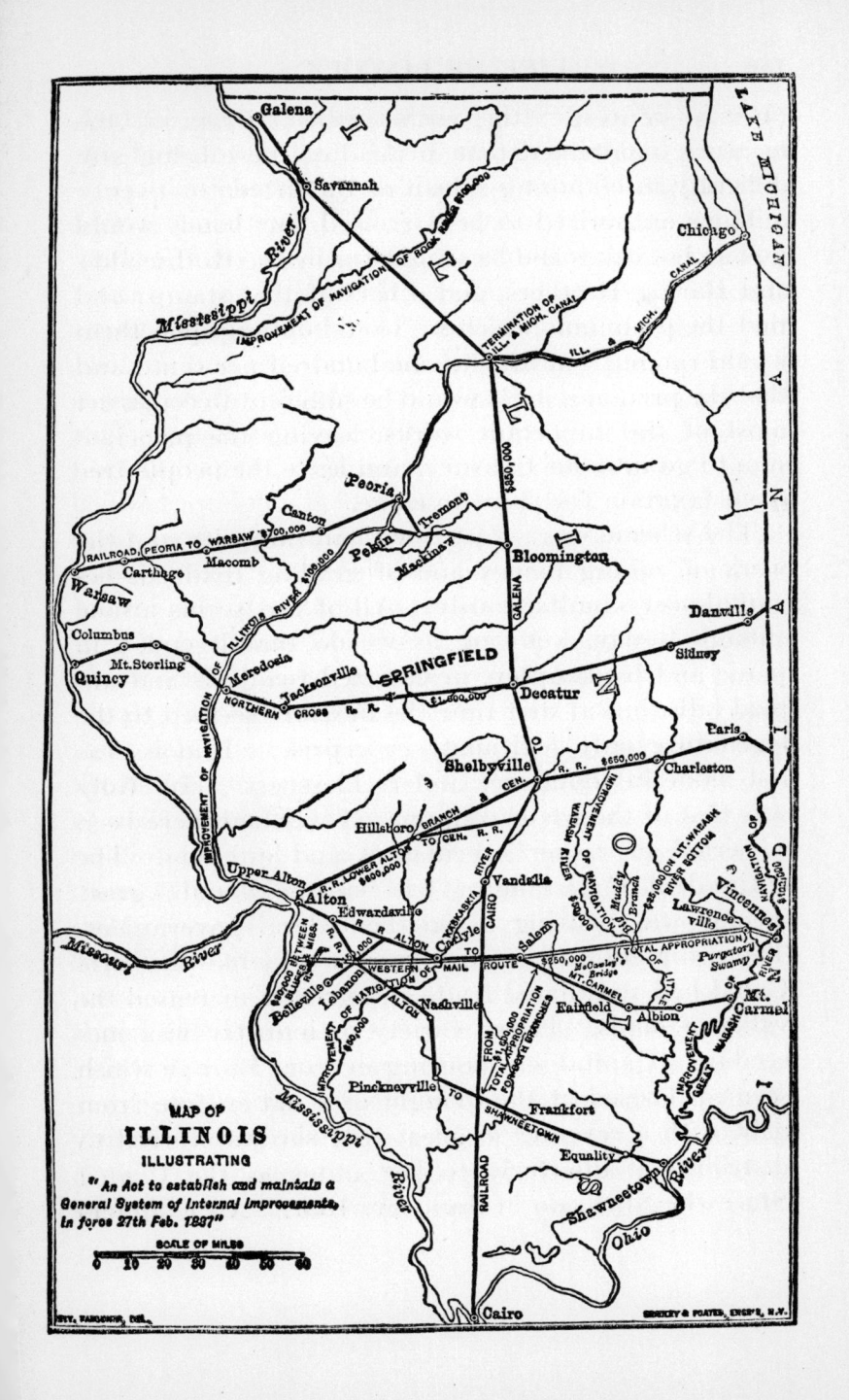

MAP OF
ILLINOIS
ILLUSTRATING
*"An Act to establish and maintain a
General System of Internal Improvements,
in force 27th Feb. 1837"*

SCALE OF MILES

"Reminiscences," "the enthusiastic friends of the measure maintained that, instead of there being any difficulty in obtaining a loan of the fifteen or twenty millions authorized to be borrowed, our bonds would go like hot cakes and be sought for by the Rothschilds, and Baring Brothers, and others of that stamp; and that the premiums which we would obtain upon them would range from fifty to one hundred per cent., and that the premium itself would be sufficient to construct most of the important works, leaving the principal sum to go into our treasury, and leave the people free from taxation for years to come."

The scheme was adopted without difficulty and the work of raising money and of grading roadbeds began almost simultaneously. All of this seems insane enough to-day, knowing as we do that it ended in panic and bankruptcy, in deserted roadbeds and unpaid bills, but at that time the measure seemed to the legislature only legitimate enterprise. Illinois was not alone in confidence and recklessness. Her folly was that of the whole country. Never had there been a period of rasher speculation and inflation. The entire debt of the country had been paid, and a great income was pouring in on the federal government. The completion of certain great works like the Erie Canal had stimulated trade and greatly increased the value of lands. Every variety of industry was succeeding. Capital was pouring in from Europe which seemed dazzled at the thought of a nation free from debt with a revenue so great that she was forced to distribute it quarterly to her states as the United States began to do in January, 1837. An exagger-

FIRST PUBLISHED ADDRESS 159

ated confidence in regard to the future of the country possessed both foreign and domestic capitalist. Credit was practically unlimited, "Debt was the road to wealth" and men could realize millions on the wildest schemes. Little wonder that Lincoln and his associates, ignorant of the history of finance and governed as they were by popular opinion, fell into the delusion of the day and sought to found a state on credit.

Although Lincoln favored and aided in every way the plan for internal improvements, his real work was in securing the removal of the capital to Springfield. The task was by no means an easy one to direct, for outside of the "Long Nine" there was, of course, nobody particularly interested in Springfield, and there were delegations from a dozen other counties hot to secure the capital for their own constituencies. It took patient and clever manipulation to put the bill through. Certain votes Lincoln, no doubt, gained for his cause by force of his personal qualities. Thus Jesse K. Dubois says that he and his colleagues voted for the bill because they liked Lincoln and wanted to oblige him; but probably the majority he won by skillful log-rolling. The few letters written by him at this time which have been preserved show this; for instance a letter to John Bennett in which he says:

"Mr. Edwards tells me you wish to know whether the act to which your town incorporation provision was attached passed into a law. It did. You can organize under the general incorporation law as soon as you choose.

"I also tacked a provision on to a fellow's bill, to authorize the relocation of the road from Salem down to your town, but I am not certain whether or not the bill passed. Neither do I suppose I can ascertain before the law will be published —if it is a law."

There is nothing in his correspondence, however, to show that he ever sacrificed his principles in these trades. Everything we know of his transactions are indeed to the contrary. General T. H. Henderson, of Illinois, says in his reminiscences of Lincoln:

"Before I had ever seen Abraham Lincoln I heard my father, who served with him in the legislature of 1838-39 and of 1840-41, relate an incident in Mr. Lincoln's life which illustrates his character for integrity and his firmness in maintaining what he regarded as right in his public acts, in a marked manner.

"I do not remember whether this incident occurred during the session of the legislature in 1836-37 or 1838-39. But I think it was in that of 1836-37, when it was said that there was a great deal of log-rolling going on among the members. But, however that may be, according to the story related by my father, an effort was made to unite the friends of capital removal with the friends of some measure which Mr. Lincoln, for some reason, did not approve. What that measure was to which he objected, I am not now able to recall. But those who desired the removal of the capital to Springfield were very anxious to effect the proposed combination, and a meeting was held to see if it could be accomplished. The meeting continued in session nearly all night, when it adjourned without accomplishing anything, Mr. Lincoln refusing to yield his objections and to support the obnoxious measure.

"Another meeting was called, and at this second meeting a number of citizens, not members of the legislature, from the central and northern parts of the state, among them my father, were present by invitation. The meeting was long protracted and earnest in its deliberations. Every argu-

FIRST PUBLISHED ADDRESS 161

ment that could be thought of was used to induce Mr. Lincoln to yield his objections and unite with his friends, and thus secure the removal of the capital to his own city; but without effect. Finally, after midnight, when everybody seemed exhausted with the discussion, and when the candles were burning low in the room, Mr. Lincoln rose amid the silence and solemnity which prevailed, and, my father said, made one of the most eloquent and powerful speeches to which he had ever listened. He concluded his remarks by saying, 'You may burn my body to ashes and scatter them to the winds of heaven; you may drag my soul down to the regions of darkness and despair to be tormented forever; but you will never get me to support a measure which I believe to be wrong, although by doing so I may accomplish that which I believe to be right.' And the meeting adjourned."

As was to be expected, the Democrats charged that the Whigs of Sangamon had won their victory by "bargain and corruption." These charges became so serious that, in an extra session called in the summer of 1837, a few months after the bill passed, Lincoln had a bitter fight over them with General L. D. Ewing, who wanted to keep the capital at Vandalia. "The arrogance of Springfield," said General Ewing, "its presumption in claiming the seat of government, is not to be endured; the law has been passed by chicanery and trickery; the Springfield delegation has sold out to the internal improvement men and has promised its support to every measure that would gain a vote to the law removing the seat of government."

Lincoln answered in a speech of such severity and keenness that the House believed he was "digging his own grave," for Ewing was a high-spirited man who would not hesitate to answer by a challenge. It was, in fact, only the interference of their friends which prevented a duel at this time between Ewing and Lincoln. This speech, to many of Lincoln's colleagues, was a revelation of his ability and character. "This was the first time," said General Linder, "that I began to conceive a very high opinion of the talents and personal courage of Abraham Lincoln."

A few months later the "Long Nine" were again attacked, Lincoln specially being abused. The assailant this time was a prominent Democrat, Mr. J. B. Thomas. When he had ended, Lincoln replied in a speech which was long known in local political circles as the "skinning of Thomas."

No one doubted after this that Lincoln could defend himself. He became doubly respected as an opponent, for his reputation for good-humored raillery had already been established in his campaigns. In a speech made in January he gave another evidence of his skill in the use of ridicule. A resolution had been offered by Mr. Linder to institute an inquiry into the management of the affairs of the state bank. Lincoln's remarks on the resolution form his first reported speech. He began his remarks by good-humored but nettling chaffing of his opponent.

"Mr. Chairman," he said. "Lest I should fall into the too common error of being mistaken in regard to which side I design to be upon, I shall make it my first care to remove all doubt on that point, by declaring that I am opposed to the resolution under consideration, *in toto*. Before I proceed to the body of the subject, I will further remark that it is not without a considerable degree of apprehension that I venture to cross the track of the gentleman from Coles

(Mr. Linder). Indeed, I do not believe I could muster a sufficiency of courage to come in contact with that gentleman, were it not for the fact that he, some days since, most graciously condescended to assure us that he would never be found wasting ammunition on *small game*. On the same fortunate occasion he further gave us to understand that he regarded *himself* as being decidedly the *superior* of our common friend from Randolph (Mr. Shields); and feeling, as I really do, that I, to say the most of myself, am nothing more than the peer of our friend from Randolph, I shall regard the gentleman from Coles as decidedly my superior also; and consequently, in the course of what I shall have to say, whenever I shall have occasion to allude to that gentleman I shall endeavor to adopt that kind of court language which I understand to be due to decided superiority. In one faculty, at least, there can be no dispute of the gentleman's superiority over me, and most other men; and that is, the faculty of entangling a subject so that neither himself or any other man can find head or tail to it."

Taking up the resolution on the bank, he declared its meaning:

"Some gentlemen have their stock in their hands, while others, who have more money than they know what to do with, want it; and this, and this alone, is the question to settle which we are called on to squander thousands of the people's money. What interest, let me ask, have the people in the settlement of this question? What difference is it to them whether the stock is owned by Judge Smith or Sam Wiggins? If any gentleman be entitled to stock in the bank, which he is kept out of possession of by others, let him assert his right in the Supreme Court, and let him or his antagonist, whichever may be found in the wrong, pay the costs of suit. It is an old maxim, and a very sound one, that he that dances should always pay the fiddler. Now, sir, in the present case, if any gentlemen whose money is a burden to them choose to lead off a dance, I am decidedly opposed to the people's money being used to pay the fiddler. No one can doubt that the examination proposed by this resolution must cost the State some ten or twelve thousand dollars; and all this to settle a question in which the people have no interest, and about which they care nothing. These capitalists generally act harmoniously and in concert to fleece the people; and now that they have got into a quarrel with themselves, we are called upon to appropriate the people's money to settle the quarrel."

The resolution had declared that the bank practised various methods which were "to the great injury of the people." Lincoln took the occasion to announce his ideas of the people and the politicians.

"If the bank really be a grievance, why is it that no one of the real people is found to ask redress of it? The truth is, no such oppression exists. If it did, our people would groan with memorials and petitions, and we would not be permitted to rest day or night till we had put it down. The people know their rights, and they are never slow to assert and maintain them when they are invaded. Let them call for an investigation, and I shall ever stand ready to respond to the call. But they have made no such call. I make the assertion boldly and without fear of contradiction that no man who does not hold an office, or does not aspire to one, has ever found any fault of the bank. It has doubled the prices of the products of their farms and filled their pockets with a sound circulating medium; and they are all well pleased with its operations. No, sir, it is the politician who is the first to sound the alarm (which, by the way, is a false one). It is he who, by these unholy means, is endeavoring to blow up a storm that he may ride upon and direct. It is he, and he alone, that here proposes to spend thousands of the people's public treasure for no other advantage to them than to make valueless in their pockets the reward of

FIRST PUBLISHED ADDRESS 165

their industry. Mr. Chairman, this work is exclusively the work of politicians—a set of men who have interests aside from the interests of the people, and who, to say the most of them, are, taken as a mass, at least one step removed from honest men. I say this with the greater freedom, because, being a politician myself, none can regard it as personal."

The speech was published in full in the "Sangamon Journal" for Jan. 28, 1837, and the editor commented:

"Mr. Lincoln's remarks on Mr. Linder's bank resolution in the paper are quite to the point. Our friend carries the true Kentucky rifle, and when he fires he seldom fails of sending the shot home."

One other act of his in this session cannot be ignored. It is a sinister note in the hopeful chorus of the Tenth Assembly. For months there had come from the Southern States violent protests against the growth of abolition agitation in the North. Garrison's paper, the "infernal Liberator," as it was called in the pro-slavery part of the country, had been gradually extending its circulation and its influence; and it already had imitators even on the banks of the Mississippi. The American Anti-slavery Society was now over three years old. A deep, unconquerable conviction of the iniquity of slavery was spreading through the North. The South felt it and protested, and the statesmen of the North joined them in their protest. Slavery could not be crushed, said the conservatives. It was sanctioned by the Constitution. The South must be supported in its claims, and agitation stopped. But the agitation went on, and riots, violence, and hatred pursued the agitators. In Illinois, in this very year, 1837, we have a printing-office raided and an anti-slavery editor, Elijah Lovejoy, killed by the citizens of Alton, who were determined that it should not be said among them that slavery was an iniquity.

To silence the storm, mass-meetings of citizens, the United States Congress, the state legislatures, took up the question and again and again voted resolutions assuring the South that the Abolitionists were not supported; that the country recognized their right to their "peculiar institution," and that in no case should they be interfered with. At Springfield, this same year (1837) the citizens convened and passed a resolution declaring that "the efforts of Abolitionists in this community are neither necessary nor useful." When the riot occurred in Alton, the Springfield papers uttered no word of condemnation, giving the affair only a laconic mention.

The Illinois Assembly joined in the general disapproval, and on March 3d passed the following resolutions:

"Resolved by the General Assembly of the State of Illinois:

"That we highly disapprove of the formation of Abolition societies, and of the doctrines promulgated by them.

"That the right of property in slaves is sacred to the slave-holding States by the Federal Constitution, and that they cannot be deprived of that right without their consent.

"That the General Government cannot abolish slavery in the District of Columbia against the consent of the citizens of said District, without a manifest breach of good faith.

"That the governor be requested to transmit to the States of Virginia, Alabama, Mississippi, New York and Connecticut a copy of the foregoing report and resolutions."

Lincoln refused to vote for these resolutions. In his judgment no expression on the slavery question should go unaccompanied by the statement that it was an evil, and he had the boldness to protest immediately against the action of the House. He found only one man in the Assembly willing to join him in his protest. These two names are joined to the document they presented:

"Resolutions upon the subject of domestic slavery having passed both branches of the General Assembly at its present session, the undersigned hereby protest against the passage of the same.

"They believe that the institution of slavery is founded on both injustice and bad policy, but that the promulgation of abolition doctrines tends rather to increase than abate its evils.

"They believe that the Congress of the United States has no power under the Constitution to interfere with the institution of slavery in the different States.

"They believe that the Congress of the United States has the power under the Constitution, to abolish slavery in the District of Columbia, but that the power ought not to be exercised, unless at the request of the people of the District.

"The difference between these opinions and those contained in the resolutions is their reason for entering this protest.

"DAN STONE,
"A. LINCOLN,
"Representatives from the County of Sangamon."

The Tenth Assembly gave Lincoln an opportunity to show his ability as a political manœuvrer, his power as a speaker and his courage in opposing what seemed to him wrong. There had never been a session of the assembly when the members had the chance to make so wide an impression. The character of the legislation on foot had called to Vandalia numbers of persons of influence from almost every part of the state. They were invariably there to secure something for their town or county, and naturally made a point of learning all they could of the members and of getting as well acquainted with them as circumstances allowed. Game suppers seem to have been the means usually employed by visitors for bringing people together, and Lincoln became a favorite guest not only because he was necessary to the success of almost any measure, but because he was so jovial a companion. It was then that he laid the foundation of his extensive acquaintance throughout the state which in after years stood him in excellent stead.

The lobbyists were not the only ones in Vandalia who gave suppers, however. Not a bill was passed nor an election decided that a banquet did not follow. Mr. John Bryant, the brother of William Cullen Bryant, was in Vandalia that winter in the interest of his county, and he attended one of these banquets, given by the successful candidate for the United States Senate. Lincoln was present, of course, and so were all the prominent politicians of the state.

"After the company had gotten pretty noisy and mellow from their imbibitions of Yellow Seal and 'corn juice,' " says Mr. Bryant, "Mr. Douglas and General Shields, to the consternation of the host and intense merriment of the guests, climbed up on the table, at one end, encircled each other's waists, and to the tune of a rollicking song, pirouetted down the whole length of the table, shouting, singing, and kicking dishes, glasses, and everything right and left, helter-skelter. For this night of entertainment to his constituents, the successful candidate was presented with a bill, in the morning, for supper, wines, liquors, and damages, which amounted to six hundred dollars."

But boisterous suppers were not by any means the only feature of Lincoln's social life that winter in Vandalia. There was another and quieter side in which he showed his rare companionableness and endeared himself to many people. In the midst of the log-rolling and jubilations of the session he would often slip away to some acquaintance's room and spend hours in talk and stories. Mr. John Bryant tells of his coming frequently to his room at the hotel and sitting "with his knees up to his chin, telling his inimitable stories and his triumphs in the House in circumventing the Democrats."

Major Newton Walker, of Lewiston, who was in Vandalia at the time, says: "I used to play the fiddle a great deal and have played for Lincoln a number of times. He used to come over to where I was boarding and ask me to play, and I would take the fiddle with me when I went over to visit him, and when he grew weary of telling stories he would ask me to give him a tune, which I never refused to do."

CHAPTER X

LINCOLN BEGINS TO STUDY LAW—MARY OWENS—A
NEWSPAPER CONTEST—GROWTH OF POLITICAL
INFLUENCE

As soon as the assembly closed, Lincoln returned to New Salem, but not to stay. He had determined to go to Springfield. Major John Stuart, the friend who had advised him to study law and who had lent him books and with whom he had been associated closely in politics, had offered to take him as a partner. It was a good opening, for Stuart was one of the leading lawyers and politicians of the state, and his influence would place Lincoln at once in command of more or less business. From every point of view the charge seems to have been wise; yet Lincoln made it with foreboding.

To practise law he must abandon his business as surveyor, which was bringing him a fair income; he must for a time, at least, go without a certain income. If he failed, what then? The uncertainty weighed on him heavily, the more so because he was burdened by the debts left from his store and because he was constantly called upon to aid his father's family. Thomas Lincoln had remained in Coles County, but he had not, in these six years in which his son had risen so rapidly, been able to get anything more than a poor livelihood from his farm. The sense of responsibility

BEGINS TO STUDY LAW

Lincoln had towards his father's family made it the more difficult for him to undertake a new profession. His decision was made, however, and as soon as the session of the Tenth Assembly was over he started for Springfield. His first appearance there is as pathetic as amusing.

"He had ridden into town," says Joshua Speed, "on a borrowed horse, with no earthly property save a pair of saddle-bags containing a few clothes. I was a merchant at Springfield, and kept a large country store, embracing dry-goods, groceries, hardware, books, medicines, bed-clothes, mattresses—in fact, everything that the country needed. Lincoln came into the store with his saddle-bags on his arm. He said he wanted to buy the furniture for a single bed. The mattress, blankets, sheets, coverlid, and pillow, according to the figures made by me, would cost seventeen dollars. He said that perhaps was cheap enough; but small as the price was, he was unable to pay it. But if I would credit him till Christmas, and his experiment as a lawyer was a success, he would pay then, saying in the saddest tone, 'If I fail in this I do not know that I can ever pay you.' As I looked up at him I thought then, and I think now, that I never saw a sadder face.

"I said to him: 'You seem to be so much pained at contracting so small a debt, I think I can suggest a plan by which you can avoid the debt and at the same time attain your end. I have a large room with a double bed upstairs, which you are very welcome to share with me.'

"'Where is your room?' said he.

"'Upstairs,' said I, pointing to a pair of winding stairs which led from the store to my room.

"He took his saddle-bags on his arm, went upstairs, set them on the floor, and came down with the most changed expression of countenance. Beaming with pleasure, he exclaimed:

"'Well, Speed, I am moved.'"

Another friend, William Butler, with whom Lincoln had become intimate at Vandalia, took him to board; life at Springfield thus began under as favorable auspices as he could hope for.

After Chicago, Springfield was at that day the most promising city in Illinois. It had some fifteen hundred inhabitants, and the removal of the capital was certain to bring many more. Already, in fact, the town felt the effect. "The owner of real estate sees his property rapidly enhancing in value," declared the "Sangamon Journal"; "the merchant anticipates a large accession to our population and a corresponding additional sale for his goods; the mechanic already has more contracts offered him for building and improvements than he can execute; the farmer anticipates the growth of a large and important town, a market for the varied products of his farm;—indeed, every class of our citizens look to the future with confidence, that, we trust, will not be disappointed."

The effect was apparent too, in society. "We used to eat all together," said an old man who in the early thirties came to Springfield as a hostler, "but about this time some one came along and told the people they oughtn't to do so, and then the hired folks ate in the kitchen." This differentiation was apparent to Lincoln and a little discouraging. He was thinking at the time of this removal of marrying, but he soon saw that it was quite out of the question for him to support a wife in Springfield.

"I am afraid you would not be satisfied," he wrote the young woman; "there is a great deal of flourishing about in carriages here, which it would be your doom to see without

LINCOLN'S SADDLE-BAGS.

These saddle-bags, now in the Lincoln Monument at Springfield, are said to have been used by Lincoln while he was a surveyor.

CABINET MADE BY ABRAHAM LINCOLN.

This cabinet is now in the possession of Captain J. W. Wartman of Evansville, Indiana. It is of walnut, two feet in height, and very well put together. Thomas Lincoln is said to have aided his son in making it.

sharing it. You would have to be poor, without the means of hiding your poverty. Do you believe you could bear that patiently?"

Lincoln's idea of marrying Mary Owens, of whom he asked this question, was the result of a quixotic sense of honor which had curiously blinded him to the girl's real feeling for him. The affair had begun in the fall of 1836, when a woman of his acquaintance who was going to Kentucky on a visit, proposed laughingly to bring back a sister of hers on condition that Lincoln marry her.

"I of course accepted the proposal," Lincoln wrote afterwards in a letter to Mrs. O. H. Browning, "for you know I could not have done otherwise had I really been averse to it; but privately, between you and me, I was most confoundedly well pleased with the project. I had seen the said sister some three years before, thought her intelligent and agreeable, and saw no good objection to plodding life through hand in hand with her. Time passed on, the lady took her journey and in due time returned, sister in company, sure enough. This astonished me a little, for it appeared to me that her coming so readily showed that she was a trifle too willing, but on reflection it occurred to me that she might have been prevailed on by her married sister to come, without anything concerning me ever having been mentioned to her, and so I concluded that if no other objection presented itself, I would consent to waive this."

Another objection did present itself as soon as he saw the lady. He was anything but pleased with her appearance.

"But what could I do?" he continues in his letter to Mrs. Browning. "I had told her sister that I would take her for better or for worse, and I made it a point of honor and conscience in all things to stick to my word, especially if others had been induced to act on it, which in this case I had no doubt they had, for I was now fairly convinced that no other man on earth would have her, and hence the conclusion that they were bent on holding me to my bargain. 'Well,' thought I, 'I have said it, and, be the consequences what they may, it shall not be my fault if I fail to do it.' At once I determined to consider her my wife, and this done, all my powers of discovery were put to work in search of perfections in her which might be fairly set off against her defects. I tried to imagine her handsome, which, but for her unfortunate corpulency, was actually true. Exclusive of this, no woman that I have ever seen has a finer face. I also tried to convince myself that the mind was much more to be valued than the person, and in this she was not inferior, as I could discover, to any with whom I had been acquainted.

"Shortly after this, without attempting to come to any positive understanding with her, I set out for Vandalia, when and where you first saw me. During my stay there I had letters from her which did not change my opinion of either her intellect or intention, but, on the contrary, confirmed it in both.

"All this while, although I was fixed 'firm as the surge-repelling rock' in my resolution, I found I was continually repenting the rashness which had led me to make it. Through life I have been in no bondage, either real or imaginary, from the thraldom of which I so much desired to be free. After my return home I saw nothing to change my opinion of her in any particular. She was the same, and so was I. I now spent my time in planning how I might get along in life after my contemplated change of circumstances should have taken place, and how I might procrastinate the evil day for a time, which I really dreaded as much, perhaps more, than an Irishman does the halter."

Lincoln was in this state of mind when he went to Springfield and discovered how unfit his resources were to support a wife there. Although he put the question of poverty so plainly he assured Miss Owens that if she married him he would do all in his power to make her happy.

"Whatever woman may cast her lot with mine," he wrote her, "should any ever do so, it is my intention to do all in my power to make her happy and contented; and there is nothing I can imagine that would make me more unhappy than to fail in the effort. I know I should be much happier with you than the way I am, provided I saw no signs of discontent in you. What you have said to me may have been in the way of jest, or I may have misunderstood it. If so, then let it be forgotten; if otherwise, I much wish you would think seriously before you decide. What I have said I will most positively abide by, provided you wish it. My opinion is that you had better not do it. You have not been accustomed to hardship, and it may be more serious than you now imagine. I know you are capable of thinking correctly on any subject, and if you deliberate maturely upon this before you decide, then I am willing to abide your decision."

This decidedly dispassionate view of their relation seems not to have brought any decision from Miss Owens, for three months later Mr. Lincoln wrote her an equally judicial letter, telling her that he could not think of her "with entire indifference," that he in all cases wanted to do right and "most particularly so in all cases with women," and summing up his position as follows:

"I now say that you can now drop the subject, dismiss your thoughts (if you ever had any) from me forever, and leave this letter unanswered, without calling forth one accusing murmur from me. And I will even go further and say that if it will add anything to your comfort or peace of mind to do so, it is my sincere wish that you should, Do not understand by this that I wish to cut your acquaintance. I mean no such thing.

"What I do wish is that our further acquaintance shall depend upon yourself. If such further acquaintance would contribute nothing to your happiness, I am sure it would not to mine. If you feel yourself in any degree bound to me, I am now willing to release you, provided you wish it; while, on the other hand, I am willing and even anxious to bind you faster, if I can be convinced that it will, in any considerable degree, add to your happiness. This, indeed, is the whole question with me. Nothing would make me more miserable than to believe you miserable—nothing more happy than to know you were so."

Miss Owens had enough discernment to recognize the disinterestedness of this love-making, and she refused Mr. Lincoln's offer. She found him "deficient in those little links which make up the chain of a woman's happiness," she said. When finally refused, Lincoln wrote the letter to Mrs. Browning from which the above citations have been taken. He concluded it with an account of the effect on himself of Miss Owens' refusal:

"I was mortified, it seemed to me, in a hundred different ways. My vanity was deeply wounded by the reflection that I had so long been too stupid to discover her intentions, and at the same time never doubting that I understood them perfectly; and also that she, whom I had taught myself to believe nobody else would have, had actually rejected me with all my fancied greatness. And, to cap the whole, I then for the first time began to suspect that I was really a little in love with her. But let it all go! I'll try and outlive it.

BEGINS TO STUDY LAW

Others have been made fools of by the girls, but this can never with truth be said of me. I most emphatically, in this instance, made a fool of myself. I have now come to the conclusion never again to think of marrying, and for this reason,—I can never be satisfied with any one who would be blockhead enough to have me."

The skill, the courage, and the good-will Lincoln had shown in his management of the bill for the removal of the capital gave him at once a position in Springfield. The entire "Long Nine," indeed, were regarded by the county as its benefactors, and throughout the summer there were barbecues and fireworks, dinners and speeches in their honor. "The service rendered Old Sangamon by the present delegation" was a continually recurring toast at every gathering. At one "sumptuous dinner" the internal improvement scheme in all its phases was toasted again and again by the banqueters. " 'The Long Nine' of Old Sangamon—well done, good and faithful servants," drew forth long applause. Among those who offered volunteer toasts at this dinner were "A. Lincoln, Esq.," and "S. A. Douglas, Esq."

At a dinner at Athens, given to the delegation, eight formal toasts and twenty-five volunteers are quoted in the report of the affair in the "Sangamon Journal." Among them were the following:

A. Lincoln. He has fulfilled the expectations of his friends and disappointed the hopes of his enemies.

A. Lincoln. One of nature's noblemen.

By A. Lincoln. Sangamon County will ever be true to her best interests, and never more so than in reciprocating the good feelings of the citizens of Athens and neighborhood.

Martin, Samb. &Co   To Stuart & Lincoln   Dr
1837 April — To attendance at trial of right }
            of J. A. Davis' property before Neffwell } $ 5.00.

Lucinda Cason   To Stuart & Lincoln   Dr
1837 Oct   To obtaining assignment of Dower. $ 5.00

Wiley & Wood   To Stuart & Lincoln   Dr
1838-8   To defense of Chancery case of &c By $ 50.00
        Stuart by cost to Stuart —   15.00
                                            $ 35.00

FACSIMILE OF PAGE FROM STUART & LINCOLN'S FEE BOOK.

From the original owned by Jesse W. Weik.

BEGINS TO STUDY LAW

Lincoln had not been long in Springfield before he was able to support himself from his law practice, a result due, no doubt, very largely to his personal qualities and to his reputation as a shrewd politician. Not that he made money. The fee-book of Lincoln and Stuart shows that the returns were modest enough, and that sometimes they even "traded out" their account. Nevertheless it was a satisfaction to earn a livelihood so soon. Of his peculiar methods as a lawyer at this date we know very little. Most of his cases are uninteresting. The first year he was in Springfield, however, he had one case which created a sensation, and which is an admirable example of the way he could combine business and politics as well as of his merciless persistency in pursuing a man whom he believed unjust.

It seems that among the offices to be filled at the August election of 1837 was that of probate justice of the peace. One of the candidates was General James Adams, a man who had come on from the East in the early twenties, and who had at first claimed to be a lawyer. He had been an aspirant for various offices, among them that of governor of the state, but with little success. A few days before the August election of 1837 an anonymous handbill was scattered about the streets. It was an attack on General Adams, charging him with having acquired the title to a ten-acre lot of ground near the town by the deliberate forgery of the name of Joseph Anderson, of Fulton County, Illinois, to an assignment of a judgment. Anderson had died, and his widow, going to Springfield to dispose of the land, had been surprised to find that it was claimed by General Adams. She had employed Stuart and Lincoln to look into the matter. The handbill, which went into all of the details at great length, concluded as follows: "I have only made these statements because I am known by many to be one of the individuals against whom the charge of forging the assignment and slipping it into the general's papers has been made; and because our silence might be construed into a confession of the truth. I shall not subscribe my name; but hereby authorize the editor of the 'Journal' to give it up to any one who may call for it."

After the election, at which General Adams was successful, the handbill was reproduced in the "Sangamon Journal," with a card signed by the editor, in which he said: "To save any further remarks on this subject, I now state that A. Lincoln, Esq., is the author of the handbill in question." The same issue of the paper contained a lengthy communication from General Adams, denying the charge of fraud.

The controversy was continued for several weeks in the newspapers, General Adams often filling six columns of a single issue of the "Springfield Republican."

He charged that the assault upon him was the result of a conspiracy between "a knot of lawyers, doctors, and others," who wished to ruin his reputation. Lincoln's answers to Adams are most emphatic. In one case, quoting several of his assertions, he pronounced them "all as false as hell, as all this community must know." Adams's replies were always voluminous. "Such is the turn which things have lately taken," wrote Lincoln, "that when General Adams writes a book I am expected to write a commentary on it." Replying to Adams's denunciation of the lawyers, he said: "He attempted to impose himself upon the community as a lawyer, and he actually carried the attempt so far as to induce a man who was under the charge of murder to entrust the defence of his life to his hands, and finally took his money and got him hanged. Is this the man that is to raise a breeze in his favor by abusing lawyers? . . . If he is not a lawyer, he *is* a liar; for he proclaimed himself a lawyer, and got a man hanged by depending on him." Lincoln concluded: "Farewell, General. I will see you again at court, if not before—when and where we will settle the question whether you or the widow shall have the land." The widow did get the land, but this was not the worst thing that happened to Adams. The climax was reached when the "Sangamon Journal" published a long editorial (written by Lincoln, no doubt) on the controversy, and followed it with a copy of an indictment found against Adams in Oswego County, New York, in 1818. The offence charged in this indictment was the forgery of a deed by Adams—"a person of evil name and fame and of a wicked disposition."

Lincoln's victory in this controversy undoubtedly did much to impress the community, not necessarily that he was a good lawyer, but rather that he was a clever strategist and a fearless enemy. It was not, in fact, as a lawyer that he was prominent in the first years after he came to Springfield. It was as a politician. The place he had taken among the leaders of the Whig Party in the winter of 1836 and 1837 he easily kept. The qualities which he had shown from the outstart of his public life were only strengthened as he gained experience and self-confidence. He was the terror of the pretentious and insincere, and had a way of exposing their shams by clever tricks which were unanswerable arguments. Thus, it was considered necessary, at that day, by a candidate to prove to the farmers that he was poor and, like themselves, horny-handed. Those politicians who wore good clothes and dined sumptuously were careful to conceal their regard for the elegancies of life from their constituents. One of the Democrats who in this period took particular pains to decry the Whigs for their wealth and aristocratic principles was Colonel Dick Taylor, generally known in Illinois as "ruffled-shirt Taylor." He was a vain and handsome man, who habitually arrayed himself as gorgeously as the fashion allowed. One day when he and Lincoln had met in debate at a countryside gathering, Colonel Dick became particularly bitter in his condemnation of Whig elegance. Lincoln listened for a time, and then, slipping near the speaker, suddenly caught his coat, which was buttoned up close, and tore it open. A mass of ruffled shirt, a gorgeous velvet vest, and a great gold chain from which dangled numerous rings and seals, were uncovered to the crowd. Lincoln needed to make no further reply that day to the charge of being a "rag baron."

Lincoln loved fair play as he hated shams, and throughout these early years in Springfield boldly insisted that friend and enemy have the chance due

BEGINS TO STUDY LAW

them. A dramatic case of this kind occurred at a political meeting held one evening in the Springfield court-room, which at that date was temporarily in a hall under Stuart and Lincoln's law office. Directly over the platform was a trapdoor. Lincoln frequently would lie by this opening during a meeting, listening to the speeches. One evening one of his friends, E. D. Baker, in speaking angered the crowd, and an attempt was made to "pull him down." Before the assailants could reach the platform, however, a pair of long legs dangled from the trapdoor, and in an instant Lincoln dropped down beside Baker, crying out, "Hold on, gentlemen, this is a land of free speech." His appearance was so unexpected, and his attitude so determined, that the crowd soon was quiet, and Baker went on with his speech.

Lincoln did not take a prominent place in his party because the Whigs lacked material. He had powerful rivals. Edward Dickinson Baker, Colonel John J. Hardin, John T. Stuart, Ninian W. Edwards, Jesse K. Dubois, O. H. Browning, were but a few of the brilliant men who were throwing all their ability and ambition into the contest for political honors in the state. Nor were the Whigs a whit superior to the Democrats. William L. D. Ewing, Ebenezer Peck, William Thomas, James Shields, John Calhoun, were in every respect as able as the best men of the Whig Party. Indeed, one of the prominent Democrats with whom Lincoln came often in contact was popularly regarded as the most brilliant and promising politician of the state—Stephen A. Douglas. His record had been phenomenal. He had amazed both parties, in

1834 by securing the appointment by the legislature to the office of State Attorney for the first judicial circuit, over John J. Hardin. In 1836 he had been elected to the legislature, and although he was at that time but twenty-three years of age, he had shown himself one of the most vigorous, capable, and intelligent members. Indeed, Douglas's work in the Tenth Assembly gave him about the same position in the Democratic Party of the state at large that Lincoln's work in the same body gave him in the Whig Party of his own district. In 1837 he had had no difficulty in being appointed registrar of the land office, a position which compelled him to make his home in Springfield. It was only a few months after Lincoln rode into town, all his earthly possessions in a pair of saddle-bags, that Douglas appeared. Handsome, polished, and always with an air of prosperity, the advent of the young Democratic official was in striking contrast to that of the sad-eyed, ill-clad, poverty-stricken young lawyer from New Salem.

From the first, Lincoln and Douglas were thrown constantly together in the social life of the town, and often pitted against each other in what were the real forums of the state at that day—the space around the huge "Franklin" stove of some obliging storekeeper, the steps of somebody's law office, a pile of lumber, or a long timber, lying in the public square, where the new State-house was going up.

In the fall of 1837 Douglas was nominated for Congress on the Democratic ticket. His Whig opponent was Lincoln's law partner, John T. Stuart. The campaign which the two conducted was one of

STUART AND LINCOLN'S LAW OFFICE.

From a photograph loaned by Jesse W. Weik. The law office of Stuart and Lincoln was in the second story of the building occupied at the time the photograph was made by "Tom Dupleaux's Furniture Store." Hoffman's Row, as this group of buildings was called, was used as a court-house at that date, 1837. The court-room was in the lower story of the two central buildings.

the most remarkable in the history of the state. For
five months of the spring and summer of 1838 they
rode together from town to town all over the northern
part of Illinois (Illinois at that time was divided into
but three congressional districts, the third, in which
Sangamon County was included, being made up of the
twenty-two northernmost counties), speaking six days
out of seven. When the election came off in August,
1838, out of thirty-six thousand votes cast, Stuart received a majority of only fourteen; but even that
majority the Democrats always contended was won
unfairly.

The campaign was watched with intense interest by
the young politicians of Springfield; no one of them
felt a deeper interest in it than Lincoln, who was himself a candidate for the state legislature, and who was
spending a great deal of his time in electioneering.

As the campaign of 1840 approached Lincoln was
more and more frequently pitted against Douglas.
He had by this time no doubt learned something of
the power of the "Little Giant," as Douglas was
already called. Certainly no man in public life between 1837 and 1860 had a greater hold on his followers. The reasons for this grasp are not hard to
find. Douglas was by nature buoyant, enthusiastic,
impetuous. He had that sunny boyishness which is
so irresistible to young and old. With it he had great
natural eloquence. When his deep, rich voice rolled
out fervid periods in support of the sub-treasury and
the convention system, or in opposition to internal
improvements by the federal government, the people
applauded out of sheer joy at the pleasure of hearing

him. He was one of the few men in Illinois whom the epithet of "Yankee" never hurt. He might be a Yankee, but when he sat down on the knee of some surly lawyer, and confidentially told him his plans; or, at a political meeting, took off his coat and rolled up his sleeves, and "pitched into" his opponent, the sons of Illinois forgot his origin in love for the man.

Lincoln undoubtedly understood the charm of Douglas, and realized his power. But he already had an insight into one of his political characteristics that few people recognized at that day. In writing to Stuart in 1839, while the latter was attending Congress, Lincoln said:

"Douglas has not been here since you left. A report is in circulation here now that he has abandoned the idea of going to Washington, though the report does not come in a very authentic form, so far as I can learn. Though, by the way, speaking of authenticity, you know that if we had heard Douglas say that he had abandoned the contest, it would not be very authentic."

At that time the local issues, which had formerly engaged Illinois candidates almost entirely, were lost sight of in national questions. In Springfield, where the leaders of both parties were living, many hot debates were held in private. Out of these grew, in December, 1839, a series of public discussions, extending over eight evenings, and in which several of the first orators of the state took part. Lincoln was the last man on the list. The people were nearly worn out before his turn came, and his audience was small. He began his speech with some melancholy, self-

BEGINS TO STUDY LAW

deprecatory reflections, complaining that the small audience cast a damp upon his spirits which he was sure he would be unable to overcome during the evening. He did better than he expected, overcoming the damp on his spirits so effectually that he made what was regarded as the best speech of the series. By a general request, it was printed for distribution. The speech is peculiarly interesting from the fact that while there is a little of the perfervid eloquence of 1840 in it, as well as a good deal of the rather boisterous humor of the time, a part of it is devoted to a careful examination of the statements of his opponents, and a refutation of them by means of public documents.

As a good Democrat was expected to do, Douglas had explained with plausibility why the Van Buren administration had in 1838 spent $40,000,000. Lincoln takes up his statements one by one and proves, as he says, that "the majority of them are wholly untrue." Douglas had attributed a part of the expenditures to the purchase of public lands from the Indians.

"Now it happens," said Lincoln, "that no such purchase was made during that year. It is true that some money was paid that year in pursuance of Indian treaties; but no more, or rather not as much as had been paid on the same account in each of several preceding years. . . . Again, Mr. Douglas says that the removal of the Indians to the country west of the Mississippi created much of the expenditure of 1838. I have examined the public documents in relation to this matter and find that less was paid for the removal of Indians in that than in some former years. The whole sum expended on that account in that year did not much exceed one quarter of a million. For this small sum, although we do not think the administration entitled to credit, because large sums have been expended in the same way in former years, we consent it may take one and make the most of it.

"Next, Mr. Douglas says that five millions of the expeditures of 1838 consisted of the payment of the French indemnity money to its individual claimants. I have carefully examined the public documents and thereby find this statement to be wholly untrue. Of the forty millions of dollars expended in 1838, I am enabled to say positively that not one dollar consisted of payments on the French indemnities. So much for that excuse.

"Next comes the Post-office. He says that five millions were expended during that year to sustain that department. By a like examination of public documents, I find this also wholly untrue. Of the so often mentioned forty millions, not one dollar went to the Post-office. . . .

"I return to another of Mr. Douglas's excuses for the expenditures of 1838, at the same time announcing the pleasing intelligence that this is the last one. He says that ten millions of that year's expenditure was a contingent appropriation, to prosecute an anticipated war with Great Britain on the Maine boundary question. Few words will settle this. First, that the ten millions appropriated was not made till 1839, and consequently could not have been expended in 1838; second, although it was appropriated, it has never been expended at all. Those who heard Mr. Douglas recollect that he indulged himself in a contemptuous expression of pity for me. 'Now he's got me,' thought I. But when he went on to say that five millions of the expenditure of 1838 were payments of the French indemnities, which I knew to be untrue; that five millions had been for the Post-office, which I knew to be untrue; that ten millions had been for the Maine boundary war, which I not only knew to be untrue, but supremely ridiculous also; and when I saw that he was stupid enough to hope that I would permit such groundless and audacious assertions to go unexposed,—I readily consented that, on the score both of veracity and sagacity, the audience should judge whether he or I were the more deserving of the world's contempt."

These citations show that Lincoln had already learned to handle public documents and to depend for at least a part of his success with an audience upon a careful statement of facts. The methods used in at least a portion of this speech are exactly those which made the irresistible strength of his speeches in 1858, 1859, and 1860.

But there was little of as good work done in the campaign of 1840, by Lincoln or anybody else, as is found in this speech. It was a campaign of fun and noise, and nowhere more so than in Illinois. Lincoln was one of the five Whig Presidential electors, and he flung himself into the campaign with confidence. "The nomination of Harrison takes first rate," he wrote to his partner Stuart, then in Washington. "You know I am never sanguine, but I believe we will carry the state. The chance of doing so appears to me twenty-five per cent. better than it did for you to beat Douglas." The Whigs, in spite of their dislike of the convention system, organized as they never had before, and even sent out a "confidential" circular of which Lincoln was the author.

This circular provided for a remarkably complete organization of the state, as the following extracts will show:

After due deliberation, the following is the plan of organization, and the duties required of each county committee:
(1) To divide their county into small districts, and to appoint in each a subcommittee, whose duty it shall be to

make a perfect list of all the voters in their respective districts and to ascertain with certainty for whom they will vote. If they meet with men who are doubtful as to the man they will support, such voters should be designated in separate lines, with the name of the man they will probably support.

(2) It will be the duty of said subcommittee to keep a constant watch on the doubtful voters, and from time to time have them talked to by those in whom they have the most confidence, and also to place in their hands such documents as will enlighten and influence them.

. . . .

(5) On the first of each month hereafter we shall expect to hear from you. After the first report of your subcommittees, unless there should be found a great many doubtful voters, you can tell pretty accurately the manner in which your county will vote. In each of your letters to us, you will state the number of certain votes both for and against us, as well as the number of doubtful votes, with your opinion of the manner in which they will be cast.

(6) When we have heard from all the counties, we shall be able to tell with similar accuracy the political complexion of the state. This information will be forwarded to you as soon as received.

Every weapon Lincoln thought of possible use in the contest he secured. "Be sure to send me as many copies of the 'Life of Harrison' as you can spare from other uses," he wrote Stuart. "Be very sure to procure and send me the 'Senate Journal' of New York, of September, 1814. I have a newspaper article which says that that document proves that Van Buren voted against raising troops in the last war. And, in general, send me everything you think will be a good 'war-club.'"

Every sign of success he quoted to Stuart; the number of subscribers to the "Old Soldier," a campaign newspaper which the Whig committee had informed the Whigs of the state that they *"must take";* the names of Van Buren men who were weakening, and to whom he wanted Stuart to send documents; the name of every theretofore doubtful person who had declared himself for Harrison. "Japh Bell has come out for Harrison," he put in a postscript to one letter; "ain't that a caution?"

The monster political meetings held throughout the state did much to widen Lincoln's reputation, particularly one held in June in Springfield. Twenty thousand people attended this meeting, delegations coming from every direction. It took fourteen teams to haul the delegation from Chicago, and they were three weeks on their journey. Each party carried some huge symbolic piece—the log cabin being the favorite. One of the cabins taken to Springfield was drawn by thirty yokes of oxen. In a hickory tree which was planted beside this cabin, coons were seen playing, and a barrel of hard cider stood by the door, continually on tap. Instead of a log cabin, the Chicago delegation dragged across country a government yawl rigged up as a two-masted ship, with a band of music and a six-pounder cannon on board.

There are many reminiscences of this great celebration and Lincoln's part in it, still afloat in Illinois. General T. J. Henderson writes, in his entertaining reminiscences of Lincoln:

"The first time I remember to have seen Abraham Lincoln was during the memorable campaign of 1840, when I was a boy fifteen years of age. It was at an immense Whig mass-meeting held at Springfield, Illinois, in the month of June of that year. The Whigs attended this meeting from all parts of the state in large numbers, and it was estimated that from forty to fifty thousand people were present. They came in carriages and wagons, on horseback and on foot. They came with log cabins drawn on wheels by oxen, and with coons, coonskins, and hard cider. They came with music and banners; and thousands of them came from long distances. It was the first political meeting I had ever attended, and it made a very strong impression upon my youthful mind.

"My father, William H. Henderson, then a resident of Stark County, Illinois, was an ardent Whig; and having served under General William Henry Harrison, the then Whig candidate for President, in the war of 1812-1815, he felt a deep interest in his election. And although he lived about a hundred miles from Springfield, he went with a delegation from Stark County to this political meeting and took me along with him. I remember that at this great meeting of the supporters of Harrison and Tyler there were a number of able and distinguished speakers of the Whig Party of the State of Illinois present. Among them were Colonel E. D. Baker, who was killed at Ball's Bluff, on the Potomac, in the late war, and who was one of the most eloquent speakers in the state; Colonel John J. Hardin, who was killed at the battle of Buena Vista, in the Mexican War; Fletcher Webster, a son of Daniel Webster, who was killed in the late war; S. Leslie Smith, a brilliant orator of Chicago; Rev. John Hogan, Ben Bond, and Abraham Lincoln. I heard all of these men speak on that occasion. And while I was too young to be a judge of their speeches, yet I thought them all to be great men, and none of them greater than Abraham Lincoln."

The late Judge Scott of Illinois says of Lincoln's speech at that gathering, in an unpublished paper "Lincoln on the Stump and at the Bar":

A HARRISON BADGE OF 1840.
From the collection of Mr. O. H. Oldroyd of
Washington, D. C.

BEGINS TO STUDY LAW

"Mr. Lincoln stood in a wagon, from which he addressed the mass of people that surrounded it. The meeting was one of unusual interest because of him who was to make the principal address. It was at the time of his greatest physical strength. He was tall, and perhaps a little more slender than in later life, and more homely than after he became stouter in person. He was then only thirty-one years of age, and yet he was regarded as one of the ablest of the Whig speakers in that campaign. There was that in him that attracted and held public attention. Even then he was the subject of popular regard because of his candid and simple mode of discussing and illustrating political questions. At times he was intensely logical, and was always most convincing in his arguments. The questions involved in that canvass had relation to the tariff, internal public improvements by the federal government, the distribution of the proceeds of the sales of public lands among the several states, and other questions that divided the political parties of that day. They were not such questions as enlisted and engaged his best thoughts; they did not take hold of his great nature, and had no tendency to develop it. At times he discussed the questions of the time in a logical way, but much time was devoted to telling stories to illustrate some phase of his argument, though more often the telling of these stories was resorted to for the purpose of rendering his opponents ridiculous. That was a style of speaking much appreciated at that early day. In that kind of oratory he excelled most of his contemporaries—indeed, he had no equal in the state. One story he told on that occasion was full of salient points and well illustrated the argument he was making. It was not an impure story, yet it was not one it would be seemly to publish; but rendered, as it was, in his inimitable way, it contained nothing that was offensive to a refined taste. The same story might have been told by another in such a way that it would probably have been regarded as transcending the proprieties of popular address. One characterizing feature of all the stories told by Mr.

Lincoln, on the stump and elsewhere, was that although the subject matter of some of them might not have been entirely unobjectionable, yet the manner of telling them was so peculiarly his own that they gave no offence even to refined and cultured people. On the contrary, they were much enjoyed. The story he told on this occasion was much liked by the vast assembly that surrounded the temporary platform from which he spoke and was received with loud bursts of laughter and applause. It served to place the opposing party and its speakers in a most ludicrous position in respect to the question being considered and gave him a most favorable hearing for the arguments he later made in support of the measures he was sustaining."

Although so active as a Whig politician Lincoln was not prominent at this period as a legislator. Few bills originated with him. Among these few, one of interest is the Illinois law requiring the examination of school teachers as to their qualifications, and providing for the granting of official certificates of authority to teach. In the pioneer days, any person whom circumstances forced into the business was permitted to teach. On December 2, 1840, Lincoln offered the following resolution in the Illinois House of Representatives:

"Resolved, That the committee on education be instructed to inquire into the expediency of providing by law for the examination as to the qualification of persons offering themselves as school teachers, that no teacher shall receive any part of the public school fund who shall not have successfully passed such examination, and that they report by bill or otherwise."

A motion to table this resolution was defeated. Within the ensuing three months the legislature passed "an act making provision for organizing and maintaining common schools"—the act which was the foundation of the common school system of Illinois. Section 81 of this act, providing for the qualification of teachers, embodied Lincoln's idea. This section made it the duty of the school trustees in every township "to examine any person proposing to teach school in their vicinity in relation to the qualifications of such

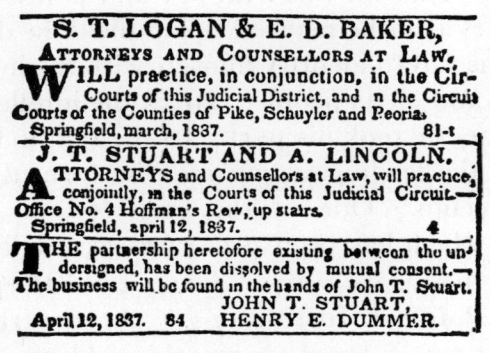

```
S. T. LOGAN & E. D. BAKER,
ATTORNEYS AND COUNSELLORS AT LAW.
WILL practice, in conjunction, in the Cir-
    Courts of this Judicial District, and n the Circuit
Courts of the Counties of Pike, Schuyler and Peoria.
    Springfield, march, 1837.                    81-t

J. T. STUART AND A. LINCOLN.
ATTORNEYS and Counsellors at Law, will practice,
    conjointly, in the Courts of this Judicial Circuit.—
Office No. 4 Hoffman's Row, up stairs.
    Springfield, april 12, 1837.                  4

THE partnership heretofore existing between the un-
    dersigned, has been dissolved by mutual consent.—
The business will be found in the hands of John T. Stuart.
                            JOHN T. STUART,
April 12, 1837.   84     HENRY E. DUMMER.
```

STUART AND LINCOLN'S PROFESSIONAL CARD

person as a teacher," or they might appoint a board of commissioners to conduct the examination; and a certificate of qualification was to be issued by a majority of the trustees or commissioners. Since then, of course, all the states have passed laws providing for the examination of teachers. In Illinois, no material change has been made in Lincoln's plan (for this section of the law was very likely drawn by Lincoln), except that the power of examination has been transferred from the trustees or commissioners to the county superintendent of schools, an office then unknown.

CHAPTER XI

LINCOLN'S ENGAGEMENT TO MARY TODD—BREAKING OF THE ENGAGEMENT—LINCOLN-SHIELDS DUEL

Busy as Lincoln was with law and politics the first three years after he reached Springfield, he did not by any means fail to identify himself with the interests of the town and of its people. In all the intellectual life of the place he took his part. In the fall of 1837 with a few of the leading young men he formed a young men's lyceum. One of the very few of his early speeches which has been preserved was delivered before this body, its subject being the "Perpetuation of Our Political Institutions." At the request of the members of the Lyceum this address was published in the "Sangamon Journal" for February 3, 1838.

The most pleasing feature of his early life in the town was the way in which he attracted all classes of people to him. He naturally, from his political importance and from his relation to Mr. Stuart, was admitted to the best society. But Lincoln was not received there from tolerance of his position only. The few members left of that interesting circle of Springfield in the thirties are emphatic in their statements that he was recognized as a valuable social factor. If indifferent to forms and little accustomed to conventional usages, he had a native dignity and self-

HIS MARRIAGE ENGAGEMENT 197

respect which stamped him at once as a superior man. He had a good will, an easy adaptability to people, which made him take a hand in everything that went

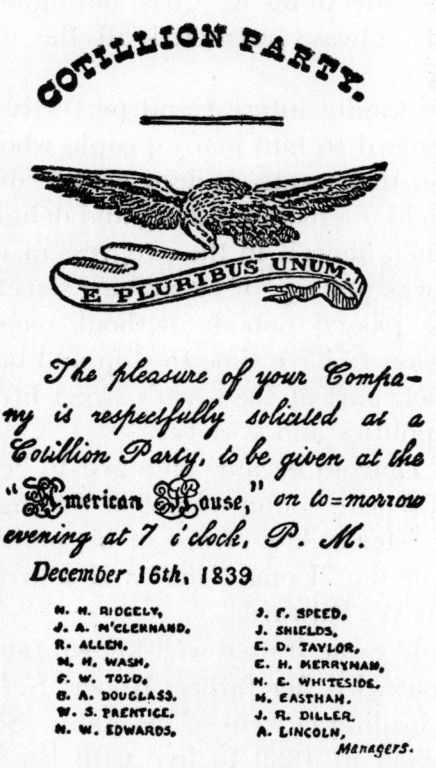

COTILLION PARTY.

E PLURIBUS UNUM.

The pleasure of your Company is respectfully solicited at a Cotillion Party, to be given at the "American House," on to-morrow evening at 7 o'clock, P. M.

December 16th, 1839

N. H. RIDGELY,	J. F. SPEED,
J. A. M'CLERNAND,	J. SHIELDS,
R. ALLEN,	E. D. TAYLOR,
M. H. WASH,	E. H. MERRYMAN,
E. W. TODD,	N. E. WHITESIDE,
B. A. DOUGLASS,	M. EASTHAM,
W. S. PRENTICE,	J. R. DILLER,
N. W. EDWARDS,	A. LINCOLN,

Managers.

FACSIMILE OF INVITATION TO A SPRINGFIELD COTILLION PARTY.
From the collection of Mr. C. F. Gunther, Chicago.

on. His name appears in every list of banqueters and merrymakers reported in the Springfield papers. He even served as committeeman for cotillion parties. "We liked Lincoln though he was not gay," said one charming and cultivated old lady to me in Springfield.

"He rarely danced, he was never very attentive to ladies, but he was always a welcome guest everywhere, and the centre of a circle of animated talkers. Indeed, I think the only thing we girls had against Lincoln was that he always attracted all the men around him."

Lincoln's kindly interest and perfectly democratic feeling attached to him many people whom he never met save on the streets. Indeed his life in the streets of Springfield is a most touching and delightful study. He concerned himself in the progress of every building which was put up, of every new street which was opened; he passed nobody without recognition; he seemed always to have time to stop and talk. He became, in fact, part of the town's street life, just as he did of its politics and society.

In 1840 Lincoln became engaged to be married to one of the favorite young women of Springfield, Mary Todd, the sister-in-law of one of his political friends, a member of the "Long Nine" and a prominent citizen, Ninian W. Edwards.

Miss Todd came from a well-known family of Lexington, Kentucky, her father, Robert S. Todd, being one of the leading citizens of his state. She had come to Springfield in 1839 to live with her sister, Mrs. Edwards. She was a brilliant, witty, highly educated girl, ambitious and spirited, with a touch of audacity which only made her more attractive, and she at once took a leading position in Springfield society. There were many young unmarried men in the town, drawn there by politics, and Mr. Edwards's handsome home was opened to them in the hospitable Southern way.

MARY TODD LINCOLN.

From a carbon enlargement, by Sherman and McHugh of New York, of a photograph by Brady. Mary Todd was born in Lexington, Kentucky, December 13, 1818. Her mother died when she was young, and she was educated at one of the best-known schools of the State, Madame Mantelli's. She remained there some four years, and as the school was conducted entirely in French, she spoke the language fluently. She was afterwards some time in the Ward Academy of Lexington. Miss Todd first visited Springfield in 1837, but remained only a few months. In 1839 she returned to make her home with her sister, Mrs. Edwards. She had two other sisters in the town, Mrs. William Wallace and Mrs. C. M. Smith.

After Mary Todd became an inmate of the Edwards house, the place was gayer than ever. She received much attention from Douglas, Shields, Lincoln, and several others. It was soon apparent, however, that Miss Todd preferred Lincoln. As the intimacy between them increased, Mr. and Mrs. Edwards protested. However honorable and able a man Lincoln might be, he was still a "plebeian." His family were humble and poor; he was self-educated, without address or polish, careless of forms, indifferent to society. How could Mary Todd, brought up in a cultured home, accustomed to the refinements of life, ambitious for social position, accommodate herself to so grave a nature, so dull an exterior? Miss Todd knew her own mind, however. She loved Lincoln and seems to have believed from the first in his future. Some time in 1840 they became engaged.

But it was not long before there came the clashing inevitable between two persons whose tastes and ambitions were so different. Miss Todd was jealous and exacting; Lincoln thoughtless and inattentive. He frequently failed to accompany her to the merrymakings which she wanted to attend and she, naturally enough, resented his neglect, interpreting it as a purposed slight. Sometimes in revenge she went with Mr. Douglas or some other escort who offered. Reproaches and tears and misunderstandings followed. If the lovers made up, it was only to fall out again. At last Lincoln became convinced that they were incompatible, and resolved that he must break the engagement. But the knowledge that the girl loved him took away his courage. He felt that he must not draw back, and he became profoundly miserable.

"Whatever woman may cast her lot with mine, should any ever do so, it is my intention to do all in my power to make her happy and contented; and there is nothing I can imagine that would make me more unhappy than to fail in the effort," Lincoln had written Miss Owens three years before. How could he make this brilliant, passionate creature to whom he was betrothed happy?

A mortal dread of the result of the marriage, a harrowing doubt of his own feelings, possessed him. The experience is not so rare in the history of lovers that it should be regarded, as it often has been, as something exceptional and abnormal in Lincoln's case. A reflective nature founded in melancholy, like Lincoln's, rarely undertakes even the simpler affairs of life without misgivings. He certainly experienced dread and doubt before entering on any new relation. When it came to forming the most delicate and intimate of all human relations, he staggered under a burden of uncertainty and suffering and finally broke the engagement.

So horrible a breach of honor did this seem to him that he called the day when it occurred the "fatal first of January, 1841," and months afterward he wrote to his intimate friend Speed: "I must regain my confidence in my own ability to keep my resolves when they are made. In that ability I once prided myself as the only or chief gem of my character; that gem I lost—how and where you know too well. I have not yet regained it, and, until I do, I cannot trust myself in any matter of much importance."

The breaking of the engagement between Miss Todd and Mr. Lincoln was known at the time to all their friends. Lincoln's melancholy was evident to them all, nor did he, indeed, attempt to disguise it. He wrote and spoke freely to his intimates of the despair which possessed him, and of his sense of dishonor. The episode caused a great amount of gossip, as was to be expected. After Mr. Lincoln's assassination and Mrs. Lincoln's sad death, various accounts of the courtship and marriage were circulated. It remained, however, for one of Lincoln's law partners, Mr. W. H. Herndon, to develop and circulate the most sensational of all the versions of the rupture. According to Mr. Herndon, the engagement between the two was broken in the most violent and public way possible, by Mr. Lincoln's failing to appear at the wedding. Mr. Herndon even describes the scene in detail:

"The time fixed for the marriage was the first day of January, 1841. Careful preparations for the happy occasion were made at the Edwards mansion. The house underwent the customary renovation; the furniture was properly arranged, the rooms neatly decorated, the supper prepared, and the guests invited. The latter assembled on the evening in question and awaited in expectant pleasure the interesting ceremony of marriage. The bride, bedecked in veil and silken gown, and nervously toying with the flowers in her hair, sat in the adjoining room. Nothing was lacking but the groom. For some strange reason he had been delayed. An hour passed, and the guests, as well as the bride, were becoming restless. But they were all doomed to disappointment. Another hour passed; messengers were sent out over town, and each returning with the same report, it became apparent that Lincoln, the principal in this little drama, had purposely failed to appear. The bride, in grief, disappeared to her room; the wedding supper was left untouched; the guests quietly and wonderingly withdrew; the lights in the Edwards mansion were blown out, and darkness settled over all for the night. What the feelings of a lady as sensitive, passionate, and proud as Miss Todd were we can only imagine; no one can ever describe them. By daybreak, after persistent search, Lincoln's friends found him. Restless, gloomy, miserable, desperate, he seemed an object of pity. His friends, Speed among the number, fearing a tragic termination, watched him closely in their rooms day and night. 'Knives and razors, and every instrument that could be used for self-destruction, were removed from his reach.' Mrs. Edwards did not hesitate to regard him as insane, and of course her sister Mary shared in that view."

No one can read this description in connection with the rest of Mr. Herndon's text and escape the impression that, if it is true, there must have been a vein of cowardice in Lincoln. The context shows that he was not insane enough to excuse such a public insult to a woman. To break his engagement was, all things considered, not an unusual or abnormal thing; to brood over the rupture, to blame himself, to feel that he had been dishonorable, was to be expected, after such an act, from one of his temperament. Nothing, however, but temporary insanity or constitutional cowardice could explain such conduct as here described. Mr. Herndon does not pretend to found his story on any personal knowledge of the affair. He was in Springfield at the time, a clerk in Speed's store, but did not have then, nor, indeed, did he ever have, any social relations with the families in which Mr. Lincoln was always a welcome guest. His authority for the story is a remark which he says Mrs. Ninian Edwards made to him in an interview: "Lincoln and Mary were engaged; everything was ready and prepared for the marriage, even to the supper. Mr. Lincoln failed to meet his engagement; cause, insanity." This remark, it should be noted, is not from a manuscript written by Mrs. Edwards, but in a report of an interview with her, written by Mr. Herndon. Supposing, however, that the statement was made in the exact words as Mr. Herndon reports, it certainly does not justify the sensational description Mr. Herndon gives.

If such a thing had ever occurred, it could not have failed to be known, of course, even to its smallest details, by all the relatives and friends of both Miss Todd and Mr. Lincoln. Nobody, however, ever heard of this wedding party until Mr. Herndon gave his story to the public.

One of the closest friends of the Lincolns throughout their lives was a cousin of Mrs. Lincoln's, Mrs. Grimsley, afterwards the wife of Dr. Brown. Mrs. Grimsley lived in Springfield, on the most intimate and friendly relations with Mr. and Mrs. Lincoln, and the first six months of their life in the White House she spent with them. She was a woman of unusual culture, and of the rarest sweetness and graciousness of character. Some months before Mrs. Brown's death, in August, 1895, a copy of Mr. Herndon's story was sent her, with a request that she write for publication her knowledge of the affair. In her reply she said:

"Did Mr. Lincoln fail to appear when the invitations were out, the guests invited, and the supper ready for the wedding? I will say emphatically, 'No.'

"There may have been a little shadow of foundation for Mr. Herndon's lively imagination to play upon, in that, the year previous to the marriage, and when Mr. Lincoln and my cousin Mary expected soon to be married, Mr. Lincoln was taken with one of those fearful, overwhelming periods of depression, which induced his friends to persuade him to leave Springfield. This he did for a time; but I am satisfied he was loyal and true to Mary, even though at times he may have doubted whether he was responding as fully as a manly, generous nature should to such affection as he knew my cousin was ready to bestow on him. And this because it had not the overmastering depth of an early love. This everybody here knows; therefore I do not feel as if I were betraying dear friends."

When the material for this work was gathered, Mrs. John Stuart, the wife of Lincoln's first law partner, was still living in Springfield, a refined, cultivated, intelligent woman, who remembered perfectly the life and events of that day. Her indignation was intense when Mr. Herndon's story was first called to her attention. She protested that she never before had heard of such a thing. Mrs. Stuart was not, however, in Springfield at that particular date, but in Washington, her husband being a member of Congress. She wrote the following statement for this biography:

"I cannot deny this, as I was not in Springfield for some months before and after this occurrence was said to have taken place; but I was in close correspondence with relatives and friends during all this time, and never heard a word of it. The late Judge Broadwell told me that he had asked Mr. Ninian Edwards about it, and Mr. Edwards told him that no such thing had ever taken place.

"All I can say is that I unhesitatingly do not believe such an event ever occurred. I thought I had never heard of this till I saw it in Herndon's book. I have since been told that Lamon mentions the same thing. I read Lamon at the time he published, and felt very much disgusted, but did not remember this particular assertion. The first chapters of Lamon's book were purchased from Herndon; so Herndon is responsible for the whole.

"Mrs. Lincoln told me herself all the circumstances of her engagement to Mr. Lincoln, of his illness, and the breaking off of her engagement, of the renewal, and her marriage. So I say I do not believe one word of this dishonorable story about Mr. Lincoln."

Another prominent member in the same circle with Mr. Lincoln and Miss Todd was Mrs. B. T. Edwards, the widow of Judge Benjamin T. Edwards, the sister-in-law of Mr. Ninian Edwards, who had married Miss Todd's sister. She came to Springfield in 1839, and was intimately acquainted with Mr. Lincoln and Miss Todd, and knew, as well as another could know, their affairs. In answer to the question, "Is Mr. Herndon's description true?" Mrs. Edwards, a woman of refinement and trustworthiness, wrote:

"I am impatient to tell you that all that he says about this wedding—the time for which was 'fixed for the first day of January'—is a fabrication. He has drawn largely upon his imagination in describing something which never took place.

"I know the engagement between Mr. Lincoln and Miss

Todd was interrupted for a time, and it was rumored among her young friends that Mr. Edwards had rather opposed it. But I am sure there had been no 'time fixed' for any wedding; that is, no preparations had ever been made until the day that Mr. Lincoln met Mr. Edwards on the street and told him that he and Mary were going to be married that evening. Upon inquiry, Mr. Lincoln said they would be married in the Episcopal church, to which Mr. Edwards replied: 'No; Mary is my ward, and she must be married at my house.'

"If I remember rightly, the wedding guests were few, not more than thirty; and it seems to me all are gone now but Mrs. Wallace, Mrs. Levering, and myself, for it was not much more than a family gathering; only two or three of Mary Todd's young friends were present. The 'entertainment' was simple, but in beautiful taste; but the bride had neither veil nor flowers in her hair, with which to 'toy nervously.' There had been no elaborate trousseau for the bride of the future President of the United States, nor even a handsome wedding grown; nor was it a gay wedding."

Two sisters of Mrs. Lincoln who were still living when this book was written, Mrs. Wallace of Springfield, and Mrs. Helm of Elizabethtown, Kentucky, denied emphatically that any wedding was ever arranged between Mr. Lincoln and Miss Todd but the one which did take place. That the engagement was broken after a wedding had been talked of, they thought possible; but Mr. Herndon's story, they denied.

"There is not a word of truth in it!" Mrs. Wallace broke out impulsively, before the question about the non-appearance of Mr. Lincoln had been finished. "I never was so amazed in my life as when I read that story. Mr. Lincoln never did such a thing. Why, Mary Lincoln never had a silk dress in her life until she went to Washington."

As Mr. Joshua Speed, of Louisville, Kentucky, was, all through this period, Mr. Lincoln's closest friend, no thought or feeling of the one ever being concealed from the other, Mrs. Joshua Speed was asked if she knew of the story. Mrs. Speed listened in surprise to Mr. Herndon's tale. "I never heard of it before," she declared. "I never heard of it. If it is true, I never heard of it."

While the above investigation was going on, quite unexpectedly a volunteer witness to the falsity of the story appeared. The Hon. H. W. Thornton of Millersburg, Illinois, was a member of the Twelfth General Assembly, which met in Springfield in 1840. During that winter he was boarding near Lincoln, saw him almost every day, was a constant visitor at Mr. Edwards's house, and he knew Miss Todd well. He wrote to the author declaring that Mr. Herndon's statement about the wedding must be false, as he was closely associated with Miss Todd and Mr. Lincoln all winter and never knew anything of it. Mr. Thornton went on to say that he knew beyond a doubt that the sensational account of Lincoln's insanity was untrue, and he quoted from the House journal to show how it was impossible that, as Lamon says, using Herndon's notes, "Lincoln went crazy as a loon, and did not attend the legislature in 1841-1842, for this reason"; or, as Herndon says, that he had to be watched constantly. According to the record taken from the journals of the House by Mr. Thornton, and which have been verified in Springfield, Mr. Lincoln was in his seat in the House on that "fatal first of January" when he is asserted to have been groping in the shadow of madness, and he was also there on the following day. The third of January was Sunday. On Monday, the fourth, he appears not to have been present—at least he did not vote; but even this is by no means conclusive evidence that he was not there. On the fifth, and on every succeeding day until the thirteenth, he was in his seat. From the thirteenth to the eighteenth, inclusive, he is not recorded on any of the roll-calls, and probably was not present. But on the nineteenth, when "John J. Hardin announced his illness to the House," as Mr. Herndon says (which announcement seems not to have gotten into the journal), Lincoln was again in his place, and voted. On the twentieth he is not recorded; but on every subsequent day, until the close of the session on the first of March, Lincoln was in the House. Thus, during the whole of the two months of January and February, he was absent not more than seven days—as good a record of attendance, perhaps, as that made by the average member.

Mr. Thornton says further: "Mr. Lincoln boarded at William Butler's, near to Dr. Henry's, where I boarded. The missing days, from January 13th to 19th, Mr. Lincoln spent several hours each day at Dr. Henry's; a part of these days I remained with Mr. Lincoln. His most intimate friends had no fears of his injuring himself. He was very sad and melancholy, but being subject to these spells, nothing serious was apprehended. His being watched, as stated in Herndon's book, was news to me until I saw it there."

But while Lincoln went about his daily duties, even

on the "fatal first of January,"—the day when he broke his word to Miss Todd—his whole being was shrouded in gloom. He did not pretend to conceal this from his friends. Writing to Mr. Stuart on January 23d, he said:

"I am now the most miserable man living. If what I feel were equally distributed to the whole human family, there would not be one cheerful face on the earth. Whether I shall ever be better, I cannot tell; I awfully forebode I shall not. To remain as I am is impossible. I must die or be better, it appears to me. The matter you speak of on my account you may attend to as you say, unless you shall hear of my condition forbidding it. I say this because I fear I shall be unable to attend to any business here, and a change of scene might help me."

In the summer he visited his friend Speed, who had sold his store in Springfield, and returned to Louisville, Kentucky. The visit did much to brighten his spirits, for, writing back in September, after his return, to his friend's sister, he was even gay.

A curious situation arose the next year (1842), which did much to restore Lincoln to a more normal view of his relation to Miss Todd. In the summer of 1841, his friend Speed had become engaged. As the time for his marriage approached, he in turn was attacked by a melancholy not unlike that from which Lincoln had suffered. He feared he did not love well enough to marry, and he confided his fear to Lincoln. Full of sympathy for the trouble of his friend, Lincoln tried in every way to persuade him that his "twinges of the soul" were all explained by nervous debility. When Speed returned to Kentucky, Lincoln wrote him several letters in which he consoled, counselled, or laughed at him. These letters abound in suggestive passages. From what did Speed suffer? From three special causes and a general one, which Lincoln proceeds to enumerate:

"The general cause is, that you are naturally of a nervous temperament; and this I say from what I have seen of you personally, and what you have told me concerning your mother at various times, and concerning your brother William at the time his wife died. The first special cause is your exposure to bad weather on your journey, which my experience clearly proves to be very severe on defective nerves. The second is the absence of all business and conversation of friends, which might divert your mind, give it occasional rest from the intensity of thought which will sometimes wear the sweetest idea threadbare and turn it to the bitterness of death. The third is the rapid and near approach of that crisis on which all your thoughts and feelings concentrate."

Speed writes that his fiancée is ill, and his letter is full of gloomy forebodings of an early death. Lincoln hails these fears as an omen of happiness.

"I hope and believe that your present anxiety and distress about her health and her life must and will forever banish those horrid doubts which I know you sometimes felt as to the truth of your affection for her. If they can once and forever be removed (and I almost feel a presentiment that the Almighty has sent your present affliction expressly for that object) surely nothing can come in their stead to fill their immeasurable measure of misery. It really appears to me that you yourself ought to rejoice, and not sorrow, at this indubitable evidence of your undying affection for her. Why, Speed, if you do not love her, although you might not wish her death, you would most certainly be resigned to it.

Perhaps this point is no longer a question with you, and my pertinacious dwelling upon it is a rude intrusion upon your feelings. If so, you must pardon me. You know the hell I have suffered on that point, and how tender I am upon it. . . . I am now fully convinced that you love her as ardently as you are capable of loving. Your ever being happy in her presence, and your intense anxiety about her health, if there were nothing else, would place this beyond all dispute in my mind. I incline to think it probable that your nerves will fail you occasionally for a while; but once you get them firmly guarded now, that trouble is over forever. I think, if I were you, in case my mind were not exactly right, I would avoid being idle. I would immediately engage in some business or go to making preparations for it, which would be the same thing."

Mr. Speed's marriage occurred in February, and to the letter announcing it Lincoln replied:

"I opened the letter with intense anxiety and trepidation; so much so, that, although it turned out better than I expected, I have hardly yet, at a distance of ten hours, become calm.

"I tell you, Speed, our forebodings (for which you and I are peculiar) are all the worst sort of nonsense. I fancied, from the time I received your letter of Saturday, that the one of Wednesday was never to come, and yet it *did* come, and what is more, it is perfectly clear, both from its tone and handwriting, that you were much happier, or, if you think the term preferable, less miserable, when you wrote it than when you wrote the last one before. You had so obviously improved at the very time I so much fancied you would have grown worse. You say that something indescribably horrible and alarming still haunts you. You will not say that three months from now, I will venture. When your nerves once get steady now, the whole trouble will be over forever. Nor should you become impatient at their being even very slow in becoming steady. Again you say, you much fear that that Elysium of which you have dreamed so much is never to be realized. Well, if it shall not, I dare swear it will not be the fault of her who is now your wife. I now have no doubt that it is the peculiar misfortune of both you and me to dream dreams of Elysium far exceeding all that anything earthly can realize."

His prophecy was true. In March Speed wrote him that he was "far happier than he had ever expected to be." Lincoln caught at the letter with pathetic eagerness.

"It cannot be told how it now thrills me with joy to hear you say you are 'far happier than you ever expected to be.' That much I know is enough. I know you too well to suppose your expectations were not, at least, sometimes extravagant, and if the reality exceeds them all, I say, Enough, dear Lord. I am not going beyond the truth when I tell you that the short space it took me to read your last letter gave me more pleasure than the total sum of all I have enjoyed since the fatal 1st of January, 1841. Since then it seems to me I should have been entirely happy, but for the never-absent idea that there is one still unhappy whom I have contributed to make so. That still kills my soul. I cannot but reproach myself for even wishing to be happy while she is otherwise. She accompanied a large party on the railroad cars to Jacksonville last Monday, and on her return spoke, so that I heard of it, of having enjoyed the trip exceedingly. God be praised for that."

Evidently Lincoln was still unreconciled to his separation from Miss Todd. In the summer of 1842, only three or four months after the above letter was written, a clever ruse on the part of certain of their friends threw the two unexpectedly together; and an understanding of some kind evidently was reached, for during the season they met secretly at the house of one of Lincoln's friends, Mr. Simeon Francis. It was while these meetings were going on that a burlesque encounter occurred between Lincoln and James Shields, for which Miss Todd was partly responsible, and which no doubt gave just the touch of comedy necessary to relieve their tragedy and restore them to a healthier view of their relations.

Among the Democratic officials then living in Springfield was the auditor of the state, James Shields. He was a hot-headed, blustering Irishman, not without ability, and certainly courageous; a good politician, and, on the whole, a very well-liked man. However, the swagger and noise with which he carried on his duties, and his habit of being continually on the defensive, made him the butt of Whig ridicule. Nothing could have given greater satisfaction to Lincoln and his friends than having an opponent who, whenever they joked him, flew into a rage and challenged them to fight.

At the time Lincoln was visiting Miss Todd at Mr. Francis's house, the Whigs were much excited over the fact that the Democrats had issued an order forbidding the payment of state taxes in state bank-notes. The bank-notes were in fact practically worthless, for the state finances were suffering a violent reaction from the extravagant legislation of 1836 and 1837. One of the popular ways of attacking an obnoxious political doctrine in that day was writing letters from some imaginary backwoods settlement, setting forth in homely vernacular the writer's views of the question and showing how its application affected his part of the world. These letters were really a rude form of the "Biglow Papers" or "Nasby Letters." Soon after the order was issued by the Illinois officials demanding silver instead of banknotes in payment of taxes, Lincoln wrote a letter to a Springfield paper from the "Lost Townships," signing it "Aunt Rebecca." In it he described the plight to which the new order had brought the neighborhood, and he intimated that the only reason for issuing such an order was that the state officers might have their salaries paid in silver. Shields was ridiculed unmercifully in the letter for his vanity and his gallantry.

It happened that there were several young women in Springfield who had received rather too pronounced attention from Mr. Shields, and who were glad to see him tormented. Among them were Miss Todd and her friend, Miss Julia Jayne. Lincoln's letter from the "Lost Townships" was such a success that they followed it up with one in which "Aunt Rebecca" proposed to the gallant auditor, and a few days later they published some very bad verses, signed "Cathleen," celebrating the wedding.

Springfield was highly entertained, less by the verses than by the fury of Shields. He would have satisfaction, he said, and he sent a friend, one General Whitesides, to the paper, to ask for the name of the writer of the communications. The editor, in a quandary, went to Lincoln, who, unwilling that Miss Todd and Miss Jayne should figure in the affair, ordered that his own name be given as the author of letters and poem. This was only about ten days after

GENERAL JAMES SHIELDS.

HIS MARRIAGE ENGAGEMENT

the first letter had appeared, on September 2d, and Lincoln left Springfield in a day or two for a long trip on the circuit. He was at Tremont when, on the morning of the seventeenth, two of his friends, E. H. Merryman and William Butler, drove up hastily. Shields and his friend Whitesides were behind, they said, the irate Irishman vowing that he would challenge Lincoln. They, knowing that Lincoln was "unpractised both as to diplomacy and weapons," had started as soon as they had learned that Shields had left Springfield, had passed him in the night, and were there to see Lincoln through.

It was not long before Shields and Whitesides arrived, and soon Lincoln received a note in which the indignant writer said: "I will take the liberty of requiring a full, positive, and absolute retraction of all offensive allusions used by you in these communications in relation to my private character and standing as a man, as an apology for the insults conveyed in them. This may prevent consequences which no one will regret more than myself."

Lincoln immediately replied that, since Shields had not stopped to inquire whether he really was the author of the articles, had not pointed out what was offensive in them, had assumed facts and hinted at consequences, he could not submit to answer the note. Shields wrote again, but Lincoln simply replied that he could receive nothing but a withdrawal of the first note or a challenge. To this he steadily held, even refusing to answer the question as to the authorship of the letters, which Shields finally put. It was inconsistent with his honor to negotiate for peace with Mr.

Shields, he said, unless Mr. Shields withdrew his former offensive letter. Seconds were immediately named: Whitesides by Shields, Merryman by Lincoln; and though they talked of peace, Whitesides declared he could not mention it to his principal. "He would challenge me next, and as soon cut my throat as not."

This was on the nineteenth, and that night the party returned to Springfield. But in some way the affair had leaked out and, fearing arrest, Lincoln and Merryman left town the next morning. The instructions were left with Butler. If Shields would withdraw his first note and write another asking if Lincoln was the author of the offensive articles, and, if so, asking for gentlemanly satisfaction, then Lincoln had prepared a letter explaining the whole affair. If Shields would not do this, there was nothing to do but fight. Lincoln left the following preliminaries for the duel:

"*First.* Weapons: Cavalry broadswords of the largest size, precisely equal in all respects, and such as now used by the cavalry company at Jacksonville.

"*Second.* Position: A plank ten feet long, and from nine to twelve inches broad, to be firmly fixed on edge, on the ground, as the line between us, which neither is to pass his foot over on forfeit of his life. Next a line drawn on the ground on either side of said plank and parallel with it, each at the distance of the whole length of the sword and three feet additional from the plank; and the passing of his own such line by either party during the fight shall be deemed a surrender of the contest.

"*Third.* Time: On Thursday evening at five o'clock, if you can get it so; but in no case to be at a greater distance of time than Friday evening at five o'clock.

"*Fourth.* Place: Within three miles of Alton, on the opposite side of the river, the particular spot to be agreed on by you."

As Mr. Shields refused to withdraw his first note, the entire party started for the rendezvous across the Mississippi. Lincoln and Merryman drove together in a dilapidated old buggy, in the bottom of which rattled a number of broadswords. It was the morning of the 22d of September when the duellists arrived in town. There are people still living in Alton who remember their coming. "The party arrived about the middle of the morning," says Mr. Edward Levis, "and soon crossed the river to a sand-bar which at the time was, by reason of the low water, a part of the Missouri mainland. The means of conveyance was an old horse-ferry that was operated by a man named Chapman. The weapons were in the keeping of the friends of the principals, and no care was taken to conceal them; in fact, they were openly displayed. Naturally, there was a great desire among the male population to attend the duel, but the managers of the affair would not permit any but their own party to board the ferryboat. Skiffs were very scarce, and but a few could avail themselves of the opportunity in this way. I had to content myself with standing on the levee and watching proceedings at long range."

As soon as the parties reached the island the seconds began preparations for the duel, the principals meanwhile seating themselves on logs on opposite sides of the field—a half-cleared spot in the timber. One of the spectators says:

"I watched Lincoln closely while he sat on his log awaiting the signal to fight. His face was grave and serious. I could discern nothing suggestive of 'Old Abe,' as we knew him. I never knew him to go so long before without making a joke, and I began to believe he was getting frightened. But presently he reached over and picked up one of the swords, which he drew from its scabbard. Then he felt along the edge of the weapon with his thumb, like a barber feels of the edge of his razor, raised himself to his full height, stretched out his long arms and clipped off a twig from above his head with the sword. There wasn't another man of us who could have reached anywhere near that twig, and the absurdity of that long-reaching fellow fighting with cavalry sabers with Shields, who could walk under his arm, came pretty near making me howl with laughter. After Lincoln had cut off the twig he returned the sword to the scabbard with a sigh and sat down, but I detected the gleam in his eye, which was always the forerunner of one of his inimitable yarns, and fully expected him to tell a side-splitter there in the shadow of the grave—Shields's grave."

The arrangements for the affair were about completed when the duellists were joined by some unexpected friends. Lincoln and Merryman, on their way to Alton, had stopped at White Hall for dinner. Across the street from the hotel lived Mr. Elijah Lott, an acquaintance of Merryman. Mr. Lott was not long in finding out what was on foot, and as soon as the duellists had departed, he drove to Carrollton, where he knew that Colonel John J. Hardin and several other friends of Lincoln were attending court, and warned them of the trouble. Hardin and one or two others immediately started for Alton. They arrived in time to calm Shields, and to aid the seconds in adjusting matters "with honor to all concerned."

That the duellists returned in good spirits is evident from Mr. Levis's reminiscences: "It was not very long," says he, "until the boat was seen returning to Alton. As it drew near I saw what was presumably a mortally wounded man lying in the bow of the boat. His shirt appeared to be bathed in blood. I distinguished Jacob Smith, a constable, fanning the supposed victim vigorously. The people on the bank held their breath in suspense, and guesses were feebly made as to which of the two men had been so terribly wounded. But suspense was soon turned to chagrin and relief when it transpired that the supposed candidate for another world was nothing more nor less than a log covered with a red shirt. This ruse had been resorted to in order to fool the people on the levee; and it worked to perfection. Lincoln and Shields came off the boat together, chatting in a nonchalant and pleasant manner."

The Lincoln-Shields duel had so many farcical features, and Miss Todd had unwittingly been so much to blame for it, that one can easily see that it might have had considerable influence on the relations of the two young people. However that may be, something had made Mr. Lincoln feel that he could renew his engagement. Early in October, not a fortnight after the duel, he wrote Speed: "You have now been the husband of a lovely woman nearly eight months. That you are happier now than the day you married her I well know, for without you would not be living. But I have your word for it, too, and the returning elasticity of spirits which is manifested in your letters. But I want to ask a close question: Are you now in feelings as well as judgment glad that you are married as you are?

"From anybody but me this would be an impudent question, not to be tolerated; but I know that you

> **THE PEOPLE OF THE STATE OF ILLINOIS.**
> To any Minister of the Gospel, or other authorised Person—GREETING.
>
> THESE are to License and permit you to join in the holy bands of Matrimony *Abraham Lincoln* and *Mary Todd* of the County of Sangamon and State of Illinois, and for so doing, this shall be your sufficient warrant.
>
> Given under my hand and seal of office, at Springfield, in said County this 4th day of November 1842
>
> N. W. Matheny, Clerk.

Solemnized on the same 4th day of Nov. 1842.   Charles Dresser

FACSIMILE OF MARRIAGE LICENSE AND CERTIFICATE OF ABRAHAM LINCOLN.
From the original on file in the County Clerk's office of Springfield, Ill.

will pardon it in me. Please answer it quickly, as I am impatient to know."

We do not know Speed's answer, nor the final struggle of the man's heart. We only know that on November 4, 1842, Lincoln was married, the wedding being almost impromptu. Mrs. Brown, Miss Todd's cousin, in the same letter quoted from above, describes the wedding:

"One morning, bright and early, my cousin came down in her excited, impetuous way and said to my father: 'Uncle, you must go up and tell my sister that Mr. Lincoln and I are to be married this evening,' and to me: 'Get on your bonnet and go with me to get my gloves, shoes, etc., and then to Mr. Edwards's.' When we reached there we found some excitement over a wedding being sprung upon them so suddenly. However, my father, in his lovely, pacific way, 'poured oil upon the waters,' and we thought everything was 'ship-shape,' when Mrs. Edwards laughingly said: 'How fortunately you selected this evening, for the Episcopal Sewing Society is to meet here, and my supper is all ordered.'

"But that comfortable little arrangement would not hold, as Mary declared she would not make a spectacle for gossiping ladies to gaze upon and talk about; there had already been too much talk about her. Then my father was despatched to tell Mr. Lincoln that the wedding would be deferred until the next evening. Clergyman, attendants and intimate friends were notified, and on Friday evening, in the midst of a small circle of friends, with the elements doing their worst in the way of rain, this singular courtship culminated in marriage. This I know to be literally true, as I was one of her bridesmaids, Miss Jayne (afterwards Mrs. Lyman Trumbull) and Miss Rodney being the others."

CHAPTER XII

LINCOLN BECOMES A CANDIDATE FOR CONGRESS AND IS DEFEATED—ON THE STUMP IN 1844—NOMINATED AND ELECTED TO THE 30TH CONGRESS

For eight successive years Lincoln had been a member of the General Assembly of Illinois. It was quite long enough, in his judgment, and his friends seem to have wanted to give him something better, for in 1841 they offered to support him as a candidate for Governor of the state. This, however, he refused. His ambition was to go to Washington. In 1842 he declined renomination for the Assembly and became a candidate for Congress. He did not wait to be asked, nor did he leave his case in the hands of his friends. He frankly announced his desire and managed his own canvass. There was no reason, in Lincoln's opinion, for concealing political ambition. He recognized, at the same time, the legitimacy of the ambition of his friends, and entertained no suspicion or rancor if they contested places with him.

"Do you suppose that I should ever have got into notice if I had waited to be hunted up and pushed forward by older men?" he wrote his friend Herndon once, when the latter was complaining that the older men did not help him on. "The way for a young man to rise is to improve himself every way he can, never suspecting that anybody wishes to hinder him. Allow me to assure you that suspicion and jealousy never did help any man in any situation. There may sometimes be ungenerous attempts to keep a young man down; and they will succeed, too, if he allows his mind to be diverted from its true channel to brood over the attempted injury. Cast about, and see if this feeling has not injured every person you have ever known to fall into it."

Lincoln had something more to do, however, in 1842, than simply to announce himself in the innocent manner of early politics. The convention system introduced into Illinois in 1835 by the Democrats had been zealously opposed by all good Whigs, Lincoln included, until constant defeat taught them that to resist organization by an every-man-for-himself policy was hopeless and wasteful, and that if they would succeed they must meet organization with organization. In 1841 a Whig State convention had been called to nominate candidates for the offices of Governor and Lieutenant Governor; and now, in March, 1843, a Whig meeting was held again at Springfield, at which the party's platform was laid, and a committee, of which Lincoln was a member, was appointed to prepare an "Address to the People of Illinois." In this address the convention system was earnestly defended. Against this rapid adoption of the abominated system many of the Whigs protested, and Lincoln found himself supporting before his constituents the tactics he had once warmly opposed. In a letter to his friend John Bennett, of Petersburg, written in March, 1843, he said:

"I am sorry to hear that any of the Whigs of your county, or of any county, should longer be against conventions. On last Wednesday evening a meeting of all the Whigs then here from all parts of the state was held, and the question of the propriety of conventions was brought up and fully discussed, and at the end of the discussion a resolution recommending the system of conventions to all the Whigs of the state was unanimously adopted. Other resolutions were also passed, all of which will appear in the next 'Journal.' The meeting also appointed a committee to draft an address to the people of the state, which address will also appear in the next 'Journal.' In it you will find a brief argument in favor of conventions, and, although I wrote it myself, I *will* say to you that it is conclusive upon the point and cannot be reasonably answered.

"If there be any good Whig who is disposed still to stick out against conventions, get him, at least, to read the argument in their favor in the 'Address.' "

The "brief argument" which Lincoln thought so conclusive, "if he did write it himself," justified his good opinion. After its circulation there were few bound to "stick out against conventions."

The Whigs of the various counties in the Congressional district met on April 5, as they had been instructed to do, and chose delegates. John J. Hardin of Jacksonville, Edward D. Baker and Abraham Lincoln of Springfield, were the three candidates for whom these delegates were instructed.

To Lincoln's keen disappointment, the delegation from Sangamon County was instructed for Baker.

A variety of social and personal influences, besides Baker's popularity, worked against Lincoln. "It would astonish, if not amuse, the older citizens," wrote Lincoln to a friend, "to learn that I (a stranger, friendless, uneducated, penniless boy, working on a flatboat at ten dollars per month) have been put down here as the candidate of pride, wealth, and aristocratic family distinction." He was not only accused of being an aristocrat, he was called "a deist." He had fought, or been about to fight, a duel. His wife's relations were Episcopalian and Presbyterian. He and she attended a Presbyterian church. These influences alone could not be said to have defeated him, he wrote, but "they levied a tax of considerable per cent. upon my strength."

The meeting that named Baker as its choice for Congress appointed Lincoln one of the delegates to the convention. "In getting Baker the nomination," Lincoln wrote to Speed, "I shall be fixed a good deal like a fellow who is made a groomsman to a man that has cut him out and is marrying his own dear 'gal.'" From the first, however, he stood bravely by Baker. "I feel myself bound not to hinder him in any way from getting the nomination; I should despise myself were I to attempt it," he wrote certain of his constituents who were anxious that he should attempt to secure the nomination in spite of his instructions. It was soon evident to both Lincoln and Baker that John J. Hardin was probably the strongest candidate in the district, and so it proved when the convention met in May, 1843, at Pekin.

It has frequently been charged that in this Pekin

THE EARLIEST PORTRAIT OF ABRAHAM LINCOLN.   ABOUT 1848.   AGE 39.

From the original daguerreotype, owned by Mr. Lincoln's son, the Hon. Robert T. Lincoln, through whose courtesy it was first published in "McClure's Magazine" for November, 1895.

convention, Hardin, Baker, and Lincoln agreed to take in turn the three next nominations to Congress, thus establishing a species of rotation in office. This charge cannot be sustained. What occurred at the Pekin convention is here related by one of the delegates, the Hon. J. M. Ruggles of Havana, Illinois.

"When the convention assembled," writes Mr. Ruggles, "Baker was there with his friend and champion delegate, Abraham Lincoln. The ayes and noes had been taken, and there were fifteen votes apiece, and one in doubt that had not arrived. That was myself. I was known to be a warm friend of Baker, representing people who were partial to Hardin. As soon as I arrived Baker hurried to me, saying: 'How is it? It all depends on you.' On being told that notwithstanding my partiality for him, the people I represented expected me to vote for Hardin, and that I would have to do so, Baker at once replied: 'You are right—there is no other way.' The convention was organized, and I was elected secretary. Baker immediately arose, and made a most thrilling address, thoroughly arousing the sympathies of the convention, and ended by declining his candidacy. Hardin was nominated by acclamation; and then came the episode.

"Immediately after the nomination, Mr. Lincoln walked across the room to my table and asked if I would favor a resolution recommending Baker for the next term. On being answered in the affirmative, he said: 'You prepare the resolution, I will support it, and I think we can pass it.' The resolution created a profound sensation, especially with the friends of Hardin. After an excited and angry discussion, the resolution passed by a majority of one."

Lincoln supported Hardin energetically in the campaign which followed. In a letter to the former written on May 11th, just after the convention, he says:

"Butler informs me that he received a letter from you in which you expressed some doubt as to whether the Whigs of Sangamon will support you cordially. You may at once dismiss all fears on that subject. We have already resolved to make a particular effort to give you the very largest majority possible in our county. From this no Whig of the county dissents. We have many objects for doing it. We make it a matter of honor and pride to do it; we do it because we love the Whig cause; we do it because we like you personally; and, last, we wish to convince you that we do not bear that hatred to Morgan County that you people have seemed so long to imagine. You will see by the 'Journal' of this week that we propose, upon pain of losing a barbecue, to give you twice as great a majority in this county as you shall receive in your own. I got up the proposal."

Lincoln was true to his promise and after Hardin was elected and in Washington he kept him informed of much that went on in the district; thus in an amusing letter written in May, 1844, while the latter was in Congress, he tells him of one disgruntled constituent who must be pacified, giving him, at the same time, a hint as to the temper of the "Locofocos."

"Knowing that you have correspondents enough, I have forborne to trouble you heretofore," he writes; "and I now only do so to get you to set a matter right which has got wrong with one of our best friends. It is old Uncle Thomas Campbell of Spring Creek (Berlin P. O.). He has received several documents from you, and he says they are old newspapers and old documents, having no sort of interest in them. He is, therefore, getting a strong impression that you treat him with disrespect. This, I know, is a mistaken impression, and you must correct it. The way, I leave to yourself. Robert W. Canfield says he would like to have a document or two from you.

"The Locos here are in considerable trouble about Van Buren's letter on Texas, and the Virginia electors. They are growing sick of the tariff question, and consequently are much confounded at Van Buren's cutting them off from the new Texas question. Nearly half the leaders swear they won't stand it. Of those are Ford, T. Campbell, Ewing, Calhoun, and others. They don't exactly say they won't go for Van Buren, but they say he will not be the candidate, and that *they* are for Texas anyhow."

The resolution passed at the Pekin convention in 1843 was remembered and respected by the Whigs when the time came to nominate Hardin's successor. Baker was selected and elected, Lincoln working for him as loyally as he had for Hardin. In this campaign—that of 1844—Lincoln was a presidential elector. He went into the canvass with unusual ardor, for Henry Clay was the candidate and Lincoln shared the popular idolatry of the man. His devotion was not merely a sentiment, however. He had been an intelligent student of Clay's public life, and his sympathy was all with the principles of the "gallant Harry of the West." Throughout the campaign he worked zealously, travelling all over the state, speaking and talking. As a rule, he was accompanied by a Democrat. The two went unannounced, simply stopping at some friendly house. On their arrival the word was sent around, "the candidates are here," and the men of the neighborhood gathered to hear the discussion, which was carried on in the most informal way, the candidates frequently sitting tipped back against the side of the house, or perched on a rail, whittling during the debates. Nor was all of this electioneering done by argument. Many votes were still cast in Illinois out of personal liking, and the wily candidate did his best to make himself agreeable, particularly to the women of the household. The Hon. William L. D. Ewing, a Democrat who travelled with Lincoln in one campaign, used to tell a story of how he and Lincoln were eager to win the favor of one of their hostesses, whose husband was an important man in his neighborhood. Neither had made much progress until at milking-time Mr. Ewing started after the woman of the house as she went to the yard, took her pail, and insisted on milking the cow himself. He naturally felt that this was a master stroke. But receiving no reply from the hostess, to whom he had been talking loudly as he milked, he looked around, only to see her and Lincoln leaning comfortably over the bars, engaged in an animated discussion. By the time he had completed his self-imposed task, Lincoln had captivated the hostess, and all Mr. Ewing received for his pains was hearty thanks for giving her a chance to have so pleasant a talk with Mr. Lincoln.

Lincoln's speeches at this time were not confined to his own state. He made several in Indiana, being invited there by prominent Whig politicians who had heard him speak in Illinois. The first and most important of his meetings in Indiana was at Bruceville. The Democrats, learning of the proposed Whig gathering, arranged one, for the same evening, with Lieutenant William W. Carr of Vincennes as speaker. As might have been expected from the excited state of politics at the moment, the proximity of the two mass-meetings aroused party loyalty to a fighting

CRAWFORD WELL.

In a field near the Crawford house is a well which is pointed out to sightseers as one which Lincoln helped to dig. Many things about the Crawford place—fences, corn-cribs, house, barn—were built in part by Mr. Lincoln.

THE CRAWFORD HOUSE.

The house of Josiah Crawford, near Gentryville, Indiana. Here Mr. Lincoln worked by the day for several months, and his sister was a "hired girl" for Mrs. Crawford. In 1829 Mr. Lincoln cut down timber and whip-sawed it into planks for a new house which his father proposed to build; but Thomas Lincoln had decided to go to Illinois before the new house was begun, and Abraham sold his planks to Mr. Crawford, who worked them into the southeast room of his house, where relic-seekers have since cut them to pieces to make canes. This picture is made after a photograph taken before the death of Mr. and Mrs. Crawford, both of whom are shown here.

pitch. "Each party was determined to break up the other's speaking," writes Miss O'Flynn, in a description of the Bruceville meeting prepared from interviews with those who took part in it. "The night was made hideous with the rattle of tin pans and bells and the blare of cow-horns. In spite of all the din and uproar of the younger element, a few grown-up male radicals and partisan women sang and cheered loudly for their favorites, who kept on with their flow of political information. Lieutenant Carr stood in his carriage and addressed the crowd around him, while a local politician acted as grand marshal of the night and urged the yelling Democratic legion to surge to the schoolhouse, where Abraham Lincoln was speaking, and run the Whigs from their headquarters. Old men now living, who were big boys then, cannot remember any of the burning eloquence of either speaker. As they now laughingly express it: 'We were far more interested in the noise than the success of the speakers, and we ran backward and forward from one camp to the other.'"

Fortunately, the remaining speeches in Indiana were made under more dignified conditions. One was delivered at Rockport; another "from the door of a harness shop" near Gentryville, Lincoln's old home in Indiana; and a third at the "Old Carter School" in the same neighborhood. At the delivery of the last many of Lincoln's old neighbors were present, and they still tell of the cordial way in which he greeted them and inquired for old friends. After his speech he drove home with Mr. Josiah Crawford, for whom he had once worked as a day laborer. His interest in every familiar spot—a saw-pit where he had once worked—the old swimming pool, the town grocery, the mill, the blacksmith shop, surprised and flattered everybody. "He went round inspecting everything," declares one of his hosts. So vivid were the memories which this visit to Gentryville aroused, so deep were Lincoln's emotions, that he even attempted to express them in verse. A portion of the lines he wrote have been preserved, the only remnants of his various early attempts at versification.

In this campaign of 1844 Lincoln for the second time in his political life met the slavery question. The chief issue of that campaign was the annexation of Texas. The Whigs, under Clay's leadership, opposed it. To annex Texas without the consent of Mexico would compromise our national reputation for fair dealing, Clay argued; it would bring on war with Mexico, destroy the existing relations between North and South and compel the North to annex Canada, and it would tend to extend rather than restrict slavery.

A large party of strong anti-slavery people in the North felt that Clay did not give enough importance to the anti-slavery argument and they nominated a third candidate, James G. Birney. This "Liberal Party" as it was called, had a fair representation in Illinois and Lincoln must have encountered them frequently, though what arguments he used against them, if any, we do not know, no extracts of his 1844 speeches being preserved.

The next year, 1845, he found the abolition sentiment stronger than ever. Prominent among the leaders of the third party in the state were two brothers, Williamson and Madison Durley of Hennepin, Illinois. They were outspoken advocates of their principles, and even operated a station of the underground railroad. Lincoln knew the Durleys, and, when visiting Hennepin, solicited their support. They set up as an obstacle, their liberty principles. On returning to Springfield, Lincoln wrote Williamson Durley a letter which sets forth with admirable clearness his exact position on the slavery question at that period. It is the most valuable document on the question which we have up to this point in Lincoln's life.

"When I saw you at home," Lincoln began, "it was agreed that I should write to you and your brother Madison. Until I then saw you I was not aware of your being what is generally called an Abolitionist, or, as you call yourself, a Liberty man, though I well knew there were many such in your county.

"I was glad to hear that you intended to attempt to bring about, at the next election in Putnam, a union of the Whigs proper and such of the Liberty men as are Whigs in principle on all questions save only that of slavery. So far as I can perceive, by such union neither party need yield anything on *the* point in difference between them. If the Whig Abolitionists of New York had voted with us last fall, Mr. Clay would now be President, Whig principles in the ascendant, and Texas not annexed; whereas, by the division, all that either had at stake in the contest was lost. And, indeed, it was extremely probable, beforehand, that such would be the result. As I always understood, the Liberty men deprecated the annexation of Texas extremely; and this being so, why they should refuse to cast their votes (so) as to prevent it, even to me seemed wonderful. What was their process of reasoning, I can only judge from what a single one of them told me. It was this: 'We are not to do *evil* that *good* may come.' This general proposition is doubtless correct; but did it apply? If by your votes you could have prevented the *extension*, etc., of slavery, would it not have been *good*, and not *evil*, so to have used your votes, even though it involved the casting of them for a slave-holder? By the *fruit* the tree is to be known. An *evil* tree cannot bring forth *good* fruit. If the fruit of electing Mr. Clay would have been to prevent the extension of slavery, could the act of electing have been evil?

"But I will not argue further. I perhaps ought to say that individually I never was much interested in the Texas question. I never could see much good to come of annexation, inasmuch as they were already a free republican people on our own model. On the other hand, I never could very clearly see how the annexation would augment the evil of slavery. It always seemed to me that slaves would be taken there in about equal numbers, with or without annexation. And if more *were* taken because of annexation, still there would be just so many the fewer left where they were taken from. It is possibly true, to some extent, that, with annexation, some slaves may be sent to Texas and continued in slavery that otherwise might have been liberated. To whatever extent this may be true, I think annexation an evil. I hold it to be a paramount duty of us in the free states, due to the Union of the states, and perhaps to liberty itself (paradox though it may seem), to let the slavery of the other states alone; while, on the other hand, I hold it to be equally clear that we should never knowingly lend ourselves, directly or indirectly, to prevent that slavery from dying a natural death—to find new places for it to live in, when it can no longer exist in the old. Of course I am not now considering what would be our duty in cases of insurrection among the slaves. To recur to the Texas question, I understand the Liberty men to have viewed annexation as a much greater evil than ever I did; and I would like to convince you, if I could, that they could have prevented it without violation of principle, if they had chosen."

At the time that Lincoln wrote the above letter to the Durley brothers he was working for a nomination to Congress. In 1843 he had helped elect his friend Hardin. He had secured the nomination for Baker in 1844 and had worked faithfully to elect him. Now he felt that his duty to his friends was discharged and that he was free to try for himself. He undoubtedly hoped that neither of his friends would contest the nomination. Baker did not, but late in 1845 it became evident that Hardin might. Lincoln was worried over the prospect. "The paper at Pekin has nominated Hardin for governor," he wrote his friend, B. F. James, in November, "and, commenting on this, the Alton papers indirectly nominated him for Congress. It would give Hardin a great start, and perhaps use me up, if the Whig papers of the district should nominate him for Congress. If your feelings toward me are the same as when you saw me (which I have no reason to doubt), I wish you would let nothing appear in your paper which may operate against me. You understand. Matters stand just as they did when I saw you. Baker is certainly off the track, and I fear Hardin intends to be on it."

Hardin certainly was free to run for Congress if he wanted to. He had voluntarily declined the nomination in 1844, because of the events of the Pekin convention, but he had made no promise to do so in 1846. Many of the Whigs of the district had not expected him to be a candidate, however, arguing that Lincoln, because of his relation to the party, should be given his turn. "We do not entertain a doubt," wrote the editor of the "Sangamon Journal," in February, 1846, "that if we could reverse the positions of the two men, a very large portion of those who now support Mr. Lincoln most warmly would support General Hardin quite as well."

As time went on and Lincoln found in all probability that Hardin would enter the race, it made him anxious and a little melancholy. In writing to his friend, Dr. Robert Boal, of Lacon, Illinois, on January 7, 1846, he said:

"Since I saw you last fall, I have often thought of writing you, as it was then understood I would; but, on reflection, I have always found that I had nothing new to tell you. All has happened as I then told you I expected it would— Baker's declining, Hardin's taking the track, and so on.

"If Hardin and I stood precisely equal—that is, if *neither* of us had been to Congress, or if we *both* had—it would not only accord with what I have always done, for the sake of peace, to give way to him; and I expect I should do it. That I *can* voluntarily postpone my pretensions, when they are no more than equal to those to which they are postponed, you have yourself seen. But to yield to Hardin under present circumstances seems to me as nothing else than yielding to one who would gladly sacrifice me altogether. This I would rather not submit to. That Hardin is talented, energetic, unusually generous and magnanimous, I have, before this, affirmed to you, and do not now deny. You know that my only argument is that 'turn about is fair play.' This he, practically at least, denies.

"If it would not be taxing you too much, I wish you would write me, telling the aspect of things in your county, or rather your district; and also send the names of some of your Whig neighbors to whom I might, with propriety, write. Unless I can get some one to do this, Hardin, with his old franking list, will have the advantage of me. My reliance for a fair shake (and I want nothing more) in your county

BECOMES A CANDIDATE FOR CONGRESS 237

is chiefly on you, because of your position and standing, and because I am acquainted with so few others. Let me hear from you soon."

Lincoln followed the vibrations of feeling in the various counties with extreme nicety, studying every individual whose loyalty he suspected or whose vote was not yet pledged. "Nathan Dresser is here," he wrote to his friend Bennett, on January 15, 1846, "and speaks as though the contest between Hardin and me is to be doubtful in Menard County. I know he is candid, and this alarms me some. I asked him to tell me the names of the men that were going strong for Hardin; he said Morris was about as strong as any. Now tell me, is Morris going it openly? You remember you wrote me that he would be neutral. Nathan also said that some man (whom he could not remember) had said lately that Menard County was again to decide the contest, and that made the contest very doubtful. Do you know who that was?

"Don't fail to write me instantly on receiving, telling me all—particularly the names of those who are going strong against me."

In January, General Hardin suggested that since he and Lincoln were the only persons mentioned as candidates, there be no convention, but the selection be left to the Whig voters of the district. Lincoln refused.

"It seems to me," he wrote Hardin, "that on reflection you will see the fact of your having been in Congress has, in various ways, so spread your name in the district as to give you a decided advantage in such a stipulation. I appreciate your desire to keep down excitement; and I promise you to 'keep cool' under all circumstances. . . . I have always been in the habit of acceding to almost any proposal that a friend would make, and I am truly sorry that I cannot in this. I perhaps ought to mention that some friends at different places are endeavoring to secure the honor of the sitting of the convention at their towns respectively, and I fear that they would not feel much complimented if we shall make a bargain that it should sit nowhere."

After General Hardin received this refusal he withdrew from the contest in a manly and generous letter which was warmly approved by the Whigs of the district. Both men were so much loved that a break between them would have been a disastrous thing for the party. "We are truly glad that a contest which in its nature was calculated to weaken the ties of friendship has terminated amicably," said the "Sangamon Journal."

The charge that Hardin, Baker, and Lincoln tried to ruin one another in this contest for Congress has often been denied by their associates, and never more emphatically than by Judge Gillespie, an influential politician of the state. "Hardin," Judge Gillespie says, "was one of the most unflinching and unfaltering Whigs that ever drew the breath of life. He was a mirror of chivalry, and so was Baker. Lincoln had boundless respect for, and confidence in, them both. He knew they would sacrifice themselves rather than do an act that could savor in the slightest degree of meanness or dishonor. These men, Lincoln, Hardin and Baker, were bosom friends, to my certain knowledge. . . . Lincoln felt that they could be actuated by nothing but the most honorable sentiments towards him. For although they were rivals, they were all three men of the most punctilious honor, and devoted friends. I knew them intimately, and can say confidently that there never was a particle of envy on the part of one towards the other. The rivalry between them was of the most honorable and friendly character, and when Hardin and Baker were killed (Hardin in Mexico, and Baker at Ball's Bluff) Lincoln felt that in the death of each he had lost a dear and true friend."

After Hardin's withdrawal, Lincoln went about in his characteristic way trying to soothe his and Hardin's friends. "Previous to General Hardin's withdrawal," he wrote one of his correspondents, "some of his friends and some of mine had become a little warm; and I felt . . . that for them now to meet face to face and converse together was the best way to efface any remnant of unpleasant feeling, if any such existed. I did not suppose that General Hardin's friends were in any greater need of having their feelings corrected than mine were."

In May, Lincoln was nominated. His Democratic opponent was Peter Cartwright, the famous Methodist exhorter, the most famous itinerant preacher of the pioneer era. Cartwright had moved from Kentucky to Illinois when still a young man to get into a free state, and had settled in the Sangamon Valley, near Springfield. For the next forty years he travelled over the state, most of the time on horseback, preaching the Gospel in his unique and rugged fashion. His district was at first so large (extending from Kaskaskia to Galena) that he was unable to traverse the whole of it in the same year. He was elected to the legislature in 1828 and again in 1832; Lincoln, in the latter year, being an opposing candidate. In 1840 when he was the Democratic nominee for Congress against Lincoln he was badly beaten. Cartwright now made an energetic canvass, his chief weapon against Lincoln being the old charges of atheism and aristocracy; but they failed of effect, and in August, Lincoln was elected.

The contest over, sudden and characteristic disillusion seized him. "Being elected to Congress, though I am grateful to our friends for having done it, has not pleased me as much as I expected," he wrote Speed.

THE BIRTHPLACE OF ABRAHAM LINCOLN.
Near Hodgenville, La Rue County, Kentucky.

CHAPTER XIII

LINCOLN IN WASHINGTON IN 1847—HE OPPOSES THE MEXICAN WAR—CAMPAIGNING IN NEW ENGLAND

IN November, 1847, Lincoln started for Washington. The city in 1848 was little more than the outline of the present Washington. The capitol was without its wings, dome, or western terrace. The White House, the City Hall, the Treasury, the Patent Office, and the Post-Office were the only public buildings standing then which have not been rebuilt or materially changed. The streets were unpaved, and their dust in summer and mud in winter are celebrated in every record of the period. The parks and circles were still unplanted. Near the White House were a few fine old homes, and Capitol Hill was partly built over. Although there were deplorable wastes between these two points, the majority of the people lived in the southeastern part of the city, on or near Pennsylvania Avenue. The winter that Lincoln was in Washington, Daniel Webster lived on Louisiana Avenue, near Sixth Street; Speaker Winthrop and Thomas H. Benton on C Street, near Third; John Quincy Adams and James Buchanan, the latter then Secretary of State, on F Street, between Thirteenth and Fourteenth. Many of the senators and congressmen were in hotels, the leading ones of which were Willard's, Coleman's Gadsby's, Brown's, Young's, Fuller's, and the United States. Stephen A. Douglas, who was in Washington for his first term as senator, lived at Willard's. So inadequate were the hotel accommodations during the sessions that visitors to the town were frequently obliged to accept most uncomfortable makeshifts for beds. Seward, visiting the city in 1847, tells of sleeping on "a cot between two beds occupied by strangers."

The larger number of members lived in "messes," a species of boarding-club, over which the owner of the house occupied usually presided. The "National Intelligencer" of the day is sprinkled with announcements of persons "prepared to accommodate a mess of members." Lincoln went to live in one of the best known of these clubs, Mrs. Spriggs's, in "Duff Green's Row," on Capitol Hill. This famous row has now entirely disappeared, the ground on which it stood being occupied by the Congressional Library.

At Mrs. Spriggs's, Lincoln had as mess-mates several congressmen: A. R. McIlvaine, James Pollock, John Strohm, and John Blanchard, all of Pennsylvania, Patrick Tompkins of Mississippi, Joshua R. Giddings of Ohio, and Elisha Embree of Indiana. Among his neighbors in messes on Capitol Hill were Andrew Johnson of Tennessee, Alexander H. Stephens of Georgia, and Jefferson Davis of Mississippi. One of the members of the mess at Mrs. Spriggs's in the winter of 1847-1848 was Dr. S. C. Busey of Washington, D. C.

"I soon learned to know and admire Lincoln," says Dr. Busey in his "Personal Reminiscences and Recollections," "for his simple and unostentatious manners, kind-heartedness, and amusing jokes, anecdotes, and witticisms. When about to tell an anecdote during a meal he would lay down his knife and fork, place his elbows upon the table, rest his face between his hands, and begin with the words, 'That reminds me,' and proceed. Everybody prepared for the explosion sure to follow. I recall with vivid pleasure the scene of merriment at the dinner after his first speech in the House of Representatives, occasioned by the descriptions, by himself and others of the congressional mess, of the uproar in the House during its delivery.

"Congressman Lincoln was always neatly but very plainly dressed, very simple and approachable in manner, and unpretentious. He attended to his business, going promptly to the House and remaining till the session adjourned, and appeared to be familiar with the progress of legislation."

The town offered then little in the way of amusement. The Adelphi Theater was opened that winter for the first time, and presented a variety of mediocre plays. At the Olympia were "lively and beautiful exhibitions of model artists." Herz and Sivori, the pianists, then touring in the United States, played several times in the season; and there was a Chinese museum. Add the exhibitions of Brown's paintings of the heroes of Palo Alto, Resaca, Monterey, and Buena Vista, and of Powers's "Greek Slave," the performances of Dr. Valentine, "Delineator of Eccentricities," a few lectures, and numerous church socials, and you have about all there was in the way of public entertainments in Washington in 1848. But of dinners, receptions, and official gala affairs there were many. Lincoln's name appears frequently in the "National Intelligencer" on committees to offer dinners to this or that great man. In the spring of 1849 he was one of the managers of the inaugural ball given to Taylor. His friend Washburne recalls an amusing incident of Lincoln at this ball. "A small number of mutual friends," says Mr. Washburne, "including Mr. Lincoln, made up a party to attend the inauguration ball together. It was by far the most brilliant inauguration ball ever given. Of course Mr. Lincoln had never seen anything of the kind before. One of the most modest and unpretending persons present, he could not have dreamed that like honors were to come to him, almost within a little more than a decade. He was greatly interested in all that was to be seen, and we did not take our departure until three or four o'clock in the morning. When we went to the cloak and hat room, Mr. Lincoln had no trouble in finding his short cloak, which little more than covered his shoulders, but, after a long search was unable to find his hat. After an hour he gave up all idea of finding it. Taking his cloak on his arm, he walked out into Judiciary Square, deliberately adjusting it on his shoulders, and started off bare-headed for his lodgings. It would be hard to forget the sight of that tall and slim man, with his short cloak thrown over his shoulders, starting for his long walk home on Capitol Hill, at four o'clock in the morning, without any hat on."

Another reminiscence of his homely and independent ways comes from the librarian of the Supreme Court at that period, through Lincoln's friend, Washburne. Mr. Lincoln, the story goes, came to the library one day for the purpose of procuring some law books which he wanted to take to his room for examination. Getting together all the books he wanted, he placed them in a pile on a table. Taking a large bandana handkerchief from his pocket, he tied them up and, putting the stick he carried through a knot made in the handkerchief, he shouldered the package and marched off from the library to his room. In a few days he returned the books in the same way.

Lincoln's simple, sincere friendliness and his quaint humor soon won him a sure, if quiet, social position in Washington. He was frequently invited to Mr. Webster's Saturday breakfasts, where his stories were highly relished for their originality and drollery. Dr. Busey recalls his popularity at one of the leading places of amusement on Capitol Hill.

"Congressman Lincoln was very fond of bowling," he says, "and would frequently join others of the mess, or meet other members in a match game, at the alley of James Casparis, which was near the boarding-house. He was a very awkward bowler, but played the game with great zest and spirit, solely for exercise and amusement, and greatly to the enjoyment and entertainment of the other players and bystanders by his criticisms and funny illustrations. He accepted success and defeat with like good nature and humor, and left the alley at the conclusion of the game without a sorrow or disappointment. When it was known that he was in the alley, there would assemble numbers of people to witness the fun which was anticipated by those who knew of his fund of anecdotes and jokes. When in the alley, surrounded by a crowd of eager listeners, he indulged with great freedom in the sport of narrative, some of which were very broad. His witticisms seemed for the most part to be impromptu, but he always told the anecdotes and jokes as if he wished to convey the impression that he had heard them from some one; but they appeared very many times as if they had been made for the immediate occasion."

Another place where he became at home and was much appreciated was in the post-office at the Capitol.

"During the Christmas holidays," says Ben. Perley Poore, "Mr. Lincoln found his way into the small room used as the post-office of the House, where a few jovial raconteurs used to meet almost every morning, after the mail had been distributed into the members' boxes, to exchange such new stories as any of them might have acquired since they had last met. After modestly standing at the door for several days, Mr. Lincoln was reminded of a story, and by New Year's he was recognized as the champion story-teller of the Capitol. His favorite seat was at the left of the open fireplace, tilted back in his chair, with his long legs reaching over to the chimney jamb. He never told a story twice, but appeared to have an endless *répertoire* of them always ready, like the successive charges in a magazine gun, and always pertinently adapted to some passing event. It was refreshing to us correspondents, compelled as we were to listen to so much that was prosy and tedious, to hear this bright specimen of western genius tell his inimitable stories, especially his reminiscences of the Black Hawk war."

But Lincoln had gone to Washington for work, and he at once interested himself in the Whig organization formed to elect the officers of the House. There was only a small Whig majority, and it took skill and energy to keep the offices in the party. Lincoln's share in achieving this result was generally recognized. As late as 1860, twelve years after the struggle, Robert C. Winthrop of Massachusetts, who was elected speaker, said in a speech in Boston discussing Lincoln's nomination to the Presidency: "You will be sure that I remember him with interest, if I may be allowed to remind you that he helped to make me the speaker of the Thirtieth Congress, when the vote was a very close and strongly contested vote."

A week after Congress organized, Lincoln wrote to Springfield: "As you are all so anxious for me to distinguish myself, I have concluded to do so before long"; and he did it—but not exactly as his Springfield friends wished. The United States was then at war with Mexico, a war that the Whigs abhorred. Lincoln had used his influence against it; but, hostilities declared, he had publicly affirmed that every loyal man must stand by the army. Many of his friends, Hardin, Baker, and Shields, among others, were at that moment in Mexico. Lincoln had gone to Washington intending to say nothing in opposition to the war. But the administration wished to secure from the Whigs not only votes of supplies and men, but a resolution declaring that the war was just and right. Lincoln, with others of his party in Congress, refused his sanction and voted for a resolution offered by Mr. Ashburn, which declared that the war had been "unnecessarily and unconstitutionally" begun. On December 22d he made his début in the House by the famous "Spot Resolutions," a series of searching questions so clearly put, so strong historically and logically, that they drove the administration from the "spot" where the war began, and showed that it had been the aggressor in the conquest. The resolution ran:—

"*Whereas,* The President of the United States, in his message of May 11, 1846, has declared that 'the Mexican Government not only refused to receive him (the envoy of the United States), or to listen to his propositions, but, after a long-continued series of menaces, has at last invaded our territory and shed the blood of our fellow-citizens on our own soil.'

"And again, in his message of December 8, 1846, that 'we had ample cause of war against Mexico long before the breaking out of hostilities; but even then we forbore to take redress into our own hands until Mexico herself became the aggressor, by invading our soil in hostile array and shedding the blood of our citizens.'

"And yet again, in his message of December 7, 1847, that 'The Mexican Government refused even to hear the terms of adjustment which he (our minister of peace) was authorized to propose, and finally, under wholly unjustifiable pretexts, involved the two countries in war, by invading the territory of the State of Texas, striking the first blow and shedding the blood of our citizens on our own soil.'

"*And whereas*, This House is desirous to obtain a full knowledge of all the facts which go to establish whether the particular spot on which the blood of our citizens was so shed was or was not at that time our own soil: therefore,

"*Resolved*, by the House of Representatives, that the President of the United States be respectfully requested to inform this House—

"First. Whether the spot on which the blood of our citizens was shed, as in his message declared, was or was not within the territory of Spain, at least after the treaty of 1819 until the Mexican revolution.

"Second. Whether that spot is or is not within the territory which was wrested from Spain by the revolutionary Government of Mexico.

"Third. Whether that spot is or is not within a settlement of people, which settlement has existed ever since long before the Texas revolution and until its inhabitants fled before the approach of the United States army.

"Fourth. Whether that settlement is or is not isolated from any and all other settlements by the Gulf and the Rio

Grande on the south and west, and by wide uninhabited regions on the north and east.

"Fifth. Whether the people of that settlement, or a majority of them, or any of them, have ever submitted themselves to the government or laws of Texas or of the United States, by consent or by compulsion, either by accepting office, or voting at elections, or paying tax, or serving on juries, or having process served upon them, or in any other way.

"Sixth. Whether the people of that settlement did or did not flee from the approach of the United States army, leaving unprotected their homes and their growing crops, *before* the blood was shed, as in the message stated; and whether the first blood, so shed, was or was not shed within the inclosure of one of the people who had thus fled from it.

"Seventh. Whether our citizens, whose blood was shed, as in his message declared, were or were not, at that time, armed officers and soldiers, sent into that settlement by the military order of the President, through the Secretary of War.

"Eighth. Whether the military force of the United States was or was not so sent into that settlement after General Taylor had more than once intimated to the War Department that, in his opinion, no such movement was necessary to the defence or protection of Texas."

In January Lincoln followed up these resolutions with a speech in support of his position. His action was much criticised in Illinois, where the sound of the drum and the intoxication of victory had completely turned attention from the moral side of the question, and Lincoln found himself obliged to defend his position with even Mr. Herndon, his law partner, who, with many others, objected to Lincoln's voting for the Ashburn resolution.

"That vote," wrote Lincoln in answer to Mr. Herndon's letter, "affirms that the war was unnecessarily and unconstitutionally commenced by the President; and I will stake my life that if you had been in my place you would have voted just as I did. Would you have voted what you felt and knew to be a lie? I know you would not. Would you have gone out of the House—skulked the vote? I expect not. If you had skulked one vote, you would have had to skulk many more before the end of the session. Richardson's resolutions, introduced before I made any move or gave any vote upon the subject, make the direct question of the justice of the war; so that no man can be silent if he would. You are compelled to speak; and your only alternative is to tell the truth or a lie. I cannot doubt which you would do.

"This vote has nothing to do in determining my votes on the questions of supplies. I have always intended, and still intend, to vote supplies; perhaps not in the precise form recommended by the President, but in a better form for all purposes, except Locofoco party purposes." . . .

This determination to keep the wrong of the Mexican War before the people even while voting supplies for it Lincoln held to steadily. In May a pamphlet was sent him in which the author claimed that "in view of all the facts" the government of the United States had committed no aggression in Mexico.

"Not in view of all the facts," Lincoln wrote him. "There are facts which you have kept out of view. It is a fact that the United States army in marching to the Rio Grande marched into a peaceful Mexican settlement and frightened the inhabitants away from their homes and their growing crops. It is a fact that Fort Brown, opposite Matamoras, was built by that army within a Mexican cotton-field, on which at the time the army reached it a young cotton crop was growing, and which crop was wholly destroyed and the field itself greatly and permanently injured by ditches, embankments, and the like. It is a fact that when the Mexicans captured Captain Thornton and his command, they found and captured them within another Mexican field.

"Now I wish to bring these facts to your notice and to ascertain what is the result of your reflections upon them. If you deny that they are facts, I think I can furnish proofs which shall convince you that you are mistaken. If you admit that they are facts, then I shall be obliged for a reference to any law of language, law of States, law of nations, law of morals, law of religions, any law, human or divine, in which an authority can be found for saying those facts constitute 'No aggression.'

"Possibly you consider those acts too small for notice. Would you venture to so consider them had they been committed by any nation on earth against the humblest of our people? I know you would not. Then I ask, Is the precept 'Whatsoever ye would that men should do to you, do ye even so to them' obsolete? of no force? of no application?"

The routine work assigned Lincoln in the Thirtieth Congress was on the committee on the post-office and post roads. Several reports were made by him from this committee. These reports, with a speech on internal improvements, cover his published work in the House up to July.

As the Whigs were to hold their national convention for nominating a candidate for the presidency in June, Lincoln gave considerable time during the spring to electioneering. In his judgment the Whigs could elect nobody but General Taylor and he urged his friends in Illinois to give up Henry Clay, to whom many of them still clung. "Mr. Clay's chance for an election," he wrote, "is just no chance at all."

Lincoln went to the convention, which was held in

Philadelphia, and as he prophesied, "Old Rough and Ready" was nominated. He went back to Washington full of enthusiasm. "In my opinion we shall have a most overwhelming, glorious triumph," he wrote a friend. "One unmistakable sign is that all the odds and ends are with us—Barnburners, Native Americans, Tyler men, disappointed office-seekers, Locofocos, and the Lord knows what. This is important, if in nothing else, in showing which way the wind blows."

In connection with Alexander H. Stephens, of whom he had become a warm friend, Toombs, and Preston, Lincoln formed the first Congressional Taylor Club, known as the "Young Indians." Campaigning had already begun on the floor of Congress, and the members were daily making speeches for the various candidates. On July 27th Lincoln made a speech for Taylor. It was a boisterous election speech, full of merciless caricaturing, and delivered with inimitable drollery. It kept the House in an uproar, and was reported the country over by the Whig press. The "Baltimore American," in giving a synopsis of it, called it the "crack speech of the day," and said of Lincoln:

"He is a very able, acute, uncouth, honest, upright man, and a tremendous wag, withal. . . . Mr. Lincoln's manner was so good-natured, and his style so peculiar, that he kept the House in a continuous roar of merriment for the last half hour of his speech. He would commence a point in his speech far up one of the aisles, and keep on talking, gesticulating, and walking until he would find himself, at the end of a paragraph, down in the centre of the area in front of the clerk's desk. He would then go back and take another *head*, and *work down* again. And so on, through his capital speech."

This speech, as well as the respect Lincoln's work in the House had inspired among the leaders of the party, brought him an invitation to deliver several campaign speeches in New England at the close of Congress, and he went there early in September. There was in New England, at that date, much strong anti-slavery feeling. The Whigs claimed to be "Free Soilers" as well as the party which appropriated that name, and Lincoln began his campaign by defining carefully his position on the slavery question. This was at Worcester, Massachusetts, on September 12th. The Whig State convention had met to nominate a candidate for governor, and the most eminent Whigs of Massachusetts were present. Curiously enough the meeting was presided over by ex-Governor Levi Lincoln, a descendant, like Abraham Lincoln, from the original Samuel of Hingham. There were many brilliant speeches made; but if we are to trust the reports of the day, Lincoln's was the one which by its logic, its clearness, and its humor did most for the Whig cause. "Gentlemen inform me," says one Boston reporter, who came too late for the exercises, "that it was one of the best speeches ever heard in Worcester, and that several Whigs who had gone off on the 'free soil' fizzle have come back again to the Whig ranks."

A report of the speech was printed in the Boston "Advertiser." According to this report, Lincoln spent the first part of his hour in defending General

Taylor against the charge of having no principles and in proving him a good Whig.

"Mr. Lincoln then passed," says the "Advertiser," "to the subject of slavery in the states, saying that the people of Illinois agreed entirely with the people of Massachusetts on this subject, except, perhaps, that they did not keep so constantly thinking about it. All agreed that slavery was an evil, but that we were not responsible for it, and cannot affect it in states of this Union where we do not live. But the question of the *extension* of slavery to new territories of this country is a part of our responsibility and care, and is under our control. In opposition to this Mr. Lincoln believed that the self-named 'Free Soil' Party was far behind the Whigs. Both parties opposed the extension. As he understood it, the new party had no principle except this opposition. If their platform held any other, it was in such a general way that it was like the pair of pantaloons the Yankee peddler offered for sale, 'large enough for any man, small enough for any boy.' They therefore had taken a position calculated to break down their single important declared object. They were working for the election of either General Cass or General Taylor. The speaker then went on to show, clearly and eloquently, the danger of extension of slavery likely to result from the election of General Cass. To unite with those who annexed the new territory, to prevent the extension of slavery in that territory, seemed to him to be in the highest degree absurd and ridiculous. Suppose these gentlemen succeed in electing Mr. Van Buren, they had no specific means to *prevent* the extension of slavery to New Mexico and California; and General Taylor, he confidently believed, would not encourage it and would not prohibit its restriction. But if General Cass was elected, he felt certain that the plans of farther extension of territory would be encouraged, and those of the extension of slavery would meet no check. The 'Free Soil' men, in claiming that name, indirectly attempt a deception, by implying that Whigs were *not* Free Soil men. In declaring that they would 'do their duty and leave the consequences to God,' they merely gave an excuse for taking a course they were not able to maintain by a fair and full argument. To make this declaration did not show what their duty was. If it did, we should have no use for judgment; we might as well be made without intellect; and when divine or human law does not clearly point out what *is* our duty, we have no means of finding out what it is but using our most intelligent judgment of the consequences. If there were divine law or human law for voting for Martin Van Buren, or if a fair examination of the consequences and first reasoning would show that voting for him would bring about the ends they pretended to wish, then he would give up the argument. But since there was no fixed law on the subject, and since the whole probable result of their action would be an assistance in electing General Cass, he must say that they were behind the Whigs in their advocacy of the freedom of the soil.

"Mr. Lincoln proceeded to rally the Buffalo convention for forbearing to say anything—after all the previous declarations of those members who were formerly Whigs—on the subject of the Mexican War because the Van Burens had been known to have supported it. He declared that of all the parties asking the confidence of the country, this new one had *less* of principle than any other.

"He wondered whether it was still the opinion of these Free Soil gentlemen, as declared in the 'whereas' at Buffalo, that the Whig and Democratic parties were both entirely dissolved and absorbed into their own body. Had the *Vermont* election given them any light? They had calculated on making as great an impression in that state as in any part of the Union, and there their attempts had been wholly ineffectual. Their failure there was a greater success than they would find in any other part of the Union.

"At the close of this truly masterly and convincing speech" the "Advertiser" goes on, "the audience gave three enthusiastic cheers for Illinois, and three more for the eloquent Whig member from that state."

After the speech at Worcester, Lincoln spoke at Lowell, Dedham, Roxbury, Chelsea and Cambridge and on September 22d, in Tremont Temple, Boston, following a splendid oration by Governor Seward. Lincoln's speech on this occasion was not reported, though the Boston papers united in calling it "powerful and convincing." His success at Worcester and Boston was such that invitations came from all over New England asking him to speak.

But Lincoln won something in New England of vastly deeper importance than a reputation for making popular campaign speeches. Here for the first time he caught a glimpse of the utter impossibility of ever reconciling the northern conviction that slavery was evil and unendurable, and the southern claim that it was divine and necessary; and he began here to realize that something must be done.

The first impression of slavery which Abraham Lincoln received was in his childhood in Kentucky. His father and mother belonged to a small company of western abolitionists, who at the beginning of the century boldly denounced the institution as an iniquity. So great an evil did Thomas and Nancy Lincoln hold slavery that to escape it they were willing to leave their Kentucky home and move to a free state. Thus their boy's first notion of the institution was that it was something to flee from, a thing so dreadful that it was one's duty to go to pain and hardship to escape it.

In his new home in Indiana he heard the debate on

THOMAS LINCOLN'S HOME IN ILLINOIS.

Built by Thomas Lincoln in 1831, on Goose Neck Prairie, Coles County, Illinois. He died here in 1851. The cabin was occupied until 1891, when it was bought by the Lincoln Log Cabin Association to be shown at the World's Fair in 1893.

slavery go on. The state he had moved into was in a territory made free forever by the ordinance of 1787, but there were still slaves and believers in slavery within its boundaries and it took many years to eradicate them. Close to his Indiana home lay Illinois and here the same struggle went on through all his boyhood. The lad was too thoughtful not to reflect on what he heard and read of the differences of opinions on slavery. By the time the Statutes of Indiana fell into his hands—some time before he was eighteen years old—he had gathered a large amount of practical information about the question which he was able then to weigh in the light of the great principles of the Constitution, the ordinance of 1787, and the laws of Indiana, which he had begun to study with passionate earnestness.

When he left Indiana for Illinois he continued to be thrown up against slavery. In his trip in 1831 to New Orleans he saw its most terrible features. As a young legislator he saw the citizens of his town and his fellows in the legislature ready to condemn as "dangerous agitators" those who dared call slavery an evil, saw them secretly sympathize with outlawry like the Alton riot and the murder of Elijah Lovejoy. So keenly did he feel the danger of passing resolutions against abolitionists which tacitly implied that slavery was as the South was beginning to claim, a divine institution that in 1837, he was one of the only two members of the Illinois Assembly who were willing to publicly declare "that the institution of slavery is founded on both injustice and bad policy."

From time to time as he travelled on the Mississippi

and Ohio he saw the workings of slavery. In 1841, coming home from a visit to Louisville, Ky., he saw in the boat a gang of chained negroes; the sight so impressed him that he described it to a friend:

"A gentleman had purchased twelve negroes in different parts of Kentucky and was taking them to a farm in the South. They were chained six and six together. A small iron clevis was around the left wrist of each, and this fastened to the main chain by a shorter one, at a convenient distance from the others, so that the negroes were strung together precisely like so many fish upon a trout-line. In this condition they were being separated forever from the scenes of their childhood, their friends, their fathers and mothers, and brothers and sisters, and many of them from their wives and children, and going into perpetual slavery, where the lash of the master is proverbially more ruthless and unrelenting than any other where; and yet amid all these distressing circumstances, as we would think them, they were the most cheerful and apparently happy creatures on board. One whose offense for which he had been sold was an overfondness for his wife, played the fiddle almost continually, and the others danced, sang, cracked jokes, and played various games with cards from day to day. How true it is that 'God tempers the wind to the shorn lamb,' or in other words, that he renders the worst of human conditions tolerable, while he permits the best to be nothing better than tolerable."

Runaway slaves, underground railway stations, masters and men tracking negroes, the occasional capture of a man or woman to be taken back to the South, trials of fugitives—all the features common in those years particularly in the states bordering on bond territory Lincoln saw. In 1847 he was even engaged to defend a slave-owner's claim, a case he lost, the negro being allowed to go free.

It was not until 1844-45, however, that the matter became an important element in his political life. Heretofore it had been for him a moral question, now, however, the annexation of Texas made it a political one. It became necessary that every politician and voter decide whether the new territory should be bond or free. The abolitionists, or Liberty party, grew rapidly in Illinois. Lincoln found himself obliged to meet not only Democratic arguments, but abolition theories and convictions. When in 1847 he went to Congress it was already evident that the Mexican War would be settled by the acquisition of large new territory. What was to be done with it? The North had tried to forestall the South by bringing in a provision that whatever territory was acquired should be free forever. This Wilmot Proviso, as it was called from the name of the originator, went through as many forms as Proteus, though its intent was always the same. From first to last Lincoln voted for it. "I may venture to say that I voted for it at least forty times during the short time I was there," he said in after years. Although he voted so persistently he did little or no debating on the question in the House and in the hot debates from which he could not escape, he acted as a peace-maker.

At Mrs. Spriggs's mess, where he boarded in Washington, the Wilmot Proviso was the topic of frequent conversation and the occasion of many angry controversies. Dr. Busey, who was a fellow boarder, says of Lincoln's part in these discussions, that though he may have been as radical as any in the household, he was so discreet in giving expression to his convictions on the slavery question as to avoid giving offence to anybody, and was so conciliatory as to create the impression, even among the pro-slavery advocates, that he did not wish to introduce or discuss subjects that would provoke a controversy.

"When such conversation would threaten angry or even unpleasant contention he would interrupt it by interposing some anecdote, thus diverting it into a hearty and general laugh, and so completely disarrange the tenor of the discussion that the parties engaged would either separate in good humor or continue conversation free from discord. This amicable disposition made him very popular with the household."

When Lincoln went to New England in 1848 he experienced for the first time the full meaning of the "free soil" sentiment. Massachusetts was quivering at that moment under the impassioned protests of the great abolitionists. Sumner was just deciding to abandon literature to devote his life to the cause of freedom and was speaking wherever he had the chance and often in scenes which were riots. "Ah me, such an assembly," wrote Longfellow in his Journal after one of these speeches of Sumner. "It was like one of Beethoven's symphonies played in a saw-mill." Whittier was laboring at Amesbury by letters of counsel and encouragement to friends, by his pure, high-souled poems of protest and promise and by his editorials to the "National Era," which he and his friends had just started in Washington. Lowell was publishing the last of the Biglow Papers and preparing the whole for the book form. He was writing, too, some of his noblest prose. Emerson, Palfrey, Hoar, Adams, Phillips, Garrison, were all at work. Giddings had been there from Ohio.

Only a few days before Lincoln arrived a great convention of Free Soilers and bolting Whigs had been held in Tremont Temple and its earnestness and passion had produced a deep impression. Sensitive as Lincoln was to every shade of popular feeling and conviction the sentiment in New England stirred him as he had never been stirred before, on the question of slavery. Listening to Seward's speech in Tremont Temple, he seems to have had a sudden insight into the truth, a quick illumination; and that night, as the two men sat talking, he said gravely to the great antislavery advocate:

"Governor Seward, I have been thinking about what you said in your speech. I reckon you are right. We have got to deal with this slavery question, and got to give much more attention to it hereafter than we have been doing."

CHAPTER XIV

LINCOLN AT NIAGARA—SECURES A PATENT FOR AN INVENTION—ABANDONS POLITICS AND DECIDES TO DEVOTE HIMSELF TO THE LAW

It was late in September when Lincoln started westward from his campaigning in New England. He stopped in Albany, N. Y., and in company with Thurlow Weed called on Fillmore, then candidate for Vice-President. From Albany he went to Niagara. Mr. Herndon once asked him what made the deepest impression on him when he stood before the falls.

"The thing that struck me most forcibly when I saw the falls," he responded, "was, where in the world did all that water come from?" The memory of Niagara remained with him and aroused many speculations. Among various notes for lectures which Nicolay and Hay found among Mr. Lincoln's papers after his death and published in his "Complete Works," is a fragment on Niagara which shows how deeply his mind was stirred by the majesty of that mighty wonder.

"Niagara Falls! By what mysterious power is it that millions and millions are drawn from all parts of the world to gaze upon Niagara Falls? There is no mystery about the thing itself. Every effect is just as any intelligent man, knowing the causes, would anticipate without seeing it. If the water moving onward in a great river reaches a point where there is a perpendicular jog of a hundred feet in descent in the bottom of the river, it is plain the water will have a violent and continuous plunge at that point. It is also plain, the water, thus plunging, will foam and roar, and send up a mist continuously, in which last, during sunshine, there will be perpetual rainbows. The mere physical of Niagara Falls is only this. Yet this is really a very small part of that world's wonder. Its power to excite reflection and emotion is its great charm. The geologist will demonstrate that the plunge, or fall, was once at Lake Ontario, and has worn its way back to its present position; he will ascertain how fast it is wearing now, and so get a basis for determining how long it has been wearing back from Lake Ontario, and finally demonstrate by it that this world is at least fourteen thousand years old. A philosopher of a slightly different turn will say, 'Niagara Falls is only the lip of the basin out of which pours all the surplus water which rains down on two or three hundred thousand square miles of the earth's surface.' He will estimate with approximate accuracy that five hundred thousand tons of water fall with their full weight a distance of a hundred feet each minute—thus exerting a force equal to the lifting of the same weight, through the same space, in the same time. . . .

"But still there is more. It calls up the indefinite past. When Columbus first sought this continent—when Christ suffered on the cross—when Moses led Israel through the Red Sea—nay, even when Adam first came from the hand of his Maker; then, as now, Niagara was roaring here. The eyes of that species of extinct giants whose bones fill the mounds of America have gazed on Niagara, as ours do now. Contemporary with the first race of men, and older than the first man, Niagara is strong and fresh to-day as ten thousand years ago. The Mammoth and Mastodon, so long dead that fragments of their monstrous bones alone testify that they ever lived, have gazed on Niagara—in that long, long time never still for a single moment, never dried, never froze, never slept, never rested."

In his trip westward to Springfield from Niagara there occurred an incident which started Lincoln's mind on a new line of thought, one which all that fall divided it with politics. It happened that the boat on which he made part of the trip stranded in shallow water. The devices employed to float her interested Lincoln much. He no doubt recalled the days when on the Ohio, the Mississippi, and the Sangamon he had seen his own or his neighbor's boats stuck on a sand-bar for hours, even days. Was there no way that these vexatious delays could be prevented in shallow streams? He set himself resolutely at the task of inventing a practical device for getting boats over shoals. When he reached Springfield he began to build a model representing his idea. He showed the deepest interest in the work and Mr. Herndon says he would sometimes bring the model into his office and while whittling on it would talk of its merits and the revolution it was going to work on the western rivers.

When Lincoln returned to Washington he took the model with him, and through Mr. Z. C. Robbins, a lawyer of Washington, secured a patent.

"He walked into my office one morning with a model of a western steamboat under his arm," says Mr. Robbins. "After a friendly greeting he placed his model on my office-table and proceeded to explain the principles embodied therein that he believed to be his own invention, and which, if new, he desired to secure by letters-patent. During my former residence in St. Louis, I had made myself thoroughly familiar with everything appertaining to the construction and equipment of the flat-bottomed steamboats that were adapted to the shallow rivers of our western and southern states, and therefore, I was able speedily to come to the

MODEL OF ABRAHAM LINCOLN'S DEVICE FOR LIFTING VESSELS OVER SHOALS.

The inscription above this model in the Model Hall of the Patent Office, reads, "6469, Abraham Lincoln, Springfield, Illinois. Improvement in method of lifting vessels over shoals. Patented May 22, 1849." The apparatus consists of a bellows placed in each side of the hull of the craft, just below the water line, and worked by an odd but simple system of ropes and pulleys. When the keel of the vessel grates against the sand or obstruction, the bellows is filled with air; and thus, buoyed up, the vessel is expected to float over the shoal. The model is about eighteen or twenty inches long, and looks as if it had been whittled with a knife out of a shingle and a cigar box.

conclusion that Mr. Lincoln's proposed improvement of that class of vessels was new and patentable, and I so informed him. Thereupon he instructed me to prepare the necessary drawings and papers and prosecute an application for a patent for his invention at the United States patent office. I complied with his instructions and in due course of proceedings procured for him a patent that fully covered all the distinguishing features of his improved steamboat. The identical model that Mr. Lincoln brought to my office can now be seen in the United States patent office."

But it was only his leisure which Lincoln spent in the fall of 1848 on his invention. All through October and the first days of November he was speaking up and down the state for Taylor. His zeal was rewarded in November by the election of the Whig ticket and a few weeks later he went back to Washington for the final session of the Thirtieth Congress. He went back resolved to do something regarding slavery. He seems to have seen but two things at that moment which could constitutionally be done. The first was to allow the slave-holder no more ground than he had; to accomplish this he continued to vote for the Wilmot Proviso. The second was to abolish slavery in the District of Columbia. Over ten years before, in 1837, Lincoln had declared, in the Assembly of Illinois, that the Congress of the United States had the power, under the constitution, to abolish slavery in the District of Columbia, but that the power should be exercised only on request of the people of the District. When he went to Washington in 1847 he found a condition of things which made him feel that Congress ought to exercise the power it had. There had existed for years in the city a slave market:

"a sort of negro livery stable, where droves of negroes were collected, temporarily kept, and finally taken to southern markets, precisely like droves of horses," Lincoln described it in later years; and this frightful place was in view from the windows of the Capitol. Morally and intellectually shocked and irritated by this spectacle, Lincoln brooded over it until now, in the second session of his term, he decided to ask that Congress exercise the power he had affirmed ten years before belonged to it, and he drew up and, on January 16, 1849, presented a bill to abolish slavery in the District of Columbia, "with the consent of the voters of the District and with compensation to owners."

The bill caused a noise in the House, but came to naught, as indeed at that date any similar bill was bound to do. It showed, however, more plainly than anything Lincoln had done so far in Congress that he was beginning to feel that aggressive action against slavery must be taken.

The inauguration of Taylor on March 4, 1849, ended Lincoln's congressional career. The principle, "turn about is fair play," which he had insisted on in 1846 when working for the nomination for himself, he regarded as quite as applicable now. It was not because he did not desire to return to Congress.

"I made the declaration that I would not be a candidate again," he wrote Herndon in January, 1848, "more from a wish to deal fairly with others, to keep peace among our friends, and to keep the district from going to the enemy, than from any cause personal to myself; so that, if it should so happen that nobody else wishes to be elected, I could not refuse the people the right of sending me again. But to enter myself as a competitor of others, or to authorize any one so to enter me, is what my word and honor forbid."

And yet he was not willing to leave public life. The term in Congress had only increased his fondness for politics. It had given him a touch of that fever for public office from which so few men who have served in Congress ever entirely recover. The Whigs owed much to him, and there was a general disposition to gratify any reasonable ambition he might have. "I believe that, so far as the Whigs in Congress are concerned, I could have the General Land Office almost by common consent," he wrote Speed; "but then Sweet and Don Morrison and Browning and Cyrus Edwards all want it, and what is worse, while I think I could easily take it myself, I fear I shall have trouble to get it for any other man in Illinois."

Although he feared his efforts would be useless, he pledged his support to his friend, Cyrus Edwards. While Lincoln was looking after Edwards's interests, a candidate appeared who was most objectionable to the Whigs, General Justin Butterfield. Lincoln did all he could to defeat Butterfield save the one thing necessary—ask the position for himself. This he would not do until he learned that Edwards had no chance. Then he applied; but it was too late. Butterfield had secured the office while Lincoln had been holding back. When Edwards found that Lincoln had finally applied for the place, he accused him of treachery. Lincoln was deeply hurt by the suspicion.

"The better part of one's life consists of his friendships," he wrote to Judge Gillespie, "and, of them, mine with Mr.

Edwards was one of the most cherished. I have not been false to it. At a word I could have had the office any time before the Department was committed to Mr. Butterfield—at least Mr. Ewing and the President say as much. That word I forbore to speak, partly for other reasons, but chiefly for Mr. Edwards's sake—losing the office that he might gain it. I was always for him; but to lose his *friendship*, by the effort for him, would oppress me very much, were I not sustained by the utmost consciousness of rectitude. I first determined to be an applicant, unconditionally, on the 2d of June; and I did so then upon being informed by a telegraphic despatch that the question was narrowed down to Mr. B. and myself, and that the Cabinet had postponed the appointment three weeks for my benefit. Not doubting that Mr. Edwards was wholly out of the question, I, nevertheless, would not then have become an applicant had I supposed he would thereby be brought to suspect me of treachery to him. Two or three days afterwards a conversation with Levi Davis convinced me Mr. Edwards was dissatisfied; but I was then too far in to get out. His own letter, written on the 25th of April, after I had fully informed him of all that had passed, up to within a few days of that time, gave assurance I had that entire confidence from him which I felt my uniform and strong friendship for him entitled me to. Among other things it says: 'Whatever course your judgment may dictate as proper to be pursued shall never be excepted to by me.' I also had had a letter from Washington saying Chambers, of the 'Republic,' had brought a rumor there, that Mr. E. had declined in my favor, which rumor I judged came from Mr. E. himself, as I had not then breathed of his letter to any living creature. In saying I had never, before the 2d of June, determined to be an applicant, *unconditionally*, I mean to admit that, before then, I had said, substantially, I would take the office rather than it should be lost to the state, or given to one in the state whom the Whigs did not want; but I aver that in every instance in which I spoke of myself I intended to keep, and now believe I did keep, Mr. E. above myself. Mr. Edwards's first suspicion was that I had allowed Baker to overreach me, as his friend, in behalf of Don Morrison. I know this was a mistake; and the result has proved it. I understand his view now is, that if I had gone to open war with Baker I could have ridden him down and had the thing all my own way. I believe no such thing. With Baker and some strong man from the Military tract and elsewhere for Morrison, and we and some strong men from the Wabash and elsewhere for Mr. E., it was not possible for either to succeed. I believed this in March, and I *know* it now. The only thing which gave either any chance was the very thing Baker and I proposed—an adjustment with themselves.

"You may wish to know how Butterfield finally beat me. I cannot tell you particulars now, but will when I see you. In the meantime let it be understood I am not greatly dissatisfied—I wish the office had been so bestowed as to encourage our friends in future contests, and I regret exceedingly Mr. Edwards's feelings towards me. These two things away, I should have no regrets—at least I think I would not."

It was not until eleven years later that Edwards forgave Lincoln. Then at Judge Gillespie's request he promised to "bury the hatchet with Lincoln" and to enter the campaign of 1860 for him.

Lincoln declared that he had no regrets about the way the General Land Office went, but, if he had not, his Whig friends in Washington had. They determined to do something for him, and in the summer of 1849 summoned him to the capital to urge him to accept the governorship of Oregon. The territory would soon be a state, it was believed, and Lincoln would then undoubtedly be chosen to represent it in the United States Senate. Unquestionably, a splendid political prospect was thus opened. Many of Lincoln's friends advised him to accept; his wife, however, disliked the idea of life in the far West, and on her account he refused the place.

The events of the summer of 1849 seemed to Lincoln to end his political career. He had no time to brood over his situation, however. The necessity of earning a livelihood was too imperative. His financial obligations were, in fact, considerable. The old debt for the New Salem store still hung over him; he had a growing family; and his father and mother, who were still living in Coles County, whither they had moved in 1831, were dependent upon him for many of the necessaries, as well as all the comforts, of their lives. At intervals ever since he had left home he had helped them; now by saving their land from the foreclosing of a mortgage, now by paying their doctor's bills, now by adding to the cheerfulness of their home.

He was equally kind to his other relatives, visiting them and aiding them in various ways. Among these relatives were two cousins, Abraham and Mordecai, the sons of his uncle Mordecai Lincoln, who lived in Hancock County, in his congressional district. At Quincy, also in his district, lived with his family a relative, possibly a brother, of his mother—Joseph Hanks. Lincoln never went to Quincy without going to see his uncle Joseph and "uncle Joe's Jake," as he called one of his cousins. "On these occasions," writes one of the latter's family, Mr. J. M. Hanks of Florence, Colorado, "mirth and jollity abounded, for Mr. Lincoln indulged his bent of story-telling to the utmost, until a late hour." His step-brother, John Johnston, he aided for many years. His help did not always take the form of money. Johnston was shiftless and always in debt, and consequently restless and discontented. In 1851 he was determined to borrow money or sell his farm, and move to Missouri. He proposed to Mr. Lincoln that he lend him eighty dollars. Mr. Lincoln answered:

"What I propose is, that you shall go to work, 'tooth and nail,' for somebody who will give you money for it. . . . I now promise you, that for every dollar you will, between this and the first of May, get for your own labor, either in money or as your own indebtedness, I will then give you one other dollar. . . . In this I do not mean you shall go off to St. Louis, or the lead mines, or the gold mines in California, but I mean for you to go at it for the best wages you can get close to home in Coles County. Now, if you will do this, you will be soon out of debt, and, what is better, you will have a habit that will keep you from getting in debt again. But, if I should now clear you out of debt, next year you would be just as deep in as ever. You say you would almost give your place in Heaven for seventy or eighty dollars. Then you value your place in Heaven very cheap, for I am sure you can, with the offer I make, get the seventy or eighty dollars for four or five months' work."

A few months later Lincoln wrote Johnston in regard to his contemplated move to Missouri:

"What can you do in Missouri better than here? Is the land any richer? Can you there, any more than here, raise corn and wheat and oats without work? Will anybody there, any more than here, do your work for you? If you intend to go to work, there is no better place than right where you are; if you do not intend to go to work, you cannot get along anywhere. Squirming and crawling about from place to place can do no good. You have raised no crop this year; and what you really want is to sell the land, get the money, and spend it. Part with the land you have, and, my life upon it, you will never after own a spot big enough to bury you in. Half you will get for the land you will spend in moving to Missouri, and the other half you will eat, drink, and wear out, and no foot of land will be bought. Now, I feel it my duty to have no hand in such a piece of foolery."

All this plain advice did not prevent Johnston trying to sell a small piece of land on which Mr. Lincoln had paid the mortgage in order to secure it to his stepmother during her life. When Mr. Lincoln received this proposition he replied:

"Your proposal about selling the east forty acres of land is all that I want or could claim for *myself;* but I am not satisfied with it on *mother's* account. I want her to have her living, and I feel that it is my duty, to some extent, to see that she is not wronged. She had a right of dower (that is, the use of one-third for life) in the other two forties; but, it seems, she has already let you take that, hook and line. She now has the use of the whole of the east forty as long as she lives, and if it be sold, of course she is entitled to the interest on *all* the money it brings as long as she lives; but you propose to sell it for three hundred dollars, take one hundred away with you, and leave her two hundred at eight per cent., making her the *enormous* sum of sixteen dollars a year. Now, if you are satisfied with treating her in that way, I am not. It is true that you are to have that forty for two hundred dollars *at* mother's death; but you are not to have it *before.* I am confident that land can be made to produce for mother at least thirty dollars a year, and I cannot, to oblige any living person, consent that she shall be put on an allowance of sixteen dollars a year."

It was these obligations which made Lincoln resume at once the practice of the law. He decided to remain in Springfield, although he had an opportunity to go in with a well-established Chicago lawyer. For many reasons life in Springfield was satisfactory to him. He had bought a home there in 1844, and was deeply attached to it. There, too, he was surrounded by scores of friends who had known him since his first appearance in the town, and to many of whom he was related by marriage; and he had the good-will of the community. In short, he was a part of Springfield. The very children knew him. "My first strong impression of Mr. Lincoln," says a lady of Springfield, "was made by one of his kind deeds. I was going with a little friend for my first trip alone on the railroad cars. It was an epoch of my life. I had planned for it and dreamed of it for weeks. The day I was to go came, but as the hour of the train approached, the hackman, through some neglect, failed to call for my trunk. As the minutes went on, I realized, in a panic of grief, that I should miss the train. I was standing by the gate, my hat and gloves on, sobbing as if my heart would break, when Mr. Lincoln came by.

" 'Why, what's the matter?' he asked, and I poured out all my story.

" 'How big's the trunk? There's still time, if it isn't too big.' And he pushed through the gate and up to the door. My mother and I took him up to my room, where my little old-fashioned trunk stood, locked and tied. 'Oh, ho,' he cried; 'wipe your eyes and come on quick.' And before I knew what he was going to do, he had shouldered the trunk, was down stairs, and striding out of the yard. Down the street he went, fast as his long legs could carry him, I trotting behind, drying my tears as I went. We reached the station in time. Mr. Lincoln put me on the train, kissed me good-bye, and told me to have a good time. It was just like him."

This sensitiveness to a child's wants made Mr. Lincoln a most indulgent father. He continually carried his boys about with him, and their pranks, even when they approached rebellion, seemed to be an endless delight to him. Like most boys, they loved to run away, and neighbors of the Lincolns tell many tales of Mr. Lincoln's captures of the culprits. One of the prettiest of all these is a story told of an escape Willie once made, when three or four years old, from the hands of his mother, who was giving him a tubbing. He scampered out of the door without the vestige of a garment on him, flew up the street, slipped under a fence into a great green field, and took across it. Mr. Lincoln was sitting on the porch and discovered the pink and white runaway as he was cutting across the greensward. He stood up, laughing aloud, while the mother entreated him to go in pursuit; then he started in chase. Half-way across the field he caught the child and, gathering him up in his long arms, he covered his rosy form with kisses. Then, mounting him on his back, the chubby legs around his neck, he rode him back to his mother and his tub.

It was a frequent custom with Lincoln, this of carrying his children on his shoulders. He rarely went down street that he did not have one of his younger boys thus mounted, while another hung to the tail of his long coat. The antics of the boys with their father, and the species of tyranny they exercised over him, are still subjects of talk in Springfield. Mr. Roland Diller, who was a neighbor of Mr. Lincoln, tells one of the best of the stories. He was called to the door one day by hearing a great noise of children crying, and there was Mr. Lincoln striding by with the boys, both of whom were wailing aloud. "Why, Mr. Lincoln, what's the matter with the boys?" he asked.

"Just what's the matter with the whole world," Lincoln replied; "I've got three walnuts and each wants two."

Another of Lincoln's Springfield acquaintances, the Rev. Mr. Alcott of Elgin, Ill., tells of seeing him coming away from church, unusually early one Sunday morning. "The sermon could not have been more than half way through," says Mr. Alcott. " 'Tad' was slung across his left arm like a pair of saddle-bags, and Mr. Lincoln was striding along with long, and deliberate steps toward his home. On one of the street corners he encountered a group of his fellow-townsmen. Mr. Lincoln anticipated the question which was about to be put by the group, and, taking his figure of speech from practices with which they were familiar, said: 'Gentlemen, I entered this colt, but he kicked around so I had to withdraw him.' "

There was no institution in Springfield in which Lincoln had not taken an active interest in the first years of his residence; and now that he had decided to remain in the town, he resumed all his old relations, from the daily visits to the drug-stores on the public square, which were the recognized rendezvous of Springfield politicians and lawyers, to his weekly attendance at the First Presbyterian Church. That he was as regular in his attendance on the latter as on the former, all his old neighbors testify. In fact, Lincoln, all his life, went regularly to church. The serious attention which he gave the sermons he heard is shown in a well-authenticated story of a visit he made in 1837, with a company of friends, to a camp-meeting held six miles west of Springfield at the "Salem Church." The sermon on this occasion was preached by one of the most vigorous and original individuals in the pulpit of that day—the Rev. Dr. Peter Akers. In this discourse was a remarkable and prophetic passage, long remembered by those who heard it. The speaker prophesied the downfall of castes, the end of tyrannies, and the crushing out of slavery. As Lincoln and his friends returned home there was a long discussion of the sermon.

"It was the most instructive sermon, and he is the most impressive preacher, I have ever heard," Lincoln said. "It is wonderful that God has given such power to men. I firmly believe his interpretation of prophecy, so far as I understand it, and especially about the breaking down of civil and religious tyrannies; and, odd as it may seem, when he described those changes and revolutions, I was deeply impressed that I should be somehow strangely mixed up with them."

If Lincoln was not at this period a man of orthodox beliefs, he certainly was, if we accept his own words, profoundly religious. In the letters which passed between Lincoln and Speed in 1841 and 1842, when the two men were doubting their own hearts and wrestling with their disillusions and forebodings, Lincoln frequently expressed the idea that the Almighty had sent their suffering for a special purpose. When Speed finally acknowledged himself happily married, Lincoln wrote to him: "I always was superstitious; I believe God made me one of the instruments of bringing your Fanny and you together, which union I have no doubt he had foreordained." Then, referring to his own troubled heart, he added: "Whatever He designs He will do for me yet. 'Stand still, and see the salvation of the Lord,' is my text just now."

Only a few months after Lincoln decided to settle permanently in Springfield his father, Thomas Lincoln, fell dangerously ill. Lincoln in writing to John Johnston, his step-brother, said: "I sincerely hope father may recover his health, but, at all events, tell him to remember to call upon and confide in our great and good and merciful Maker, who will not turn away from him in any extremity. He notes the fall of a sparrow, and numbers the hairs of our heads, and He will not forget the dying man who puts his trust in Him."

Lincoln's return to the law was characterized by a marked change in his habits. He gave much more attention to study than he ever had before. His colleagues in Springfield and on the circuit noticed this change. After court closed in the town on the circuit, and the lawyers were gathered in the bar-room or on the veranda of the tavern, telling stories and chaffing one another, Lincoln would join them, though often but for a few minutes. He would tell a story as he passed, and while they were laughing at its climax, would slip away to his room to study. Frequently this work was carried on far into the night. "Placing a candle on a chair at the head of the bed," says Mr. Herndon, "he would study for hours. I have known him to study in this position until two o'clock in the morning. Meanwhile, I and others who chanced to occupy the same room would be safely and soundly asleep." Although he worked so late, "he was in the habit of rising earlier than his brothers of the bar," says Judge Weldon. "On such occasions he was wont to sit by the fire, having uncovered the coals, and muse, ponder, and soliloquize."

But it was not only the law that occupied him. He began a serious course of general education, studying mathematics, astronomy, poetry, as regularly as a school-boy who had lessons to recite. In the winter of 1849-50 he even joined a club of a dozen gentlemen of Springfield who had begun the study of German, the meetings of the class being held in his office.

Much of Lincoln's devotion to study at this period was due to his desire to bring himself in general culture up to the men whom he had been meeting in the East. No man ever realized his own deficiencies in knowledge and experience more deeply than Abraham Lincoln, nor made a braver struggle to correct them. He often acknowledged to his friends the consciousness he had of his limitations in even the simplest matters of life. Mr. H. C. Whitney, one of his old friends, gives a touching example of this. They were on the circuit and Lincoln's friends missed him after supper. When he returned, some one asked where he had been.

"Well, I have been to a little show up at the Academy," he said.

"He sat before the fire," says Mr. Whitney, "and narrated all the sights of that most primitive of county shows, given chiefly to school children. Next night he was missing again; the show was still in town, and he stole in as before, and later entertained us with a description of new sights—a magic lantern, electrical machine, etc. I told him I had seen all these sights at school. 'Yes,' said he sadly, 'I now have an advantage over you, for the first time in my life seeing these things which are, of course, common to those who had, what I did not, a chance at an education when they were young."

It was to make up for the "chance at an education" which he did not have in youth that Abraham Lincoln at forty years of age, after having earned the reputation of being one of the ablest politicians in Illinois, spent his leisure in study.

CHAPTER XV

LINCOLN ON THE CIRCUIT—HIS HUMOR AND PERSUASIVENESS—HIS MANNER OF PREPARING CASES, EXAMINING WITNESSES, AND ADDRESSING JURIES

When in 1849 Lincoln decided to abandon politics finally and to devote himself to the law, he had been practising for thirteen years. In spite of the many interruptions electioneering and office-holding had caused he was well-established. Rejoining his partner Herndon—the firm of Lincoln and Herndon had been only a name during Lincoln's term in Washington—he took up the law with a singleness of purpose which had never before characterized his practice.

Lincoln's headquarters were in Springfield, but his practice was itinerant. The arrangements for the administration of justice in Illinois in the early days were suited to the conditions of the country, the state being divided into judicial circuits including more or less territory according to the population. To each circuit a judge was appointed, who each spring and fall travelled from county-seat to county-seat holding court. With the judge travelled a certain number of the best-known lawyers of the district. Each lawyer had, of course, a permanent office in one of the county-seats, and often at several of the others he had partners, usually young men of little experience, for whom he acted as counsel in special cases. This peripatetic court prevailed in Illinois until the beginning of the fifties; but for many years after, when the towns had grown so large that a clever lawyer might have enough to do in his own county, a few lawyers, Lincoln among them, who from long association felt that the circuit was their natural habitat refused to leave it.

Lincoln travelled what was known as the "Eighth Judicial Circuit." It included fifteen counties in 1845, though the territory has since been divided into more. It was about one hundred and fifty miles long by as many broad. There were no railroads in the Eighth Circuit until about 1854, and the court travelled on horseback or in carriages. Lincoln had no horse in the early days of his practice. It was his habit then to borrow one, or to join a company of a half dozen or more in hiring a "three-seated spring wagon." Later he owned a turn-out of his own, which figures in nearly all the traditions of the Eighth Circuit, the horse being described as "poky" and the buggy as "rattling."

There was much that was irritating and uncomfortable in the circuit-riding of the Illinois court, but there was more which was amusing to a temperament like Lincoln's. The freedom, the long days in the open air, the unexpected if trivial adventures, the meeting with wayfarers and settlers—all was an entertainment to him. He found humor and human interest on the route where his companions saw nothing but commonplaces. "He saw the ludicrous in an assemblage of fowls," says H. C. Whitney, one of his fellow-itinerants, "in a man spading his garden, in a clothes-line full of clothes, in a group of boys, in a lot of pigs rooting at a mill door, in a mother duck teaching her brood to swim—in everything and anything." The sympathetic observations of these long rides furnished humorous settings for some of his best stories. If frequently on these trips he fell into sombre reveries and rode with head bent, ignoring his companions, generally he took part in all the frolicking which went on, joining in practical jokes, singing noisily with the rest, sometimes even playing a Jew's-harp.

When the county-seat was reached, the bench and bar quickly settled themselves in the town tavern. It was usually a large two-story house with big rooms and long verandas. There was little exclusiveness possible in these hostelries. Ordinarily judge and lawyer slept two in a bed, and three or four beds in a room. They ate at the common table with jurors, witnesses, prisoners out on bail, travelling peddlers, teamsters, and laborers. The only attempt at classification on the landlord's part was seating the lawyers in a group at the head of the table. Most of them accepted this distinction complacently. Lincoln, however, seemed to be indifferent to it. One day, when he had come in and seated himself at the foot with the "fourth estate," the landlord called to him, "You're in the wrong place, Mr. Lincoln; come up here."

"Have you anything better to eat up there, Joe?" he inquired quizzically; "if not, I'll stay here."

The accommodations of the taverns were often unsatisfactory—the food poorly cooked, the beds hard. Lincoln accepted everything with uncomplaining good nature, though his companions habitually growled at the hardships of the life. It was not only repugnance to criticism which might hurt others, it

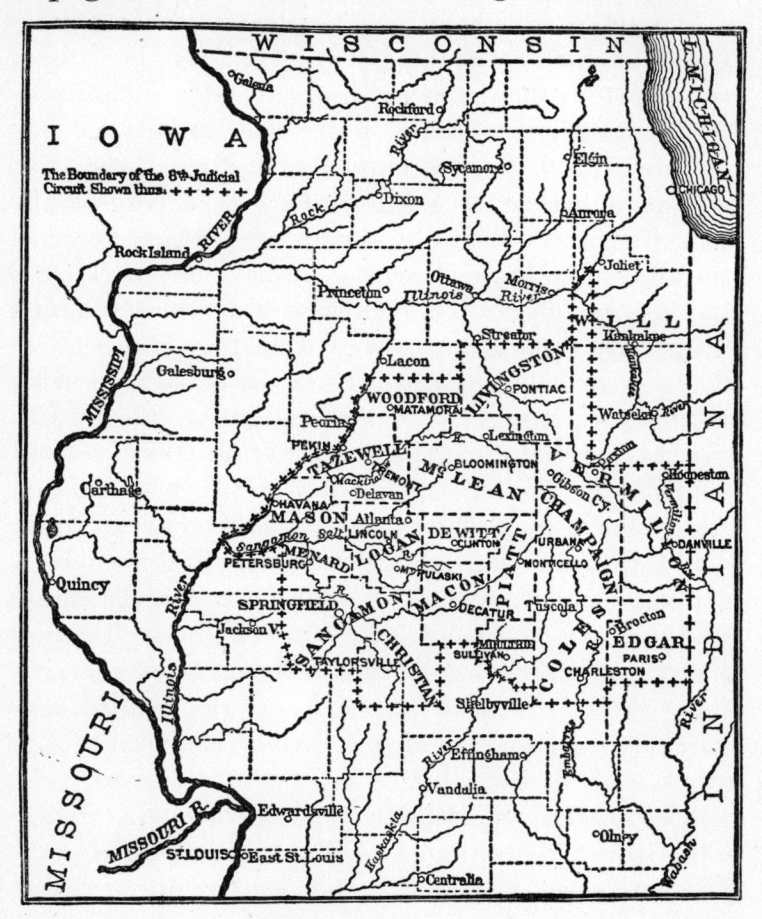

FACSIMILE OF MAP OF CIRCUIT WHICH LINCOLN TRAVELLED IN PRACTISING LAW.

was the indifference of one whose thoughts were always busy with problems apart from physical comfort, who had little notion of the so-called "refinements of life," and almost no sense of luxury and ease.

The judge naturally was the leading character in these nomadic groups. He received all the special consideration the democratic spirit of the inhabitants bestowed on any one and controlled his privacy and his time to a degree. Judge David Davis, who from 1848 presided over the Eighth Circuit as long as Mr. Lincoln travelled it, was a man of unusual force of character, of large learning, quick impulses, and strong prejudices. Lincoln was from the beginning of their association a favorite with Judge Davis. Unless he joined the circle which the judge formed in his room after supper, his honor was impatient and distraught, interrupting the conversation constantly by demanding: "Where's Lincoln?" "Why don't Lincoln come?" And when Lincoln did come, the judge would draw out story after story, quieting everybody who interrupted with an impatient, "Mr. Lincoln's talking." If any one came to the door to see the host in the midst of one of Lincoln's stories he would send a lawyer into the hall to see what was wanted, and as soon as the door closed, order Lincoln to "go ahead."

The appearance of the court in a town was invariably a stimulus to its social life. In all of the county-seats there were a few fine homes, the dignity, spaciousness, and elegance of which still impress the traveller through Illinois. The hospitality of these houses was generous. Dinners, receptions, and suppers followed one another as soon as the court began. Lincoln was a favorite figure at all these gatherings.

TRAVELLING ON THE CIRCUIT 285

His favorite field, however, was the court. The court-houses of Illinois in which he practised were not log houses, as has been frequently taken for granted. "It is not probable," says a leading member of the Illinois bar, "Mr. Lincoln ever saw a log court-house in central Illinois, where he practised law, unless he saw one at Decatur, in Macon County. In a conversation between three members of the Supreme Court of Illinois, all of whom had been born in this state and had lived in it all their lives, and who were certainly familiar with the central portions of the state, all declared they had never seen a log court-house in the state."

The court-houses in which Lincoln practised were stiff, old-fashioned wood or brick structures, usually capped by cupola or tower, and fronted by verandas with huge Doric or Ionic pillars. They were finished inside in the most uncompromising style—hard white walls, unpainted woodwork, pine floors, wooden benches. Usually they were heated by huge Franklin stoves, with yards of stove-pipe running wildly through the air, searching for an exit, and threatening momentarily to unjoint and tumble in sections. Few of the lawyers had offices in the town; and a corner of the court-room, the shade of a tree in the court-yard, a sunny side of a building, were where they met their clients and transacted business.

In the courts themselves there was a certain indifference to formality engendered by the primitive surroundings, which, however, the judges never allowed to interfere with the seriousness of the work. Lincoln habitually, when not busy, whispered stories to his neighbors, frequently to the annoyance of Judge Davis. If Lincoln persisted too long, the judge would rap on the chair and exclaim: "Come, come, Mr. Lincoln, I can't stand this! There is no use trying to carry on two courts; I must adjourn mine or you yours, and I think you will have to be the one." As soon as the group had scattered, the judge would call one of the men to him and ask: "What was that Lincoln was telling?"

"I was never fined but once for contempt of court," says one of the clerks of the court in Lincoln's day. "Davis fined me five dollars. Mr. Lincoln had just come in, and leaning over my desk had told me a story so irresistibly funny that I broke out into a loud laugh. The judge called me to order in haste, saying, 'This must be stopped. Mr. Lincoln, you are constantly disturbing this court with your stories.' Then to me, 'You may fine yourself five dollars for your disturbance.' I apologized, but told the judge that the story was worth the money. In a few minutes the judge called me to him. 'What was the story Lincoln told you?' he asked. I told him, and he laughed aloud in spite of himself. 'Remit your fine,' he ordered."

The partiality of Judge Davis for Lincoln was shared by the members of the court generally. The unaffected friendliness and helpfulness of his nature had more to do with this than his wit and cleverness. If there was a new clerk in court, a stranger unused to the ways of the place, Lincoln was the first—sometimes the only one—to shake hands with him and congratulate him on his election.

"No lawyer on the circuit was more unassuming

than was Mr. Lincoln," says one who practised with him. "He arrogated to himself no superiority over anyone—not even the most obscure member of the bar. He treated everyone with that simplicity and kindness that friendly neighbors manifest in their relations with one another. He was remarkably gentle with young lawyers becoming permanent residents at the several county-seats in the circuit where he had practised for so many years. . . . The result was, he became the much-beloved senior member of the bar. No young lawyer ever practised in the courts with Mr. Lincoln who did not in all his after life have a regard for him akin to personal affection."

"I remember with what confidence I always went to him," says Judge Lawrence Weldon, who first knew Lincoln at the bar in 1854, "because I was certain he knew all about the matter and would most cheerfully help me. I can see him now, through the decaying memories of thirty years, standing in the corner of the old court-room; and as I approached him with a paper I did not understand, he said, 'Wait until I fix this plug of my "gallis" and I will pitch into that like a dog at a root.' While speaking he was busily engaged in trying to connect his suspenders with his pants by making a plug perform the function of a button."

If for any reason Lincoln was absent from court, he was missed perhaps as no other man on the Eighth Circuit would have been, and his return greeted joyously. He was not less happy himself to rejoin his friends. "Ain't you glad I've come?" he would call out, as he came up to shake hands.

The cases which fell to Lincoln on the Eighth Circuit were of the sort common to a new country—litigation over border lines, over deeds, over damages by wandering cattle, over broils at country festivities. Few of the cases were of large importance. When a client came to Lincoln his first effort was to arrange matters, if possible, so as to avoid a suit. In a few notes for a law lecture prepared about 1850, he says:

"Discourage litigation. Persuade your neighbors to compromise whenever you can. Point out to them how the nominal winner is often a real loser—in fees, expenses, and waste of time. As a peacemaker the lawyer has a superior opportunity of being a good man. There will still be business enough.

"Never stir up litigation. A worse man can scarcely be found than one who does this. Who can be more nearly a fiend than he who habitually overhauls the register of deeds in search of defects in titles, whereon to stir up strife, and put money in his pocket? A moral tone ought to be infused into the profession which should drive such men out of it."

He carried out this in his practice. "Who was your guardian?" he asked a young man who came to him to complain that a part of the property left him had been withheld. "Enoch Kingsbury," replied the young man.

"I know Mr. Kingsbury," said Lincoln, "and he is not the man to have cheated you out of a cent, and I can't take the case, and advise you to drop the subject." And it was dropped.

"We shall not take your case," he said to a man who had shown that by a legal technicality he could win property worth six hundred dollars. "You must than was Mr. Lincoln," says one who practised with him. "He arrogated to himself no superiority over anyone—not even the most obscure member of the bar. He treated everyone with that simplicity and kindness that friendly neighbors manifest in their relations with one another. He was remarkably gentle with young lawyers becoming permanent residents at the several county-seats in the circuit where he had practised for so many years. . . . The result was, he became the much-beloved senior member of the bar. No young lawyer ever practised in the courts with Mr. Lincoln who did not in all his after life have a regard for him akin to personal affection."

"I remember with what confidence I always went to him," says Judge Lawrence Weldon, who first knew Lincoln at the bar in 1854, "because I was certain he knew all about the matter and would most cheerfully help me. I can see him now, through the decaying memories of thirty years, standing in the corner of the old court-room; and as I approached him with a paper I did not understand, he said, 'Wait until I fix this plug of my "gallis" and I will pitch into that like a dog at a root.' While speaking he was busily engaged in trying to connect his suspenders with his pants by making a plug perform the function of a button."

If for any reason Lincoln was absent from court, he was missed perhaps as no other man on the Eighth Circuit would have been, and his return greeted joyously. He was not less happy himself to rejoin his friends. "Ain't you glad I've come?" he would call out, as he came up to shake hands.

The cases which fell to Lincoln on the Eighth Circuit were of the sort common to a new country—litigation over border lines, over deeds, over damages by wandering cattle, over broils at country festivities. Few of the cases were of large importance. When a client came to Lincoln his first effort was to arrange matters, if possible, so as to avoid a suit. In a few notes for a law lecture prepared about 1850, he says:

"Discourage litigation. Persuade your neighbors to compromise whenever you can. Point out to them how the nominal winner is often a real loser—in fees, expenses, and waste of time. As a peacemaker the lawyer has a superior opportunity of being a good man. There will still be business enough.

"Never stir up litigation. A worse man can scarcely be found than one who does this. Who can be more nearly a fiend than he who habitually overhauls the register of deeds in search of defects in titles, whereon to stir up strife, and put money in his pocket? A moral tone ought to be infused into the profession which should drive such men out of it."

He carried out this in his practice. "Who was your guardian?" he asked a young man who came to him to complain that a part of the property left him had been withheld. "Enoch Kingsbury," replied the young man.

"I know Mr. Kingsbury," said Lincoln, "and he is not the man to have cheated you out of a cent, and I can't take the case, and advise you to drop the subject." And it was dropped.

"We shall not take your case," he said to a man who had shown that by a legal technicality he could win property worth six hundred dollars. "You must remember that some things legally right are not morally right. We shall not take your case, but will give you a little advice for which we will charge you nothing. You seem to be a sprightly, energetic man; we would advise you to try your hand at making six hundred dollars in some other way."

Where he saw injustice he was quick to offer his services to the wronged party. A pleasant example of this is related by Joseph Jefferson in his "Autobiography." In 1839, Jefferson, then a lad of ten years, travelled through Illinois with his father's theatrical company. After playing at Chicago, Quincy, Peoria and Pekin, the company went in the fall to Springfield, where the sight of the legislature tempted the elder Jefferson and his partner to remain throughout the season. But there was no theatre. Not to be daunted they built one. But hardly had they completed it before a religious revival broke out in the town, and the church people turned all their influence against the theatre. So effectually did they work that a law was passed by the municipality imposing a license which was practically prohibitory. "In the midst of our trouble," says Jefferson, "a young lawyer called on the managers. He had heard of the injustice, and offered, if they would place the matter in his hands, to have the license taken off, declaring that he only desired to see fair play, and he would accept no fee whether he failed or succeeded. The young lawyer began his harangue. He handled the subject with tact, skill, and humor, tracing the history of the drama from the time when Thespis acted in a cart to the stage of to-day. He illustrated his speech with a number of anecdotes, and kept the council in a roar of laughter. His good humor prevailed, and the exorbitant tax was taken off." The "young lawyer" was Lincoln.

Having accepted a case, Lincoln's first object seemed to be to reduce it to its simplest elements. "If I can clean this case of technicalities and get it properly swung to the jury, I'll win it," he told his partner Herndon one day. He began by getting at what seemed to him the pivot on which it rested. Sure of that, he cared little for anything else. He trusted very little to books; a great deal to common sense and his ideas of right and wrong.

"In the make of his character Mr. Lincoln had many elements essential to the successful circuit lawyer," says one of his fellow-practitioners. "He knew much of the law as written in the books, and had that knowledge ready for use at all times. That was a valuable possession in the absence of law books, where none were obtainable on the circuit. But he had more than a knowledge of the law. He knew right and justice, and knew how to make their application to the affairs of every-day life. That was an element in his character that gave him power to prevail with the jury when arguing a case before them. Few lawyers ever had the influence with a jury that Mr. Lincoln had."

When a case was clear to him and he was satisfied of its justice, he trusted to taking advantage of the developments of the trial to win. For this reason he made few notes beforehand, rarely writing out his plan of argument. Those he left are amusingly brief;

for instance, the notes made for a suit he had brought against a pension agent who had withheld as fee half of the pension he had obtained for the aged widow of a Revolutionary soldier. Lincoln was deeply indignant at the agent and had resolved to win his suit. He read up the Revolutionary War afresh, and when he came to address the jury drew a harrowing picture of the private soldier's sufferings and of the trials of his separation from his wife. The notes for this argument ran as follows:

When you can't find it anywhere else look into this

FACSIMILE OF A LINCOLN MEMORANDUM.

From the Lincoln collection in the law offices of Messrs. Vanuxem & Potter, of Philadelphia. This characteristic memorandum was found by Messrs. Herndon & Weik in looking over the papers in Lincoln's law office. It was the label to a package of letters, pamphlets, and newspapers which he had tied together and marked.

"No contract—Not professional services. Unreasonable charge,—Money retained by Def't not given by Pl'ff.—Revolutionary War.—Soldier's bleeding feet.—Pl'ff's husband.—Soldier leaving home for army.—*Skin def't.*—Close."

Lincoln's reason for not taking notes, as he told it to H. W. Beckwith, when a student in the Danville office of Lincoln and Lamon, was: "Notes are a bother, taking time to make, and more to hunt them up afterwards; lawyers who do so soon get the habit of referring to them so much that it confuses and tires the jury." "He relied on his well-trained memory," says Mr. Beckwith, "that recorded and indexed every passing detail. And by his skilful questions, a joke, or pat retort as the trial progressed, he steered his jury from the bayous and eddies of side issues and kept them clear of the snags and sandbars, if any were put in the real channel of his case."

Much of his strength lay in his skill in examining witnesses. "He had a most remarkable talent for examining witnesses," says an intimate associate; "with him it was a rare gift. It was a power to compel a witness to disclose the whole truth. Even a witness at first unfriendly, under his kindly treatment would finally become friendly, and would wish to tell nothing he could honestly avoid against him, if he could state nothing for him."

He could not endure an unfair use of testimony or the misrepresentation of his own position. "In the Harrison murder case," says Mr. T. W. S. Kidd of Springfield, a crier of the court in Lincoln's day, "the prosecuting attorney stated that such a witness made a certain statement, when Mr. Lincoln rose and made such a plaintive appeal to the attorney to correct the statement, that the attorney actually made the *amende honorable,* and afterwards remarked to a brother lawyer that he could deny his own child's appeal as quickly as he could Mr. Lincoln's."

Sometimes under provocation he became violently angry. In the murder case referred to above, the judge ruled contrary to his expectations, and, as Mr. Lincoln said, contrary to the decision of the Supreme Court in a similar case. "Both Mr. Lincoln and Judge Logan, who was with him in the case," says Mr. Kidd, "rose to their feet quick as thought. I do think he was the most unearthly looking man I had ever seen. He roared like a lion suddenly aroused from his lair and said and did more in ten minutes than I ever heard him say or saw him do before in an hour."

He depended a great deal upon stories in his pleading, using them as illustrations which demonstrated the case more conclusively than argument could have done. Judge H. W. Beckwith of Danville, Illinois, in his "Personal Recollections of Lincoln," tells a story which is a good example of Lincoln's way of condensing the law and the facts of an issue in a story.

"A man, by vile words, first provoked and then made a bodily attack upon another. The latter in defending himself gave the other much the worst of the encounter. The aggressor, to get even, had the one who thrashed him tried in our circuit court upon a charge of assault and battery. Mr. Lincoln defended. His client, he told the jury, was in the fix of a man who, in going along the highway with a pitchfork on his shoulder, was attacked by a fierce dog that ran out at him from a farmer's dooryard. In parrying off the brute with the fork its prongs stuck into the brute and killed him.

" 'What made you kill my dog?' said the farmer.

" 'What made him try to bite me?'

" 'But why did you not go at him with the other end of the pitchfork?'

" 'Why did he not come after me with his other end?' At this Mr. Lincoln whirled about in his long arms an imaginary dog and pushed its tail end toward the jury. This was the defensive plea of *'son assault demesne'*—loosely, that 'the other fellow brought on the fight,'—quickly told, and in a way the dullest mind would grasp and retain."

Mr. T. W. S. Kidd says that he once heard a lawyer opposed to Lincoln trying to convince a jury that precedent was superior to law, and that custom made things legal in all cases. When Lincoln arose to answer him he told the jury he would argue his case in the same way. Said he: "Old 'Squire Bagly, from Menard, came into my office and said, 'Lincoln, I want your advice as a lawyer. Has a man what's been elected justice of the peace a right to issue a marriage license?' I told him he had not; when the old 'squire threw himself back in his chair very indignantly, and said: 'Lincoln, I thought you was a lawyer. Now Bob Thomas and me had a bet on this thing, and we agreed to let you decide; but if this is your opinion I don't want it, for I know a thunderin' sight better, for I have been 'squire now eight years and have done it all the time.'"

His manner of telling stories was most effective. "When he chose to do so," writes Judge Scott, "he could place the opposite party, and his counsel too, for that matter, in a most ridiculous attitude by relating in his inimitable way a pertinent story. That often gave him a great advantage with the jury. A young lawyer had brought an action in trespass to recover damages done to his client's growing crops by defendant's hogs. The right of action under the law of Illinois, as it was then, depended on the fact whether plaintiff's fence was sufficient to turn ordinary stock. There was some little conflict in the evidence on that question; but the weight of the testimony was decidedly in favor of plaintiff and sustained beyond all doubt his cause of action. Mr. Lincoln appeared for defendant. There was no controversy as to the damage done by defendant's stock. The only thing in the case that could possibly admit of any discussion was the condition of plaintiff's fence; and as the testimony on that question seemed to be in favor of plaintiff, and as the sum involved was little in amount, Mr. Lincoln did not deem it necessary to argue the case seriously, but by way of saying something in behalf of his client he told a little story about a *fence* that was so *crooked* that when a hog went through an opening in it, invariably it came out on the same side from whence it started. His description of the confused look of the hog after several times going through the fence and still finding itself on the side from which it had started was a humorous specimen of the best story-telling. The effect was to make plaintiff's case appear ridiculous; and while Mr. Lincoln did not attempt to apply the story to the case, the jury seemed to think it had some kind of application to the fence in controversy—otherwise he would not have told it—and shortly returned a verdict for the defendant."

Those unfamiliar with his methods frequently took his stories as an effort to wring a laugh from the jury. A lawyer, a stranger to Mr. Lincoln, once expressed to General Linder the opinion that this practice of Lincoln was a waste of time. "Don't lay that flattering unction to your soul," Linder answered; "Lincoln is like Tansey's horse, he 'breaks to win.'"

But it was not his stories, it was his clearness which was his strongest point. He meant that the jury should see that he was right. For this reason he never used a word which the dullest juryman could not understand. Rarely, if ever, did a Latin term creep into his arguments. A lawyer quoting a legal maxim one day in court, turned to Lincoln, and said: "That is so, is it not, Mr. Lincoln?"

"If that's Latin," Lincoln replied, "you had better call another witness."

His illustrations were almost always of the homeliest kind. He did not care to "go among the ancients for figures," he said.

"Much of the force of his argument," writes Judge Scott, "lay in his logical statement of the facts of a case. When he had in that way secured a clear understanding of the facts, the jury and the court would seem naturally to follow him in his conclusions as to the law of the case. His simple and natural presentation of the facts seemed to give the impression that the jury were themselves making the statement. He had the happy and unusual faculty of making the jury believe *they*—and not *he*—were trying the case. Mr. Lincoln kept himself in the background and apparently assumed nothing more than to be an *assistant* counsel to the court or the jury, on whom the primary responsibility for the final decision of the case in fact rested."

He rarely consulted books during a trial, lest he lose the attention of the jury, and if obliged to, translated their statements into the simplest terms. In his desire to keep his case clear he rarely argued points

MR. LINCOLN IN 1857.

From an ambrotype made in the fall of 1857 at Urbana, Illinois. Mr. Lincoln is wearing the photographer's coat, he having gone to the gallery in a light linen garment which would not "take" well. This accounts for the peculiar "fit"!

which seemed to him unessential. "In law it is good policy never to plead what you need not, lest you oblige yourself to prove what you can not," he wrote. He would thus give away point after point with an indifferent "I reckon that's so," until the point which he considered pivotal was reached, and there he hung.

"In making a speech," says Mr. John Hill, "Mr. Lincoln was the plainest man I ever heard. He was not a speaker but a talker. He talked to jurors and to political gatherings plain, sensible, candid talk, almost as in conversation, no effort whatever in oratory. But his talking had wonderful effect. Honesty, candor, fairness, everything that was convincing, were in his manner and expressions."

This candor of which Mr. Hill speaks characterized his entire conduct of a trial. "It is well understood by the profession," says General Mason Brayman, "that lawyers do not read authorities favoring the opposing side. I once heard Mr. Lincoln, in the Supreme Court of Illinois, reading from a reported case some strong points in favor of his argument. Reading a little too far, and before becoming aware of it, he plunged into an authority against himself. Pausing a moment, he drew up his shoulders in a comical way, and half laughing, went on, 'There, there, may it please the court, I reckon I've scratched up a snake. But, as I'm in for it, I guess I'll read it through.' Then, in his most ingenious and matchless manner, he went on with his argument and won his case, convincing the court that it was not much of a snake after all."

CHAPTER XVI

LINCOLN'S IMPORTANT LAW CASES—DEFENCE OF A SLAVE GIRL—THE MC CORMICK CASE—THE ARMSTRONG MURDER CASE—THE ROCK ISLAND BRIDGE CASE

ABRAHAM LINCOLN's place in the legal circle of Illinois long went undefined. The impression prevailed that, though a faithful and trusted lawyer, he never rose to the first rank of his profession. This idea came from imperfect information concerning his legal career. An examination of the reports of the Illinois Supreme Court from 1840, when he tried his first case before that body, to 1861, when he gave up his profession to become President of the United States, shows that in this period of twenty years, broken as it was, from 1847 to 1849, by a term in Congress, and interrupted constantly, from 1854 to 1860, by his labors in opposition to the repeal of the Missouri Compromise, Lincoln was engaged in nearly one hundred cases before that court, some of them of great importance. This fact alone shows him to have been one of the leading lawyers of his state. Between ninety and one hundred cases before the Supreme Court of a state in twenty years is a record surpassed by but few lawyers. It was exceeded by none of Lincoln's Illinois contemporaries.

Among the cases in which he was prominent and of which we have reports, there are several of dramatic

IMPORTANT LAW CASES 299

import, viewing them, as we can now, in connection with his later life. One of the first in which he appeared before the Illinois Supreme Court involved the freedom of a negro girl called Nance. In spite of the fact that Illinois had been free since its admission as a state, many traces of slavery still remained, particularly in the southern and central parts of the state. Among the scattered slaveholders was one Nathan Cromwell of Tazewell County, who for some years had in his service a negro girl, Nance. He claimed that Nance was bound to him by indenture, and that he had the right to sell her as any other property, a right he succeeded finally in exercising. One of his neighbors, Baily by name, bought the girl; but the purchase was conditional: Baily was to pay for his property only when he received from Cromwell title papers showing that Nance was bound to serve under the laws of the state. These papers Cromwell failed to produce before his death. Later his heirs sued Baily for the purchase price. Baily employed Lincoln to defend him. The case was tried in September, 1839, and decided against Baily. Then in July, 1841, it was tried again, before the Supreme Court of the state. Lincoln proved that Nance had lived for several years in the state, that she was over twenty-one years of age, that she had declared herself to be free, and that she had even purchased goods on her own account. The list of authorities he used in the trial to prove that Nance could not be held in bondage shows that he was already familiar with both Federal and state legislation on the slavery question up to that date. He went back to the Ordinance of 1787 to show that slavery was forbidden in the Northwest Territory; he recalled the Constitution that had made the state free in 1818; he showed that by the law of nations no person can be sold in a free state. His argument convinced the court; the judgment of the lower court was overruled, and Nance was free.

After Lincoln's return from Congress in 1849, he was engaged in some of the most important cases of the day. One of these was a contest between the Illinois Central Railroad, at that time building, and McLean County, Illinois. This road had been exempted by the legislature from all state taxation on condition that it pay perpetually into the state treasury seven per cent. of its annual gross earnings. When the line was laid in McLean County the county authorities declared that the state legislature could not excuse the railroad company from paying county taxes; accordingly the company's property was assessed and a tax levied. If this claim of the county could be sustained, it was certain to kill the railroad; and great preparations were made for the defence. The solicitor of the Illinois Central at that time was General Mason Brayman, who retained Lincoln. The case was tried at Bloomington, before the Supreme Court, and, largely through the efforts of Lincoln, was won for the road. According to Herndon, Lincoln charged for his services a fee of two thousand dollars. Going to Chicago he presented his bill. "Why," said the officer to whom he applied, "this is as much as a first-class lawyer would have charged."

Stung by the ungrateful speech, Lincoln withdrew the bill, left the office, and at the first opportunity

LINCOLN'S OFFICE BOOK-CASE, CHAIR, AND INK STAND.

(In the Lincoln collection of Mr. William H. Lambert of Philadelphia, Pa.)

They formerly belonged to the Lincoln Memorial Collection of Chicago. Accompanying the ink stand is a letter saying that Mr. Lincoln wrote from it the famous "house-divided-against-itself" speech.

submitted the matter to his friends. Five thousand dollars, they all agreed, was a moderate fee, considering what he had done for the road, and six leading lawyers of the state signed a paper in which they declared that such a charge would not be "unreasonable." Lincoln then sued the road for that amount and won his case. "He gave me my half," says Herndon; "and as much as we deprecated the avarice of great corporations, we both thanked the Lord for letting the Illinois Central Railroad fall into our hands."

The current version of this story names General George B. McClellan as the testy official who snubbed Lincoln when he presented the bill. This could not have been. The incident occurred in 1855; that year Captain McClellan spent in the Crimea, as one of a commission of three sent abroad to study the European military service as displayed in the Crimean War. It was not until January, 1857, that McClellan resigned his commission in the United States army to become the chief engineer, and afterwards vice-president, of the Illinois Central Railroad. It was when an officer of the Illinois Central, however, that McClellan first met Lincoln. "Long before the war," he says, in "McClellan's Own Story," "when vice-president of the Illinois Central Railroad, I knew Mr. Lincoln, for he was one of the counsel of the company. More than once I have been with him in out-of-the-way county-seats where some important case was being tried, and, in the lack of sleeping accommodations, have spent the night in front of a stove, listening to the unceasing flow of anecdotes from his lips.

He was never at a loss, and I could never quite make up my mind how many of them he had really heard before, and how many he invented on the spur of the moment. His stories were seldom refined, but were always to the point."

It was through his legal practice that Lincoln first met still another man who was to sustain a relation of the greatest importance to him in the war. This man was Edwin M. Stanton. The meeting occurred in Cincinnati in 1855 in connection with a patent case which is famous in the manufacturing history of the country, and in which both Lincoln and Stanton had been retained as counsel. So much that is false has been written of this meeting, that a full and exact statement of the circumstances was obtained for this work from Mr. George Harding of Philadelphia, the only one of the counsel in the case living when this book was written.

"Cyrus H. McCormick owned reaping-machine patents granted in 1845 and 1847," says Mr. Harding, "upon which he sued John M. Manny and Co. of Rockford, Illinois. Mr. Manny had obtained patents also. Manny and Co. were large manufacturers of reaping-machines under Manny's patents. McCormick contended that his patents were valid and secured to him a virtual monopoly of all practical reaping machines as constructed at that date. If McCormick had been successful in his contention, Manny would have been enjoined, his factory stopped, and a claim of four hundred thousand dollars damages demanded from his firm. McCormick's income from that monopoly would have been vastly increased. Hence the suit was very important to all parties and to the farming public. The plaintiff McCormick had retained Mr. E. N. Dickerson and Reverdy Johnson. The former was entrusted with the preparation of the plaintiff's case and the argument before the court on the mechanics of the case. Mr. P. H. Watson, who had procured Manny's patents, was given by Manny the entire control of the defendant's case. He employed Mr. George Harding to prepare the defence for Manny and to argue the mechanics of the case before the court. In those times it was deemed important in patent cases to employ associate counsel not specially familiar with mechanical questions, but of high standing in the general practice of the law, and of recognized forensic ability. If such counsel represented the defendant he urged upon the court the importance of treating the patentee as a quasi-monopolist, whose claims should be limited to the precise mechanical contributions which he had made to the art; while, on the other hand, the plaintiff's forensic counsel was expected to dwell upon the privations and labor of the patentee, and insist on a very liberal view of his claims, and to hold that defendants who had appropriated any of his ideas should be treated as pirates. The necessity of the forensic contributions in the argument of patent cases is not now recognized.

"McCormick had selected Mr. Reverdy Johnson for the forensic part of his case. Mr. Watson was in doubt as to whom to select to perform this duty for the defendants. At the suggestion of Mr. Manny, Mr. Watson wrote to Mr. Lincoln, sending to him a retainer of five hundred dollars, and requesting him to read the testimony, which was sent to him from time to time as taken, so that if Mr. Watson afterward concluded to have him argue the case he would be prepared. Mr. Harding had urged the employment of Mr. Stanton, who was personally known to him, and who then resided at Pittsburg.

"With a view to determining finally who should argue the forensic part of Manny's case, Mr. Watson personally visited Springfield and conferred with Mr. Lincoln. On his way back from Springfield he called upon Mr. Stanton at Pittsburg, and, after a conference, retained Mr. Stanton, and informed him distinctly that he was to make the closing argument in the case. Nevertheless Mr. Lincoln was sent copies of the testimony; he studied the testimony and was paid for so doing, the same as Mr. Stanton. Mr. Watson considered that it would be prudent for Mr. Lincoln to be prepared, in case of Mr. Stanton's inability, for any cause, to argue the case; so that, at the outset, Mr. Stanton was selected by Mr. Manny's direct representative to perform this duty.

"When all the parties and counsel met at Cincinnati, Mr. Lincoln was first definitely informed by Mr. Watson of his determination that Mr. Stanton was to close the case for defendants. Mr. Lincoln was evidently disappointed at Mr. Watson's decision. Mr. Lincoln had written out his argument in full. He was anxious to meet Mr. Reverdy Johnson in forensic contest. The case was important as to the amount in dispute, and of widespread interest to farmers. Mr. Lincoln's feelings were embittered, moreover, because the plaintiff's counsel subsequently, in open court, of their own motion, stated that they perceived that there were three counsel present for defendant, and that plaintiff had only two counsel present; but they were willing to allow all three of defendant's counsel to speak, provided Mr. Dickerson, who had charge of the mechanical part of McCormick's case, were permitted to make two arguments, besides Mr. Johnson's argument. Mr. Watson, who had charge of defendant's case, declined this offer, because the case ultimately depended upon mechanical questions; and he thought that if Mr. Dickerson were allowed to open the mechanical part of the case and then make a subsequent argument on the mechanics, the temptation would be great to make an insufficient or misleading mechanical opening of the case at first, and, after Mr. Harding had replied thereto, to make a fuller or different mechanical presentation, which could not be replied to by Mr. Harding. It was conceded that neither Mr. Lincoln nor Mr. Stanton was prepared to handle the mechanics of the case either in opening or reply. In view of these facts, Mr. Watson decided that only two arguments

IMPORTANT LAW CASES

would be made for Manny, and that Mr. Harding would open the case for defendant on the mechanical part, and Mr. Stanton would close on the general propositions of law applicable to the case. Mr. Stanton said in court that personally he had no desire to speak, but he agreed with Mr. Watson that only two arguments should be made for defendants whether he spoke or not. Mr. Lincoln, knowing Mr. Watson's wishes, insisted that Mr. Stanton should make the closing argument, and that he would not himself speak. Mr. Stanton accepted the position and did speak, because he knew that such was the expressed wish and direction of Mr. Watson, who controlled the conduct of defendant's case.

"Mr. Lincoln kindly and gracefully, but regretfully, accepted the situation. He attended and exhibited much interest in the case as it proceeded. He sent to Mr. Harding the written argument which he had prepared, that he might have the benefit of it before he made his opening argument; but requested Mr. Harding not to show it to Mr. Stanton. The chagrin of Mr. Lincoln at not speaking continued, however, and he felt that Mr. Stanton should have insisted on his, Mr. Lincoln's, speaking also; while Mr. Stanton merely carried out the positive direction of his client that there should be only two arguments for defendant, and that he, Mr. Stanton, should close the case, and Mr. Harding should open the case. Mr. Lincoln expressed to Mr. Harding satisfaction at the manner in which the mechanical part of the case had been presented by him, and after Mr. Lincoln had been elected President, he showed his recollection of it by tendering Mr. Harding, of his own motion, a high position.

"In regard to the personal treatment of Mr. Lincoln while in attendance at Cincinnati, it is to be borne in mind that Mr. Lincoln was known to hardly any one in Cincinnati at that date, and that Mr. Stanton was probably not impressed with the appearance of Mr. Lincoln. It is true there was no personal intimacy formed between them while at Cincinnati. Mr. Lincoln was disappointed and unhappy while in Cincinnati, and undoubtedly did not receive the attention which he should have received. Mr. Lincoln felt all this, and particularly, but unjustly, reflected upon Mr. Stanton as the main cause. When Mr. Lincoln was nominated for President, Mr. Stanton, like many others in the country, sincerely doubted whether Mr. Lincoln was equal to the tremendous responsibility which he was to be called upon to assume as President. This is to be borne in mind, in view of events subsequent to the case at Cincinnati. Mr. Stanton never called upon Mr. Lincoln after he came to Washington as President. Mr. Lincoln in alluding to Mr. Stanton (both before and after his election as President) did not attempt to conceal his unkind feeling towards him, which had its origin at Cincinnati. This feeling did not undergo a change until after he met Mr. Stanton as Secretary of War.

"The occurrences narrated show how one great man may underrate his fellow man. Mr. Stanton saw at Cincinnati in Mr. Lincoln only his gaunt, rugged features, his awkward dress and carriage, and heard only his rural jokes; but Stanton lived to perceive in those rugged lineaments only expressions of nobility and loveliness of character, and to hear from his lips only wisdom, prudence, and courage, couched in language unsurpassed in literature. But above all they show the nobility of Mr. Lincoln's character in forgetting all unkind personal feeling engendered at Cincinnati towards Mr. Stanton, and subsequently appointing him his Secretary of War.

"The above was narrated by Mr. Harding for the main purpose of correcting the popular impression that Mr. Stanton, of his own motion, rode over and displaced Mr. Lincoln in the case at Cincinnati; for the truth is that Mr. Stanton, in the course he pursued, was directed by his clients' representative, Mr. Watson, who believed that he was serving the best interests of his clients."

Lincoln was first suggested to Mr. Manny as counsel in this case by a younger member of the firm, Mr. Ralph Emerson, of Rockford, Illinois. Mr. Emerson, as a student of law, had been thrown much into Lincoln's company and had learned to respect his judgment and ability. Indeed, it was Lincoln who was instrumental in deciding him to abandon the law. The young man had seen much in the practice of his chosen profession which seemed to him unjust, and he had begun to feel that the law was incompatible with his ideals. One evening, after a particularly trying day in court, he walked out with Lincoln. Suddenly turning to his companion, he said: "Mr. Lincoln, I want to ask you a question. Is it possible for a man to practice law and always do by others as he would be done by?" Lincoln's head dropped on his breast, and he walked in silence for a long way; then he heaved a heavy sigh. When he finally spoke, it was of a foreign matter. "I had my answer," said Mr. Emerson, "and that walk turned the course of my life."

During the trial at Cincinnati, Lincoln and Mr. Emerson were thrown much together, and Mr. Emerson's recollections are particularly interesting.

"As I was the sole intimate friend of Mr. Lincoln in the case, when it was decided that he should not take part in the argument, he invited me to his room to express his bitter disappointment; and it was with difficulty that I persuaded him to remain as counsel during the hearing. We generally spent the afternoons together. The hearing had hardly progressed two days before Mr. Lincoln expressed to me his satisfaction that he was not to take part in the argument. So many and so deep were the questions involved that he realized he had not given the subject sufficient study to have done himself justice.

"The court-room, which during the first day or two was

well filled, greatly thinned out as the argument proceeded day after day. But as the crowd diminished, Mr. Lincoln's interest in the case increased. He appeared entirely to forget himself, and at times, rising from his chair, walked back and forth in the open space of the court-room, as though he were in his own office, pausing to listen intently as one point after another was clearly made out in our favor. He manifested such delight in countenance and unconscious action that its effect on the judges, one of whom at least already highly respected him, was evidently stronger than any set speech of his could possibly have been. The impression produced on the judges was evidently that Mr. Lincoln was thoroughly convinced of the justice of our side and anxious that we should prevail, not merely on account of his interest in his clients, but because he thought our case was just and should triumph.

"The final summing up on our side was by Mr. Stanton; and though he took but about three hours in its delivery, he had devoted as many, if not more, weeks to its preparation. It was very able, and Mr. Lincoln was throughout the whole of it a rapt listener. Mr. Stanton closed his speech in a flight of impassioned eloquence. Then the court adjourned for the day, and Mr. Lincoln invited me to take a long walk with him. For block after block he walked rapidly forward, not saying a word, evidently deeply dejected.

"At last he turned suddenly to me, exclaiming, 'Emerson, I am going home.' A pause. 'I am going home to study law.'

"'Why,' I exclaimed, 'Mr. Lincoln, you stand at the head of the bar in Illinois now! What are you talking about?'

"'Ah, yes,' he said, 'I do occupy a good position there, and I think that I can get along with the way things are done there now. But these college-trained men, who have devoted their whole lives to study, are coming West, don't you see? And they study their cases as we never do. They have got as far as Cincinnati now. They will soon be in Illinois.' Another long pause; then stopping and turning

IMPORTANT LAW CASES

toward me, his countenance suddenly assuming that look of strong determination which those who knew him best sometimes saw upon his face, he exclaimed, 'I am going home to study law! I am as good as any of them, and when they get out to Illinois I will be ready for them.' "

The fee which Lincoln received in the McCormick case, including the retainer, which was five hundred dollars—the largest retainer ever received by Lincoln—amounted to nearly two thousand dollars. Except the sum paid him by the Illinois Central Railroad it was probably the largest fee he ever received. The two sums came to him about the same time and undoubtedly helped to tide over the rather unfruitful period, from a financial standpoint which followed—the period of his contest with Douglas for the Senate. Lincoln never made money. From 1850 to 1860 his income averaged from two thousand to three thousand dollars a year. In the forties it was considerably less. The fee-book of Lincoln and Herndon for 1847 shows total earnings of only fifteen hundred dollars. The largest fee entered was one of one hundred dollars. There are several of fifty dollars, a number of twenty, more of ten, still more of five, and a few of three dollars.

But Lincoln's fees were as a rule smaller than his clients expected or his fellow lawyers approved of. Mr. Abraham Brokaw of Bloomington, Illinois, tells the following story illustrating Lincoln's idea of a proper fee. One of Mr. Brokaw's neighbors had borrowed about $500 from him and given his note. When it became due the man refused to pay. Action was brought, and the sheriff levied on the property of the debtor and finally collected the entire debt; but at about that time the sheriff was in need of funds and used the money collected. When Brokaw demanded it from him he was unable to pay it and was found to be insolvent. Thereupon Brokaw employed Stephen A. Douglas to sue the sureties on the official bond of the sheriff. Douglas brought the suit and soon collected the claim. But Douglas was at that time in the midst of a campaign for Congress and the funds were used by him with the expectation of being able to pay Brokaw later. However, he neglected the matter and went to Washington without making any settlement. Brokaw, although a life-long and ardent Democrat and a great admirer of Douglas, was a thrifty German and did not propose to lose sight of his money. After fruitlessly demanding the money from Douglas, Brokaw went to David Davis, then in general practice at Bloomington, told him the circumstances and asked him to undertake the collection of the money from Douglas. Davis protested that he could not do it, that Douglas was a personal friend and a brother lawyer and Democrat and it would be very disagreeable for him to have anything to do with the matter. He finally said to Brokaw, "You wait until the next term of court and Lincoln will be here. He would like nothing better than to have this claim for collection. I will introduce you to him and I have no doubt he will undertake it." Shortly after, Brokaw was presented to Lincoln, stated his case and engaged his services. Lincoln promptly wrote Douglas, still at Washington, that he had the claim for collection and that he must insist upon prompt payment. Douglas,

IMPORTANT LAW CASES

very indignant, wrote directly to Brokaw that he thought the placing of the claim in Lincoln's hands a gross outrage, that he and Brokaw were old friends and Democrats and that Brokaw ought not to place any such weapon in the hands of such an Abolitionist opponent as Lincoln and if he could not wait until Douglas returned he should at least have placed the claim for collection in the hands of a Democrat. Brokaw's thrift again controlled and he sent Douglas' letter to Lincoln. Thereupon Lincoln placed the claim in the hands of "Long" John Wentworth, then a Democratic member of Congress from Chicago. Wentworth called upon Douglas and insisted upon payment, which shortly after was made, and Brokaw at last received his money. "And what do you suppose Lincoln charged me?" Brokaw says in telling the story. After hearing a few guesses he answered, "He charged me exactly $3.50 for collecting nearly $600."

Such charges were felt by the lawyers of the Eighth Circuit, with some reason, to be purely quixotic. They protested and argued, but Lincoln went on serenely charging what he thought his services worth. Ward Lamon who was one of Lincoln's numerous circuit partners says that he and Lincoln frequently fell out on the matter of fees. On one occasion Lamon was particularly incensed. He had charged and received a good-sized fee for a case which the two had tried together and won. When Lamon offered Lincoln his share he refused it. The fee was too large, he said, part of it must be refunded and he would not accept a cent until that had been done. Judge Davis heard of this transaction. He was himself a shrewd money-maker, never hesitating to take all he could legally get, and he felt strong disgust at this disinterested attitude about money. Calling Lincoln to him the judge scolded roundly. "You are pauperizing this court, Mr. Lincoln, you are ruining your fellows. Unless you quit this ridiculous policy, we shall all have to go to farming." But not even the ire of the bench moved Lincoln.

If a fee was not paid, Lincoln did not believe in suing for it. Mr. Herndon says that he would consent to be swindled before he would contest a fee. The case of the Illinois Central Railroad, however, was an exception to this rule. He was careless in accounts, never entering anything on the book. When a fee was paid to him, he simply divided the money into two parts, one of which he put into his pocket, and the other into an envelope which he labelled "Herndon's half." Lincoln's whole theory of the conduct of a lawyer in regard to money is summed up in the "notes" for a law lecture which he left among his papers:

"The matter of fees is important, far beyond the mere question of bread and butter involved. Properly attended to, fuller justice is done to both lawyer and client. An exorbitant fee should never be claimed. As a general rule never take your whole fee in advance, nor any more than a small retainer. When fully paid beforehand, you are more than a common mortal if you can feel the same interest in the case, as if something was still in prospect for you, as well as for your client. And when you lack interest in the case the job will very likely lack skill and diligence in the performance. Settle the amount of fee and take a note in advance.

IMPORTANT LAW CASES 313

Then you will feel that you are working for something, and you are sure to do your work faithfully and well. Never sell a fee note—at least not before the consideration service is performed. It leads to negligence and dishonesty—negligence by losing interest in the case, and dishonesty in refusing to refund when you have allowed the consideration to fail."

If a client was poor, and Lincoln's sympathies were aroused, he not infrequently refused pay. There are a few well authenticated cases of his offering his services to those whom he believed he could help, stipulating when he did it that he would make no charge. The best known example of this is the Armstrong murder case.

William, or "Duff" Armstrong, as he was generally called, was the son of Lincoln's New Salem friends, Jack and Hannah Armstrong. In August, 1857, Duff and a number of his mates had joined a crowd of ruffians who had gathered on the outskirts of a camp-meeting held near Havana, in Macon County. He had drunk heavily for some days, and, finally, in a broil on the night of August 29, had beaten a comrade, one Metzker, who had provoked him to a fight. That same night Metzker was hit with an ox-yoke by another drunken reveller, Norris by name. Three days later he died. Both Armstrong and Norris were arrested. Marks of two blows were on the victim, either of which might have killed him. That Norris had dealt one was proved. Did Armstrong deal the other? He claimed he had used nothing but his fists in the broil; but both the marks on Metzker were such as must have been made by some instrument. The theory was developed that one blow was from a slungshot used by Armstrong, and that he and Norris had acted in concert, deliberately planning to murder Metzker. Outraged by the cruelty of the deed, the whole countryside demanded the punishment of the prisoners. Just at the time that Armstrong was thrown into prison his father died, his last charge to his wife Hannah being, "Sell everything you have and clear Duff." True to her trust, Hannah engaged two Havana lawyers, both living when this book was written, to defend her boy. Anxious lest the violence of public feeling should injure Duff's chances, the lawyers secured a change of venue to Cass County, their client remaining in prison until spring. Norris, in the meantime, was convicted and sentenced to eight years in the penitentiary.

When Lincoln heard of the arrest of Duff Armstrong he at once wrote his mother:

"Dear Mrs. Armstrong: I have just heard of your deep affliction, and the arrest of your son for murder. I can hardly believe that he can be capable of the crime alleged against him. It does not seem possible. I am anxious that he should be given a fair trial at any rate; and gratitude for your long-continued kindness to me in adverse circumstances prompts me to offer my humble services gratuitously in his behalf.

"It will afford me an opportunity to requite, in a small degree, the favors I received at your hand, and that of your lamented husband, when your roof afforded me a grateful shelter, without money and without price."

The trial came off in May, 1858, at Beardstown, and Lincoln was on hand. At that moment he was, after Stephen A. Douglas, the most conspicuous man in Illinois. His future course in politics was a source of interest both in the East and West. The coming contest with Douglas for the senatorship—for it was already probable that he would be the candidate in the convention which was only a month away—was causing him intense anxiety. Yet occupied as he was with his profession and harassed by the critical political situation, he did not hesitate to keep the promise that he had made nine months before to Hannah Armstrong. Going to her lawyers, he said that he should like to assist them. They asked nothing better than to have his aid. He seems to have taken full charge at the start. His first care was the selection of a jury. Not knowing the neighborhood well, he could not discriminate closely as to individuals; but he took pains, as far as he could control the choice, to have only young men chosen, believing that they would be more favorable to the prisoner. A surviving witness in the case estimates that the average age of the jury was not over twenty-three years.

The jury empanelled, the examination of witnesses on behalf of the defence seems to have been conducted chiefly by Lincoln. Many of the witnesses bore familiar names. Some were sons of "Clary's Grove Boys," and Lincoln had known their fathers. "The witnesses were kept out of the court-room until called to testify," says William A. Douglas. "I happened to be the first witness called, and so heard the whole trial. When William Killian was called to the stand, Lincoln asked him his name.

" 'William Killian,' was the reply.

"'Bill Killian,' Lincoln repeated in a familiar way; 'tell me, are you a son of old Jake Killian?'

"'Yes, sir,' answered the witness.

"'Well,' said Lincoln, somewhat aside, 'you are a smart boy if you take after your dad.'"

As the trial developed it became evident that there could have been no collusion between Armstrong and Norris, but there was strong evidence that Armstrong had used a slung-shot. The most damaging evidence was that of one Allen, who swore that he had seen Armstrong strike Metzker about ten or eleven o'clock in the evening. When asked how he could see, he answered that the moon shone brightly. Under Lincoln's questioning he repeated the statement until it was impressed on the jury. If Allen's testimony stood, conviction seemed certain.

Lincoln's address to the jury was full of genuine pathos. It was not as a hired attorney that he was there, he said, but to discharge a debt of friendship. "Uncle Abe," says Duff Armstrong himself, "did his best talking when he told the jury what true friends my father and mother had been to him in the early days. . . . He told how he used to go out to 'Jack' Armstrong's and stay for days; how kind mother was to him; and how, many a time, he had rocked me to sleep in the old cradle."

But Lincoln was not relying on sympathy alone to win his case. In closing he reviewed the evidence, showing that all depended on Allen's testimony, and this he said he could prove to be false. Allen never saw Armstrong strike Metzker by the light of the moon, for at the hour when he said he saw the fight, between ten and eleven o'clock, the moon was not in the heavens. Then producing an almanac, he passed it to the judge and jury. The moon, which was on that night in its first quarter, had set before midnight. This unexpected overthrow of the testimony by which Lincoln had taken care that the jury should be most deeply impressed, threw them into confusion. There was a complete change of feeling. Lincoln saw it; and as he finished his address, and the jury left the room, turning to the boy's mother, he said, "Aunt Hannah, your son will be free before sundown."

Lincoln had not misread his jury. Duff Armstrong was discharged as not guilty.

There has long been a story current that the dramatic introduction of the almanac, by which certainly the audience and the jury were won, was a piece of trickery on Lincoln's part; that the almanac was not one of 1857, but of 1853, in which the figure three had been changed throughout to seven. The best reply to this charge of forgery is the very evident one that it was utterly unnecessary. The almanac for August, 1857, shows that the moon was in the position where it served Lincoln's client's interests best. He did not need to forge an almanac, the one of the period being all that he could want.

Another murder case in which Lincoln defended the accused occurred in August, 1859. The victim was a student in his own law office, Greek Crafton. The murderer, Peachy Harrison, was the grandson of Lincoln's old political antagonist, Peter Cartwright. Both young men were connected with the best families of the county; the brother of one was married to the sister of the other; they had been lifelong friends. In an altercation upon some political question hot words were exchanged, and Harrison, beside himself, stabbed Crafton, who three days later died from the wound. The best known lawyers of the state were engaged for the case. Senator John M. Palmer and General A. McClernand were on the side of the prosecution. Among those who represented the defendant were Lincoln, Herndon, Logan, and Senator Shelby M. Cullom. The tragic pathos of a case which involved, as this did, the deepest affections of almost an entire community, reached its climax in the appearance in court of the venerable Peter Cartwright. No face in Illinois was better known than his, no life had been spent in a more relentless war on evil. Eccentric and aggressive as he was, he was honored far and wide; and when he arose in the witness stand, his white hairs crowned with this cruel sorrow, the most indifferent spectator felt that his examination would be unbearable. It fell to Lincoln to question Cartwright. With the rarest gentleness he began to put his questions.

"How long have you known the prisoner?"

Cartwright's head dropped on his breast for a moment; then straightening himself, he passed his hand across his eyes and answered in a deep, quavering voice:

"I have known him since a babe, he laughed and cried on my knee."

The examination ended by Lincoln drawing from the witness the story of how Crafton had said to him, just before his death: "I am dying; I will soon part

IMPORTANT LAW CASES

with all I love on earth, and I want you to say to my slayer that I forgive him. I want to leave this earth with a forgiveness of all who have in any way injured me."

This examination made a profound impression on the jury. Lincoln closed his argument by picturing the scene anew, appealing to the jury to practice the same forgiving spirit that the murdered man had shown on his death-bed. It was undoubtedly to his handling of the grandfather's evidence that Harrison's acquittal was due.

A class of legal work which Lincoln enjoyed particularly was that in which mathematical or mechanical problems were involved. He never lost interest in his youthful pot-boiling profession of surveying, and would go out himself to make sure of boundaries if a client's case required particular investigation. Indeed, he was generally recognized by his fellow lawyers as an authority on surveying, and as late as 1859 his opinion on a disputed question was sought by a convention of surveyors who had met in Springfield. One of the most interesting cases involving mechanical problems which Lincoln ever argued was that of the Rock Island Bridge. It was not, however, the calculations he used which made it striking. The case was a dramatic episode in the war long waged by the Mississippi against the plains beyond. For decades the river had been the willing burden-bearer of the West. Now, however, the railroad had come. The Rock Island Railroad had even dared to bridge the stream to carry away the traffic which the river claimed.

In May, 1856, a steamboat struck one of the piers of the bridge and was wrecked and burned. One pier of the bridge was also destroyed. The boat owners sued the railroad company. The suit was the beginning of the long and violent struggle for commercial supremacy between St. Louis and Chicago. In Chicago it was commonly charged that the St. Louis Chamber of Commerce had bribed the captain of the boat to run upon the pier; and it was said that later, when the bridge itself was burned, the steamers gathered near and whistled for joy. The case was felt to involve the future course of western commerce; and when it was called in September, 1857, at Chicago, people crowded there from all over the West. Norman B. Judd, afterwards so prominent in the politics of the state, was the attorney of the road, and he engaged Lincoln, among others, as counsel. Lincoln made an address to the jury which those who remember it declare to have been one of his strongest legal arguments.

"The two points relied upon by the opponents of the bridge," says Judge Blodgett of Chicago, "were:
"First. That the river was the great waterway for the commerce of the valley, and could not legally be obstructed by a bridge.
"Second. That this particular bridge was so located with reference to the channel of the river at that point as to make it a peril to all water craft navigating the river and an unnecessary obstruction to navigation.
"The first proposition had not at that time been directly passed upon by the Supreme Court of the United States, although the Wheeling Bridge case involved the question; but the court had evaded a decision upon it, by holding that

the Wheeling Bridge was so low as to be an unnecessary obstruction to the use of the river by steamboats. The discussion of the first proposition on the part of the bridge company devolved mainly upon Mr. Abraham Lincoln.

"I listened with much interest to his argument on this point, and while I was not impressed by it as a specially eloquent effort (as the word eloquent is generally understood), I have always considered it as one of the ablest efforts I ever heard from Mr. Lincoln at the bar. His illustrations were apt and forcible, his statements clear and logical, and his reasons in favor of the policy (and necessarily the right) to bridge the river, and thereby encourage the settlement and building up of the vast area of fertile country to the west of it, were broad and statesmanlike.

"The pith of his argument was in his statement that *one man had as good a right to cross a river as another had to sail up or down it;* that these were equal and mutual rights which must be exercised so as not to interfere with each other, like the right to cross a street or highway and the right to pass along it. From this undeniable right to cross the river he then proceeded to discuss the means for crossing. Must it always be by canoe or ferryboat? Must the products of all the boundless fertile country lying west of the river for all time be compelled to stop on its western bank, be unloaded from the cars and loaded upon a boat, and after the transit across the river, be reloaded into cars on the other side, to continue their journey East? In this connection he drew a vivid picture of the future of the great West lying beyond the river, and argued that the necessities of commerce demanded that the bridges across the river be a conceded right, which the steamboat interests ought not to be allowed to successfully resist, and thereby stay the progress of development and civilization in the region of the West.

"While I cannot recall a word or sentence of the argument, I well remember its effect on all who listened to it, and the decision of the court fully sustained the right to bridge so long as it did not unnecessarily obstruct navigation."

All the papers in regard to the trial are supposed to have been burned in the Chicago fire of 1871, but the speech, which was reported by Congressman Hitt of Illinois, at that time court stenographer, was published on September 24, 1857, in the Chicago "Daily Press," afterwards united with the "Tribune."

According to this report the first part of the speech was devoted to the points Judge Blodgett outlines; the second part was given to a careful explanation of the currents of the Mississippi at the point where the bridge crossed. Lincoln succeeded in showing that had the pilot of the boat been as familiar as he ought to have been with the river, he could easily have prevented the accident. His argument was full of nice mathematical calculations clearly put, and was marked by perfect candor. Indeed, the honesty with which he admitted the points made by the opposite counsel caused considerable alarm to some of his associates. Mrs. Norman B. Judd (Mr. Judd was the attorney of the road) says that Mr. Joseph B. Knox, who was also engaged with Mr. Lincoln in the defence, dined at her house the day that Lincoln made his speech. "He sat down at the dinner table in great excitement," writes Mrs. Judd, "saying, 'Lincoln has lost the case for us. The admissions he made in regard to the currents in the Mississippi at Rock Island and Moline will convince the court that a bridge at that point will always be a serious and constant detriment to navigation on the river.' 'Wait until you hear the conclusion of his speech,' replied Mr. Judd;

'you will find his admission is a strong point instead of a weak one, and on it he will found a strong argument that will satisfy you.' " And as it proved, Mr. Judd was right.

The few cases briefly outlined here show something of the range of Lincoln's legal work. They show that not only his friends like Hannah Armstrong believed in his power with a jury, but that great corporations like the Illinois Central Railroad were willing to trust their affairs in his hands; that he was not only a "jury lawyer," as has been often stated, but trusted when it came to questions of law pure and simple. If this study of his cases were continued, it would only be to accumulate evidence to prove that Lincoln was considered by his contemporaries one of the best lawyers of Illinois.

It is worth notice, too, that he made his reputation as a lawyer and tried his greatest cases *before* his debate with Douglas gave him a national reputation. It was in 1855 that the Illinois Central engaged him first as counsel; in 1855 that he went to Cincinnati on the McCormick case; in 1857 that he tried the Rock Island Bridge case. Thus his place was won purely on his legal ability unaided by political prestige. His success came, too, in middle life. Lincoln was forty years old in 1849, when he abandoned politics definitely, as he thought, for the law. He tried his greatest cases when he was from forty-five to forty-eight.

CHAPTER XVII

LINCOLN RE-ENTERS POLITICS

FROM 1849 to 1854 Abraham Lincoln gave almost his entire time to his profession. Politics received from him only the attention which any public-spirited citizen without personal ambition should give. He kept close watch upon Federal, state and local affairs. He was active in the efforts made in Illinois in 1851 to secure a more thorough party organization. In 1852 he was on the Scott electoral ticket and did some canvassing. But this was all. He was yearly becoming more absorbed in his legal work, losing more and more of his old inclination for politics, when in May, 1854, the Repeal of the Missouri Compromise aroused him as he had never been before in all his life. The Missouri Compromise was the second in that series of noble provisions for making new territory free territory, which liberty-loving men had wrested from the United States Congress, whenever the thirst for expansion had seized this country. The first of these was the "Ordinance of 1787," prohibiting slavery in all the great Northwest Territory. The second the Missouri Compromise, passed in 1820, was the result of a struggle to keep the Louisiana Purchase free. It provided that Missouri might come in as a slave state if slavery was never allowed north of 36° 30′ north latitude. The next great expansion of the United States after the Louisiana Purchase resulted from the annexation of Texas, and of the territory acquired by the Mexican War. The North was determined that this new territory should be free. The South wanted it for slaves. The struggle between them threatened the Union for a time, but it was adjusted by the Compromise of 1850, in which, according to Mr. Lincoln's summing up, "the South got their new fugitive-slave law, and the North got California (by far the best part of our acquisition from Mexico) as a free state. The South got a provision that New Mexico and Utah, when admitted as states, may come in with or without slavery, as they may then choose; and the North got the slave-trade abolished in the District of Columbia. The North got the western boundary of Texas thrown farther back eastward than the South desired; but, in turn, they gave Texas ten millions of dollars with which to pay her old debts."

For three years matters were quiet. Then Nebraska sought territorial organization. Now by the Missouri Compromise slavery was forbidden in that section of the Union, but in spite of this fact, Stephen A. Douglas, then a member of the United States Senate, added to a bill which he had introduced giving Kansas and Nebraska the state governments they desired, an amendment repealing the Missouri Compromise, permitting the people who should settle in the new territories to reject or establish slavery as they should see fit. It was the passage of this bill which brought Abraham Lincoln from the court-room to the stump. His friend Richard Yates was running for re-election to Congress. Lincoln began to speak for him, but in accepting invitations he stipulated that it should be against the Kansas-Nebraska Bill that he talk. His earnestness surprised his friends. Lincoln was coming back into politics, they said, and when Douglas, the author of the repeal, was announced to speak in Springfield in October of 1854, they called on Lincoln to meet him.

Douglas was having a serious struggle to reconcile his Illinois constituency. All the free sentiment of the state had been bitterly aroused by his part in the repeal of the Missouri Compromise, and when he first returned to Illinois it looked as if he would not be given even a hearing. Indeed, when he first attempted to speak in Chicago, September 1, he was hooted from the platform. With every day in the state, however, he won back his friends, so great was his power over men, and he was beginning to arouse something of his old enthusiasm when he went to Springfield to speak at the annual State Fair. There was a great crowd present from all parts of the state, and Douglas spoke for three hours. When he closed it was announced that Lincoln would answer him the next day. Lincoln's friends expected him to do well in his reply, but his speech was a surprise even to those who knew him best. It was profound, finished, vigorous, eloquent. When had he mastered the history of the slavery question so completely? they asked each other. "The anti-Nebraska speech of Mr. Lincoln," said the "Springfield Journal" the next day, "was the profoundest, in our opinion, that he has made in his whole life. He felt upon his soul the truths burn which he uttered, and all present felt that he was true to his own soul. His feelings once or twice swelled within and came near stifling utterance. He quivered with emotion. The whole house was as still as death. He attacked the Nebraska Bill with unusual warmth and energy; and all felt that a man of strength was its enemy, and that he intended to blast it if he could by strong and manly efforts. He was most successful, and the house approved the glorious triumph of truth by loud and continued huzzas."

The vigor and earnestness of Lincoln's speech aroused the crowd to such enthusiasm that Senator Douglas felt obliged to reply to him the next day. These speeches of October 3, 4 and 5, 1854, form really the first of the series of Lincoln-Douglas Debates. They proved conclusively to the anti-Nebraska politicians in Illinois that Lincoln was to be their leader in the fight they had begun against the extension of slavery.

Although the speech of October 4 was not preserved, we know from Paul Selby, at that time editor of an independent paper in Jacksonville, Illinois, which had been working hard against the repeal of the Missouri Compromise, that Lincoln's speech at Springfield was practically the same as one delivered twelve days later at Peoria in reply to Douglas. Of this latter a full report was preserved.

In his reply at Peoria, Lincoln began by a brief but sufficient résumé of the efforts of the North to apply the Declaration of Independence to all new territory which it acquired, and failing in that to provide for the sake of peace a series of compromises reserving as much territory as possible to freedom. He showed that the Kansas-Nebraska Bill was a direct violation of one of the greatest of these solemn compromises. This he declared was "wrong." "Wrong in its direct effect, letting slavery into Kansas and Nebraska, and wrong in its prospective principle, allowing it to spread to every other part of the wide world where men can be found inclined to take it. This declared indifference, but, as I must think, covert real zeal, for the spread of slavery, I cannot but hate. I hate it because of the monstrous injustice of slavery itself. I hate it because it deprives our republican example of its just influence in the world; enables the enemies of free institutions with plausibility to taunt us as hypocrites; causes the real friends of freedom to doubt our sincerity; and especially because it forces so many men among ourselves into an open war with the very fundamental principles of civil liberty, criticizing the Declaration of Independence, and insisting that there is no right principle of action but self-interest."

Disavowing all "prejudice against the Southern people," he generously declared:

"They are just what we would be in their situation. If slavery did not exist among them, they would not introduce it. If it did now exist among us, we should not instantly give it up. . . . I surely will not blame them for not doing what I should not know how to do myself. If all earthly power were given me, I should not know what to do as to the existing institution. My first impulse would be to free all the slaves and send them to Liberia, to their own native land. But a moment's reflection would convince me that whatever of high hope . . . there may be in this in the long run, its sudden execution is impossible. If they were all landed there in a day, they would all perish in the next ten days, and there are not surplus shipping and surplus money enough to carry them there in many times ten days. . . . I think I would not hold one in slavery at any rate, yet the point is not clear enough for me to denounce people upon. . . . It does seem to me that systems of gradual emancipation might be adopted, but for their tardiness in this I will not undertake to judge our brethren of the South. . . . The law which forbids the bringing of slaves from Africa, and that which has so long forbidden the taking of them into Nebraska, can hardly be distinguished on any moral principle, and the repeal of the former could find quite as plausible excuses as that of the latter."

Taking up the arguments by which the repeal of the Missouri Compromise was justified, he answered them one by one with clearness and a great array of facts. The chief of these arguments was that the repeal was in the interest of the "sacred right of self-government" that the people of Nebraska had a right to govern themselves as they chose, voting for or against slavery as they pleased.

"The doctrine of self-government is right," Lincoln said, "absolutely and eternally right, but it has no just application as here attempted. Or perhaps I should rather say that whether it has such application depends upon whether a negro is not or is a man. If he is not a man, in that case he who is a man may as a matter of self-government do just what he pleases with him. But if the negro is a man, is it not to that extent a total destruction of self-government to say that he too shall not govern himself? When the white man governs himself, that is self-government; but when he governs himself and also governs another man, that is more than self-government—that is despotism. If the negro is a man, why then my ancient faith teaches me that 'all men are created equal,' and that there can be no moral right in connection with one man's making a slave of another.

"Judge Douglas frequently, with bitter irony and sarcasm, paraphrases our argument by saying: 'The white people of Nebraska are good enough to govern themselves, but they are not good enough to govern a few miserable negroes!'

"Well! I doubt not that the people of Nebraska are and will continue to be as good as the average of people elsewhere. I do not say the contrary. What I do say is that no man is good enough to govern another man without that other's consent. I say this is the leading principle, the sheet-anchor of American republicanism."

This Peoria speech, which is very long, is particularly interesting to students of Mr. Lincoln's speeches, because in it is found the germ of many of the arguments which he elaborated in the next six years and used with tremendous effect.

With the Peoria speech Douglas had had enough of Lincoln as an antagonist, and he made a compact with him that neither should speak again in the campaign. It was characteristic of Douglas that on his way to Chicago he should stop and deliver a speech at Princeton!

But though Lincoln had temporarily withdrawn from the stump he was by no means abandoning the struggle. The iniquity of the Kansas-Nebraska Bill grew greater to him every day. He meant to fight it to the end and he wanted to go where he could fight it directly. He became a candidate for the General Assembly of Illinois from Sangamon County and was elected by a large majority in November. A little later he saw an opportunity for a larger position. Although Illinois was strongly Democratic, the revolt against the Nebraska Bill had driven from the party a number of men, members of the Legislature who had signified their determination to vote only for an anti-Nebraska Senator. This gave the Whigs a chance, and several candidates offered themselves— among them Lincoln. Resigning from the Legislature (members of the Legislature could not become candidates for the senatorship), he began his electioneering in the frank western style of those days by requesting his friends to support him, usually writing them characteristic letters.

"I have really got it into my head to try to be United States Senator," he wrote his friend Gillespie, "and, if I could have your support, my chances would be reasonably good. But I know and acknowledge that you have as just claims to the place as I have; and therefore I cannot ask you to yield to me, if you are thinking of becoming a candidate yourself. If, however, you are not, then I should like to be remembered affectionately by you; and also to have you make a mark for me with the anti-Nebraskan members, down your way."

He sent a large number of similar letters to friends, and by the first of January, when the Legislature reassembled, he felt his chances of election were good. "I have more committals than any other man," he wrote his friend Washburne. Nevertheless he failed of the election. Just how he explained to Washburne early in February:

"I began with 44 votes, Shields (Democratic) 41, and Trumbull (Anti-Nebraska) 5,—yet Trumbull was elected. In fact, 47 different members voted for me,—getting three new ones on the second ballot, and losing four old ones. How came my 47 to yield to Trumbull's 5? It was Governor Matteson's work. He has been secretly a candidate ever since (before, even) the fall election. All the members round about the canal were Anti-Nebraska, but were nevertheless nearly all Democrats and old personal friends of his. His plan was to privately impress them with the belief that he was as good Anti-Nebraska as any one else—at least could be secured to be so by instructions, which could be easily passed.

"The Nebraska men, of course, were not for Matteson; but when they found they could elect no avowed Nebraska man, they tardily determined to let him get whomever of our men he could, by whatever means he could, and ask him no questions. . . . The Nebraska men were very confident of the election of Matteson, though denying that he was a candidate, and we very much believing also that they would elect him. But they wanted first to make a show of good faith to Shields by voting for him a few times, and our secret Matteson men also wanted to make a show of good faith by voting with us a few times. So we led off. On the seventh ballot, I think, the signal was given to the Nebraska men to turn to Matteson, which they acted on to a man, with one exception. . . . Next ballot the remaining Nebraska man and one pretended Anti went over to him, giving him 46. The next still another, giving him 47, wanting only three of an election. In the meantime our friends, with a view of detaining our expected bolters, had been turning from me to Trumbull till he had risen to 35 and I had been reduced to 15. These would never desert me except by my direction; but I became satisfied that if we could prevent Matteson's election one or two ballots more, we could not possibly do so a single ballot after my friends should begin to return to me from Trumbull. So I determined to strike at once, and accordingly advised my remaining friends to go for him, which they did and elected him on the tenth ballot.

"Such is the way the thing was done. I think you would have done the same under the circumstances. . . . I could have headed off every combination and been elected, had it not been for Matteson's double game—and his defeat now gives me more pleasure than my own gives me pain. On the whole, it is perhaps as well for our general cause that Trumbull is elected. The Nebraska men confess that they hate it worse than anything that could have happened. It is a great consolation to see them worse whipped than I am."

Not only had Lincoln made the leading orator of the Nebraska cause cry enough, he had by his quick wit and his devotion to the cause secured an Anti-Nebraska Senator for the state.

Although for the time being campaigning was over, Lincoln by no means dropped the subject. The struggle between North and South over the settlement of Kansas grew every day more bitter. Violence was beginning, and it was evident that if the people of the new territory should vote to make the state free it would be impossible to enforce the decision without bloodshed. Lincoln watched the developments with a growing determination never to submit to the repeal of the Missouri Compromise. He would advocate its restoration so long as Kansas remained a territory, and if it ever sought to enter the Union as a slave state he would oppose it. He discussed the subject incessantly with his friends as he travelled the circuit; and wrestled with it day and night in solitude. A new conviction was gradually growing upon him. He had long held that slavery was wrong but that it would not be touched in the state where it was recognized by the Constitution; all that the free states could require, in his judgment, was that no new territory should be opened to slavery. He held that all compromises adjusting difficulties between the North and South on the slavery question were as sacred as the Constitution. Now he saw the most important of them all violated. Was it possible to devise a compromise which would settle forever the conflicting interests? He turned over the question continually. Judge T. Lyle Dickey of Illinois once told the Hon. William Pitt Kellogg that when the excitement over the Kansas-Nebraska Bill first broke out, he was with Lincoln and several friends attending court. One evening several persons, including himself and Lincoln, were discussing the slavery question. Judge Dickey contended that slavery was an institution, which the Constitution recognized, and which could not be disturbed. Lincoln argued that ultimately slavery must become extinct. "After a while," said Judge Dickey, "we went upstairs to bed. There were two beds in our room, and I remember that Lincoln sat up in his night shirt on the edge of the bed arguing the point with me. At last, we went to sleep. Early in the morning I woke up and there was Lincoln half sitting up in bed. 'Dickey,' he said, 'I tell you this nation cannot exist half slave and half free.' 'Oh, Lincoln,' said I, 'go to sleep.'"

As the months went on this idea took deeper root, and in August, 1855, we find it expressed in a letter to George Robertson of Kentucky: "Our political problem now is, 'Can we as a nation continue together permanently—forever—half slave and half free?' The problem is too mighty for me—may God, in His mercy, superintend the solution."

Not only was he beginning to see that the Union could not exist "divided against itself," he was beginning to see that in order to fight effectively against the repeal of the Missouri Compromise and the admission of Kansas as a slave state, he might be obliged to abandon the Whigs. All his life he had been a loyal Henry Clay Whig, ardent in his devotion to the party, sincerely attached to its principles. His friends were of that party, and never had a man's party friends been more willing than his to aid his ambition. But the Whigs were afraid of the Anti-Nebraska agitation. Was he being forced from his party? He hardly knew. "I think I am a Whig," he wrote his friend Speed, who had inquired where he stood, "but others say there are no Whigs and that I am an Abolitionist." This was in August, 1855. The events of the next few months showed him that he must stand by the body of men of all parties— Whig, Democratic, Abolition, Free Soil—who opposed the repeal of the Missouri Compromise, and were slowly uniting into the new Republican Party to fight it.

The first decisive step to organize these elements in Illinois was an editorial convention held on February 22, 1856, at Decatur. One of the editors interested, Paul Selby, relates the history of the convention in an heretofore unpublished manuscript on the "Formation of the Republican Party in Illinois," from which the following account is quoted:

"This movement, first suggested by 'The Morgan Journal' at Jacksonville, having received the approval of a considerable number of the Anti-Nebraska papers of the state, resulted in the issue of the following call:

" *'Editorial Convention.*—All editors in Illinois opposed to the Nebraska bill are requested to meet in Convention at Decatur, Illinois, on the 22d of February next, for the purpose of making arrangements for organizing the Anti-Nebraska forces in this state for the coming contest. All editors favoring the movement will please forward a copy of their paper containing their approval to the office of the Illinois 'State Chronicle,' Decatur.

"Twenty-five papers indorsed the call, but on the day of the meeting only about half that number of editors put in an appearance. One reason for the small number was the fact that, on the night before a heavy snow-storm had fallen throughout the state, obstructing the passage of trains on the two railroads centering at Decatur. The meeting was held in the parlor of the 'Cassell House'—afterwards the 'Oglesby House,' now called the 'St. Nicholas Hotel.' Those present and participating in the opening proceedings, as shown by the official report, were: E. C. Dougherty, 'Register,' Rockford; Charles Faxon, 'Post,' Princeton; A. N. Ford, 'Gazette,' Lacon; Thomas J. Pickett, 'Republican,' Peoria; Virgil Y. Ralston, 'Whig,' Quincy; Charles H. Ray, 'Tribune,' Chicago; George Schneider, 'Staats Zeitung,' Chicago; Paul Selby, 'Journal,' Jacksonville; B. F. Shaw, 'Telegraph,' Dixon; W. J. Usrey, 'Chronicle,' Decatur, and O. P. Wharton, 'Advertiser,' Rock Island. In the organization Paul Selby was made Chairman and W. J. Usrey, Secretary, while Messrs. Ralston, Ray, Wharton, Dougherty, Pickett and Schneider constituted a Committee on Resolutions. The platform adopted as 'a basis of common and concerted action' among the members of the new organization, embraced a declaration of principles that would be regarded in this day as most conservative Republicanism, recognizing 'The legal rights of the slave states to hold and enjoy their property in slaves under their state laws'; reaffirming the principles of the Declaration of Independence, with its correlative doctrine that 'Freedom is national and slavery sectional'; declaring assumption of the right to extend slavery on the plea that it is essential to the security of the institution 'an invasion of our rights' which 'must be resisted'; demanding the restoration of the Missouri Compromise and 'the restriction of slavery to its present authorized limits'; advocating the maintenance of 'the naturalization laws as they are' and favoring 'the widest tolerance in matters of religion and faith' (a rebuke to Know-Nothingism); pledging resistance to assaults upon the common school system, and closing with a demand for reformation in the administration of the state Government as 'second only in importance to the question of slavery itself.' Mr. Lincoln was present in Decatur during the day, and, although he did not take part in the public deliberations of the convention, he was in close conference with the Committee on Resolutions, and the impress of his hand is seen in the character of the platform adopted. Messrs. Ray and Schneider, of the Chicago press, were also influential factors in shaping the declaration of principles with which the new party in Illinois started on its long career of almost uninterrupted success.

"The day's proceedings ended with a complimentary banquet given to the editors at the same hotel by the citizens of Decatur. Speeches were made in response to toasts by Mr. Lincoln, R. J. Oglesby (afterward Major-General of Volunteers and three times Governor of Illinois—then a young lawyer of Decatur), Ray of the Chicago 'Tribune,' Ralston of the Quincy 'Whig' and others among the editors. In the course of his speech, referring to a movement which some of the editors present had inaugurated to make him the Anti-Nebraska candidate for Governor at the ensuing election, Mr. Lincoln spoke (in substance) as follows: 'I wish to say why I should not be a candidate. If I should be chosen, the Democrats would say it was nothing more than an attempt to resurrect the dead body of the old Whig Party. I would secure the vote of that party and no more, and our defeat will follow as a matter of course. But I can suggest a name that will secure not only the old Whig vote, but enough Anti-Nebraska Democrats to give us the victory. That man is Colonel William H. Bissell.'

"Here Mr. Lincoln again displayed his characteristic unselfishness and sagacity. That he would, at that time, have regarded an election to the Governorship of the great State of Illinois as an honor not worth contending for, will scarcely be presumed. He was seeking more important results, however, in the interest of freedom and good government—the ending of the political chaos that had prevailed for the past two years and the consolidation of the forces opposed to slavery extension in a compact political organization. Bissell had been an officer in the Mexican War with a good record; had afterwards, as a member of Congress from the Belleville District, opposed the Kansas-Nebraska Bill, and had refused to be brow-beaten by Jefferson Davis into the retraction of statements he had made on the floor of Congress. As will appear later, he was nominated and Lincoln's judgment vindicated by his election and the unification of the elements which afterwards composed the Republican Party.

"One of the last acts of the editorial convention was the appointment of a State Central Committee, consisting of one member for each Congressional District and two for the state at large. Some of the names were suggested by Mr. Lincoln, while the others received his approval. . . . A supplementary resolution recommended the holding of a State Convention at Bloomington, on the 29th of May following, and requested the committee just appointed to issue the necessary call. . . .

"It is a coincidence of some interest that on the day the Illinois editors were in session at Decatur, a convention of representatives from different states, with a similar object in view for the country at large, was in session at Pittsburg,

Pa. The latter was presided over by the venerable Francis P. Blair, of Maryland, while among its most prominent members appear such names as those of Governor E. D. Morgan of New York, Horace Greeley, Preston King, David Wilmot, Oliver P. Morton, Joshua R. Giddings, Zachariah Chandler and many others of national reputation. A National Committee there appointed called the first National Convention of the Republican Party, held at Philadelphia on the 17th of June."

In the interval between the Decatur meeting and the Bloomington Convention called for May 29, the excitement in the county over Kansas grew almost to a frenzy. The new state was in the hands of a pro-slavery mob, her Governor a prisoner, her capital in ruins, her voters intimidated. The newspapers were full of accounts of the attack on Sumner in the United States Senate by Brooks. One of the very men who had been expected to be a leader in the Bloomington Convention, Paul Selby, was lying at home prostrated by a cowardly blow from a political opponent. Little wonder then that when the convention met its members were resolved to take radical action. The convention was opened with John M. Palmer, afterwards United States Senator, in its chair, and in a very short time it had adopted a platform, appointed delegates to the National Convention, nominated a state ticket, completed, in short, all the work of organizing the Republican Party in Illinois. After this work of organizing and nominating was finished, there was a call for speeches. The convention felt the need of some powerful amalgamating force which would weld its discordant elements. In spite of the best intentions of the members, their most manful efforts, they knew in their hearts that they were still political enemies, that the Whig was still a Whig, the Democrat a Democrat, the Abolitionist an Abolitionist. Man after man was called to the platform and spoke without producing any marked effect, when suddenly there was a call raised of a name not on the program—"Lincoln"— "Lincoln"—"give us Lincoln!" The crowd took it up and made the hall ring until a tall figure rose in the back of the audience and slowly strode down the aisle. As he turned to his audience there came gradually a great change upon his face. "There was an expression of intense emotion," Judge Scott, of Bloomington, once told the author. "It was the emotion of a great soul. Even in stature he seemed greater. He seemed to realize it was a crisis in his life."

Lincoln, in fact, had come to the parting of the ways in his political life, to the moment when he must publicly break with his party. For two years he had tried to fight slavery extension under the name of a Whig. He had found it could not be done, and now in spite of the efforts of his conservative friends who had vainly tried to keep him away from the Bloomington Convention, he was facing that convention, was openly ackowledging that henceforth he worked with the Republican Party.

Lincoln's extraordinary human insight and sympathy told him as he looked at his audience that what this body of splendid, earnest, but groping men needed was to feel that they had undertaken a cause of such transcendent value that beside it all previous alliances, ambitions and duties were as nothing. If he could make them see the triviality of their differences as compared with the tremendous principle of the new party, he was certain they would go forth Republicans in spirit as well as in name.

He began his speech, then, deeply moved, and with a profound sense of the importance of the moment. At first he spoke slowly and haltingly, but gradually he grew in force and intensity until his hearers arose from their chairs and with pale faces and quivering lips pressed unconsciously towards him. Starting from the back of the broad platform on which he stood, his hands on his hips, he slowly advanced towards the front, his eyes blazing, his face white with passion, his voice resonant with the force of his conviction. As he advanced he seemed to his audience fairly to grow, and when at the end of a period he stood at the front line of the stage, hands still on the hips, head back, raised on his tiptoes, he seemed like a giant inspired. "At that moment he was the handsomest man I ever saw," Judge Scott declared.

So powerful was his effect on his audience that men and women wept as they cheered and children there that night still remember the scene, though at the time they understood nothing of its meaning. As he went on there came upon the convention the very emotion he sought to arouse. "Every one in that before incongruous assembly came to feel as one man, to think as one man and to purpose and resolve as one man," says one of his auditors. He had made every man of them pure Republican. He did something more. The indignation which the outrages in

Kansas and throughout the country had aroused was uncontrolled. Men talked passionately of war. It was at this meeting that Lincoln, after firing his hearers by an expression which became a watchword of the campaign, "We won't go out of the Union, and you shan't," poured oil on the wrath of the Illinois opponents of the Nebraska Bill by advising "ballots, not bullets."

Nothing illustrates better the extraordinary power of Lincoln's speech at Bloomington than the way he stirred up the newspaper reporters. It was before the stenographer had become acclimated in Illinois, though long-hand reports were regularly taken. Of course, all the leading papers of the state leaning towards the new party, had reporters at the convention. Among these was Mr. Joseph Medill.

"It was my journalistic duty," says Mr. Medill, "though a delegate to the convention, to make a 'long-hand' report of the speeches delivered for the Chicago 'Tribune.' I did make a few paragraphs of what Lincoln said in the first eight or ten minutes, but I became so absorbed in his magnetic oratory that I forgot myself and ceased to take notes; and joined with the convention in cheering and stamping and clapping to the end of his speech.

"I well remember that after Lincoln sat down and calm had succeeded the tempest, I waked out of a sort of hypnotic trance, and then thought of my report for the 'Tribune.' There was nothing written but an abbreviated introduction.

"It was some sort of satisfaction to find that I had not been 'scooped,' as all the newspaper men present had been equally carried away by the excitement caused by the wonderful oration and had made no report or sketch of the speech."

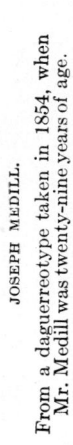

JOSEPH MEDILL.
From a daguerreotype taken in 1854, when Mr. Medill was twenty-nine years of age.

H. C. WHITNEY.
From a photograph taken by Copelin, Chicago, in 1874.

RE-ENTERS POLITICS 343

A number of Lincoln's friends, young lawyers, most of them, were accustomed to taking notes of speeches, and as usual sharpened their pencils as he began. "I attempted for about fifteen minutes," says Mr. Herndon, Lincoln's law partner, "as was usual with me then to take notes, but at the end of that time I threw pen and paper away and lived only in the inspiration of the hour." The result of this excitement was that when the convention was over there was no reporter present who had anything for his newspaper. They all went home and wrote burning editorials about the speech and its great principle, but as to reproducing it they could not. Men came to talk of it all over Illinois. They realized that it had been a purifying fire for the party, but as to what it contained no one could say. Gradually it became known as Lincoln's "lost speech." From the very mystery of it its reputation grew greater as time went on.

But though the convention so nearly to a man lost its head, there was at least one auditor who had enough control to pursue his usual habit of making notes of the speeches he heard. This was a young lawyer on the same circuit as Lincoln, Mr. H. C. Whitney. For some three weeks before the convention Lincoln and Whitney had been attending court at Danville. They had discussed the political situation in the state carefully, and to Whitney Lincoln had stated his convictions and determinations. In a way Whitney had absorbed Lincoln's speech beforehand, as indeed any one must have done who was with Lincoln when he was preparing an address, it being his habit to discuss points and to repeat them aloud indifferent to who heard him. Whitney had gone to the convention intending to make notes, knowing, as he did, that Lincoln had not written out what he was going to say. Fortunately he had a cool enough head to keep to his purpose. He made his notes, and on returning to Judge Davis's home in Bloomington, where he, with Lincoln and one or two others, were staying, he enlarged them while the others discussed the speech. These notes Whitney kept for many years, always intending to write them out, but never attending to it until the author, in 1896, learned that he had them and urged him to expand them. This Mr. Whitney did, and the speech was first published in "McClure's Magazine" for September, 1896. Mr. Whitney did not claim that he had made a full report. He did claim that the argument was correct and that in many cases the expressions were exact. A few quotations will show any one familiar with Lincoln's speeches that Mr. Whitney has caught much of their style, for instance, the following:

. . . .

"We come—we are here assembled together—to protest as well as we can against a great wrong, and to take measures, as well as we now can, to make that wrong right; to place the nation, as far as it may be possible now, as it was before the repeal of the Missouri Compromise; and the plain way to do this is to restore the Compromise, and to demand and determine that *Kansas shall be free!* While we affirm, and reaffirm, if necessary, our devotions to the principles of the Declaration of Independence, let our practical work here be limited to the above. We know that there is not a perfect agreement of sentiment here on the public questions which might be rightfully considered in this convention, and that the indignation which we all must feel cannot be helped; but all of us must give up something for the good of the cause. There is one desire which is uppermost in the mind, one wish common to us all—to which no dissent will be made; and I counsel you earnestly to bury all resentment, to sink all personal feeling, make all things work to a common purpose in which we are united and agreed about, and which all present will agree is absolutely necessary—which *must* be done by any rightful mode if there be such: *Slavery must be kept out of Kansas!* The test—the pinch—is right there. If we lose Kansas to freedom, an example will be set which will prove fatal to freedom in the end. We, therefore, in the language of the *Bible*, must 'lay the axe to the root of the tree.' Temporizing will not do longer; now is the time for decision—for firm, persistent, resolute action.

.   .   .   .

"We have made a good beginning here to-day. As our Methodist friends would say, 'I feel it is good to be here.' While extremists may find some fault with the moderation of our platform, they should remember that 'the battle is not always to the strong, nor the race to the swift.' In grave emergencies, moderation is generally safer than radicalism; and as this struggle is likely to be long and earnest, we must not, by our action, repel any who are in sympathy with us in the main, but rather win all that we can to our standard. We must not belittle nor overlook the facts of our condition —that we are new and comparatively weak, while our enemies are entrenched and relatively strong. They have the administration and the political power; and, right or wrong, at present they have the numbers. Our friends who urge an appeal to arms with so much force and eloquence, should recollect that the government is arrayed against us, and that the numbers are now arrayed against us as well; or, to state it nearer to the truth, they are not yet expressly and affirmatively for us; and we should repel friends rather than gain them by anything savoring of revolutionary methods. As it now stands, we must appeal to the sober sense and patriotism of the people. We will make converts day by day; we will grow strong by calmness and moderation; we will grow strong by the violence and injustice of our adversaries. And, unless truth be a mockery and justice a hollow lie, we will be in the majority after a while, and then the revolution which we will accomplish will be none the less radical from being the result of pacific measures. The battle of freedom is to be fought out on principle. Slavery is a violation of the eternal right. We have temporized with it from the necessities of our condition, but *as sure as God reigns and school children read*, THAT BLACK FOUL LIE CAN NEVER BE CONSECRATED INTO GOD'S HALLOWED TRUTH!

. . . .

"I will not say that we may not sooner or later be compelled to meet force by force; but the time has not yet come, and if we are true to ourselves, may never come. Do not mistake that the ballot is stronger than the bullet. Therefore, let the legions of slavery use bullets; but let us wait patiently till November, and fire ballots at them in return; and by that peaceful policy, I believe we shall ultimately win.

. . . .

"Did you ever, my friends, seriously reflect upon the speed with which we are tending downwards? Within the memory of men now present the leading statesmen of Virginia could make genuine, red-hot abolitionist speeches in old Virginia; and, as I have said, now even in 'free Kansas' it is a crime to declare that it is 'free Kansas.' The very sentiments that I and others have just uttered would entitle us, and each of us, to the ignominy and seclusion of a dungeon; and yet I suppose that, like Paul, we were 'free born.' But if this thing is allowed to continue, it will be but one step further to impress the same rule in Illinois.

"The conclusion of all is, that we must restore the Missouri Compromise. We must highly resolve that *Kansas must be free!* We must reinstate the birthday promise of the Republic; we must reaffirm the Declaration of Inde-

LINCOLN IN 1857.

From a photograph loaned by H. W. Fay of De Kalb, Illinois. The original was taken early in 1857 by Alexander Hesler of Chicago. Mr. Fay writes of the picture: "I have a letter from Mr. Hesler stating that one of the lawyers came in and made arrangements for the sitting, so that the members of the bar could get prints. Lincoln said at the time that he did not know why the boys wanted such a homely face." Mr. Joseph Medill of Chicago went with Mr. Lincoln to have the picture taken. He says that the photographer insisted on smoothing down Lincoln's hair, but Lincoln did not like the result, and ran his fingers through it before sitting. The original negative was burned in the Chicago fire.

pendence; we must make good in essence as well as in form Madison's avowal that 'the word *slave* ought not to appear in the Constitution'; and we must even go further, and decree that only local law, and not that time-honored instrument, shall shelter a slave-holder. We must make this a land of liberty in fact, as it is in name. But in seeking to attain these results—so indispensable if the liberty which is our pride and boast shall endure—we will be loyal to the Constitution and to the 'flag of our Union,' and no matter what our grievance—even though Kansas shall come in as a slave state; and no matter what theirs—even if we shall restore the Compromise—WE WILL SAY TO THE SOUTHERN DISUNIONISTS, WE WON'T GO OUT OF THE UNION, AND YOU SHAN'T!!!"

•   •   •   ◂   •   ▸   •

CHAPTER XVIII

THE LINCOLN-DOUGLAS DEBATES

"THE greatest speech ever made in Illinois, and it puts Lincoln on the track for the Presidency," was the comment made by enthusiastic Republicans on Lincoln's speech before the Bloomington Convention. Conscious that it was he who had put the breath of life into their organization, the party instinctively turned to him as its leader. The effect of this local recognition was at once perceptible in the national organization. Less than three weeks after the delivery of the Bloomington speech, the national convention of the Republican Party met in Philadelphia June 17, to nominate candidates for the presidency and vice-presidency. Lincoln's name was the second proposed for the latter office, and on the first ballot he received one hundred and ten votes. The news reached him at Urbana, Ill., where he was attending court, one of his companions reading from a daily paper just received from Chicago, the result of the ballot. The simple name Lincoln was given, without the name of the man's state. Lincoln said indifferently that he did not suppose it could be himself; and added that there was "another great man" of the name, a man from Massachusetts. The next day, however, he knew that it was himself to whom the convention had given so strong an endorsement. He

THE LINCOLN-DOUGLAS DEBATES 349

knew also that the ticket chosen was Frémont and Dayton.

The campaign of the following summer and fall was one of intense activity for Lincoln. In Illinois and the neighboring states he made over fifty speeches, only fragments of which have been preserved. One of the first of importance was delivered on July 4, 1856, at a great mass meeting at Princeton, the home of the Lovejoys and the Bryants. The people were still irritated by the outrages in Kansas and by the attack on Sumner in the Senate, and the temptation to deliver a stirring and indignant oration must have been strong. Lincoln's speech was, however, a fine example of political wisdom, an historical argument admirably calculated to convince his auditors that they were right in their opposition to slavery extension, but so controlled and sane that it would stir no impulsive radical to violence. There probably was not uttered in the United States on that critical 4th of July, 1856, when the very foundation of the government was in dispute and the day itself seemed a mockery, a cooler, more logical speech than this by the man who, a month before, had driven a convention so nearly mad that the very reporters had forgotten to make notes. And the temper of this Princeton speech Lincoln kept throughout the campaign.

In spite of the valiant struggle of the Republicans, Buchanan was elected; but Lincoln was in no way discouraged. The Republicans had polled 1,341,264 votes in the country. In Illinois, they had given Frémont nearly 100,000 votes, and they had elected their candidate for governor, General Bissell. Lincoln turned from arguments to encouragements and good counsel.

"All of us," he said at a Republican banquet in Chicago, a few weeks after the election, "who did not vote for Mr. Buchanan, taken together, are a majority of four hundred thousand. But in the late contest we were divided between Frémont and Fillmore. Can we not come together for the future? Let every one who really believes and is resolved that free society is not and shall not be a failure, and who can conscientiously declare that in the last contest he has done only what he thought best—let every such one have charity to believe that every other one can say as much. Thus let bygones be bygones; let past differences as nothing be; and with steady eye on the real issue let us reinaugurate the good old 'central idea' of the republic. We can do it. The human heart is with us; God is with us. We shall again be able, not to declare that 'all states as states are equal,' nor yet that 'all citizens as citizens are equal,' but to renew the broader, better declaration, including both these and much more, that 'all men are created equal.' "

The spring of 1857 gave Lincoln a new line of argument. Buchanan was scarcely in the Presidential chair before the Supreme Court, in the decision of the Dred Scott case, declared that a negro could not sue in the United States courts and that Congress could not prohibit slavery in the Territories. This decision was such an evident advance of the slave power that there was a violent uproar in the North. Douglas went at once to Illinois to calm his constituents. "What," he cried, "oppose the Supreme Court! Is it not sacred? To resist it is anarchy."

Lincoln met him fairly on the issue in a speech at Springfield in June, 1857.

STEPHEN A. DOUGLAS.

"We believe as much as Judge Douglas (perhaps more) in obedience to and respect for the judicial department of government. . . . But we think the Dred Scott decision is erroneous. We know the court that made it has often overruled its own decisions, and we shall do what we can to have it overrule this. We offer no resistance to it. . . . If this important decision had been made by the unanimous concurrence of the judges, and without any apparent partisan bias, and in accordance with legal public expectation and with the steady practice of the departments throughout our history, and had been in no part based on assumed historical facts which are not really true; or if, wanting in some of these, it had been before the court more than once, and had there been affirmed and reaffirmed through a course of years, it then might be, perhaps would be, factious, nay, even revolutionary, not to acquiesce in it as a precedent. But when, as is true, we find it wanting in all these claims to the public confidence, it is not resistance, it is not factious, it is not even disrespectful, to treat it as not having yet quite established a settled doctrine for the country."

Let Douglas cry "awful," "anarchy," "revolution," as much as he would, Lincoln's arguments against the Dred Scott decision appealed to common sense and won him commendation all over the country. Even the radical leaders of the party in the East —Seward, Sumner, Theodore Parker—began to notice him, to read his speeches, to consider his arguments.

With every month of 1857 Lincoln grew stronger, and his election in Illinois as United States senatorial candidate in 1858 against Douglas would have been insured if Douglas had not suddenly broken with Buchanan and his party in a way which won him the hearty sympathy and respect of a large part of the

Republicans of the North. By a flagrantly unfair vote the pro-slavery leaders of Kansas had secured the adoption of the Lecompton Constitution allowing slavery in the state. President Buchanan urged Congress to admit Kansas with her bogus Constitution. Douglas, who would not sanction so base an injustice, opposed the measure, voting with the Republicans steadily against the admission. The Buchananists, outraged at what they called "Douglas's apostasy," broke with him. Then it was that a part of the Republican Party, notably Horace Greeley at the head of the New York "Tribune," struck by the boldness and nobility of Douglas's opposition, began to hope to win him over from the Democrats to the Republicans. Their first step was to counsel the leaders of their party in Illinois to put up no candidate against Douglas for the United States senatorship in 1858.

Lincoln saw this change on the part of the Republican leaders with dismay. "Greeley is not doing me right," he said. " . . . I am a true Republican, and have been tried already in the hottest part of the anti-slavery fight; and yet I find him taking up Douglas, a veritable dodger,—once a tool of the South, now its enemy,—and pushing him to the front." He grew so restless over the returning popularity of Douglas among the Republicans that Herndon, his law-partner, determined to go East to find out the real feeling of the eastern leaders towards Lincoln. Herndon had, for a long time, been in correspondence with the leading abolitionists and had no difficulty in getting interviews. The returns he brought back from his canvass were not altogether reassuring. Seward,

Sumner, Phillips, Garrison, Beecher, Theodore Parker, all spoke favorably of Lincoln, and Seward sent him word that the Republicans would never take up so slippery a quantity as Douglas had proved himself. But Greeley—the all-important Greeley—was lukewarm. "The Republican standard is too high," he told Herndon. "We want something practical. . . . Douglas is a brave man. Forget the past and sustain the righteous." "Good God, *righteous,* eh!" groaned Herndon in his letter to Lincoln.

But though the encouragement which came to Lincoln from the East in the spring of 1858 was meagre, that which came from Illinois was abundant. There the Republicans supported him in whole-hearted devotion. In June, the State convention, meeting in Springfield to nominate a candidate for Senator, declared that Abraham Lincoln was its *first and only choice* as the successor of Stephen A. Douglas. The press was jubilant. "Unanimity is a weak word," wrote the editor of the Bloomington "Pantagraph," "to express the universal and intense feeling of the convention. 'Lincoln! LINCOLN!! LINCOLN!!!' was the cry everywhere, whenever the senatorship was alluded to. Delegates from Chicago and from Cairo, from the Wabash and the Illinois, from the north, the center, and the south, were alike fierce with enthusiasm, whenever that loved name was breathed. Enemies at home and misjudging friends abroad, who have looked for dissension among us on the question of the senatorship, will please take notice that our nomination is a *unanimous* one; and that, in the event of a Republican majority in the next Legislature, no other name than Lincoln's will be mentioned, or thought of, by a solitary Republican legislator. One little incident in the convention was a pleasing illustration of the universality of the Lincoln sentiment. Cook County had brought a banner into the assemblage inscribed, 'Cook County for Abraham Lincoln.' During a pause in the proceedings, a delegate from another county rose and proposed, with the consent of the Cook County delegation, *to amend the banner* by substituting for "Cook County" the word which I hold in my hand,' at the same time unrolling a scroll, and revealing the word 'Illinois' in huge capitals. The Cook delegation promptly *accepted the amendment,* and amidst a perfect hurricane of hurrahs, the banner was duly altered to express the sentiment of the whole Republican Party of the state, thus: 'Illinois for Abraham Lincoln.' "

On the evening of the day of his nomination, Lincoln addressed his constituents. The first paragraph of his speech gave the key to the campaign he proposed. "A house divided against itself cannot stand. I believe this government cannot endure permanently half slave and half free. I do not expect the house to fall—but I do expect it will cease to be divided. It will become all one thing or all the other."

Then followed the famous charge of conspiracy against the slavery advocates, the charge that Pierce, Buchanan, Chief Justice Taney, and Douglas had been making a concerted effort to legalize the institution of slavery "in all the states, old as well as new, North as well as South." He marshalled one after another of the measures that the pro-slavery leaders

THE LINCOLN AND DOUGLAS MEETING AT GALESBURG, ILLINOIS, OCTOBER 7, 1858.

The fifth debate between Lincoln and Douglas was held at Galesburg, Illinois, on October 7, 1858. The platform from which they spoke was erected at the end of Knox College. The students took a lively interest in the contest, decorating the college gayly with flags and streamers. Immediately over the heads of the speakers, extending across the end of the building, was placed a large banner bearing the words: "KNOX COLLEGE FOR LINCOLN."

had secured in the past four years and clinched the argument by one of his inimitable illustrations:

"When we see a lot of framed timbers, different portions of which we know have been gotten out at different times and places and by different workmen,—Stephen, Franklin, Roger and James,* for instance,—and we see these timbers joined together, and see they exactly make the frame of a house or a mill, all the tenons and mortises exactly fitting, and all the lengths and proportions of the different pieces exactly adapted to their respective places, and not a piece too many or too few, not omitting even scaffolding—or, if a single piece be lacking, we see the place in the frame exactly filled and prepared yet to bring such a piece in—in such a case we find it impossible not to believe that Stephen and Franklin and Roger and James all understood one another from the beginning, and all worked upon a common plan or draft, drawn up before the first blow was struck."

The speech was severely criticised by Lincoln's friends. It was too radical. It was sectional. He heard the complaints unmoved. "If I had to draw a pen across my record," he said, one day, "and erase my whole life from sight, and I had one poor gift or choice left as to what I should save from the wreck, I should choose that speech and leave it to the world unerased."

The speech was, in fact, one of great political adroitness. It forced Douglas to do exactly what he did not want to do in Illinois: explain his own record during the past four years; explain the true meaning of the Kansas-Nebraska Bill; discuss the Dred Scott decision; say whether or not he thought slavery so good a thing that the country could afford to extend

* *Stephen* A. Douglas, *Franklin* Pierce, *Roger* Taney, *James* Buchanan.

it instead of confining it where it would be in course of gradual extinction. Douglas wanted the Republicans of Illinois to follow Greeley's advice: "Forgive the past." He wanted to make the most among them of his really noble revolt against the attempt of his party to fasten an unjust constitution on Kansas. Lincoln would not allow him to bask for an instant in the sun of that revolt. He crowded him step by step through his party's record, and compelled him to face what he called the "profound central truth" of the Republican Party, "slavery is wrong and ought to be dealt with as wrong."

But it was at once evident that Douglas did not mean to meet the issue squarely. He called the doctrine of Lincoln's "house-divided-against-itself" speech "sectionalism"; his charge of conspiracy "false"; his talk of the wrong of slavery extension "abolitionism." This went on for a month. Then Lincoln resolved to force Douglas to meet his arguments, and challenged him to a series of joint debates. Douglas was not pleased. His reply to the challenge was irritable, even slightly insolent. To those of his friends who talked with him privately of the contest, he said: "I do not feel, between you and me, that I want to go into this debate. The whole country knows me, and has me measured. Lincoln, as regards myself, is comparatively unknown, and if he gets the best of this debate,—and I want to say he is the ablest man the Republicans have got,—I shall lose everything and Lincoln will gain everything. Should I win, I shall gain but little. I do not want to go into a debate with Abe." Publicly, however, he carried off the prospect confidently, even jauntily. "Mr. Lincoln," he said patronizingly, "is a kind, amiable, intelligent gentleman." In the meantime his constituents boasted loudly of the fine spectacle they were going to give the state—"the Little Giant chawing up Old Abe!"

Many of Lincoln's friends looked forward to the encounter with foreboding. Often, in spite of their best intentions, they showed anxiety. "Shortly before the first debate came off at Ottawa," says Judge H. W. Beckwith of Danville, Ill., "I passed the Chenery House, then the principal hotel in Springfield. The lobby was crowded with partisan leaders from various sections of the state, and Mr. Lincoln, from his greater height, was seen above the surging mass that clung about him like a swarm of bees to their ruler. He looked careworn, but he met the crowd patiently and kindly, shaking hands, answering questions, and receiving assurances of support. The day was warm, and at the first chance he broke away and came out for a little fresh air, wiping the sweat from his face.

"As he passed the door he saw me, and, taking my hand, inquired for the health and views of his 'friends over in Vermilion County.' He was assured they were wide awake, and further told that they looked forward to the debate between him and Senator Douglas with deep concern. From the shadow that went quickly over his face, the pained look that came to give quickly way to a blaze of eyes and quiver of lips, I felt that Mr. Lincoln had gone beneath my mere words and caught my inner and current fears as to the result. And then, in a forgiving, jocular way peculiar to him, he said, 'Sit down; I have a moment to spare and will tell you a story.' Having been on his feet for some time, he sat on the end of the stone step leading into the hotel door, while I stood closely fronting him.

" 'You have,' he continued, 'seen two men about to fight?'

" 'Yes, many times.'

" 'Well, one of them brags about what he means to do. He jumps high in the air cracking his heels together, smites his fists, and wastes his breath trying to scare somebody. You see the other fellow, he says not a word,'—here Mr. Lincoln's voice and manner changed to great earnestness, and repeating—'you see the other man says not a word. His arms are at his side, his fists are closely doubled up, his head is drawn to the shoulder, and his teeth are set firm together. He is saving his wind for the fight, and as sure as it comes off he will win it, or die a-trying.'

"He made no other comment, but arose, bade me good-by, and left me to apply the illustration."

It was inevitable that Douglas's friends should be sanguine, Lincoln's doubtful. The contrast between the two candidates was almost pathetic. Senator Douglas was the most brilliant figure in the political life of the day. Winning in personality, fearless as an advocate, magnetic in eloquence, shrewd in political manœuvring, he had every quality to captivate the public. His resources had never failed him. From his entrance into Illinois politics in 1834, he had been the recipient of every political honor his party had to bestow. For the past eleven years he had been a member of the United States Senate, where he had influenced all the important legislation of the day and met in debate every strong speaker of North and South. In 1852, and again in 1856, he had been a strongly supported, though unsuccessful, candidate for the Democratic presidential nomination. In 1858 he was put at or near the head of every list of possible presidential candidates made up for 1860.

How barren Lincoln's public career in comparison! Three terms in the lower house of the State Assembly, one term in Congress, then a failure which drove him from public life. Now he returns as a bolter from his party, a leader in a new organization which the conservatives are denouncing as "visionary," "impractical," "revolutionary."

No one recognized more clearly than Lincoln the difference between himself and his opponent. "With me," he said sadly, in comparing the careers of himself and Douglas, "the race of ambition has been a failure—a flat failure. With him it has been one of splendid success." He warned his party at the outset that, with himself as a standard-bearer, the battle must be fought on principle alone, without any of the external aids which Douglas's brilliant career gave. "Senator Douglas is of world-wide renown," he said. "All the anxious politicians of his party, or who have been of his party for years past, have been looking upon him as certainly, at no distant day, to be the President of the United States. They have seen in his round, jolly, fruitful face, post-offices, land-offices, marshalships, and cabinet appointments, chargéships and foreign missions, bursting and sprouting out in wonderful exuberance, ready to be laid hold of by their greedy hands. And as they have been gazing upon this attractive picture so long, they cannot, in the little distraction that has taken place in the party, bring themselves to give up the charming hope; but with greedier anxiety they rush about him, sustain him, and give him marches, triumphal entries, and receptions beyond what even in the days of his highest prosperity they could have brought about in his favor. On the contrary, nobody has ever expected me to be President. In my poor, lean, lank face, nobody has ever seen that any cabbages were sprouting out. These are disadvantages, all taken together, that the Republicans labor under. We have to fight this battle upon principle, and upon principle alone."

If one will take a map of Illinois and locate the points of the Lincoln and Douglas debates held between August 21 and October 15, 1858, he will see that the whole state was traversed in the contest. The first took place at Ottawa, about seventy-five miles southwest of Chicago, on August 21; the second at Freeport, near the Wisconsin boundary, on August 27. The third was in the extreme southern part of the state, at Jonesboro, on September 15. Three days later the contestants met one hundred and fifty miles northeast of Jonesboro, at Charleston. The fifth, sixth, and seventh debates were held in the western part of the state; at Galesburg, October 7; Quincy, October 13; and Alton, October 15.

Constant exposure and fatigue were unavoidable in meeting these engagements. Both contestants spoke almost every day through the intervals between the

ABRAHAM LINCOLN IN 1858.

From an ambrotype taken by C. Jackson, in Pittsfield, Ill., October 1, 1858, immediately after Lincoln had made a speech in the public square. Lincoln was the guest in Pittsfield of his friend, D. H. Gilmer, a lawyer for whom the picture was finished.

THE LINCOLN-DOUGLAS DEBATES 361

joint debates; and as railroad communication in Illinois in 1858 was still very incomplete, they were often obliged to resort to horse, carriage, or steamer to reach the desired points. Judge Douglas succeeded, however, in making this difficult journey something of a triumphal procession. He was accompanied throughout the campaign by his wife—a beautiful and brilliant woman—and by a number of distinguished Democrats. On the Illinois Central Railroad he had always a special car, sometimes a special train. Frequently he swept by Lincoln, side-tracked in an accommodation or freight train. "The gentleman in that car evidently smelt no royalty in our carriage," laughed Lincoln one day, as he watched from the caboose of a laid-up freight train the decorated special of Douglas flying by.

It was only when Lincoln left the railroad and crossed the prairie, to speak at some isolated town, that he went in state. The attentions he received were often very trying to him. He detested what he called "fizzlegigs and fireworks," and would squirm in disgust when his friends gave him a genuine prairie ovation. Usually, when he was going to a point distant from the railway, a "distinguished citizen" met him at the station nearest the place with a carriage. When they were come within two or three miles of the town, a long procession with banners and band would appear winding across the prairie to meet the speaker. A speech of greeting was made, and then the ladies of the entertainment committee would present Lincoln with flowers, sometimes even winding a garland about his head and lank figure. His embarrassment at these attentions was thoroughly appreciated by his friends. At the Ottawa debate the enthusiasm of his supporters was so great that they insisted on carrying him from the platform to the house where he was to be entertained. Powerless to escape from the clutches of his admirers, he could only cry, "Don't, boys; let me down; come now, don't." But the "boys" persisted, and they told proudly in later years of their exploit and of the cordial hand-shake Lincoln, all embarrassed as he was, gave each of them when at last he was free.

On arrival at the towns where the joint debates were held, Douglas was always met by a brass band and a salute of thirty-two guns (the Union was composed of thirty-two states in 1858), and was escorted to the hotel in the finest equipage to be had. Lincoln's supporters took delight in showing their contempt of Douglas's elegance by affecting a Republican simplicity, often carrying their candidate through the streets on a high and unadorned hay-rack drawn by farm horses. The scenes in the towns on the occasion of the debates were perhaps never equalled at any other of the hustings of this country. No distance seemed too great for the people to go; no vehicle too slow or fatiguing. At Charleston there was a great delegation of men, women, and children present which had come in a long procession from Indiana by farm wagons, afoot, on horseback, and in carriages. The crowds at three or four of the debates were for that day immense. There were estimated to be from eight thousand to fourteen thousand people at Quincy, some six thousand at Alton, from ten thousand to fifteen thousand at Charleston, some twenty thousand at Ottawa. Many of those at Ottawa came the night before. "It was a matter of but a short time," says Mr. George Beatty of Ottawa, "until the few hotels, the livery stables, and private houses were crowded, and there were no accommodations left. Then the campaigners spread out about the town, and camped in whatever spot was most convenient. They went along the bluff and on the bottom-lands, and that night the camp-fires, spread up and down the valley for a mile, made it look as if an army was gathered about us."

When the crowd was massed at the place of the debate, the scene was one of the greatest hubbub and confusion. On the corners of the squares, and scattered around the outskirts of the crowd, were fakirs of every description, selling pain-killers and ague cures, watermelons and lemonade; jugglers and beggars plied their trades, and the brass bands of all the four corners within twenty-five miles tooted and pounded at "Hail Columbia, Happy Land," or "Columbia, the Gem of the Ocean."

Conspicuous in the processions at all the points was what Lincoln called the "Basket of Flowers," thirty-two young girls in a resplendent car, representing the Union. At Charleston, a thirty-third young woman rode behind the car, representing Kansas. She carried a banner inscribed: "I will be free;" a motto which brought out from nearly all the newspaper reporters the comment that she was too fair to be long free.

The mottoes at the different meetings epitomized the popular conception of the issues and the candidates. Among the Lincoln sentiments were:

Illinois born under the Ordinance of '87.

Free Territories and Free Men,
 Free Pulpits and Free Preachers,
Free Press and a Free Pen,
 Free Schools and Free Teachers.

"Westward the star of empire takes its way;
 The girls link on to Lincoln, their mothers were for Clay."

Abe the Giant-Killer.

Edgar County for the Tall Sucker.

A striking feature of the crowds was the number of women they included. The intelligent and lively interest they took in the debates caused much comment. No doubt Mrs. Douglas's presence had something to do with this. They were particularly active in receiving the speakers, and at Quincy, Lincoln, on being presented with what the local press described as a "beautiful and elegant bouquet," took pains to express his gratification at the part women everywhere took in the contest.

While this helter-skelter outpouring of prairiedom had the appearance of being little more than a great jollification, a lawless country fair, in reality it was with the majority of the people a profoundly serious matter. With every discussion it became more vital. Indeed, in the first debate, which was opened and

Ottawa, Aug. 22. 1858

J. O. Cunningham, Esq,
My dear Sir
 Yours of the 18th signed as Secretary of the Republican, is received. In the matter of making speeches I am a good deal pressed by invitations from almost all quarters; and while I hope to be at Urbana some time during the canvass, I cannot yet say when. Can you not see me at Monticello on the 6th of Sept?

Douglas and I, for the first time this canvass, crossed swords here yesterday; the fire flew some, and I am glad to know I am yet alive. There was a vast concourse of people — more than could near enough to hear. Yours as ever
 A. Lincoln

LINCOLN'S ESTIMATE OF THE FIRST JOINT DEBATE WITH DOUGLAS.

closed by Douglas,* the relation of the two speakers became dramatic. It was here that Douglas, hoping to fasten on Lincoln the stigma of "abolitionist," charged him with having undertaken to abolitionize the old Whig Party, and having been in 1854 a subscriber to a radical platform proclaimed at Springfield. This platform Douglas read. Lincoln, when he replied, could only say he was never at the convention—knew nothing of the resolutions; but the impression prevailed that he was cornered. The next issue of the Chicago "Press and Tribune" dispelled it. That paper had employed to report the debates the first shorthand reporter in Chicago, Mr. Robert L. Hitt—later a Member of Congress and the Chairman of the Committee on Foreign Affairs. Mr. Hitt, when Douglas began to read the resolutions, took an opportunity to rest, supposing he could get the original from the speaker. He took down only the first line of each resolution. He missed Douglas after the debate, but on reaching Chicago, where he wrote out his report, he sent an assistant to the files to find the platform adopted at the Springfield Convention. It was brought, but when Mr. Hitt began to transcribe it he saw at once that it was widely different from the one Douglas had read. There was great excitement in the office, and the staff, ardently Republican, went to work to discover where the resolutions had come from. It was found that they

* By the terms agreed upon by Douglas and Lincoln for regulating the debates Douglas opened at Ottawa, Jonesboro, Galesburg, and Alton with an hour's speech; was followed by Lincoln with a speech of one and a half hours, and closed with a half-hour speech. At the three remaining points, Freeport, Charleston, and Quincy, Lincoln opened and closed.

originated at a meeting of radical abolitionists with whom Lincoln had never been associated.

The "Press and Tribune" announced the "forgery," as it was called in a caustic editorial, "The Little Dodger Cornered and Caught." Within a week even the remote school-districts of Illinois were discussing Douglas's action, and many of the most important papers of the nation had made it a subject of editorial comment.

Almost without exception Douglas was condemned. No amount of explanation on his part helped him. "The particularity of Douglas's charge," said the Louisville "Journal," "precludes the idea that he was simply and innocently mistaken." Lovers of fair play were disgusted, and those of Douglas's own party who would have applauded a trick too clever to have been discovered could not forgive him for one which had been found out. Greeley came out bitterly against him, and before long wrote to Lincoln and Herndon that Douglas was "like the man's boy who (he said) didn't weigh so much as he expected and he always knew he wouldn't."

Douglas's error became a sharp-edged sword in Lincoln's hand. Without directly referring to it, he called his hearers' attention to the forgery every time he quoted a document by his elaborate explanation that he believed, unless there was some mistake on the part of those with whom the matter originated and which he had been unable to detect, that this was correct. Once when Douglas brought forward a document, Lincoln blandly remarked that he could scarcely

THE LINCOLN-DOUGLAS DEBATES 367

be blamed for doubting its genuineness since the introduction of the Springfield resolutions at Ottawa.

It was in the second debate, at Freeport, that Lincoln made the boldest stroke of the contest. Soon after the Ottawa debate, in discussing his plan for the next encounter, with a number of his political friends, —Washburne, Cook, Judd, and others,—he told them he proposed to ask Douglas four questions, which he read. One and all cried halt at the second question. Under no condition, they said, must he put it. If it were put, Douglas would answer it in such a way as to win the senatorship. The morning of the debate, while on the way to Freeport, Lincoln read the same questions to Mr. Joseph Medill. "I do not like this second question, Mr. Lincoln," said Mr. Medill. The two men argued to their journey's end, but Lincoln was still unconvinced. Even after he reached Freeport several Republican leaders came to him pleading, "Do not ask that question." He was obdurate; and he went on the platform with a higher head, a haughtier step than his friends had noted in him before. Lincoln was going to ruin himself, the committee said despondently; one would think he did not want the senatorship.

The mooted question ran in Lincoln's notes: "Can the people of a United States territory in any lawful way, against the wish of any citizen of the United States, exclude slavery from its limits prior to the formation of a State Constitution?" Lincoln had seen the irreconcilableness of Douglas's own measure of popular sovereignty, which declared that the people of a territory should be left to regulate their domestic concerns in their own way subject only to the Constitution, and the decision of the Supreme Court in the Dred Scott case that slaves, being property, could not under the Constitution be excluded from a territory. He knew that if Douglas said *no* to this question, his Illinois constituents would never return him to the Senate. He believed that if he said *yes,* the people of the South would never vote for him for President of the United States. He was willing himself to lose the senatorship in order to defeat Douglas for the Presidency in 1860. "I am after larger game; the battle of 1860 is worth a hundred of this," he said confidently.

The question was put, and Douglas answered it with rare artfulness. "It matters not," he cried, "what way the Supreme Court may hereafter decide as to the abstract question whether slavery may or may not go into a territory under the Constitution; the people have the lawful means to introduce it or exclude it as they please, for the reason that slavery cannot exist a day or an hour anywhere unless it is supported by local police regulations. Those police regulations can only be established by the local legislature, and if the people are opposed to slavery, they will elect representatives to that body who will, by unfriendly legislation, effectually prevent the introduction of it into their midst. If, on the contrary, they are for it, their legislation will favor its extension."

His Democratic constituents went wild over the clever way in which Douglas had escaped Lincoln's

LINCOLN IN 1858. AGE 49.

From photograph loaned by W. J. Franklin of Macomb, Illinois, and taken in 1866 from an ambrotype made in 1858, at Macomb.

trap. He now practically had his election. The Republicans shook their heads. Lincoln only was serene. He alone knew what he had done. The Freeport debate had no sooner reached the pro-slavery press than a storm of protest went up. Douglas had betrayed the South. He had repudiated the Supreme Court decision. He had declared that slavery could be kept out of the territories by other legislation than a State Constitution. "The Freeport doctrine," or "the theory of unfriendly legislation," as it became known, spread month by month, and slowly but surely made Douglas an impossible candidate in the South. The force of the question was not realized in full by Lincoln's friends until the Democratic Party met in Charleston, S. C., in 1860, and the southern delegates refused to support Douglas because of the answer he gave to Lincoln's question in the Freeport debate of 1858.

"Do you recollect the argument we had on the way up to Freeport two years ago over the question I was going to ask Judge Douglas?" Lincoln asked Mr. Joseph Medill, when the latter went to Springfield a few days after the election of 1860.

"Yes," said Medill, "I recollect it very well."

"Don't you think I was right now?"

"We were both right. The question hurt Douglas for the Presidency, but it lost you the senatorship."

"Yes, and I have won the place he was playing for."

From the beginning of the campaign Lincoln supplemented the strength of his arguments by inexhaustible good-humor. Douglas, physically worn, harassed by the trend which Lincoln had given the discussions, irritated that his adroitness and eloquence could not so cover the fundamental truth of the Republican position but that it would up again, often grew angry, even abusive. Lincoln answered him with most effective raillery. At Havana, where he spoke the day after Douglas, he said:

"I am informed that my distinguished friend yesterday became a little excited—nervous, perhaps—and he said something about *fighting*, as though referring to a pugilistic encounter between him and myself. Did anybody in this audience hear him use such language? [Cries of "Yes."] I am informed further, that somebody in *his* audience, rather more excited and nervous than himself, took off his coat, and offered to take the job off Judge Douglas's hands, and fight Lincoln himself. Did anybody here witness that warlike proceeding? [Laughter and cries of "Yes."] Well, I merely desire to say that I shall fight neither Judge Douglas nor his second. I shall not do this for two reasons, which I will now explain. In the first place, a fight would prove *nothing* which is in issue in this contest. It might establish that Judge Douglas is a more muscular man than myself, or it might demonstrate that I am a more muscular man than Judge Douglas. But this question is not referred to in the Cincinnati platform, nor in either of the Springfield platforms. Neither result would prove him right nor me wrong; and so of the gentleman who volunteered to do this fighting for him. If my fighting Judge Douglas would not prove anything, it would certainly prove nothing for me to fight his bottle-holder.

"My second reason for not having a personal encounter with the judge is, that I don't believe he wants it himself. He and I are about the best friends in the world, and when we get together he would no more think of fighting me than of fighting his wife. Therefore, ladies and gentlemen, when the judge talked about fighting, he was not giving vent to any ill feeling of his own, but merely trying to excite—well, *enthusiasm* against me on the part of his audience. And as I find he was tolerably successful, we will call it quits."

More difficult for Lincoln to take good-naturedly than threats and hard names were the irrelevant matters which Douglas dragged into the debates to turn attention from the vital arguments. Thus Douglas insisted repeatedly on taunting Lincoln because his zealous friends had carried him off the platform at Ottawa. "Lincoln was so frightened by the questions put to him," said Douglas, "that he could not walk." He tried to arouse the prejudice of the audience by absurd charges of abolitionism. Lincoln wanted to give negroes social equality; he wanted a negro wife; he was willing to allow Fred Douglass to make speeches for him. Again he took up a good deal of Lincoln's time by forcing him to answer a charge of refusing to vote supplies for the soldiers in the Mexican War. Lincoln denied and explained, until at last, at Charleston, he turned suddenly to Douglas's supporters, dragging one of the strongest of them— the Hon. O. B. Ficklin, with whom he had been in Congress in 1848—to the platform.

"I do not mean to do anything with Mr. Ficklin," he said, "except to present his face and tell you that he personally knows it to be a lie." And Mr. Ficklin had to acknowledge that Lincoln was right.

"Judge Douglas," said Lincoln in speaking of this policy, "is playing cuttlefish—a small species of fish that has no mode of defending himself when pursued except by throwing out a black fluid which makes the water so dark the enemy cannot see it, and thus it escapes."

The question at stake was too serious in Lincoln's judgment for platform jugglery. Every moment of time which Douglas forced him to spend answering irrelevant charges he gave begrudgingly. He struggled constantly to keep his speeches on the line of solid argument. Slowly but surely those who followed the debates began to understand this. It was Douglas who drew the great masses to the debates in the first place; it was because of him that the public men and the newspapers of the East, as well as of the West, watched the discussions. But as the days went on it was not Douglas who made the impression.

During the hours of the speeches the two men seemed well mated. "I can recall only one fact of the debates," says Mrs. William Crotty of Seneca, Illinois, "that I felt so sorry for Lincoln while Douglas was speaking, and then to my surprise I felt *so* sorry for Douglas when Lincoln replied." The disinterested to whom it was an intellectual game felt the power and charm of both men. Partisans had each reason enough to cheer. It was afterwards, as the debates were talked over by auditors as they lingered at the country store or were grouped on the fence in the evening, or when they were read in the generous reports which the newspapers of Illinois and even of other states gave, that the thoroughness of Lincoln's argument was understood. Even the first debate at Ottawa had a surprising effect. "I tell you," says Mr. George Beatty of Ottawa, "that debate set people thinking on these important questions

LINCOLN IN 1859.

From a photograph in the collection of H. W. Fay, custodian of the Lincoln Monument, Springfield, Ill. The original was made by S. M. Fassett of Chicago; the negative was destroyed in the Chicago fire. This picture was made at the solicitation of D. B. Cook, who says that Mrs. Lincoln pronounced it the best likeness she had ever seen of her husband. Rajan used the Fassett picture as the original of his etching, and Kruell has made a fine engraving of it.

in a way they hadn't dreamed of. I heard any number of men say: 'This thing is an awfully serious question, and I have about concluded Lincoln has got it right.' My father, a thoughtful, God-fearing man, said to me, as we went home to supper, 'George, you are young, and don't see what this thing means, as I do. Douglas's speeches of "squatter sovereignty" please you younger men, but I tell you that with us older men it's a great question that faces us. We've either got to keep slavery back or it's going to spread all over the country. That's the real question that's behind all this. Lincoln is right.' And that was the feeling that prevailed, I think, among the majority, after the debate was over. People went home talking about the danger of slavery getting a hold in the North. This territory had been Democratic; La Salle County, the morning of the day of the debate, was Democratic; but when the next day came around, hundreds of Democrats had been made Republicans, owing to the light in which Lincoln had brought forward the fact that slavery threatened."

It was among Lincoln's own friends, however, that his speeches produced the deepest impression. They had believed him to be strong, but probably there was no one of them who had not felt dubious about his ability to meet Douglas. Many even feared a fiasco. Gradually it began to be clear to them that Lincoln was the stronger. Could it be that Lincoln really was a great man? The young Republican journalists of the "Press and Tribune"—Scripps, Hitt, Medill—began to ask themselves the question. One evening as they talked over Lincoln's arguments a letter was received. It came from a prominent eastern statesman. "Who is this man that is replying to Douglas in your state?" he asked. "Do you realize that no greater speeches have been made on public questions in the history of our country; that his knowledge of the subject is profound, his logic unanswerable, his style inimitable?" Similar letters kept coming from various parts of the country. Before the campaign was over Lincoln's friends were exultant. Their favorite was a great man, "a full-grown man," as one of them wrote in his paper.

The country at large watched Lincoln with astonishment. When the debates began there were Republicans in Illinois of wider national reputation. Judge Lyman Trumbull, then Senator, was better known. He was an able debater, and a speech which he had made in August against Douglas's record called from the New York "Evening Post" the remark: "This is the heaviest blow struck at Senator Douglas since he took the field in Illinois; it is unanswerable, and we suspect that it will be fatal." Trumbull's speech the "Post" afterwards published in pamphlet form. Besides Trumbull, Owen Lovejoy, Oglesby, and Palmer were all speaking. That Lincoln should not only have so far outstripped men of his own party, but should have out-argued Douglas was the cause of comment everywhere. "No man of this generation," said the "Evening Post" editorially, at the close of the debate, "has grown more rapidly before the country than Lincoln in this canvass." As a matter of fact, Lincoln had attracted the attention of all the thinking men of the country. "The first thing that really awakened my interest in him," says Henry Ward Beecher, "was his speech parallel with Douglas in Illinois, and indeed it was that manifestation of ability that secured his nomination to the presidency."

But able as were Lincoln's arguments, deep as was the impression he had made, he was not elected to the senatorship. Douglas won fairly enough; though it is well to note that if the Republicans did not elect a senator they gained a substantial number of votes over those polled in 1856.

Lincoln accepted the result with a serenity inexplicable to his supporters. To him the contest was but one battle in a "durable" struggle. Little matter who won now, if in the end the right triumphed. From the first he had looked at the final result—not at the senatorship. "I do not claim, gentlemen, to be unselfish," he said at Chicago in July. "I do not pretend that I would not like to go to the United States Senate; I make no such hypocritical pretense; but I do say to you that in this mighty issue, it is nothing to you, nothing to the mass of the people of the nation, whether or not Judge Douglas or myself shall ever be heard of after this night; it may be a trifle to either of us, but in connection with this mighty question upon which hang the destinies of the nation perhaps, it is absolutely nothing."

The intense heat and fury of the debates, the defeat in November, did not alter a jot this high view. "I am glad I made the late race," he wrote Dr. A. G. Henry. "It gave me a hearing on the great and durable question of the age which I would have had in no other way; and though I now sink out of view and shall be forgotten, I believe I have made some marks which will tell for the cause of civil liberty long after I am gone."

At that date perhaps no one appreciated the value of what Lincoln had done as well as he did himself. He was absolutely sure he was right and that in the end people would see it. Though he might not rise, he knew his cause would. "Douglas had the ingenuity to be supported in the late contest both as the best means to break down and to uphold the slave interest," he wrote. "No ingenuity can keep these antagonistic elements in harmony long. Another explosion will soon occur." His whole attention was given to conserving what the Republicans had gained,—"We have some one hundred and twenty thousand clear Republican votes. That pile is worth keeping together;" to consoling his friends,—"You are feeling badly," he wrote to N. B. Judd, Chairman of the Republican Committee, "and this too shall pass away, never fear;" to rallying for another effort,—"The cause of civil liberty must not be surrendered at the end of one or even one hundred defeats."

If Lincoln had at times a fear that his defeat would cause him to be set aside, it soon was dispelled. The interest awakened in him was genuine, and it spread with the wider reading and discussion of his arguments. He was besieged by letters from all parts of the Union, congratulations, encouragements, criticisms. Invitations for lectures poured in upon him, and he became the first choice of his entire party for political speeches.

The greater number of these invitations he declined.

THE LINCOLN-DOUGLAS DEBATES 377

He had given so much time to politics since 1854 that his law practice had been neglected and he was feeling poor; but there were certain of the calls which could not be resisted. Douglas spoke several times for the Democrats of Ohio in the 1859 campaign for governor and Lincoln naturally was asked to reply. He made but two speeches, one at Columbus on September 16 and the other at Cincinnati on September 17, but he had great audiences on both occasions. The Columbus speech was devoted almost entirely to answering an essay by Douglas which had been published in the September number of "Harper's Magazine," and which began by asserting that—"Under our complex system of government it is the first duty of American statesmen to mark distinctly the dividing-line between Federal and local authority." It was an elaborate argument for "popular sovereignty" and attracted national attention. Indeed, at the moment it was the talk of the country. Lincoln literally tore it to bits.

"What is Judge Douglas's popular sovereignty?" he asked. "It is, as a principle, no other than that if one man chooses to make a slave of another man, neither that other man nor anybody else has a right to object. Applied in government, as he seeks to apply it, it is this: If, in a new territory into which a few people are beginning to enter for the purpose of making their homes, they choose to either exclude slavery from their limits or to establish it there, however one or the other may affect the persons to be enslaved, or the infinitely greater number of persons who are afterward to inhabit that territory, or the other members of the families of communities, of which they are but an incipient member, or the general head of the family of states as parent of all—however their action may affect one or the other of these, there is no power or right to interfere. That is Douglas's popular sovereignty applied."

It was in this address that Lincoln uttered the oft-quoted paragraphs:

"I suppose the institution of slavery really looks small to him. He is so put up by nature that a lash upon his back would hurt him, but a lash upon anybody else's back does not hurt him. That is the build of the man, and consequently he looks upon the matter of slavery in this unimportant light.

"Judge Douglas ought to remember, when he is endeavoring to force this policy upon the American people, that while he is put up in that way, a good many are not. He ought to remember that there was once in this country a man by the name of Thomas Jefferson, supposed to be a Democrat—a man whose principles and policy are not very prevalent amongst Democrats to-day, it is true; but that man did not take exactly this view of the insignificance of the element of slavery which our friend Judge Douglas does. In contemplation of this thing, we all know he was led to exclaim, 'I tremble for my country when I remember that God is just!' We know how he looked upon it when he thus expressed himself. There was danger to this country, danger of the avenging justice of God, in that little unimportant popular-sovereignty question of Judge Douglas. He supposed there was a question of God's eternal justice wrapped up in the enslaving of any race of men, or any man, and that those who did so braved the arm of Jehovah—that when a nation thus dared the Almighty, every friend of that nation had cause to dread his wrath. Choose ye between Jefferson and Douglas as to what is the true view of this element among us."

One interesting point about the Columbus address is that in it appears the germ of the Cooper Institute speech delivered five months later in New York City.

Lincoln made so deep an impression in Ohio by his speeches that the State Republican Committee asked permission to publish them together with the Lincoln-Douglas Debates as campaign documents in the presidential election of the next year.

In December he yielded to the persuasion of his Kansas political friends and delivered five lectures in that state, only fragments of which have been preserved.

Unquestionably the most effective piece of work he did that winter was the address at Cooper Institute, New York, on February 27. He had received an invitation in the fall of 1859 to lecture at Plymouth Church, Brooklyn. To his friends it was evident that he was greatly pleased by the compliment, but that he feared that he was not equal to an eastern audience. After some hesitation he accepted, provided they would take a political speech if he could find time to get up no other. When he reached New York he found that he was to speak there instead of Brooklyn, and that he was certain to have a distinguished audience. Fearful lest he was not as well prepared as he ought to be, conscious, too, no doubt, that he had a great opportunity before him, he spent nearly all of the two days and a half before his lecture in revising his matter and in familiarizing himself with it. In order that he might be sure that he was heard he arranged with his friend, Mason Brayman, who had come on to New York with him, to sit in the back of the hall and in case he did not speak loud enough to raise his high hat on a cane.

Mr. Lincoln's audience was a notable one even for New York. It included William Cullen Bryant, who introduced him, Horace Greeley, David Dudley Field and many more well known men of the day. It is doubtful if there were any persons present, even his best friends, who expected that Lincoln would do more than interest his hearers by his sound arguments. Many have confessed since that they feared his queer manner and quaint speeches would amuse people so much that they would fail to catch the weight of his logic. But to the surprise of everybody Lincoln impressed his audience from the start by his dignity and his seriousness. "His manner was, to a New York audience, a very strange one, but it was captivating," wrote an auditor. "He held the vast meeting spellbound, and as one by one his oddly expressed but trenchant and convincing arguments confirmed the soundness of his political conclusions, the house broke out in wild and prolonged enthusiasm. I think I never saw an audience more thoroughly carried away by an orator."

The Cooper Union speech was founded on a sentence from one of Douglas's Ohio speeches:—"Our fathers when they framed the government under which we live understood this question just as well, and even better, than we do now." Douglas claimed that the "fathers" held that the Constitution forbade the Federal Government controlling slavery in the territories. Lincoln with infinite care had investigated the opinions and votes of each of the "fathers" —whom he took to be the thirty-nine men who signed the Constitution—and showed conclusively that a

LINCOLN IN FEBRUARY, 1860, AT THE TIME OF THE COOPER INSTITUTE SPEECH.

From photograph by Brady. The debate with Douglas in 1858 had given Lincoln a national reputation, and the following year he received many invitations to lecture. One came from a young men's Republican club in New York. Lincoln consented, and in February, 1860 (about three months before his nomination for the presidency), delivered what is known, from the hall in which it was delivered, as the "Cooper Institute speech." While in New York he was taken by the committee of entertainment to Brady's gallery, and sat for the portrait reproduced above. It was a frequent remark with Lincoln that this portrait and the Cooper Institute speech made him President.

majority of them "certainly understood that no proper division of local from Federal authority nor any part of the Constitution forbade the Federal Government to control slavery in the Federal territories." Not only did he show this of the thirty-nine framers of the original Constitution, but he defied anybody to show that one of the seventy-six members of the Congress which framed the amendments to the Constitution ever held any such view.

"Let all," he said, "who believe that 'our fathers who framed the government under which we live understood this question just as well, and even better, than we do now,' speak as they spoke, and act as they acted upon it. This is all Republicans ask—all Republicans desire—in relation to slavery. As those fathers marked it, so let it be again marked, as an evil not to be extended, but to be tolerated and protected only because of and so far as its actual presence among us makes that toleration and protection a necessity. Let all the guaranties those fathers gave it be not grudgingly, but fully and fairly, maintained. For this Republicans contend, and with this, so far as I know or believe, they will be content."

One after another he took up and replied to the charges the South was making against the North at the moment:—Sectionalism, radicalism, giving undue prominence to the slave question, stirring up insurrection among slaves, refusing to allow constitutional rights, and to each he had an unimpassioned answer impregnable with facts.

The discourse was ended with what Lincoln felt to be a precise statement of the opinion of the question on both sides, and of the duty of the Republican

Party under the circumstances. This portion of his address is one of the finest early examples of that simple and convincing style in which most of his later public documents were written.

"If slavery is right," he said, "all words, acts, laws, and constitutions against it are themselves wrong, and should be silenced and swept away. If it is right, we cannot justly object to its nationality—its universality; if it is wrong, they cannot justly insist upon its extension—its enlargement. All they ask we could readily grant, if we thought slavery right; all we ask they could as readily grant, if they thought it wrong. Their thinking it right and our thinking it wrong is the precise fact upon which depends the whole controversy. Thinking it right, as they do, they are not to blame for desiring its full recognition as being right; but thinking it wrong, as we do, can we yield to them? Can we cast our votes with their view, and against our own? In view of our moral, social, and political responsibilities, can we do this?

"Wrong, as we think slavery is, we can yet afford to let it alone where it is, because that much is due to the necessity arising from its actual presence in the nation; but can we, while our votes will prevent it, allow it to spread into the national territories, and to overrun us here in these free states? If our sense of duty forbids this, then let us stand by our duty fearlessly and effectively. Let us be diverted by none of those sophistical contrivances wherewith we are so industriously plied and belabored—contrivances such as groping for some middle ground between the right and the wrong: vain as the search for a man who should be neither a living man nor a dead man; such as a policy of 'don't care' on a question about which all true men do care; such as Union appeals beseeching true Union men to yield to Disunionists, reversing the divine rule, and calling, not the sinners, but the righteous to repentance; such as invocations to Washington, imploring men to unsay what Washington said and undo what Washington did.

THE LINCOLN-DOUGLAS DEBATES

"Neither let us be slandered from our duty by false accusations against us, nor frightened from it by menaces of destruction to the government, nor of dungeons to ourselves. Let us have faith that right makes might, and in that faith let us to the end dare to do our duty as we understand it."

From New York Lincoln went to Providence, R. I., where he spoke on the evening of February 28th and from there on to New Hampshire to visit his son Robert, then at Phillips Exeter Academy. His coming was known only a short time before he arrived and hurried arrangements were made for him to speak at Concord, Manchester, Exeter and Dover. At Concord the address was made in the afternoon on only a few hours' notice; nevertheless, he had a great audience, so eager were men at the time to hear anybody who had serious arguments on the slavery question. Something of the impression Lincoln made in New Hampshire may be gathered from the following article, "Mr. Lincoln in New Hampshire," which appeared in the Boston "Atlas and Bee" for March 5:

"The Concord 'Statesman' says that notwithstanding the rain of Thursday, rendering travelling very inconvenient, the largest hall in that city was crowded to hear Mr. Lincoln. The editor says it was one of the most powerful, logical and compact speeches to which it was ever our fortune to listen; an argument against the system of slavery, and in defence of the position of the Republican Party, from the deductions of which no reasonable man could possibly escape. He fortified every position assumed, by proofs which it is impossible to gainsay; and while his speech was at intervals enlivened by remarks which elicited applause at the expense of the Democratic Party, there was, nevertheless, not a single word which tended to impair the dignity of the speaker, or weaken the force of the great truths he uttered.

"The 'Statesman' adds that the address 'was perfect and was closed by a peroration which brought his audience to their feet. We are not extravagant in the remark, that a political speech of greater power has rarely if ever been uttered in the Capital of New Hampshire. At its conclusion nine roof-raising cheers were given; three for the speaker, three for the Republicans of Illinois, and three for the Republicans of New Hampshire.'

"On the same evening Mr. Lincoln spoke at Manchester, to an immense gathering in Smyth's Hall. The 'Mirror,' a neutral paper, gives the following enthusiastic notice of his speech: 'The audience was a flattering one to the reputation of the speaker. It was composed of persons of all sorts of political notions, earnest to hear one whose fame was so great, and we think most of them went away thinking better of him than they anticipated they should. He spoke an hour and a half with great fairness, great apparent candor, and with wonderful interest. He did not abuse the South, the Administration, or the Democrats, or indulge in any personalities, with the solitary exception of a few hits at Douglas's notions. He is far from prepossessing in personal appearance, and his voice is disagreeable, and yet he wins your attention and good will from the start.

"'He indulges in no flowers of rhetoric, no eloquent passages; he is not a wit, a humorist or a clown; yet, so great a vein of pleasantry and good nature pervades what he says, gilding over a deep current of practical argument, he keeps his hearers in a smiling good mood with their mouths open ready to swallow all he says. His sense of the ludicrous is very keen, and an exhibition of that is the clincher of all his arguments; not the ludicrous acts of persons, but ludicrous ideas. Hence he is never offensive, and steals away willingly into his train of belief persons who are opposed to him. For the first half hour his opponents would agree with every word he uttered, and from that point he began to lead them off, little by little, cunningly, till it seemed as if he had got them all into his fold. He displays more shrewdness, more knowledge of the masses of mankind than any public speaker we have heard since Long Jim Wilson left for California.'"

From New Hampshire Lincoln went to Connecticut, where he spent a week, speaking at Hartford, New Haven, Meridian, Woonsocket, Norwich and Bridgeport. There are no reports of the New Hampshire speeches, but two of the Connecticut speeches were published in part and one in full. Their effect was very similar, according to the newspapers of the day, to that in New Hampshire, described by the "Atlas and Bee."

By his debates with Douglas and the speeches in Ohio, Kansas, New York and New England, Lincoln had become a national figure in the minds of all the political leaders of the country, and of the thinking men of the North. Never in the history of the United States had a man come to the front in a more logical and intelligent way. At the beginning of the struggle against the repeal of the Missouri Compromise in 1854, Abraham Lincoln was scarcely known outside of his own state. Even most of the men whom he had met in his brief term in Congress had forgotten him. Yet in four years he had become one of the central figures of his party; and now, by worsting the greatest orator and politician of his time, he had drawn the eyes of the nation to him.

It had been a long road he had travelled to make himself a national figure. Twenty-eight years before he had deliberately entered politics. He had been beaten, but had persisted; he had succeeded and failed;

he had abandoned the struggle and returned to his profession. His outraged sense of justice had driven him back, and for six years he had travelled up and down Illinois trying to prove to men that slavery extension was wrong. It was by no one speech, by no one argument that he had wrought. Every day his ceaseless study and pondering gave him new matter, and every speech he made was fresh. He could not repeat an old speech, he said, because the subject enlarged and widened so in his mind as he went on that it was "easier to make a new one than an old one." He had never yielded in his campaign to tricks of oratory—never played on emotions. He had been so strong in his convictions of the right of his case that his speeches had been arguments pure and simple. Their elegance was that of a demonstration in Euclid. They persuaded because they proved. He had never for a moment counted personal ambition before the cause. To insure an ardent opponent of the Kansas-Nebraska Bill in the United States Senate, he had at one time given up his chance for the senatorship. To show the fallacy of Douglas's argument, he had asked a question which his party pleaded with him to pass by, assuring him that it would lose him the election. In every step of these six years he had been disinterested, calm, unyielding, and courageous. He knew he was right, and could afford to wait. "The result is not doubtful," he told his friends. "We shall not fail—if we stand firm. We shall not fail. Wise counsels may accelerate or mistakes delay it; but, sooner or later, the victory is sure to come."

The country, amazed at the rare moral and intel-

THE LINCOLN-DOUGLAS DEBATES 387

lectual character of Lincoln, began to ask questions about him, and then his history came out: a pioneer home, little schooling, few books, hard labor at all the many trades of the frontiersman, a profession mastered o' nights by the light of a friendly cooper's fire, an early entry into politics and law—and then twenty-five years of incessant poverty and struggle.

The homely story gave a touch of mystery to the figure which loomed so large. Men felt a sudden reverence for a mind and heart developed to these noble proportions in so unfriendly a habitat. They turned instinctively to one so familiar with strife for help in solving the desperate problem with which the nation had grappled. And thus it was that, at fifty years of age, Lincoln became a national figure.

CHAPTER XIX

LINCOLN'S NOMINATION IN 1860

THE possibility of Abraham Lincoln becoming the presidential candidate of the Republican Party in 1860 was probably first discussed by a few of his friends in 1856. The dramatic speech which in May of that year gave him the leadership of his party in Illinois, and the unexpected and flattering attention he received a few weeks later at the Republican National Convention suggested the idea; but there is no evidence that anything more was excited than a little speculation. The impression Lincoln made two years later in the Lincoln and Douglas debates kindled a different feeling. It convinced a number of astute Illinois politicians that judicious effort would make Lincoln strong enough to justify the presentation of his name as a candidate in 1860 on the ground of pure availability.

One of the first men to conceive this idea was Jesse W. Fell, a local politician of Bloomington, Illinois. During the Lincoln and Douglas debates, Fell was travelling in the Middle and Eastern States. He was surprised to find that Lincoln's speeches attracted general attention, that many papers quoted liberally from them, and that on all sides men plied him with questions about the career and personality of the new man. Before Fell left the East he had made up his mind that Lincoln must be pushed by his own state as its presidential candidate. One evening, soon after returning home, he met Lincoln in Bloomington, where the latter was attending court and drew him into a deserted law-office for a confidential talk.

"I have been East, Lincoln," said he, "as far as Boston, and up into New Hampshire, travelling in all the New England States, save Maine; in New York, New Jersey, Pennsylvania, Ohio, Michigan and Indiana; and everywhere I hear you talked about. Very frequently I have been asked, 'Who is this man Lincoln, of your state, now canvassing in opposition to Senator Douglas?' Being, as you know, an ardent Republican and your friend, I usually told them we had in Illinois *two* giants instead of one; that Douglas was the *little* one, as they all knew, but that you were the *big* one, which they didn't all know.

"But, seriously, Lincoln, Judge Douglas being so widely known, you are getting a national reputation *through him,* and the truth is, I have a decided impression that if your popular history and efforts on the slavery question can be sufficiently brought before the people, you can be made a formidable, if not a successful, candidate for the presidency."

"What's the use of talking of me for the presidency," was Lincoln's reply, "whilst we have such men as Seward, Chase, and others, who are so much better known to the people, and whose names are so intimately associated with the principles of the Republican Party? Everybody knows them; nobody scarcely outside of Illinois knows me. Besides, is it not, as a matter of justice, due to such men, who have carried this movement forward to its present status, in spite of fearful opposition, personal abuse, and hard names? I really think so."

Fell continued his persuasions, and finally requested Lincoln to furnish him a sketch of his life which could be put out in the East. The suggestion grated on Lincoln's sensibilities. He had no chance. Why force himself? "Fell," he said, rising and wrapping his old gray shawl around his tall figure, "I admit that I am ambitious and would like to be President. I am not insensible to the compliment you pay me and the interest you manifest in the matter; *but there is no such good luck in store for me as the presidency of these United States.* Besides, there is nothing in my early history that would interest you or anybody else; and, as Judge Davis says, 'it won't pay.' Good night." And he disappeared into the darkness.

Lincoln's defeat in November, 1858, in the contest for the United States senatorship, in no way discouraged his friends. A few days after the November election, when it was known that Douglas had been reëlected senator, the Chicago "Democrat," then edited by "Long John" Wentworth, printed an editorial, nearly a column in length, headed "Abraham Lincoln." His work in the campaign then just closed was reviewed and commended in the highest terms.

"His speeches," the "Democrat" declared, "will be recognized for a long time to come as the standard authorities upon those topics which overshadow all others in the political world of our day; and our children will read them and appreciate the great truths which they so forcibly inculcate, with even a higher appreciation of their worth than their fathers possessed while listening to them.

NOMINATION IN 1860

"We, for our part," said the "Democrat" further, "consider that it would be but a partial appreciation of his services to our noble cause that our next State Republican Convention should nominate him for Governor as unanimously and enthusiastically as it did for Senator. With such a leader and with our just cause, we would sweep the state from end to end, with a triumph so complete and perfect that there would be scarce enough of the scattered and demoralized forces of the enemy left to tell the story of its defeat. And this state should also present his name to the National Republican Convention, first for President and next for Vice-President. We should then say to the United States at large that in our opinion the Great Man of Illinois is Abraham Lincoln, and none other than **Abraham Lincoln.**"

All through the year 1859 a few men in Illinois worked quietly but persistently to awaken a demand throughout the state for Lincolns' nomination. The greater number of these were lawyers on Lincoln's circuit, his life-long friends, men like Judge Davis, Leonard Swett, and Judge Logan, who not only believed in him, but loved him, and whose efforts were doubly effective because of their affection. In addition to these were a few shrewd politicians who saw in Lincoln the "available" man the situation demanded; and a group represented by John M. Palmer, who, remembering Lincoln's magnanimity in throwing his influence to Trumbull in 1854, in order to send a sound Anti-Nebraska man to the United States Senate, wanted, as Senator Palmer himself put it, to "pay Lincoln back." Then there were a few young men who had been won by Lincoln in the debates with Douglas, and who threw youthful enthusiasm and conviction into their support. The first time his name was suggested as a candidate in the newspapers, indeed, was because the young editor of the Central Illinois "Gazette," Mr. W. O. Stoddard, had caught a glimpse of Lincoln's inner might and concluding in a sudden burst of boyish exultation that Lincoln was "the greatest man he had ever seen or heard of," had rushed off and written an editorial nominating him for the presidency; this editorial was published on May 4, 1859.

The work which these men did at this time cannot be traced with any definiteness. It consisted mainly in "talking up" their candidate. They were greatly aided by the newspapers. The press, indeed, followed a concerted plan that had been carefully laid out by the Republican State Committee in the office of the Chicago "Tribune." To give an appearance of spontaneity to the newspaper canvass it was arranged that the country papers should first take up Lincoln's name. Joseph Medill, editor of the "Tribune," and secretary of the committee, says that a Rock Island paper opened the campaign.

Lincoln soon felt the force of this effort in his behalf. Letters came to him from unexpected quarters, offering aid. Everywhere he went on the circuit, men sought him to discuss the situation. In the face of an undoubted movement for him he quailed. The interest was local; could it ever be more? Above all, had he the qualifications for President of the United States? He asked himself these questions as he pondered a reply to an editor who had suggested announcing his name, and he wrote: "I must in all candor say I do not think myself fit for the presidency."

This was in April, 1859. In the July following he still declared himself unfit. Even in the following November he had little hope of nomination. "For my single self," he wrote to a correspondent who had suggested the putting of his name on the ticket, "I have enlisted for the permanent success of the Republican cause, and for this object I shall labor faithfully in the ranks, unless, as I think not probable, the judgment of the party shall assign me a different position."

The last weeks of 1859 and the first of 1860 convinced Lincoln, however, that, fit or not, he was in the field. Fell, who as corresponding secretary of the Republican State Central Committee had been travelling constantly in the interests of the organization, brought him such proof that his candidacy was generally approved of, that in December, 1859, he consented to write the "little sketch" of his life now known as Lincoln's "autobiography."

He wrote it with a little inward shrinking, a half shame that it was so meagre. "There is not much of it," he apologized in sending the document, "for the reason, I suppose, that there is not much of me. If anything be made out of it, I wish it to be modest, and not to go beyond the material."

By the opening of 1860 Lincoln had concluded that, though he might not be a very promising candidate, at all events he was now in so deep that he must have the approval of his own state, and he began to work in earnest for that. "I am not in a position where it would hurt much for me to not be nominated on the national ticket," he wrote to Norman B. Judd, "but I am where it would hurt some for me to not get the Illinois delegates. . . . Can you help me a little in your end of the vineyard?"

The plans of the Lincoln men were well matured. About the first of December, 1859, Medill had gone to Washington, ostensibly as a "Tribune" correspondent, but really to promote Lincoln's nomination. "Before writing any Lincoln letters for the 'Tribune,'" says Mr. Medill in his "Reminiscences," "I began preaching Lincoln among the Congressmen. I urged him chiefly upon the ground of availability in the close and doubtful states, with what seemed like reasonable success."

February 16, 1860, the "Tribune" came out editorially for Lincoln, and Medill followed a few days later with a ringing letter from Washington, naming Lincoln as a candidate on whom both conservatives and radicals could unite, and declaring that he now heard Lincoln's name mentioned for President in Washington "ten times as often as it was one month ago." About the time when Medill was writing thus, Norman B. Judd, as member of the Republican National Committee, was executing a manœuvre the importance of which no one realized but the Illinois politicians. This was securing the convention for Chicago.

As the spring passed and the counties of Illinois held their conventions, Lincoln found that, save in the North, where Seward was strong, he was unanimously recommended as the candidate at Chicago. When the State Convention met at De-

LINCOLN IN 1860.
From a photograph loaned by H. W. Fay of De Kalb, Illinois.

catur, May 9 and 10, he received an ovation of so picturesque and unique a character that it colored all the rest of the campaign. The delegates were in session when Lincoln came in as a spectator and was invited to a seat on the platform. Soon after, Richard Oglesby, one of Lincoln's ardent supporters, asked that an old Democrat of Macon County be allowed to offer a contribution to the convention. The offer was accepted, and a curious banner was borne up the hall, its standard made of two weather-worn fence-rails, decorated with flags and streamers; its inscription read:

ABRAHAM LINCOLN

THE RAIL CANDIDATE

FOR PRESIDENT IN 1860

Two rails from a lot of 3,000 made in 1830 by Thos. Hanks and Abe Lincoln—whose father was the first pioneer of Macon County.

A storm of applause greeted the carrier, followed by cries of "Lincoln! Lincoln!" Rising, Lincoln said, pointing to the banner, "I suppose I am expected to reply to that. I cannot say whether I made those rails or not, but I am quite sure I have made a great many just as good." The speech was warmly applauded, and one delegate, an influential German and an ardent Seward man, George Schneider, turned to his neighbor and said, "Seward has lost the Illinois delegation." He was right; for when, later, John M. Palmer brought in a resolution that "Abraham Lincoln is the choice of the Republican Party of Illinois for the presidency, and the delegates from this state are instructed to use all honorable means to secure his nomination by the Chicago Convention, and to vote as a unit for him," it was enthusiastically adopted.

While the politicians of Illinois were thus preparing for the campaign, the Republicans of the East hardly realized that Lincoln was or could be made a possibility. In the first four months of 1860 his name was almost unmentioned as a presidential candidate in the public prints of the East. In a list of twenty-one "prominent candidates for the presidency in 1860," prepared by D. W. Bartlett and published in New York towards the end of 1859, Lincoln's name is not mentioned; nor does it appear in a list of thirty-four of "our living representative men," prepared for presidential purposes by John Savage, and published in Philadelphia in 1860. The most important notice at this period of which we know was a casual mention in an editorial in the New York "Evening Post," February 15. The "Post" considered it time for the Republicans to speak out about the nominee at the coming convention, and remarked: "With such men as Seward and Chase, Banks and *Lincoln,* and others in plenty, let us have two Republican representative men to vote for." This was ten days before the Cooper Union speech and the New England tour, which undoubtedly did much to recommend Lincoln as a logical and statesmanlike thinker and debater, though there is no evidence that it created him a presidential following in the East, save, perhaps, in New Hampshire. Indeed it was scarcely to be expected that prudent and conservative men would conclude that, because he could make a good speech, he would make a good President. They knew him to be comparatively untrained in public life and comparatively untried in large affairs. They naturally preferred a man who had experience and a record of successful statesmanship.

Up to the opening of the convention in May there was, in fact, no specially prominent mention of Lincoln by the eastern press. Greeley, intent on undermining Seward, though as yet nobody perceived him to be so, printed in the "New York Weekly Tribune" —the paper which went to the country at large— correspondence favoring the nomination of Bates and Read, McLean and Bell, Cameron, Frémont, Dayton, Chase, Wade; but not Lincoln. The New York "Herald" of May 1, in discussing editorially the nominee of the "Black Republicans," recognized "four living, two dead, aspirants." The "living" were Seward, Banks, Chase, and Cameron; the "dead," Bates and McLean. May 10 "The Independent," in an editorial on "The Nomination at Chicago," said: "Give us a man known to be true upon the only question that enters into the canvass—a Seward, a Chase, a Wade, a Sumner, a Fessenden, a Banks." But it did not mention Lincoln. His most conspicuous eastern recognition before the convention was in "Harper's Weekly" of May 12, his face being included in a double page of portraits of "eleven prominent candidates for the Republican presidential nomination at Chicago." Brief biographical sketches appeared in the same number—the last and the shortest of them being of Lincoln.

It was on May 16 that the Republican Convention of 1860 formally opened at Chicago, but for days before the city was in a tumult of expectation and preparation. The audacity of inviting a national convention to meet there, in the condition in which Chicago chanced to be at that time, was purely Chicagoan. No other city would have risked it. In ten years Chicago had nearly quadrupled its population, and it was believed that the feat would be repeated in the coming decade. In the first flush of youthful energy and ambition the town had undertaken the colossal task of raising itself bodily out of the grassy marsh, where it had been originally placed, to a level of twelve feet above Lake Michigan, and of putting underneath a good, solid foundation. When the invitation to the convention was extended, half the buildings in Chicago were on stilts; some of the streets had been raised to the new grade, others still lay in the mud; half the sidewalks were poised high on piles, and half were still down on a level with the lake. A city with a conventional sense of decorum would not have cared to be seen in this demoralized condition, but Chicago perhaps conceived that it would but prove her courage and confidence to show the country what she was doing; and so she had the convention come.

But it was not the convention alone which came. Besides the delegates, the professional politicians, the newspaper men, and the friends of the several candidates, there came a motley crowd of men hired to march and to cheer for particular candidates,—a kind of out-of-door *claque* which did not wait for a point to be made in favor of its man, but went off in rounds of applause at the mere mention of his name. New York brought the greatest number of these professional applauders, the leader of them being a notorious prize-fighter and street politician,—"a sort of white black-bird," says Bromley,—one Tom Hyer. With the New York delegation, which numbered all told fully two thousand Seward men, came Dodworth's Band, one of the celebrated musical organizations of that day.

While New York sent the largest number, Pennsylvania was not far behind, there being about one thousand five hundred persons present from that state. From New England, long as was the distance, there were many trains of excursionists. The New England delegation took Gilmore's Band with it, and from Boston to Chicago stirred up every community in which it stopped with music and speeches. Several days before the convention opened fully one-half of the members of the United States House of Representatives were in the city. To still further increase the throng were hundreds of merely curious spectators whom the flattering inducements of the fifteen railroads centring in Chicago at that time had tempted to take a trip. There were fully forty thousand strangers in the city during the sitting of the convention.

The streets for a week were the forum of this multitude. Processions for Seward, for Cameron, for Chase, for Lincoln, marched and counter-marched, brave with banners and transparencies, and noisy with country bands and hissing rockets. Every street corner became a rostrum, where impromptu harangues for any of a dozen candidates might be happened upon. In this hurly-burly two figures were particularly prominent: Tom Hyer, who managed the open-air Seward demonstration, and Horace Greeley, who was conducting independently his campaign against Seward. Greeley, in his fervor, talked incessantly. It was only necessary for some one to say in a rough but friendly way, "There's old Greeley," and all within hearing distance grouped about him. Not infrequently the two or three to whom he began speaking increased until that which had started as a conversation ended as a speech.

In this half-spontaneous, half-organized demonstration of the streets, Lincoln's followers were conspicuous. State pride made Chicago feel that she must stand by her own. Lincoln banners floated across every street, and buildings and omnibuses were decorated with Lincoln emblems. When the Illinois delegation saw that New York and Pennsylvania had brought in so many outsiders to create enthusiasm for their respective candidates, they began to call in supporters from the neighboring localities. Leonard Swett says that they succeeded in getting together fully ten thousand men from Illinois and Indiana, ready to march, shout, or fight for Lincoln, as the case required.

Not only was the city full of people days before the convention began, but the delegations had organized and actual work was in progress. Every device conceivable by an ingenious opposition was resorted to in order to weaken Seward, the most formidable of the candidates. The night before the opening of the convention a great mass meeting was held in the Wigwam. The Seward men had arranged to have only advocates of their own candidate speak. But the clever opposition detected the game, and William D. Kelley, of Pennsylvania, who was for Lincoln or for Wade, got the floor and held it until nearly midnight, doggedly talking against time until an audience of twelve thousand had dwindled to less than one thousand.

One of the first of the delegations to begin activities was that of Illinois. The Tremont House had been chosen as its headquarters, and here were gathered almost all the influential friends Lincoln had in the state. They came determined to win if human effort could compass it, and men never put more intense and persistent energy into a cause. Judge Davis was naturally the head of the body; but Judge Logan, Leonard Swett, John M. Palmer, Richard Oglesby, N. B. Judd, Jesse W. Fell, and a score more were with him. "We worked like nailers," Governor Oglesby often declared in after years.

The effort for Lincoln had to begin in the Illinois delegation itself. In spite of the rail episode at Decatur, the state convention was by no means unanimous for Lincoln.

"Our delegation was instructed for him," wrote Leonard Swett to Josiah Drummond,* "but of the twenty-two votes in

* This letter, written by Mr. Swett on May 27, 1860, to Josiah Drummond of Maine, is one of the best documents on the convention. It was published in the New York "Sun" of July 26, 1891, and is printed in O. H. Oldroyd's "Lincoln's Campaign."

it, by incautiously selecting the men, there were *eight* who would have gladly gone for Seward. The reason of this is in this fact: the northern counties of this state are more overwhelmingly Republican than any other portion of the continent. I could pick twenty-five contiguous counties giving larger Republican majorities than any other adjacent counties in any state. The result is, many people there are for Seward, and such men had crept upon the delegation. They intended in good faith to go for Lincoln, but talked despondently, and really wanted and expected finally to vote as I have indicated. We had also in the north and about Chicago a class of men who always want to turn up on the winning side, and who would do no work, although their feelings were really for us, for fear it would be the losing element and would place them out of favor with the incoming power. These men were dead weights. The centre and south, with many individual exceptions to the classes I have named, were warmly for Lincoln, whether he won or lost.

"The lawyers of our circuit went there determined to leave no stone unturned; and really they, aided by some of our state officers and a half dozen men from various portions of the state, were the only tireless, sleepless, unwavering, and ever vigilant friends he had."

The situation which the Illinois delegation faced, briefly put, was this: the Republican Party had in 1860 but one prominent candidate, William H. Seward. By virtue of his great talents, his superior cultivation, and his splendid services in anti-slavery agitation, he was the choice of the majority of the Republican Party. It was certain that at the opening of the convention he would have nearly enough votes to nominate him. But still there was a considerable and resolute opposition. The grounds of this were several, but the most substantial and convincing was that Illinois, Indiana, Pennsylvania, and New Jersey all declared that they could not elect Seward if he was nominated. Andrew G. Curtin of Pennsylvania, and Henry S. Lane of Indiana, candidates for governor in their respective states, were both his active opponents, not from dislike of him, but because they were convinced that they would themselves be defeated if he headed the Republican ticket. It was clear to the entire party that Pennsylvania and Indiana were essential to Republican success; and since many states with which Seward was the first choice held success in November as more important than Seward, they were willing to give their support to an "available" man. But the difficulty was to unite this opposition. Nearly every state which considered Seward an unsafe candidate had a "favorite son" whom it was pushing as "available." Pennsylvania wanted Cameron; New Jersey, Dayton; Ohio, Chase, McLean, or Wade; Massachusetts, Banks; Vermont, Collamer. Greeley, who alone was as influential as a state delegation, urged Bates of Missouri.

Illinois's task was to unite this opposition on Lincoln. She began her work with a next-door neighbor. "The first state approached," says Mr. Swett, "was Indiana. She was about equally divided between Bates and McLean.* Saturday, Sunday, and Monday were spent upon her, when finally she came to us, unitedly, with twenty-six votes, and from that time acted efficiently with us."

With Indiana to aid her, Illinois now succeeded in

* Mr. Joseph Medill once told the writer that half the Indiana delegation had been won for Lincoln on the ground of availability before the convention met.

drawing a few scattering votes, in making an impression on New Hampshire and Virginia, and in persuading Vermont to think of Lincoln as a second choice. Matters began to look decidedly cheerful. May 14 (Monday) the New York "Herald's" last despatch declared that the contest had narrowed down to Seward, Lincoln, and Wade. The Boston "Herald's" despatch of the same day reported: "Abe Lincoln is booming up to-night as a compromise candidate, and his friends are in high spirits." And this was the situation when the convention finally opened on Wednesday, May 16.

The assembly-room in which the convention met was situated conveniently at the corner of Market and Lake Streets. It had been built especially for the occasion by the Chicago Republican Club, and in the fashion of the West in that day was called by the indigenous name of Wigwam. It was a low, characterless structure, fully one hundred and eighty feet long by one hundred feet wide. The roof rose in the segment of a circle, so that one side was higher than the other; and across this side and the two ends were deep galleries. Facing the ungalleried side was a platform reserved for the delegates—a great floor one hundred and forty feet long and thirty-five feet deep, raised some four feet from the ground level, with committee-rooms at each end. This vast structure of pine boards had been rescued from ugliness by the energetic efforts of the committee, assisted by the Republican women of the city, who, scarcely less interested than their husbands and brothers, strove in every way to contribute to the success of the convention. They wreathed the pillars and the galleries with masses of green, with banners and flags; brought in busts of American notables; hung great allegorical paintings of Justice, Liberty, and the like, on the walls; borrowed the whole series of Healy portraits of

CHAIR OCCUPIED BY THE CHAIRMAN OF THE REPUBLICAN NATIONAL CONVENTION OF 1860.

It was the first chair made in the State of Michigan.—Reproduced from "Harper's Weekly" of May 19, 1860, by permission of Messrs. Harper and Brothers.

American statesmen—in short, made the Wigwam gay and festive. Foreign interest added something to the furnishings; the chair placed on the platform for the use of the chairman of the convention was donated by Michigan, the first chair made in that state. It was an arm-chair of the most primitive description, the seat dug out of an immense log and mounted on large rockers. Another chair, one made for the occasion, attracted a great deal of attention. It was constructed of thirty-four kinds of wood, each piece from

LIFE OF LINCOLN

a different state or territory, Kansas being appropriately represented by the "weeping willow" a symbol of her grief at being still excluded from the sisterhood of states. The gavel used by the chairman was more interesting even than his chair, having been made from a fragment of Commodore Perry's brave *Lawrence*.

Into the Wigwam, on the morning of the 16th of May, there crowded fully ten thousand persons. To the spectator in the gallery the scene was vividly picturesque and animated. Around him were packed hundreds of women, gay in the high-peaked, flower-filled bonnets and the bright shawls and plaids of the day. Below, on the platform and floor, were many of the notable men of the United States—William M. Evarts, Thomas Corwin, Carl Schurz, David Wilmot, Thaddeus Stevens, Joshua Giddings, George William Curtis, Francis P. Blair and his two sons, Andrew H. Reeder, George Ashmun, Gideon Welles, Preston King, Cassius M. Clay, Gratz Brown, George S. Boutwell, Thurlow Weed. In the multitude the newspaper representatives outnumbered the delegates. Fully nine hundred editors and reporters were present, a body scarcely less interesting than the convention itself. Horace Greeley, Samuel Bowles, Murat Halstead, Isaac H. Bromley, Joseph Medill, Horace White, Joseph Hawley, Henry Villard, A. K. McClure, historic names in American journalism, represented various newspapers at Chicago in 1860, and in some cases were active workers in the caucuses. It was evident at once that the members of the conven-

THE "WIGWAM," CHICAGO—THE BUILDING IN WHICH THE REPUBLICAN CONVENTION of 1860 WAS HELD.

tion—some five hundred out of the attendant ten thousand—were not more interested in its proceedings than the spectators, whose approval and disapproval, quickly and emphatically expressed, swayed, and to a degree controlled the delegates. Wednesday and Thursday mornings were passed in the usual opening work of a convention. While officers were formally elected and a platform adopted, the real interest centred in the caucuses, which were held almost uninterruptedly. Illinois was in a frenzy of anxiety. "No men ever worked as our boys did," wrote Mr. Swett; "I did not, the whole week, sleep two hours a night." They ran from delegation to delegation, haranguing, pleading, promising. But do their best they could not concentrate the opposition. "Our great struggle," says Senator Palmer, "was to prevent Lincoln's nomination for the vice-presidency. The Seward men were perfectly willing that he should go on the tail of the ticket. In fact, they seemed determined that he should be given the vice-presidential nomination. We were not troubled so much by the antagonism of the Seward men as by the overtures they were constantly making to us. They literally overwhelmed us with kindness. Judge David Davis came to me in the Tremont House, greatly agitated at the way things were going. He said: 'Palmer, you must go with me at once to see the New Jersey delegation.' I asked what I could do. 'Well,' said he, 'there is a grave and venerable judge over there who is insisting that Lincoln shall be nominated for Vice-President and Seward for President.

We must convince the judge of his mistake.' We went; I was introduced to the gentleman, and we talked about the matter for some time. He praised Seward, but he was especially effusive in expressing his admiration for Lincoln. He thought that Seward was clearly entitled to first place and that Lincoln's eminent merits entitled him to second place. I listened for some time, and then said: 'Sir, you may nominate Mr. Lincoln for Vice-President if you please. But I want you to understand that there are 40,000 Democrats in Illinois who will support this ticket if you give them an opportunity. We are not Whigs, and we never expect to be Whigs. We will never consent to support two old Whigs on this ticket. We are willing to vote for Mr. Lincoln with a Democrat on the ticket, but we will not consent to vote for two Whigs.' I have seldom seen a more indignant man. Turning to Judge Davis he said: 'Judge Davis, is it possible that party spirit so prevails in Illinois that Judge Palmer properly represents public opinion?' 'Oh,' said Davis, affecting some distress at what I had said, 'oh, Judge, you can't account for the conduct of these old Locofocos.' 'Will they do as Palmer says?' 'Certainly. There are 40,000 of them, and, as Palmer says, not one of them will vote for two Whigs.' We left the New Jersey member in a towering rage. When we were back at the Tremont House I said: 'Davis, you are an infernal rascal to sit there and hear that man berate me as he did. You really seemed to encourage him.' Judge Davis said nothing, but chuckled as if he had greatly enjoyed the joke. This incident is illustrative of the kind of work we had to do. We were compelled to resort to this argument—that the old Democrats then ready to affiliate with the Republican Party would not tolerate two Whigs on the ticket—in order to break up the movement to nominate Lincoln for Vice-President. The Seward men recognized in Lincoln their most formidable rival, and that was why they wished to get him out of the way by giving him second place on the ticket."

The uncertainty on Thursday was harrowing, and if the ballot had been taken on the afternoon of that day, as was at first intended, Seward probably would have been nominated. Illinois, Indiana, and Pennsylvania all felt this, and shrewdly managed to secure from the convention a reluctant adjournment until Friday morning. In spite of the time this manœuvre gave, however, Seward's nomination seemed sure; so Greeley telegraphed the "Tribune" at midnight on Thursday. At the same hour the correspondent of the "Herald" (New York) telegraphed: "The friends of Seward are firm, and claim ninety votes for him on the first ballot. Opposition to Seward not fixed on any man. Lincoln is the strongest, and may have altogether forty votes. The various delegations are still caucusing."

It was after these messages were sent that Illinois and Indiana summoned all their energies for a final desperate effort to unite the uncertain delegates on Lincoln, and that Pennsylvania went through the last violent throes of coming to a decision. The night was one of dramatic episodes of which none, perhaps, was more nearly tragic than the spectacle of Seward's followers, confident of success, celebrating in advance the nomination of their favorite, while scores of determined men laid the plans ultimately effective, for his overthrow. All night the work was kept up. "Hundreds of Pennsylvanians, Indianians, and Illinoisans," says Murat Halstead, "never closed their eyes. I saw Henry S. Lane at one o'clock, pale and haggard, with cane under his arm, walking as if for a wager from one caucus-room to another at the Tremont House. In connection with them he had been operating to bring the Vermonters and Virginians to the point of deserting Seward."

In the Pennsylvania delegation, which on Wednesday had agreed on McLean as its second choice and Lincoln as its third, a hot struggle was waged to secure the vote of the delegation *as a unit* for Cameron until a majority of the delegates directed otherwise. Judge S. Newton Pettis, who proposed this resolution, worked all night to secure votes for it at the caucus to be held early in the morning. The Illinois men ran from delegate to caucus, from editor to outsider. No man who knew Lincoln and believed in him, indeed, was allowed to rest, but was dragged away to this or that delegate to persuade him that the "rail candidate," as Lincoln had already begun to be called, was fit for the place. Colonel Hoyt, then a resident of Chicago, spent half the night telling Thaddeus Stevens of Pennsylvania what he knew of Lincoln. While all this was going on, a committee of twelve men from Pennsylvania, New York, Ohio, Indiana, Illinois, and Iowa were consulting in the upper story of the Tremont House. Before their session

NOMINATION IN 1860

was over they had agreed that in case Lincoln's votes reached a specified number on the following day, the votes of the states represented in that meeting, so far as these twelve men could effect the result, should be given to him.

The night was over at last, and at ten o'clock the convention reassembled. The great Wigwam was packed with a throng hardly less excited than the members of the actual convention, while without, for blocks away, a crowd double that within pushed and strained, every nerve alert to catch the movements of the convention.

The nominations began at once, the Hon. William M. Evarts presenting the name of William H. Seward. The New Yorkers had prepared a tremendous *claque,* which now broke forth—"a deafening shout which," says Leonard Swett, "I confess, appalled us a little." But New York in preparing her *claque* had only given an idea to Illinois. The Illinois committee, to offset it, had made secret but complete preparations for what was called a "spontaneous demonstration." From lake front to prairie the committee had collected every stentorian voice known, and early Friday morning, while Seward's men were marching exultantly about the streets, the owners of these voices had been packed into the Wigwam, where their special endowment would be most effective. The women present had been requested to wave their handkerchiefs at every mention of Lincoln's name, and hundreds of flags had been distributed to be used in the same way. A series of signals had been arranged to communicate to the thousands without the moment when a roar from them might influence the convention within. When N. B. Juda nominated Lincoln this machinery began to work. It did well; but a moment later, in greeting the seconding of Seward's nomination, New York out-bellowed Illinois. "Caleb B. Smith of Indiana then seconded the nomination of Lincoln," says Mr. Swett, "and the West came to his rescue. No mortal ever before saw such a scene. The idea of us Hoosiers and Suckers being outscreamed would have been as bad to them as the loss of their man. Five thousand people at once leaped to their seats, women not wanting in the number, and the wild yell made soft vesper breathings of all that had preceded. No language can describe it. A thousand steam whistles, ten acres of hotel gongs, a tribe of Comanches, headed by a choice vanguard from pandemonium, might have mingled in the scene unnoticed."

As the roar died out a voice cried, "Abe Lincoln has it by the sound now; let us ballot!" and Judge Logan, beside himself with screeching and excitement, called out: "Mr. President, in order or out of order, I propose this convention and audience give three cheers for the man who is evidently their nominee."

The balloting followed without delay. The Illinois men believed they had one hundred votes to start with; on counting they found they had 102. More hopeful still, no other opposition candidate approached them. Pennsylvania's man, according to the printed reports of that day, had but fifty and one-half votes; Greeley's man, forty-eight; Chase, forty-nine; while McLean, Pennsylvania's second choice, had but

WILLIAM H. SEWARD.

Seward's name was presented to the Chicago convention of 1860, which finally nominated Lincoln, by William M. Evarts of New York. On the first ballot he received 173½ votes, on the second 184½, on the third, 180; 234 votes were necessary for a choice.

SALMON P. CHASE.

Chase's name was presented to the Chicago convention of 1860 by D. K. Cartter of Ohio. On the first ballot he received 49 votes, on the second 42½, on the third 24½.

EDWARD BATES.

F. P. Blair of Missouri nominated Mr. Bates in the Chicago convention. He received on the first ballot 48 votes, on the second 35, and on the third 22. At Lincoln's inauguration as President in March, 1861, Bates became a member of his cabinet, as did also three other of his competitors for the nomination in the convention of 1860 — Seward, Chase and Cameron.

SIMON CAMERON.

Andrew H. Reeder of Pennsylvania presented Cameron's name to the Chicago convention. On the first ballot he received 50½ votes. On the second ballot his name was withdrawn, although two votes were cast for him. He received no votes on the third ballot.

twelve. If Seward was to be beaten, it must be now; and it was for Pennsylvania to say. The delegation hurried to a committee-room, where Judge Pettis, disregarding the action of the caucus by which McLean had been adopted as the delegation's second choice, moved that, on the second ballot, Pennsylvania's vote be cast solidly for Lincoln. The motion was carried. Returning to the hall the delegation found the second ballot under way. In a moment the name of Pennsylvania was called. The whole Wigwam heard the answer: "Pennsylvania casts her fifty-two votes for Abraham Lincoln." The meaning was clear. The break to Lincoln had begun. New York sat as if stupefied, while all over the hall cheer followed cheer.

It seemed but a moment before the second ballot was ended, and it was known that Lincoln's vote had risen from 102 to 181. The tension as the third ballot was taken was almost unbearable. A hundred pencils kept score while the delegations were called, and it soon became apparent that Lincoln was outstripping Seward. The last vote was hardly given before the whisper went around, "Two hundred and thirty-one and one-half for Lincoln; two and one-half more will give him the nomination." An instant of silence followed, in which the convention grappled with the idea and tried to pull itself together to act. The chairman of the Ohio delegation was the first to get his breath. "Mr. President," he cried, springing on his chair and stretching out his arm to secure recognition, "I rise to change four votes from Mr. Chase to Mr. Lincoln."

It took a moment to realize the truth. New York

saw it, and the white faces of her noble delegation were bowed in despair. Greeley saw it, and a guileless smile spread over his features as he watched Thurlow Weed press his hand hard against his wet eyelids. Illinois saw it, and tears poured from the eyes of more than one of the overwrought, devoted men as they grasped one another's hands and vainly struggled against the sobs which kept back their shouts. The crowd saw it, and broke out in a mad hurrah. "The scene which followed," wrote one spectator, "baffles all human description. After an instant's silence, as deep as death, which seemed to be required to enable the assembly to take in the full force of the announcement, the wildest and mightiest yell (for it can be called by no other name) burst forth from ten thousand voices which we ever heard from mortal throats. This strange and tremendous demonstration, accompanied with leaping up and down, tossing hats, handkerchiefs, and canes recklessly into the air, with the waving of flags, and with every other conceivable mode of exultant and unbridled joy, continued steadily and without pause for perhaps ten minutes.

"It then began to rise and fall in slow and billowing bursts, and for perhaps the next five minutes these stupendous waves of uncontrollable excitement, now rising into the deepest and fiercest shouts, and then sinking like the ground swell of the ocean into hoarse and lessening murmurs, rolled through the multitude. Every now and then it would seem as though the physical power of the assembly was exhausted and that quiet would be restored, when all at once a new hurricane would break out, more prolonged and terrific than anything before. If sheer exhaustion had not prevented, we don't know but the applause would have continued to this hour."

Without, the scene was repeated. At the first instant of realization in the Wigwam a man on the platform had shouted to a man stationed on the roof, "Hallelujah! Abe Lincoln is nominated!" A cannon boomed the news to the multitude below, and twenty thousand throats took up the cry. The city heard it, and one hundred guns on the Tremont House, innumerable whistles on the river and lake front, on locomotives and factories, and the bells in all the steeples broke forth. For twenty-four hours the clamor never ceased. It spread to the prairies, and before morning they were afire with pride and excitement.

And while all this went on, where was Lincoln? Too much of a candidate, as he had told Swett, to go to Chicago, yet hardly enough of one to stay away, he had ended by remaining in Springfield, where he spent the week in restless waiting and discussion. He drifted about the public square, went often to the telegraph office, looked out for every returning visitor from Chicago, played occasional games of ball, made fruitless efforts to read, went home at unusual hours. He felt in his bones that he had a fighting chance, so he told a friend, but the chance was not so strong that he could indulge in much exultation. By Friday morning he was tired and depressed, but still eager for news. One of his friends, the Hon. James C. Conkling, returned early in the day from Chicago, and Lincoln soon went around to his law office. "Upon entering," says Mr. Conkling, "Lincoln threw himself upon the office lounge and remarked rather wearily, 'Well, I guess I'll go back to practising law.' As he lay there on the lounge, I gave him such information as I had been able to obtain. I told him the tendency was to drop Seward; that the outlook for him was very encouraging. He listened attentively, and thanked me, saying I had given him a clearer idea of the situation than he had been able to get from any other source. He was not very sanguine of the result. He did not express the opinion that he would be nominated."

But he could not be quiet and soon left Mr. Conkling to join the throng around the telegraph office, where the reports from the convention were coming in. The nominations were being reported, his own among the others. Then news came that the balloting had begun. He could not endure to wait for the result. He remembered a commission his wife had given him that morning and started across the square to execute it. His errand was done, and he was standing in the door of the shop, talking, when a shout went up from the group at the telegraph office. The next instant an excited boy came rushing pell-mell down the stairs of the office, and, plunging through the crowd, ran across the square, shouting, "Mr. Lincoln, Mr. Lincoln, you are nominated!" The cry was repeated on all sides. The people came flocking about him, half laughing, half crying, shaking his hand when they could get it, and one another's when they could not. For a few minutes, carried away by excitement, Lincoln seemed simply one of the proud and exultant

From a photograph by Sarony, N. Y.
HORACE GREELEY.

In the Republican national convention of 1860 Horace Greeley sat as the alternate of an absent delegate from Oregon. He had failed to be chosen as a delegate from his own State (New York), through the opposition of the Seward men. As editor of the New York "Tribune," it was supposed, until a short time before the convention, that he would support Seward for the nomination to the Presidency, but he turned against Seward on the plea that he could not be elected. In the convention he labored ardently for Bates.

JESSE W. FELL.

Mr. Fell, a Pennsylvanian by birth, settled in Bloomington, Illinois. Here he became acquainted with Lincoln, who was frequently in the town during court terms. He was one of the first Republicans of the State; he first introduced Lincoln's name in Pennsylvania as a candidate for the Presidency, and it was to him that Lincoln addressed his well-known autobiography.

crowd. Then remembering what it all meant, he said, "My friends, I am glad to receive your congratulations, and as there is a little woman down on Eighth Street who will be glad to hear the news, you must excuse me until I inform her." He slipped away, telegram in hand, his coat-tails flying out behind, and strode towards home, only to find when he reached there that his friends were before him, and that the "little woman" already knew that the honor which for twenty years and more she had believed and stoutly declared her husband deserved, and which a great multitude of men had sworn to do their best to obtain for him, at last had come.

CHAPTER XX

THE CAMPAIGN OF 1860

THIRTY-SIX hours after Lincoln received the news of his nomination, an evening train from Chicago brought to Springfield a company of distinguished-looking strangers. As they stepped from their coach cannon were fired, rockets set off, bands played, and enthusiastic cheering went up from a crowd of waiting people. A long and noisy procession accompanied them to their hotel and later to a modest two-storied house in an unfashionable part of the town. The gentlemen whom the citizens of Springfield received with such demonstration formed the committee sent by the Republican National Convention to notify Abraham Lincoln that he had been nominated as its candidate for the presidency of the United States.

The delegation had in its number some of the most distinguished workers of the Republican Party of that day:—Mr. George Ashmun, Samuel Bowles, and Governor Boutwell of Massachusetts, William M. Evarts of New York, Judge Kelley of Pennsylvania, David K. Carter of Ohio, Francis P. Blair of Missouri, the Hon. Gideon Welles of Connecticut, Amos Tuck of New Hampshire, Carl Schurz of Wisconsin. Only a few of these gentlemen had ever seen Mr. Lincoln and to many of them his nomination had been a bitter disappointment.

THE CAMPAIGN OF 1860 419

As the committee filed into Mr. Lincoln's simple home there was a sore misgiving in more than one heart, and as Mr. Ashmun, their chairman, presented to him the letter notifying him of his nomination they eyed their candidate with critical keenness. They noted his great height, his huge hands and feet, his peculiar lankness of limb. His shoulders drooped as he stood, giving his form a look of irresolution. His smooth-shaven face seemed of bronze as he listened to their message and amazed them by its ruggedness. The cheeks were sunken, the cheek bones high, the nose large, the mouth unsymmetrical, the under lip protruding a little. Irregular seams and lines cut and creased the skin in every direction. The eyes, downcast as he listened, were sunken and somber. Shaded by its mass of dark hair, the face gave an impression of a sad impenetrable man.

Mr. Ashmun finished his speech and Mr. Lincoln, lifting his bent head, began to reply. The men who watched him thrilled with surprise at the change which passed over him. His drooping form became erect and firm. The eyes beamed with fire and intelligence. Strong, dignified and self-possessed, he seemed transformed by the act of self-expression.

His remarks were brief, merely a word of thanks for the honor done him, a hint that he felt the responsibility of his position, a promise to respond formally in writing and the expression of a desire to take each one of the committee by hand, but his voice was calm and clear, his bearing frank and sure. His auditors saw in a flash that here was a man who was master of himself. For the first time they understood that he whom they had supposed to be little more than a loquacious and clever state politician, had force, insight, conscience, that their misgivings were vain. "Why, sir, they told me he was a rough diamond," said Governor Boutwell to one of Lincoln's townsmen; "nothing could have been in better taste than that speech." And a delegate who had voted against Lincoln in the convention, turning to Carl Schurz, said, "Sir, we might have done a more daring thing, but we certainly could not have done a better thing," and it was with that feeling that the delegation, two hours later, left Mr. Lincoln's home, and it was that report they carried to their constituents.

But one more formality now remained to complete the ceremony of Abraham Lincoln's nomination to the presidency,—his letter of acceptance. This was soon written. The candidates of the opposing parties all sent out letters of acceptance in 1860 which were almost political platforms in themselves. Lincoln decided to make his acceptance merely an expression of his intention to stand by the party's declaration of principles. He held himself rigidly to this decision, his first address to the Republican Party being scarcely one hundred and fifty words in length. Though so short, it was prepared with painstaking attention. He even carried it when it was finished to a Springfield friend, Dr. Newton Bateman, the State Superintendent of Education, for correction.

"Mr. Schoolmaster," he said, "here is my letter of acceptance; I am not very strong on grammar and I wish you to see if it is all right. I wouldn't like to have any mistakes in it."

THE CAMPAIGN OF 1860

The doctor took the manuscript and, after reading it, said:

"There is only one change I should suggest, Mr. Lincoln; you have written 'It shall be my care *to not* violate or disregard it in any part'; you should have written 'not to violate.' Never split an infinitive, is the rule."

Mr. Lincoln took the manuscript, regarding it a moment with a puzzled air, "So you think I better put those two little fellows end to end, do you?" he said as he made the change.

His nomination an accomplished fact, the all-important question for Mr. Lincoln was "Can I be elected?" Six months before when he had asked himself, "Can I be nominated?" he had been forced to reply, "Not probable." Even the very morning of the nomination he had said despondently to a friend, "I guess I'll go back to practising law," but now when he asked himself, "Can I be elected?" the answer he gave was far from uncertain. With the tables of the popular vote since 1856 before him he reckoned his chances. Twenty-four states out of the thirty-three which then formed the Union had taken part in the Chicago Convention. These twenty-four states held 234 of the 303 electoral votes to be cast. On how many of them could he depend? In 1856 the first time the party had appeared in a presidential contest it had secured for Frémont eleven states,[*] 114 electoral votes. On these Lincoln felt he still could count. But that was not enough, nor was it all the Republi-

[*] The states which went for Frémont in 1856 were Connecticut, Iowa, Maine, Massachusetts, Michigan, New Hampshire, New York, Ohio, Rhode Island, Vermont, Wisconsin.

cans claimed. The growth of the party had been steady and vigorous since 1856. The whole country saw that if the Chicago Convention chose a presidential candidate acceptable to New Jersey, Pennsylvania, Indiana and Illinois, those states would certainly go Republican. Lincoln added their votes to the 114 of the certain states. It gave him 169—a respectable majority of the 303 which the electoral college would cast.

The tables were in his favor; but that was not all in the situation which encouraged him. Lincoln saw that, as his nomination in Chicago had been largely the result of disagreement among the Republicans, so there was a possibility of his election being the result of quarrels among the Democrats. The National Democratic Convention had met in Charleston, South Carolina, on April 23. From the opening, the sessions were stormy. One vital difference divided the body. The South was determined that a platform should be adopted stating unequivocally that slaves could be carried into the territories and that neither Congressional nor territorial legislation could interfere with them. The Democracy of the North was determined to adopt a platform in which Douglas's doctrine of popular sovereignty was the central plank. The time had been when the South had been thoroughly satisfied with the Douglas theory; that it was not so now was due largely to Lincoln. He had discovered that Douglas in presenting his attractive dogma that the people of the states should be left to regulate their domestic concerns in their own way, subject only to the Constitution, gave one interpretation in the South, another in the North. Knowing that Illinois would never consent to the doctrine as the South understood it, nor the South to the Northern notion, Lincoln forced Douglas in 1858 in a debate at Freeport, Illinois, to explain his meaning. Illinois was satisfied with the explanation, but the South saw the deceit. From the day of the Freeport Debate Douglas's power in the South declined. When the Charleston Convention met the Southern Democrats were fully determined to defeat the man who had so nearly persuaded them to a doctrine which he interpreted according to the prejudices of the section in which he spoke. When a Douglas platform was adopted by the convention they withdrew. The upshot of this secession was that the two factions called fresh conventions to meet in Baltimore in June. There the Northern Democracy nominated as its candidates Douglas and Johnson. A few days later the Southern Democrats named Breckinridge and Lane.

Thus when Lincoln was nominated his opponents were divided. The opposition to him was still further weakened by the appearance of a sporadic party, the Constitutional Union, which in a vague and general platform shirked the very precise and vital question at issue and declared finely for "the Constitution of the country, the Union of the states, and the enforcement of the laws." This party nominated Bell and Everett, known as the "Kangaroo Ticket" because "the hind part was the stronger."

The tables were in his favor. If his own party stood by him, he felt sure of his election. There was every sign that it would. "So far as I can learn," he wrote his friend Washburne a few days after the convention, "the nominations start well everywhere; and, if they get no back-set, it would seem as if they were going through."

The "start" of the nominations had in fact been very good. Nothing more jubilant could have been conceived than the reception given Lincoln's name in the Northwest. "There won't be a tar barrel left in Illinois to-night," said Douglas, in Washington, to his senatorial friends, who asked him when the news of the nomination reached them, "Who is this man Lincoln, anyhow?" Douglas was right. Not only the tar barrels but half the fences of the state went up in the fire of rejoicing.

The demonstrations in the Middle States and in the East were hardly less exultant. There was a striking difference in them, however. In the Northwest it was the candidate, in the rest of the country the platform and the probability of its success, which inspired the popular outbursts. And this was inevitable, so little was Lincoln known outside of his own part of the country. The orators at the ratification meetings of the East found it necessary to look up his history to tell their audiences who he was. The newspapers printed biographical sketches, and very meagre ones they were; for up to this time almost no details of his life had been published. These facts filled many a serious-minded Republican with dismay. To them there seemed but one explanation for the choice of Lincoln over the heads of so many more experienced and distinguished men—it had been a political trick born of the sentiment, "Anything to beat

Seward." "I remember," says a Republican of 1860, "that when I first read the news on a bulletin board as I came down street in Philadelphia that I experienced a moment of intense physical pain; it was as though some one had dealt me a heavy blow over the head, then my strength failed me. I believed our cause was doomed."

The opposition press found in Lincoln's obscurity abundant editorial material. He was a "third-rate country lawyer, poorer even than poor Pierce," said the New York "Herald." Of course, he would be a "nullity" if he were elected. How could a man be otherwise who had never done anything but deliver a few lectures and get himself beaten by Douglas in the campaign of '58. They hooted at his "coarse and clumsy jokes," declared that he "could not speak good grammar," and that all he was really distinguished for was rail-splitting, running a "broad-horn," and bearing the sobriquet of "honest old Abe." The snobbishness of the country came out in full. He was not a gentleman; that is, he did not know how to wear clothes, perhaps sat at times in shirt sleeves, tilted back his chair. He could quote neither Latin nor Greek, had never travelled, had no pedigree.

The Republican press took up the gauntlet. To the charge that he would be a "nullity" the "Tribune" replied, "A man who by his own genius and force of character has raised himself from being a penniless and uneducated flat boatman on the Wabash River to the position Mr. Lincoln now occupies is not likely to be a nullity anywhere." And Bryant answered all the sneering by a noble editorial in which he claimed Mr. Lincoln to be "A Real Representative Man."

Nevertheless the eagerness with which the Republican press hastened to show that Lincoln was not the coarse backwoodsman the Democrats painted him showed how much they winced under the charges. Reporters were sent West to describe his home, his family, and his habits, in order to prove that he did not live in "low Hoosier style." They told with great satisfaction that he wore daily a broadcloth suit "almost elegant," they described his modest home as a "mansion" and "an elegant two-story dwelling" and they never failed to note that Mrs. Lincoln spoke French fluently and that he had a son in Harvard College. When they could with reasonable certainty connect him with the Lincolns of Hingham, Mass., they heralded his "good blood" with pride and marshalled the Lincolns who had distinguished themselves in the history of the country.

Among the common people the jeers that Lincoln was but a rail-splitter was a spur to enthusiasm. Too many of the solid men of the North had swung an axe, too many of them had passed from log hut to mansion, not to blaze with sympathetic indignation when the party was taunted with nominating a backwoodsman. The rail became their emblem and their rallying cry, and the story of the rail fence Lincoln had built a feature of every campaign speech and every country store discussion. In a week after his nomination two rails declared to have been split by Lincoln were on exhibition in New York, and certain zealous Pennsylvanians had sent to Macon, Ill., asking to buy the whole fence and have it shipped East. It was the rail which decorated campaign medals, inspired campaign songs, appeared in campaign cartoons. There was something more than a desire to "stand by the candidate" in the enthusiasm. At bottom it was a popular vindication of the American way of making a man.

More important to Lincoln than any popular enthusiasm was the ratification given his nomination by the rival candidates. What would they do? The whole party held its breath until Seward was heard from. No man could have taken a crushing defeat more wisely. He was at his home in Auburn, New York, on May 18, the day of the nomination, and when the news of Lincoln's success was brought him, his informer told him that there was not a Republican to be found in the town who had the heart left to write an editorial for the "Daily Advertiser" approving the nomination. Seward smilingly took his pen and wrote the following paragraph, which appeared that evening:—

"No truer exposition of the Republican creed could be given than the platform adopted by the convention contains. No truer or firmer defenders of the Republican faith could have been found in the Union than the distinguished and esteemed citizens on whom the honors of the nomination have fallen. Their election, we trust by a decisive majority, will restore the Government of the U. S. to its Constitutional and ancient course. Let the watchword of the Republican Party be 'Union and Liberty,' and onward to victory."

A few days later Seward went to Washington where a number of disappointed and rebellious Republicans called upon him to offer their condolence. "Mr. Seward," they said, "we cannot accept this situation. We want you to bolt the nomination and run on an independent ticket."

Mr. Seward smiled: "Gentlemen," he said, "your zeal outruns your discretion. There are many of you giving this advice now, say, perhaps three hundred. Two weeks hence there would be one hundred and fifty and the next week fifty. After that only William H. Seward. No, gentlemen, the Republican Party was not made for William H. Seward, but Mr. Seward, if he is worth anything, for the Republican Party, and I believe I have still work to do, I must therefore decline to accept your advice. I have had some experience of this kind. I ran once as a candidate for the nomination to the governorship of New York; I was defeated; my friends wanted me to bolt and run independently, but I declined. My opponent who had received the nomination, was defeated in the election. I would have been defeated. Another year I did receive the nomination and I was elected, but if I had consented in the first place to bolt the regular nominee I would never have received the nomination regularly a second time and so would never have been Governor of New York."*

Seward wrote Lincoln very soon congratulating him and promising support. So did the other leading rivals. The letters were grateful to Lincoln. "Holding myself the humblest of all those whose names were before the convention," he wrote Chase, "I feel in

* The Hon. H. L. Dawes in interview corrected by him and published with his permission.

special need of the assistance of all; and I am glad—very glad—of the indication that you stand ready."

With these congratulations and promises of support from his rivals came others from men not less known. Joshua Giddings wrote Lincoln an admirable letter on May 19:

"Dear Lincoln: You're nominated. You will be elected. After your election, thousands will crowd around you, claiming rewards for services rendered. I, too, have my claims upon you. I have not worked for your nomination, nor for that of any other man. I have labored for the establishment of principles; and when men came to me asking my opinion of you, I only told them, 'Lincoln is an honest man.' All I ask of you in return for my services is, *make my statement good through your administration.* Yours, GIDDINGS."

Lincoln soon saw that not only the strong men of his party were supporting him, but that they were working harmoniously in an excellent organization. The Republicans all agreed with the "Tribune" that "the election of Mr. Lincoln though it could not be accomplished without work, was eminently a thing that could be done," and they set themselves vigorously to do it. As the party was composed largely of young men who felt that the cause was worthy of their best efforts, great zest and ingenuity were thrown into the campaigning. Arrangements were immediately made for a systematic stumping of the whole country. The speakers engaged were of a high order, among them Sumner, Seward, Chase, Cassius M. Clay, Greeley, Stevens. Many of the speeches were of more than usual dramatic interest. Such was

Sumner's great speech at Cooper Institute, July 11, on "The Origin, Necessity and Permanence of the Republican Party." It was the first speech Sumner had made in public since the attack on him in the Senate in 1856, and attracted immense attention. Seward made a five weeks' trip through the West, often speaking several times a day. No one worked harder than Carl Schurz. "I began speaking shortly after the convention," Mr. Schurz once told the author, "and continued until the day of the election, making from one to three speeches, with the exception of about ten days in September when I was so fatigued that I had to stop for a little while. I spoke in both English and German, under the auspices of the National Committee and not only in the larger towns, but frequently also in country districts." No speaker of the campaign touched the people more deeply. "Young, ardent, aspiring," said the New York "Evening Post" of Mr. Schurz, "the romances connected with his life and escape from his fatherland, his scholarly attainments, and, above all, his devotion to the principles which cast him an exile on our shores, have all combined to render him dear to the hearts of his countrymen and to place him in the foremost rank of their leaders."

Besides this educational work on the stump was that by pamphlets. After the campaign lives of Lincoln and Hamlin, of which there were many,* the

* On May 19, the day after the nominations were made, five different lives of Lincoln were announced by the New York "Evening Post." The first to appear was the Wigwam Edition, which was ready at the beginning of June. The best were those by W. D. Howells and David W. Bartlett.
The Illinois "State Journal" of June 5, 1860, quoted a paragraph

"campaign tracts" issued by the "Tribune" were the most widely circulated documents. There were several of these, the most popular being Carl Schurz's speech on the "Doom of Slavery," and Seward's on the "Irrepressible Conflict." There was at the same time, an immense amount done in the press, and much of it by the ablest literary men the United States has produced, thus Lowell wrote essays for the "Atlantic," Whittier verses for the "Tribune" and the "Atlantic," Bryant, Greeley, Raymond, Bowles, editorials for their journals.

The Republican campaign of 1860 had one distinguishing feature,—the Wide-Awakes, bands of torch-bearers who in a simple uniform of glazed cap and cape, and carrying colored lanterns or blazing coal-oil torches, paraded the streets of almost every town of the North throughout the summer and fall, arousing everywhere the wildest enthusiasm. Their origin was purely accidental. In February, Cassius M. Clay spoke in Hartford, Connecticut. A few ardent young Republicans accompanied him as a kind of body-guard, and to save their garments from the dripping of the torches a few of them wore improvised capes of black glazed cambric. The uniform attracted so much attention that a campaign club formed in Hartford soon after adopted it. This club called itself the Wide-Awakes. Other clubs took up the

---

from the Cincinnati "Commercial" to the effect that "it is stated that there have already been fifty-two applications to Mr. Lincoln to write his biography."

The "Journal" of June 15, 1860, said that none of the numerous biographies announced by publishers as "authorized" or the "only authorized" has been in fact authorized by Mr. Lincoln. "He is ignorant of their contents and is not responsible for anything they contain."

idea, and soon there were Wide-Awakes drilling regularly from one end of the North to the other.

A great many fantastic movements were invented by them, a favorite one being a peculiar zig-zag march—an imitation of the party emblem—the rail-fence. Numbers of the clubs adopted the rules and drills of the Chicago Zouaves—one of the most popular military organizations of the day. In the summer of 1860 Colonel Ellsworth, the commanding officer of the Zouaves, brought them East. The Wide-Awake movement was greatly stimulated by this tour of the Zouaves.

Almost all of the clubs had their peculiar badges, Lincoln splitting rails or engineering a flat-boat being a favorite decoration for them. There were many medals worn as well. Many of these combined business and politics adroitly, the obverse advising you to "vote for the rail-splitter," the reverse to buy somebody's soap, or tea, or wagons.

Many of the clubs owned Lincoln rails which were given the place of honor on all public occasions and the "Originals," as the Hartford Wide-Awakes were called, possessed the identical maul with which Lincoln had split the rails for the famous fence. It had been secured in Illinois together with such weighty credentials that nobody could dispute its claim, and was the pride of the club. It still is to be seen in Hartford occupying a conspicuous place in the collection of the Connecticut Historical Society.

Campaign songs set to familiar airs were heard on every hand. Many of these never had more than a local vogue, but others were sung generally. One of the most ringing was E. C. Stedman's "Honest Abe of the West," sung to the air of "The Star Spangled Banner":

"Then on to the holy Republican strife!
  And again, for a future as fair as the morning,
For the sake of that freedom more precious than life,
  Ring out the grand anthem of Liberty's warning!
Lift the banner on high, while from mountain and plain,
  The cheers of the people are sounded again;
Hurrah! for our cause—of all causes the best!
Hurrah! for Old Abe, Honest Abe of the West!"

One of the campaign songs which will never be forgotten was Whittier's "The Quakers Are Out":

"Give the flags to the winds!
  Set the hills all aflame!
Make way for the man with
  The Patriarch's name!
Away with misgivings—away
  With all doubt,
For Lincoln goes in when the
  Quakers are out!"

In many of the states great rallies were held at central points, at which scores of Wide-Awake clubs and a dozen popular speakers were present. The most enthusiastic of all these was held in Mr. Lincoln's own home, Springfield, on August 8. Fully 75,000 people gathered for the celebration, by far the greater number coming across the prairies on horseback or in wagons. A procession eight miles long filed by Mr. Lincoln's door.

Mr. E. B. Washburne, who was with Mr. Lincoln in Springfield that day, says of this mass meeting:

"It was one of the most enormous and impressive gatherings I had ever witnessed. Mr. Lincoln, surrounded by some intimate friends, sat on the balcony of his humble home. It took hours for all the delegations to file before him, and there was no token of enthusiasm wanting. He was deeply touched by the manifestations of personal and political friendships, and returned all his salutations in that off-hand and kindly manner which belonged to him. I know of no demonstration of a similar character that can compare with it except the review by Napoleon of his army for the invasion of Russia, about the same season of the year in 1812."

From May until November this work for the ticket went on steadily and ardently. Mr. Lincoln during all this time remained quietly in Springfield. The conspicuous position in which he was placed made almost no difference in his simple life. He was the same genial, accessible, modest man as ever, his habits as unpretentious, his friendliness as great. The chief outward change in his daily round was merely one of quarters. It seemed to his friends that neither his home nor his dingy law office was an appropriate place in which to receive his visitors and they arranged that a room in the State House which stood on the village green in the centre of the town, be put at his disposal. He came down to this office every morning about eight o'clock, always stopping on his way in his old cordial fashion to ask the news or exchange a story when he met an acquaintance. Frequently he went to the post-office himself before going to his office and came out, his arms loaded with letters and papers.

He had no regular hours for visitors; there was no ceremony for admittance to his presence. People

THE CAMPAIGN OF 1860

came when they would. Usually they found the door open; if it was not, it was Mr. Lincoln's own voice which answered, "come in," to their knock. These visitors were a strange medley of the curious, the interested and the friendly. Many came simply to see him, to say they had shaken hands with him; numbers to try to find out what his policy would be if elected; others to wish him success. All day long they filed in and out leaving him some days no time for his correspondence, which every day grew larger. He seemed never to be in a hurry, never to lose patience, however high his table was piled with mail, however closely his room was crowded with visitors. He even found time to give frequent sittings to the artists sent from various parts of the country to paint his portrait. Among those who came in the summer after the nomination were Berry, of Boston; Hicks, of New York; Conant, of St. Louis; Wright, of Mobile; Brown, and Atwood, of Philadelphia; Jones, of Cincinnati. Mr. Lincoln took the kindliest interest in these men, and later when President, did more than one of them a friendly turn; thus in March, 1865, he wrote to Seward in regard to Jones and Piatt, that he had "some wish" that they might have "some of those moderate sized consulates which facilitate artists a little in their profession." They in their turn never forgot him. Sitting over their easels by the hour in the corner of his office assigned them they got many glimpses into the man's great heart, and nowhere do we get pleasanter pictures of Mr. Lincoln in this period than from their journals.

To those who observed Mr. Lincoln closely as he

received his visitors one thing was apparent: he always remained master of the interview. While his visitors told him a great deal, they learned nothing from him which he did not wish to give. The following observations, published in the Illinois "State Journal" in November, 1860, illustrate very well what happened almost every day in his office:

"While talking to two or three gentlemen and standing up, a very hard-looking customer rolled in and tumbled into the only vacant chair and the one lately occupied by Mr. Lincoln. Mr. Lincoln's keen eye took in the fact, but gave no evidence of the notice. Turning around at last he spoke to the odd specimen, holding out his hand at such a distance that our friend had to vacate the chair if he accepted the proffered shake. Mr. Lincoln quietly resumed his chair. It was a small matter, yet one giving proof more positively than a larger event of that peculiar way the man has of mingling with a mixed crowd.

"He converses fluently on all subjects, illustrates everything by a merry anecdote, of which article he has an abundant supply. I said on all subjects. He does not talk politics. He passes from that gracefully the moment it is introduced. Hundreds seek him every week to get his opinion on this or that subject. He has a jolly way of disposing of that matter by saying, 'Ah! you haven't read my speeches. Let me make you a present of my speeches.' And the earnest inquirer finds himself the happy possessor of some old documents."

Among his daily visitors there were usually men of eminence from North and South. He received them all with perfect simplicity and always even on his busiest days found a moment to turn away from them to greet old friends who had known him when he kept grocery in New Salem or acted as deputy-surveyor of Sangamon County. One day as he talked to a company of distinguished strangers an old lady in a big sun-bonnet, heavy boots and short skirts walked into the office. She carried a package wrapped in brown paper and tied with a white string. As soon as Mr. Lincoln saw her he left the group, went to meet her and, shaking her hand cordially, inquired for her "folks." After a moment the old lady opened the package and taking out a pair of coarse wool socks she handed them to him. "I wanted to give you somethin', Mr. Linkin," she said, "to take to Washington, and that's all I hed. I spun that yarn and knit them socks myself." Thanking her warmly, Mr. Lincoln took the socks and holding them up by the toes, one in each hand, he turned to the astonished celebrities and said in a voice full of kindly amusement, "The lady got my latitude and longitude about right, didn't she, gentlemen?"

The old lady was not the only one, however, who gave Mr. Lincoln "something to carry to Washington." From the time of his nomination gifts poured in on him. Many of these came in the form of wearing apparel. Mr. George Lincoln, of Brooklyn, who in January carried a handsome silk hat to the President-elect, the gift of a New York hatter, says that in receiving the hat, Mr. Lincoln laughed heartily over the gifts of clothing and remarked to Mrs. Lincoln:

"Well, wife, if nothing else comes out of this scrape, we are going to have some new clothes, are we not?"

To those who observed Mr. Lincoln superficially in this period, it might have seemed that he was doing nothing of any value to himself or to his party. Certainly he was taking no active part in the campaign. He was making no speeches—writing no letters—giving no interviews. This policy of silence he had adopted at the outset. The very night of his nomination his townspeople in serenading him had called for a speech. Standing in the doorway of his house he said to them that he did not suppose the honor of such a visit was intended particularly for himself as a private citizen, but rather as the representative of a great party; that as to his position on the political questions of the day he could only refer them to his previous speeches, and he added:—"Fellow citizens and friends: The time comes upon every public man, when it is best for him to keep his lips closed. That time has come upon me." When in August the monster mass meeting was held in Springfield every effort was made to persuade Mr. Lincoln to speak. All he would consent to do was to appear and in a few words excuse himself. Up to the time he left for Washington to be inaugurated, he kept his resolve.

Nor would he write letters explaining his position, or defending himself. So many letters were received asking his political opinion that he found it necessary soon after his nomination to prepare the following form of reply to be sent out by his secretary:

"Dear Sir: Your letter to Mr. Lincoln of ———, and by which you seek to obtain his opinions on certain political points, has been received by him. He has received others of a similar character, but he also has a greater number of the exactly opposite character. The latter class beseech him to write nothing whatever upon any point of political

doctrine. They say his positions were well known when he was nominated, and that he must not now embarrass the canvass by undertaking to shift or modify them. He regrets that he cannot oblige all, but you perceive it is impossible for him to do so. Yours, etc.
"JNO. G. NICOLAY."

To one gentleman who asked him to write something disclaiming all intention to interfere with slaves or slavery in the states, he replied, "I have already done this many, many times; and it is in print and open to all who will read. Those who will not read or heed what I have already publicly said would not read or heed a repetition of it. If they hear not Moses and the prophets, neither will they be persuaded though one rose from the dead."

And to another correspondent who suggested that he set forth his conservative views, he wrote:—

". . . I will not forbear from doing so merely on punctilio and pluck. If I do finally abstain, it will be because of apprehension that it would do harm. For the good men of the South—and I regard the majority of them as such—I have no objection to repeat seventy and seven times. But I have bad men to deal with, both North and South; men who are eager for something new upon which to base new misrepresentations; men who would like to frighten me, or at least to fix upon me the character of timidity and cowardice. They would seize upon almost any letter I could write as being an 'awful coming down.' I intend keeping my eye upon these gentlemen, and to not unnecessarily put any weapons in their hands."

Nor would he defend himself against the "campaign stories" which appeared in numbers. One of which his enemies made much was that he had received two hundred dollars for the Cooper Union speech in February, 1860. They claimed that as it was a political speech it was contrary to political etiquette to accept pay. Lincoln explained the affair in a letter to a gentleman who had been disturbed by it and added:—

"I have made this explanation to you as a friend, but I wish no explanation made to our enemies. What they want is a squabble and a fuss, and that they can have if we explain; and they cannot have it if we don't."

Another foolish tale which caused Lincoln's partisans unrest was that when he was a member of Congress he had charged several pairs of *boots* to his stationery account and that they had been paid for out of public funds. One of Lincoln's friends took the trouble to examine the stationery account for the Thirtieth Congress and to publish a certified denial of the story.

Lincoln's silence and inactivity were merely external. As a matter of fact no one was busier than he. No one was following more intently and thoughtfully the gradual development of the situation and the daily fluctuation of opinion. By correspondence, from the press, through his visitors many of whom came to Springfield at his request, he kept himself informed of how the campaign was going from Maine to California. Whenever he feared a break in the ranks he put in a word of warning or of advice. He warned Thurlow Weed that Douglas was "managing the Bell element with great adroitness." He cautioned Hannibal Hamlin against a break the latter feared in Maine, "Such a result as you seem to predict in Maine"—he wrote, "would, I fear, put us on the down-hill track, lose us the state elections in Pennsylvania and Indiana, and probably ruin us on the main turn in November." While he gave the strictest attention to the progress of the elections all over the country, he managed to keep above local issues and to hold himself aloof from the personal contests and rivalries within the party.

In fact Lincoln kept in perfect touch with the progress of his party from May to November and was able to say at any time with accuracy just what his chances were in each state. He seems at no time to have had any serious fear that he would be defeated.

There was a tragic side to this very certainty of election which Lincoln felt deeply. In the Convention which had nominated him, nine states of the Union had not been represented. If he should be elected these states would have had no voice in his choice. He knew that he was pledged to a platform whose principles these states stigmatized as "deception and fraud," and that if elected he must deny what they claimed as rights. He knew that in at least one state, Alabama, the legislature two months before his nomination had pledged itself by an almost unanimous vote in case of his election to call a convention to consider what should be done for "the protection of their rights, interests and honor." He knew that numbers of influential Southern men were repeating daily with Wm. L. Yancey, "I want the cotton states precipitated in a revolution," or declaring with Mr. Crawford of Georgia, "We will never submit to the inauguration of a Black Republican President."

From May to November he watched anxiously for every sign that the South was preparing to make good the threats with which its orators were inflaming their audiences, which a hostile press reiterated day by day, which teemed in his mail, and which brought scores of timorous men to Springfield to advise and warn him. How serious was it all? He did his utmost to discover; even writing in October to Major David Hunter to find out how much truth there was in the report of disaffection in a Western fort: "I have a letter from a writer unknown to me," he said, "saying the officers of the army at Fort Kearney have determined, in case of Republican success, at the approaching presidential election, to take themselves, and the arms at that point, South, for the purpose of resistance to the government. While I think there are many chances to one that this is a humbug, it occurs to me that any real movement of this sort in the army would leak out and become known to you. In such case, if it would not be unprofessional, or dishonorable (of which you are to be judge), I shall be much obliged if you will apprise me of it."

In spite of all that Lincoln knew of the temper of the South, in spite of his close study of events there through the summer of 1860, he did not believe secession probable. "The people of the South have too much good sense and good temper to attempt the ruin of the government rather than see it administered as it was administered by the men who made it. At least so I hope and believe," he wrote a correspondent

THE CAMPAIGN OF 1860   443

in August. And in September he said to a visitor, "There are no real disunionists in the country."

There were reasons for this confidence. In every state of the South there was a Union Party working to meet the crisis which Lincoln's election was sure to produce; many of the members sent him cheering letters. In acknowledging such a letter in August, Lincoln wrote: "It contains one of the many assurances I receive from the South, that in no probable event will there be any very formidable effort to break up the Union."

Then, too, Lincoln had heard this threat of secession for so long that he had grown slightly indifferent to it. He remembered that in the Frémont campaign it had been employed with even more violence than now. Again in 1858 the clamor of disunion had risen. He believed that now much of the noise about disunion was merely political, raised by the friends of Breckenridge, Douglas, or Bell to drive voters from him. The leading men of the party sustained Lincoln in this belief. Seward and Schurz both confidently assured Republicans in their speeches that they might vote for Lincoln without fear, and Bryant, in the "Evening Post," laughed at the "conservative distresses" of those who supposed that Lincoln's election would cause secession and war; reminding them that when Jefferson was a candidate it was said his election would "let loose the flood-gates of French Jacobinism" and that Henry Clay had declared that "nothing short of universal commercial ruin" would follow Jackson's election. Lincoln was sustained not only by the assurances of the Union Party of the South and by the buoyant hopefulness of the Republicans of the North, he had a powerful moral support of his own conviction that no matter what effort the South made to secede the North could and would prevent it. He was and had been for years perfectly clear on this subject. In the Frémont campaign he had said in reply to the threat of disunion, "No matter what our grievance—even though Kansas shall come in as a slave state; and no matter what theirs—even if we shall restore the compromise—we will say to the Southern disunionists we won't go out of the Union and you *shan't*."

It was then with the belief that he was going to be elected and that while his election would produce a serious uproar in the South, that no successful resistance would follow, that Lincoln approached election day. He had grown materially in the estimation of the country in the interval between May and November. Many of the leading men of his party who had deplored his nomination had come to believe him a wise, strong man. Those who sought personal interviews with him, and they were many, went home feeling like Thurlow Weed who, heart-sick over Seward's defeat and full of distrust, not to say contempt, of Lincoln's ability, visited him soon after the nomination at the earnest request of David Davis and Leonard Swett. "I found Mr. Lincoln," wrote Weed afterward, "sagacious and practical. He displayed throughout the conversation so much good sense, such intuitive knowledge of human nature, and such familiarity with the virtues and infirmities of politicians, that I became impressed very favorably with his fitness for the duties which he was not unlikely to be called upon to discharge. This conversation lasted some five hours, and when the train arrived in which we were to depart, I rose all the better prepared to 'go to work with a will' in favor of Mr. Lincoln's election, as the interview had inspired me with confidence in his capacity and integrity." . . .

In the very South where a fury of prejudce had burst and where, as was to be expected, Lincoln was popularly regarded as an odious and tyrannical monster, much as later the North regarded Jefferson Davis, there were signs that he was at least considered honest in his views.

"It may seem strange to you," wrote a Kentuckian, who was quoted by the New York "Evening Post," August 17, 1860, "but it is nevertheless true that the South looks for the election of Lincoln by the people and would prefer him to Douglas. Our most ultra Southern men seem to respect him and to have confidence in his honesty, fairness and conservatism. They concede that he stands on a moderate platform, that his antecedents are excellent, and that he is not likely to invade the rights of any one; but they can't go for him because he holds opinions relative to the rights of slavery in the territories directly opposite to the Southern view; still he is an open and candid opponent, and therefore commands Southern respect."

"Some of the most interesting interviews which Mr. Lincoln has had," wrote some one to the Baltimore "Patriot," "have been with extreme Southern gentlemen, who came full of prejudice against him, and who left satisfied with his loyalty to all the constitutional rights of the South. I could tell you of some most interesting cases, but it is enough to know that the general sentiment of all Southern men who have conversed with him is the same as that publicly expressed by Mr. Goggin, of Virginia; Mr. Perry, of South Carolina; Mr. McRae, of North Carolina, and many others, who have not hesitated to avow their intention of accepting Mr. Lincoln's election and holding him to the constitutional discharge of the presidential office. . . ."

The most significant element in the estimate of Lincoln which the country formed between May and November was the respect and affection which was awakened among the common people. There sprang up all over the country among plain people a feeling for him not unlike that which had long existed in Illinois. The general distribution made of his speeches had something to do with this. There was published in 1860 in Columbus, Ohio, an edition of the Lincoln and Douglas debates of 1858, which was used freely as a campaign document. Lincoln himself gave away scores of these books to his friends and to persons who came to him begging for an expression of his views. To-day copies bearing his autograph are to be seen, treasured volumes in the libraries of many public men. The Cooper Union speech was published by the Young Men's Republican Club of New York and circulated widely. To the hard-working farmer, mechanic, store-keeper, who thought slowly but surely, and whose sole political ambition was to cast an honest vote, these speeches were like a personal face-to-face talk. The argument was so clear, the illustration so persuasive, the statement so colloquial and natural, that they could not get away from them. "Lincoln's right," was the general verdict among masses of people who, hesitating between Re-

THE CAMPAIGN OF 1860

publicanism and Popular Sovereignty, read the speeches as a help to a decision.

While Lincoln's speeches awakened respect for and confidence in his ability, the story of his life stirred something deeper in men. Here was a man who had become a leader of the nation by the labor of his hands, the honesty of his intellect, the uprightness of his heart. Plain people were touched by the hardships of this life so like their own, inspired by the thought that a man who had struggled as they had done, who had remained poor, who had lived simply, could be eligible to the highest place in the nation. They had believed that it could be done. Here was a proof of it. They told the story to their boys. This, they said, is what American institutions make possible; not glitter or wealth, trickery or demagogy is necessary, only honesty, hard thinking, a fixed purpose. Affection and sympathy for Lincoln grew with respect. It was the beginning of that peculiar sympathetic relation between him and the common people which was to become one of the controlling influences in the great drama of the Civil War.

Election day in 1860 fell on the 6th. Springfield, although a town of strong Democratic sympathy, realized the importance of the occasion, and by daylight was booming away with cannon; before noon numbers of bands which came, the citizens hardly knew from where, were playing on the corners of every street. Mr. Lincoln, as was his custom, came down to his room at the State House by eight o'clock, where he went over his big mail as coolly as if it were not election day and he a candidate for the presidency of the United States. He had not been there long before his friends began to flock in in such numbers that it was proposed that the doors be closed and he be allowed to remain by himself, but he said he had never done such a thing in his life as to close the door on his friends and that he did not intend to begin now, and so the day wore away in the entertainment of visitors.

It had not been Mr. Lincoln's intention to vote, the obstacle which he found in the way being that his own name headed the Republican ticket and that he did not want to vote for himself. One of his friends suggested that his name might be cut off and he vote for the rest of the ticket. He fell in with this suggestion, and late in the afternoon, when the crowd around the polls, which were just across the street from his office, had subsided somewhat, he went over to cast his ballot. He was recognized immediately and his friends were soon about him, cheering wildly and contending good-naturedly for an opportunity to shake his hand. Even the Democrats, with their hands full of documents which they were distributing, joined in this enthusiastic demonstration and cheered at the top of their voices for their beloved townsman.

No returns were expected before seven o'clock, and it was a little later than that when Mr. Lincoln returned from his supper to the State House. The first despatches that came were from different parts of Illinois, the very first being from Decatur, where a Republican gain was announced. Soon after, Alton, which was expected to go for Douglas, sent in a majority of twelve for Lincoln. There was a tremendous sensation in the company, and Mr. Lincoln asked that the despatch be sent out to the "boys," meaning the crowd which had gathered in and about the State House. After an hour or more news began to come from Missouri. "Now," said Mr. Lincoln, "they should get a few licks back at us." But to everybody's surprise, there was more good news from Missouri than had been expected. Towards midnight news began to come from Pennsylvania: "Allegheny County, 10,000 majority for Lincoln;" "Philadelphia, 15,000 plurality, 5,000 majority over all;" then a telegram from Simon Cameron, "Pennsylvania 70,000 for you. New York safe. Glory enough." This was the first news from New York, and since ten o'clock the company had been waiting impatiently for it. A fusion ticket, it was feared, might go through there, and if it did the disaster to the Republicans would be serious.

While waiting anxiously for something definite from New York, a delegation of Springfield ladies came in to invite Mr. Lincoln and his friends to a hall near by, where they had prepared refreshments for all the Republican politicians of the town. The party had not been there long before there came a telegram announcing that New York City had gone Republican. Such a cheering was probably never heard in Springfield before. The hall full of people, beside themselves with joy, began a romping promenade around the tables, singing at the top of their voices the popular campaign song, "Oh, ain't you glad you joined the Republicans?" Here at intervals further telegrams came from New York, all announcing large majorities. The scene became one of the wildest excitement, and Mr. Lincoln and his friends soon withdrew to a little telegraph office on the square, where they could receive reports more quietly. Up to this time the only anxiety Mr. Lincoln had shown about the election was in the returns from his state and town. He didn't "feel quite easy," as he said, "about Springfield." Towards morning, however, the announcement came that he had a majority in his own precinct. Then it was that he showed the first emotion, a jubilant chuckle, and soon after he remarked cheerfully to his friends, that he "guess'd he'd go home now," which he did. But Springfield was not content to go home. Cannon banged until daylight, and on every street corner and in every alley could be heard groups of men shouting at the top of their voices, "Oh, ain't you glad you joined the Republicans?"

Twenty-four hours later and the full result of that Tuesday's work was known. Out of 303 electoral votes, Lincoln had received 180. Of the popular vote he had received 1,866,452—nearly a half million over Douglas, a million over Breckenridge, a million and a quarter over Bell. It was a victory, but there were facts about the victory which startled the thoughtful. If Lincoln had more votes than any one opposing candidate, they together had nearly 1,000,000 over him. Fifteen states of the Union gave him no electoral votes, and in ten states he had not received a single popular vote.

View Of Sangamon River